D0884255

TEACHING MINDFULNESS SKILLS TO KIDS AND TEENS

Teaching Mindfulness Skills to Kids and Teens

edited by
Christopher Willard
Amy Saltzman

Foreword by Susan Kaiser Greenland

THE GUILFORD PRESS
New York   London

© 2015 The Guilford Press
A Division of Guilford Publications, Inc.
370 Seventh Avenue, Suite 1200, New York, NY 10001
www.guilford.com

All rights reserved

No part of this book may be reproduced, translated, stored in a retrieval system, or transmitted, in any form or by any means, electronic, mechanical, photocopying, microfilming, recording, or otherwise, without written permission from the publisher.

Printed in the United States of America

This book is printed on acid-free paper.

Last digit is print number: 9   8   7   6   5   4   3   2   1

The authors have checked with sources believed to be reliable in their efforts to provide information that is complete and generally in accord with the standards of practice that are accepted at the time of publication. However, in view of the possibility of human error or changes in behavioral, mental health, or medical sciences, neither the authors, nor the editors and publisher, nor any other party who has been involved in the preparation or publication of this work warrants that the information contained herein is in every respect accurate or complete, and they are not responsible for any errors or omissions or the results obtained from the use of such information. Readers are encouraged to confirm the information contained in this book with other sources.

Library of Congress Cataloging-in-Publication Data

Teaching mindfulness skills to kids and teens / edited by Christopher Willard, Amy Saltzman ; foreword by Susan Kaiser Greenland.
     pages cm
  Includes bibliographical references and index.
  ISBN 978-1-4625-2238-5 (hardback)
  1. Meditation for children.   2. Meditation—Therapeutic use.   3. Stress in children.   4. School psychology.   5. Child mental health services.   I. Willard, Christopher (Psychologist)   II. Saltzman, Amy, 1958–
  BF723.M37T43 2015
  204.´35071—dc23
                                                                  2015015974

About the Editors

Christopher Willard, PsyD, is a clinical psychologist and educational consultant with a specialty in mindfulness and self-compassion. He speaks on the topic of mindfulness and meditation with young people nationally and internationally, and holds teaching appointments at Lesley University and Harvard Medical School. Dr. Willard is on the board of directors of the Institute for Meditation and Psychotherapy and the Mindfulness in Education Network. He has been practicing sitting meditation since 1999. Dr. Willard is the author of *Child's Mind: Mindfulness Practices to Help Our Children Be More Focused, Calm, and Relaxed*; *The Mindfulness and Anxiety Workbook for Teens*; and the forthcoming *Growing Up Mindful*. His website is *www.drchristopherwillard.com*.

Amy Saltzman, MD, is a holistic physician and mindfulness coach whose passion is supporting people of all ages in enhancing their well-being and discovering the Still Quiet Place within. She is recognized by her peers as a visionary and pioneer in the fields of holistic medicine and mindfulness for youth, and her current work focuses on sharing mindfulness with school-age youth in socioeconomically diverse school and community settings. In collaboration with the Department of Psychology at Stanford University, she has conducted two research studies evaluating the benefits of teaching mindfulness to child–parent pairs and to children in low-income elementary schools. To support others in discovering the joy and peace of the Still Quiet Place, Dr. Saltzman has written the book *A Still Quiet Place: A Mindfulness Program for Teaching Children and Adolescents to Ease Stress and Difficult Emotions* and created two CDs, *Still Quiet Place: Mindfulness for Young Children* and *Still Quiet Place: Mindfulness for Teens*. Her website is *www.stillquietplace.com*.

Contributors

Marvin G. Belzer, PhD, is Adjunct Associate Professor in the Department of Psychiatry and Biobehavioral Sciences at the University of California, Los Angeles (UCLA), and Associate Director of the UCLA Mindful Awareness Research Center.

Mark Bertin, MD, is a developmental pediatrician and author of the books *The Family ADHD Solution* and *Mindful Parenting for ADHD*, integrating mindfulness into evidence-based care. Dr. Bertin is on the editorial board of Common Sense Media and a faculty member at the Windward Teacher Training Institute. He blogs for *The Huffington Post, Mindful.org,* and *Psychology Today*. His website is *www.developmentaldoctor.com.*

David S. Black, PhD, MPH, is Assistant Professor of Medicine at the Keck School of Medicine at the University of Southern California. He is Founding Director of the American Mindfulness Research Association (*goAMRA.org*) and Editor-in-Chief of *Mindfulness Research Monthly.*

Susan Bögels, PhD, is a clinical psychologist, psychotherapist, and Professor in Developmental Psychopathology at the University of Amsterdam, as well as Director of UvA minds, the Academic Treatment Center for Parents and Children. She is coauthor of the book *Mindful Parenting: A Guide for Mental Health Practitioners.*

Willoughby Britton, PhD, is Assistant Professor of Psychiatry and Public Health and Director of the Clinical and Affective Neuroscience Laboratory at Brown University. Her website is *www.brittonlab.com.*

Richard Burnett, MA, is Cofounder and Creative Director of the Mindfulness in Schools Project, which has been brought to thousands of students in multiple countries. He cowrote the highly acclaimed 9-week mindfulness course .b (pronounced *dot-b*), designed to engage adolescents in the classroom, which then led to Paws .b, a new curriculum for primary and prep schools. His website is *www.mindfulnessinschools.org.*

Jennifer Cohen Harper, MA, is Founder of New York–based Little Flower Yoga and The School Yoga Project, and Cofounder and board member of the Yoga Service Council. She is the author of *Little Flower Yoga for Kids: A Yoga and Mindfulness Program to Help Your Child Improve Attention and Emotional Balance.* Her website is *www.littlefloweryoga.com.*

Christen Coscia, BS, is a compassionate educator who has integrated mindfulness into many diverse educational and community settings. She has been creating and conducting Wellness Works in Schools classes, including at a juvenile detention facility, for over a decade.

Marcella Cox, MS, LMFT, RYT, is a psychotherapist, yoga teacher, and mindful self-compassion instructor. She specializes in mindfulness- and compassion-oriented psychotherapy for children, adolescents, and adults, and she teaches mindful eating to help clients cultivate a healthier relationship with food and improve the quality of their life. Her website is *www.marcellacox.com.*

Brian M. Galla, PhD, is Assistant Professor of Applied Developmental Psychology in the School of Education at the University of Pittsburgh. His research focuses on mindfulness, self-control, and their relationship to academic achievement and positive youth development.

Matthew S. Goodman, BS, is a doctoral student in clinical psychology at Alliant International University, San Diego. His research interests include mindfulness with elementary-age students and clinical interventions for children with autism spectrum disorders.

Lesley Grant, ECD, is Founder and Director of the Marin Mindfulness Institute and the Mindfulness and Child Development Institute, which offer certification in mindfulness in adolescent and child psychotherapy and education to psychologists, psychotherapists, social workers, and teachers for county mental health agencies, educational organizations, and to those in private practice. Her website is *www.mindfulness-education.org.*

Susan Kaiser Greenland, JD, is Cofounder of the InnerKids Foundation and author of *The Mindful Child: How to Help Your Kid Manage Stress and Become Happier, Kinder, and More Compassionate.* She teaches worldwide on mindfulness with young people.

Betsy Hanger, MEd, is an instructor certified by Mindful Schools, teaching mindfulness in the Los Angeles Unified School District and working with transgender youth and their families.

JoAnna Harper, BA, has been practicing mindfulness since 1999. She is a graduate of Noah Levine's Against the Stream teacher training and is currently in the Spirit Rock/IMS/IMC 4-year teacher training. She leads adult and teen silent retreats and daylong and weekly classes, and works with all kinds of youth.

Sam Himelstein, PhD, is a licensed psychologist at the Alameda County Juvenile Justice Center who works with incarcerated youth suffering from trauma, addiction, and other psychological/systemic issues. He has written multiple articles and two books, *A Mindfulness-Based Approach to Working with High-Risk Adolescents* and the forthcoming *Mindfulness-Based Substance Abuse Treatment with Adolescents: A Guide for Clinicians, Teachers, and Mentors*, and presents nationally on these topics. His websites are *www.samhimelstein.com* and *www.mbaproject.org*.

Iman L. Khan, MS, LPC, is founder and owner of Blooming Minds, where she is a mindfulness meditation coach and instructor, a certified family mediator, a speaker, and a learning and behavior consultant. She is a psychotherapist at Johansen and Fleming Psychological Services in Kenosha, Wisconsin, specializing in interpersonal neurobiology and contemplative neuroscience. She works with adults, children, couples, and families treating and preventing a variety of psychological diagnoses. Her website is *www.bloomingminds.org*.

Wynne Kinder, BA, Ed, a former classroom teacher, teaches the mindful awareness program Wellness Works in Schools in settings including urban, general education, special education, and alternative classrooms. She developed mindful brain breaks with *www.GoNoodle.com*, a free online digital tool for teachers and their students; FLOW is a new category of 3- to 5-minute activities with self-care and self-regulation in mind and in practice. Her website is *www.WellnessWorksinSchools. com*.

Lindsey M. Knowles, MEd, is a doctoral student in clinical psychology at the University of Arizona. She is certified as a mindfulness facilitator by the UCLA Mindful Awareness Research Center, and is a staff member for Inward Bound Mindfulness Education (iBme) retreats. Her research interests include mindfulness, bereavement, attachment, and psychoneuroimmunology.

Gregory Kramer, PhD, is Founder and Guiding Teacher of The Metta Foundation and has been teaching insight meditation since 1980. He is the author of multiple books and the developer of Insight Dialogue practice, which he has been teaching since 1995, offering retreats in North America, Asia, Europe, and Australia. His website is *www.metta.org*.

Jeffrey Pflaum, BA, has been an inner-city elementary school teacher in the New York City Department of Education for over 30 years. He is the author of *Motivating Teen and Preteen Readers: How Teachers and Parents Can Lead the Way* and is a featured blogger on The BAM Radio Network's EDWords (*www. bamradionetwork.com/edwords-blog/blogger/listings/jeffpaul*), where he writes about the mindfulness curricula that he started in the 1970s. His website is *www. JeffreyPflaum.com*.

Deborah M. Plummer, BSc, is a writer, Imagework practitioner, and workshop facilitator. She is formerly a clinical lead speech and language therapist working within the NHS in the United Kingdom and senior lecturer in health psychology and counseling at De Montfort University, Leicester. She is the author of 10 books, including *Focusing and Calming Games for Children: Mindfulness Strategies and Activities to Help Children to Relax, Concentrate and Take Control*. Her website is *www.deborahplummer.co.uk*.

Betsy Rose, MA, is a singer, songwriter, and mindfulness educator. Her in-school programs and trainings for teachers, parents, and youth invoke the magic of song, breath, and presence—mindfulness with a beat! Her recordings include *Calm Down*

Boogie and *Heart of a Child*. Her websites are *www.betsyrosemusic.org* and *www.mindfulsongs.org*.

Amy Saltzman, MD (*see* "About the Editors").

Randye J. Semple, PhD, is Assistant Professor at the University of Southern California, Los Angeles. She is the codeveloper of mindfulness-based cognitive therapy for children and Mindfulness Matters, Associate Editor of the journal *Mindfulness*, Consulting Editor of the journal *Spirituality in Clinical Practice*, and past president of the Mindfulness and Acceptance special interest group of the Association for Behavioral and Cognitive Therapies.

Arielle Sydnor, BA, works for Teach for America and is pursuing a master's degree in teaching.

Suzi Tortora, EdD, LMHC, is a dance movement and creative arts therapist, working with Memorial Sloan-Kettering Cancer Center, the New School for Continuing Studies, the Pratt Institute, the 92nd Street Y, and the Harkness Dance Center in New York City. She is the author of *The Dancing Dialogue: Using the Communicative Power of Movement with Young Children*. Her website is *www.suzitortora.com*.

Ozum Ucok-Sayrak, PhD, is Assistant Professor at the Department of Communication and Rhetorical Studies at Duquesne University, where she teaches courses on intercultural communication, integrated marketing communication, business and professional communication, and public speaking.

Vanessa CL Weiner is Founder and Executive Director of the ResilientKids organization. Her website is *ResilientKids.org*.

Char Wilkins, MSW, LCSW, is a mindfulness-based psychotherapist working with women with childhood trauma and disordered eating. She is a senior teacher of mindful eating–conscious living and mindfulness-based stress reduction professional trainings for the Mindfulness-Based Professional Training Institute at the University of California, San Diego. For information on mindful eating, visit *www.me-cl.com*.

Christopher Willard, PsyD (*see* "About the Editors").

Foreword

Susan Kaiser Greenland

Reading this excellent volume has been like catching up with old friends. Many of the authors were among the first to advance the once slightly wacky, yet remarkably commonsensical, idea that mindfulness could benefit youth. It almost felt hubristic to think we could teach children mindfulness at that time, especially since meditation was rarely taught to youth in the Eastern cultures where it had originated. As Willoughby Britton and Arielle Sydnor explain in Chapter 21, "Most young monastics spend their preteen and teen-age years engaged in the memorization of liturgical and philosophical texts and are rarely required to meditate as part of their training" (p. 412). We knew this was the historical truth. Yet, we were emboldened by our own meditation practices and trained by teachers who were respectfully bucking the conventional wisdom in a similar way. Those Eastern cultures that rarely taught meditation to young people didn't teach meditation to lay people much either. So it made sense that the more inclusive, experimental approach spearheaded by teachers in the West would spawn a new wave of practitioners eager to share what we had learned with the youngest generation.

We came from various backgrounds, trained in different traditions, were spread out across the globe, and met infrequently, if at all. However, we shared important commonalities. Notably, we were influenced and inspired by Jon Kabat-Zinn's secular approach to mindfulness training, specifically mindfulness-based stress reduction, and by the mindful parenting book he wrote with his wife, Myla Kabat-Zinn, entitled *Everyday Blessings*. Perhaps the most striking common characteristic we held was that we were absolutely certain that mindfulness would benefit young people even though there was no scientific evidence to prove it.

For starters, we hoped that mindfulness would address a common complaint we heard from our students. Adults told them time and again to "pay attention," but no one taught them how. We knew from our own practices that meditation trained two stances of attention, both of which had been helpful to us: a focused stance that had helped us concentrate and manage distractions and a more open, receptive one that had helped us calm down when we were upset, manage stress, and navigate strong, difficult emotions. Based on our positive experiences we threw caution to the wind, simplified the adult practices, and began trying them out on our kids, in their schools and community centers. Sure enough, parents, teachers, and the children themselves reported back that mindful strategies were helping them at home, at school, and with friends. There's now empirical evidence to support what was then merely anecdotal. In Chapter 19, David Black and his colleagues review the scientific findings with respect to mindfulness training and youth, including those related to the development of attention and cognitive control. In Chapter 20, Mark Bertin delves deeper into the relationship between mindfulness and executive functioning and examines how mindfulness can be integrated into care and treatment of attention-deficit/hyperactivity disorder.

Attention training wasn't the only thing we were asked about in the beginning. "Isn't mindfulness the same as teaching kids to stop and count to 10 when they feel angry or upset?" was another common question. The two strategies are similar. But what is missing in the count to 10 approach that is inherent in a mindful approach is noticing what happens in your mind and body during that 10-second interval. Rather than clenching down on the anger and hoping to wait it out by counting to 10, mindfulness suggests a different approach. We notice we're angry or upset and then stop what we're doing, relax, and breathe into a more open, receptive perspective. It's from there that our nervous systems can settle down and we can watch our strong feelings come and go. When prompted, children can then see how, if given a chance, challenging thoughts and emotions tend to morph and fade away. We were certain that teaching kids this other way of attending to their experiences—coupled with a worldview in which an understanding of compassion, impermanence, interdependence, cause and effect, and less binary thinking is baked in—could change how they relate to challenging situations and people. We saw meaningful applications in the classroom and clinic (see Chapter 1, by Lindsey Knowles and colleagues; Chapter 4, by Betsy Hanger; Chapter 13, by Marcella Cox and Char Wilkins; and the Introduction by Christopher Willard) and with populations generally considered difficult to reach (see Chapter 6, by JoAnna Harper; Chapter 3, by Wynne Kinder and Christen Coscia; and Chapter 7, by Sam Himelstein).

Getting parents and school administrations to buy into the "why" of mindfulness for youth was the first hurdle. Once that hurdle was jumped, the question of "how" to teach mindfulness in an age-appropriate, secular manner emerged. In Chapter 5, Lesley Grant provides a helpful look at mindfulness training through a child development lens while presenting games and activities appropriate for specific age groups. Suzi Tortora (Chapter 11), Jennifer Cohen Harper (Chapter 10), Betsy Rose (Chapter 15), Iman Khan (Chapter 14), Vanessa Weiner (Chapter 16), Deborah Plummer (Chapter 17), Jeffrey Pflaum (Chapter 18), and Amy Saltzman (Chapter 12) combine mindfulness with the established disciplines of dance, yoga, music, writing, art, nature studies, and competitive sports to offer joyous and ingenious ways to engage children in practice. These chapters are a generous, multidisciplinary treasure trove of creative ideas for sharing mindfulness in playful, powerful, and developmentally appropriate ways.

Working with children who don't want to be in your class is challenging for a teacher regardless of the subject matter. It is especially common in our field, given that students are often required to attend mindfulness classes because their teachers, parents, or therapists think it will be good for them. Like it or not, these students are stuck in a "conscript classroom" and would rather be anyplace but there. In Chapter 2, Richard Burnett suggests strategies that encourage resistant students to give mindfulness a chance. He urges us to start by explaining to our charges how mindfulness will help them manage the stress and strain of daily life. He continues by answering practical questions on classroom management ranging from "What do I do if a pupil starts crying?" to "What do I do when a pupil starts giggling?"

Whether working with a child who is resistant at the beginning or with one who starts out enthusiastically, the key to nurturing continued engagement is connectedness. Students generally begin mindfulness training by learning to bring awareness to their minds, bodies, and surroundings and in so doing they better connect with their present-moment experiences. But mindfulness doesn't stop with our own life experiences (intrapersonal mindfulness). Equally important is how we integrate mindful awareness into our actions and relationships (interpersonal mindfulness). In Chapter 8, Ozum Ucok-Sayrak and Gregory Kramer unpack the practice of both intra- and interpersonal mindfulness, while Susan Bögels, in Chapter 9, explores the interpersonal practice of mindfulness in the context of parenting. Working with kids on their own, outside of their homes, has its limitations, and Bögels's work reminds us that when mindfulness is offered to the entire family system the possibilities for transformation increase exponentially.

In Bögels's mindful parenting program, parents begin by practicing themselves before sharing mindfulness with their families. That approach is echoed throughout the book. To borrow from J. B. Priestley, "It's not what is taught but what's emphasized," and the authors' common emphasis on the development of your own practice first and foremost is no coincidence. Sam Himelstein points out that "one of the most important factors in developing trusting relationships . . . is the degree to which you are authentic" (p. 124) and, further, that "authenticity begets authenticity" (p. 125). Personal practice is the threshold for authenticity in this work, and the moments that we embody a worldview that supports mindfulness are when the strongest, most authentic teaching can take place.

I came to this work via meditation. In the tradition in which I was trained you needed years of practice, experience, and permission from your meditation teachers in order to teach others. When I received permission, one of my teachers gave me a specific instruction that remains a daily lesson in humility. She told me to only "serve the child in front of me now." Lindsey Knowles and her colleagues echo this wisdom:

> We do not know what we someday will know about teaching mindfulness to children. As we learn more, we adults can simply do our best to bring our own mindful attention to the complexities and uniqueness of each child we work with. (p. 40)

When teachers bring their full attention to the children in front of them now it throws the commonality they share with their students into sharp relief. JoAnna Harper's description of what it was like to practice with youth labeled "at risk," "challenging," or "troubled" after having worked with "typical' kids" illustrates this:

> Though it might seem hard to believe, the years of working with "typical" kids informed my teaching with this [at-risk] population more than I can say. They ["at-risk," "troubled," or "challenging" youth] *truly* feel no different to me; I can see the innocence, joy, and curiosity just below the surface that takes only a little encouragement and care to draw out. Many times I have walked into a room of tough, shutdown, and disinterested faces, yet within an hour, they look like different people, literally transformed. By the time they left our circle these kids were calm and had laughter in their eyes. One young man that I am working with now told me that the class gives him hope, and he now believes that he can have a better life. (p. 108)

Wynne Kinder and her colleagues, who also have extensive experience working with "atypical" and "at-risk" students offer another example of how working with kids can be humbling when they point to the opportunities for co-teaching and co-learning that emerge in a classroom:

> So often students will chime in, "I have an idea . . ." and announce something relevant, creative, and innovative. They may think of an extension of what we are doing or envision another way of doing it that makes much more sense. With their permission and blessing, we have adopted many of our students' insights. Their judging minds do not get in the way of what they have to offer. (p. 56)

The theme of approaching this work with humility is echoed throughout this book. Given that consumer enthusiasm has outpaced the science, it is crucial that we foster caution in this emerging field. Evidence now supports what was once only a belief: that mindfulness offers strategies to help children, teens, and families focus, relax, and better regulate their emotions. These are remarkably helpful life skills. In the context of popular mindfulness training, however, they are often taught outside of the worldview in which they were developed. We don't know what this unbundling of classical practice to emphasize some elements and deemphasize others will mean in the long run. Nor, as Willoughby Britton and Arielle Sydnor point out in Chapter 21, do we know whether it makes sense to wait to train some aspects of mindful attention until children reach a certain age or whether mindfulness practice is equally beneficial for everyone. These are just a few of the questions that will need to be answered for the field to mature.

In closing, a heartfelt thanks to Christopher Willard, Amy Saltzman, and The Guilford Press for integrating the work of these talented authors into the comprehensive volume that you're holding in your hands. It is an invaluable resource and serves as a reminder of how much has been accomplished in a relatively short period of time. Yet there is much more to be done. If the development of secular mindfulness tracks the development of classical meditation in only the smallest of ways, this is just the beginning. Hopefully this volume will inspire parents and professionals to continue the spadework that's needed to answer the open questions, foster new ones, and, through that process, develop best practices for sharing mindfulness with children and families. May this effort benefit children, teens, and families everywhere.

Contents

Introduction

Toward a Model of Teaching and Learning Mindfulness

Christopher Willard

Until I began working with young people, it never occurred to me that mindfulness could be, well, *fun*. Certainly it could be pleasant, and the benefits to my own life were clear, and practices were often interesting, but rarely fun. In the decade since I began experimenting with introducing young minds to contemplative practices, I've found it has only grown more joyful, not just for the kids, but for me too. Amy Saltzman and I created this book with that very idea in mind: that mindfulness, whether we teach children or adults, should mirror life itself—playful and joyous at times, reflective at others.

If you are holding this book, you may not need much convincing that mindfulness will benefit you and the young people you serve. Certainly, there is objective scientific evidence, as seen in the thousands of studies in the past decades on the physical and psychological benefits of mindfulness for adults. Some of the data regarding the benefits of mindfulness for children and adolescents are reviewed in this book. Then there is the compelling historical evidence; there must be some reason that these practices have existed for millennia, and not only remain with us, but are expanding into every facet of the modern world. Then there is your own experience when you greet the world with an authentic and open presence. While approaching this world with an open heart and mind may initially seem to make you vulnerable, mindfulness builds emotional and spiritual resilience in a world that is far from the compassionate place we might like it to be.

Beyond the benefits listed above, many of us have an intuitive sense of why it is so important to pass these practices on to the younger generation, particularly in our culture right now. Many of the reasons that mindfulness for young people is gaining momentum are the same reasons as those for adults. We adults spend so much of our time rushing around, *doing*, with less and less time to be, to quote Kabat-Zinn (2011), "becoming more of a human doing than human being." Sadly, as a society we are now creating younger and younger human "doings." You don't need to spend much time with young people today to see how overbooked, overscheduled, stressed, and distracted from their true experience they are. What we idealize as childhood, a time of play and ease, is shrinking away; it is now available only to younger and younger children. Young people no longer have the privilege of slowing down, investigating, and learning about their own experience and the world around them through exploration. We see this everywhere, from the impoverished inner-city where kids are often raised by violent videogames inside or gangs on the streets outside, to the leafy suburbs where helicopter parents frequently enter their children in the college rat race, the nanny shuttling kids from soccer practice, to SAT tutors, to piano lessons. Meanwhile, almost every child or teen I encounter is too wired from anxiety, screen stimulation, or both to sleep well enough to function inside or outside the classroom. Many of our young friends are worried not only about their personal futures, but also about the future of planet, the environment, war, poverty, racism, and violence. In a culture like this, it's no surprise that third graders come to my office with panic attacks. There is little room for childhood as we knew it, and precious moments to slow down and observe are increasingly rare. This leaves kids lacking in emotional intelligence and underprepared for the tasks of development and learning, let alone adulthood.

Mindfulness offers awareness and calm in the frantic and distracted modern world. Mindfulness is a practice of being. If it is "doing" anything at all, it is slowing down and single-tasking. Such practices can at first feel strange, because doing one thing at a time has become so unfamiliar to us. This single-tasking runs counter to the stream of our increasingly fractured attention spans that tempt us into multitasking in spite of the evidence showing that multitasking is impossible. With this context in mind, I invite you and the children with whom you work to try single-tasking just for a moment: Place one finger in the center of your forehead, close your eyes, and simply place your attention on the sensations.

> "Notice what your forehead feels like against your finger. . . .
> "Notice what your finger feels like against your forehead. . . .
> "Bring awareness to the sensations. . . .

"Notice temperature. . . .
"Texture. . . .
"Pressure. . . .
"Moisture. . . .
"Can you feel your pulse?
"Stay with this for a moment . . . and if your mind wanders, just
   notice that and bring your attention gently back to the sensation
   of your finger on your forehead.
"And then open your eyes and notice how you feel."

If you could do this practice, then you can and already have practiced mindfulness. This exercise quickly demonstrates what happens when
we begin to focus on our experience; it is simple, short, and demonstrates
immediately the power of slowing down and single-tasking—essentially,
being mindful. This is a great short practice for kids who may struggle with
settling in and starting a task such as homework; many young people may
find this a little more interesting than the more typical instruction to "focus
on the breath." Others may find their minds instantly starting to wander. In
that case, they have had their first lesson in the nature of mind: The nature
of mind is to wander. I heard someone once say that the nature of the pan-
creas is to secrete insulin, and the nature of the mind is to secrete thoughts.
Through these practices, we are training young minds to remain still, so that
our young friends can more closely examine thoughts, emotions, and urges
as they arise.

Our culture's current relationship to technology complicates the temptation toward multitasking. Sherry Turkle, a sociologist from the Massachusetts
Institute of Technology (MIT) who studies our relationship to technology,
writes: "If we don't teach kids to be alone, they are only going to know how
to be lonely" (Turkle, 2012). As a therapist, I see this problem over and over,
not just in the record rates of mental illness among children and teens in
the so-called "developed" world, but also in young adults who simply never
learned how to be alone. When they finally have the independence to figure
out who they are, what they want, and to make their own life decisions, they
become overwhelmed with anxiety.

Sadly, our culture is teaching adults and children to be lonely, teaching
them to be too busy to attend to themselves and the world around them. We
teach them to deal with their uncomfortable or confusing emotions by checking *out* and clicking through, rather than checking *in*. Even positive emotions
are to be shared instantly online, rather than fully experienced. However,
with mindfulness, we can offer youth something different: a way to observe
their internal experience, become curious about it, tolerate it, maybe even
learn from it and have fun in the process. In this way we raise happier, healthier children, teens, and young adults, and change the world for the better.

How to Use This Book

It would be easy to pick up this book, scan the table of contents, and find a chapter that looks relevant to your passions or profession and read only that. We realize many readers will do just that. Yet we strongly encourage you to read this book from start to finish, deepening and expanding your understanding of mindfulness, absorbing the wisdom of experienced teachers in a wide range of settings, exploring various ways to work with kids from all kinds of backgrounds, in a variety of creative ways. We also strongly believe that facilitators should have the a depth and breadth of personal experience and techniques for teaching and leading mindfulness, as well as experience with the challenges or discomforts of practice. As adults, we encourage kids to write, participate in sports, or play music. If we are skillful we encourage them to explore activities at which they excel, and others at which they may at first struggle. Challenge yourself in the same healthy way you challenge your kids; get out of your comfort zone and do some artwork even if you haven't lifted a paintbrush to paper since age 11; learn some brain science even if you majored in music. We ask our kids on a daily basis to be vulnerable; now we ask that you practice this principle yourself.

How We Put This Book Together

Though this book is thorough, it is in many ways still incomplete. There are so many more potential contributors out there who do not have chapters, and more still who contributed ideas that didn't make it into the book in formal ways, but whose voices echo in these pages. We have included many, but by no means all, of the talented and creative people pioneering the work of bringing mindfulness to youth from many perspectives and through many mediums. Meanwhile, even as we assembled and edited this volume, programs proliferated and blossomed like wildflowers, and the task of capturing all of it grew out from underneath us. Still others, perhaps you among them, are quietly teaching mindfulness to young people in your work, your play, or your home. While you may not be a writer or speaker, we nonetheless encourage you to share this wisdom for the benefit of all beings, young and old. *Methods of teaching mindfulness to young people are endless, and we vow to continue learning.*

This book is meant to inspire as well as instruct. For that reason, we chose not to spent much time on the "alphabet soup" of manualized programs that are already out there and have been written about extensively. We honor the value of such programs, and have asked many of their authors to contribute to this book. We also do not want you, dear reader, to feel limited by curricula that may not apply to your setting. Rather, we want you to finish this book and wisely pick and choose what speaks uniquely to you and to the children with whom you work. We realize that we all work within constraints in our schools and offices, and applying a comprehensive program in its entirety is not always realistic. Thus, we offer you many tools and building blocks to create your own unique offering.

To that end, we organized the book into sections thematically. We open with chapters on bringing practices to different kinds of kids, teens, and parents, in schools and other settings. From there, we turn to childhood activities that can incorporate mindfulness, and ways to bring mindfulness into a broad range of activities such as movement; sports; and musical, artistic, and written expression. Finally, in the concluding chapters, we review the research documenting the benefits of offering mindfulness to youth, and the scientific explanations for how mindfulness works.

Defining Mindfulness: A Bow to Tradition and a Nod to Science

The task of defining mindfulness has grown easier over time; even a few years ago, offering a definition of mindfulness could take up a substantial portion of a lecture or workshop. These days, mindfulness has entered the mainstream vernacular. For that I believe we owe a debt to Jon Kabat-Zinn, who popularized mindfulness outside of any specific spiritual tradition. As far as definitions are concerned, the most commonly referenced adult definition of mindfulness is "paying attention on purpose in the present moment and non-judgmentally" (Kabat Zinn, 2011). My coeditor, Amy Saltzman, offers a kid-friendly definition: "Mindfulness is paying attention, here and now, with kindness and curiosity, so that we can choose our behavior" (Saltzman, 2014). "Choosing our behavior" identifies the critical element of responding, rather than reacting, that is an essential aspect of adult mindfulness often not emphasized in the primary definition. This element of choice is particularly important for children as thoughts and feelings lead all too frequently toward less than skillful behavior.

There are two components to mindfulness: formal practice, which involves engaging in a guided or self-guided exercise; and informal practice, applying what is learned during formal practice to daily life. Some practices in this book emphasize specific aspects of mindfulness such as beginner's mind, nonjudgment, and intention. Some emphasize mindfulness with a specific population, others emphasize ways of incorporating mindfulness into a child's existing activities and interests. Specifically, although many people find mindfulness practice relaxing, the intention of mindfulness practice is not to be relaxed; rather the intention is to be aware of what is present in the moment—whether relaxation, tension, ease, or anxiety. Additionally, when visual images are used in mindfulness, they are used to support awareness of the practitioner's present-moment experience, rather than diminish or alter this experience.

In secularizing mindfulness, there is risk of watering down definitions and practices, or not honoring the historical origins of many practices. Our contributors offer their own unique views and experiences, and reasonable people, experts even, may disagree about certain definitions and distinctions. Yet, we feel it is important to distinguish mindfulness from other techniques with some similar aspects and benefits, and we have asked our contributors to do so.

Intentions

As we begin, I want to offer a few words about intentions and expectations when it comes to bringing mindfulness to young people. Repeat after me: "If my kids are not meditating at home, they may still be learning mindfulness." In fact, if your kids are not meditating in a therapy session or in class, they may still be learning mindfulness. When we consider intentions rather than goals, we focus on the process, which we *can* influence, rather than an outcome, over which we have little control. Intentions tell us not just where we are going, but where we are in the present moment, keeping the focus on the journey rather than the destination.

When we consider intentions, we also must examine our own intentions for teaching and work with our attachment to outcomes, which can be quite strong. For me, when I first thought about bringing mindfulness to young people, I was a wide-eyed, naïve, and frankly grandiose recent college graduate who thought he was going to change the world by teaching kids to focus on their breath. The students at the residential school where I worked had other ideas, not to mention the staff.

It's now been over a decade since I started on the path of the therapist, and bringing mindfulness to young people in practice looks very different from how it looked in the imagination of an eager and occasionally ego-driven 20-something. Sometimes it looks like two people practicing together, other times like one person guiding a practice and another following, and often it looks like an adult trying to maintain and demonstrate mindfulness in the face of strong emotional currents in the room.

I'm still not enlightened, and frankly, my clients seem to be a lot closer to that state than I am. Meanwhile, I've come to accept that many kids are unlikely to want to sit still and breathe deeply for more than a few minutes. Initially they may not want to engage the "fun" practices that this book offers. Some schools may never allow mindfulness by any name in their classrooms, whether due to feared religious connotations or to fear of it disrupting their test preparation regimen. Of course, many young people are eager to learn, and many institutions are inspired to offer mindfulness. In situations where we meet resistance, what can we do? We can practice, or as Amy says, "Listen, breathe, respond," and work with the one student whom we can really influence: ourselves. Regardless of the eagerness or skepticism of our audience, we want to always build teaching on the foundation of our own practice.

Boundaries

We all work within boundaries that describe and proscribe the limits of our professions as we engage with young people. Then there are the personal boundaries with which we each feel comfortable in terms of the kids we work with, knowing that teens especially will push on these boundaries. Parents have different boundaries than teachers, who have different boundaries and professional expectations from therapists and other professionals. While we all share dedication, affection, and often love for the children we work with, an important part of our work is that we remain within certain boundaries of our professional relationship to maintain everyone's emotional safety.

We want to move ourselves and the kids out of our and their comfort zones, yet remain well within the safety zone. If you are a therapist, know where your job ends. Encourage teachers and families to integrate mindfulness into their schedules; respect their parental and professional expertise and the limits on their time. If you are a teacher, coach, or other professional, you may find that these practices unexpectedly open kids up emotionally; be prepared for conversations that challenge the limits of your own training, and don't promise to keep secrets that could leave you and the child in an ethical dilemma. In these cases, be the best *teacher* you can be, seek support, and know when it's time for a counselor, therapist, or psychiatrist to step in. Whatever your role, know and remember your ethical and legal obligations about mandated reporting when you hear sensitive or worrisome information. And remember the common-sense obligation not to stray beyond your area of expertise or training. Help and support are available. Find and use your local resources.

Stages of Teaching and Learning:
Self, System, Awareness, Integration, Life

I have found it helpful to conceptualize teaching and learning mindfulness in terms of five domains: mindful *self*, mindful *system*, mindful *awareness* instruction, *informal* mindfulness *integration*, and mindful *living* (see Figure I.1).

Note that the stages represented by the figure narrows from bottom to top and that the wide base of the triangle indicates that, in all likelihood, more of us will practice mindfulness ourselves than will see our students live mindfully, and practicing ourselves is still teaching mindfulness. In fact, our own practice cultivates the most valuable asset we can bring to the young people in our lives: our authentic presence.

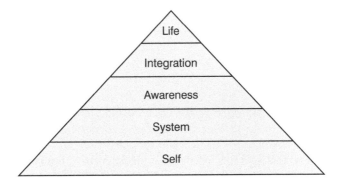

FIGURE I.1. Stages of teaching and learning mindfulness.

Self

Those of us interested in bringing mindfulness to young people are frequently asked, "What is the best mindfulness practice for a kid in the midst of a meltdown?" The answer to this question, however, may be unexpected. The best practice for that kid is your, the caregiver's, practice. And thus the first stage of bringing mindfulness to young people is to start with ourselves. Certainly, and with good reason, it is conventional wisdom in mindfulness circles, and emphasized and reiterated by the contributors to this volume, that you must practice what you teach. Not many among us would send a child into the ocean for swimming lessons from a lifeguard whose only knowledge came from reruns of *Baywatch*. Mindfulness, especially the deeper practices, may take us to some beautiful places and to some dark places, and the young people we bring on this inner journey need experienced guides. Furthermore, we demonstrate both the practices and the benefits of practice explicitly and implicitly. Are we more credible if we tell kids that we find mindfulness has made us more creative, calm, concentrated, and compassionate, or if we *show* them these qualities through our actions and interactions? Will kids be more likely to do a practice we recite to them off a script, or one that we plan, tailor for them, and then sit down and *do* with them? The effects of mindfulness are contagious: Therapists who practice have patients who recover faster (Grepmair et al., 2007), teachers who practice are better able to respond to students, who then perform better on a number of measures (Flook et al., 2013), and parents who practice have happier families with better communication (Bogels et al., 2013). There are countless reasons for us to practice, and these are just a few. If you simply use the offerings in this book to deepen your own practice, you are doing more for your students, clients, and children than you could possibly imagine.

A solid practice allows us know our own strengths and teach from these. Work within your own professional purview and be open to learning from other professionals. As a therapist I have learned more about leading groups from conversations with classroom teachers than I ever did in a group therapy class. Teachers I meet are often excited to learn about ideas we in psychotherapy consider basics, such as countertransference and transference—the ways we unconsciously react to the children in our lives, and the ways we unknowingly trigger them. It has been our great privilege to learn from our skillful, wise, and compassionate contributors, and to share this learning with you.

Systems

The second level of teaching and learning mindfulness comes at the systemic or institutional level. Thich Nhat Hanh (Hanh, 2011) describes teaching children mindfulness as "planting seeds." If we follow this metaphor further, we can think of families as soil, schools as sunlight, and the presence of compassionate adults in the community as rainwater and fertilizer that will create the conditions under which mindfulness practice is most likely to blossom. Yet, it is helpful to keep in mind that even with all of these in place, some seeds may blossom, and others may not. In his play *Admiral Guinea*, Robert Louis Stevenson said, "Don't judge each day by the harvest you reaped, but by the seeds you planted."

For that reason, we encourage you to educate and engage the larger community where you teach by sharing some research mentioned in this book and elsewhere, or explaining the science behind the beautiful images of brain scans. More powerful still is offering community members a direct experience of mindfulness. Usually, offering decision makers a personal experience with practice dispels myths and misconceptions, and directly demonstrates the power of mindfulness. The more enthusiastic your school, clinic, hospital, or family is, the more likely mindful awareness is to flourish in the rich environment of community reinforcement. We realize it can sometimes feel awkward to approach coworkers and supervisors who are unfamiliar or skeptical, and returning to your own practice can guide you and build your confidence.

There are many simple ways you can introduce mindfulness in your specific setting, such as offering workshops to staff or parents; leading sitting meditations on lunch breaks once a week; or creating a mindfulness working group, study group, or ideally a *practice* group with coworkers. If you are in a leadership position, open and close staff meetings with short practices, bring mindfulness in-service training to your staff, or recommend a book on mindfulness for the community to read together when there is time. Given what you know about your community, you may discover other creative ways to introduce mindfulness; I've seen long-lasting programs flourish when just one or two interested individuals within an organization find each other and work together. Remember, the young people you serve will benefit from almost anything that fosters a mindful community, whether they are formally taught mindfulness or not. And in moments of discouragement, compassion practices for the people in your workplace, particularly those who are dubious about mindfulness, always help.

Leading Awareness Exercises

The next level of teaching kids mindful awareness is, well, teaching and leading kids in mindful awareness. For some of us, the transition from practicing to teaching is natural. Still, for others it can feel like a significant step from being a long-term student of mindfulness to a teacher or leader of mindfulness practices. Doubt can creep in: "Who am I to teach mindfulness to these kids? They'll laugh me at me. . . . They'll think I'm a crazy old hippie." If you have doubts about your ability to teach, check in with a respected mindfulness teacher or mentor. If you don't have doubts, *definitely* check in and establish a relationship with a mentor or teacher. Along the way, continue to consult with mentors and supervisors. By seeking out guidance, we demonstrate humility and the importance of asking for support when we need it.

Before you teach or lead, practice in higher-stakes setting; your initial audience can be a friend or colleague, a neighbor, niece or nephew, or it can be a collection of stuffed animals. Consider factors such as volume (it can be easy to speak softly as we become relaxed), speed (many of us have a tendency to speed up when nervous), and tone (too monotonous a tone can invite sleepiness or silliness).

Eventually, from our personal practice we begin to teach mindful awareness practices in our classroom or clinic office, from our unique professional, parental, and personal perspectives, through breath awareness or creative expression, whether our clients are kindergarteners or juvenile offenders. If possible, try to *do* the practices along with your students, although closing your eyes and fully engaging in the practice is not always realistic or safe. The kids may or may not take these practices home, and you are still giving them an experience of presence together. The intention at this point is to offer an experience of mindful awareness. If you do that for a few of the kids in your session or your class, consider your intention met, and know that you have planted seeds that may blossom in time, if not on your timeline. If it feels like a strain and the kids are passively or actively resistant, remember the diagram, and consider taking a step or two back. Is there a way that you can engage the system to better reinforce practice? Is there anything to be learned, or do skillful ideas arise from returning to your own practice?

Integration/Informal Practices

The next level or domain of practice—encouraging integration of mindfulness into daily life—offers tremendous benefits to young people. This is how life itself becomes a mindfulness practice. Still, this stage presents its own set of challenges. It can feel like another stretch of our teaching ability as we encourage kids to practice informally at home, come back to us, and integrate the insights they are beginning to have. Doubts may arise again: "Will they do the home practice? Will they want to talk about it, or even have anything to say?" Trust the process, the practice, and yourself. Most of all, trust your students to let you know the best pace for their learning and practice. If home practice falters, don't give up on the work you are doing in sessions or classes together, and continue on as you have been doing. Work to create the space for vulnerability and growth, but do not force any particular experience.

Offer simple home practices of short, fun, mindful moments or check-ins that are interesting, relevant, and *reasonable* in terms of expectation. Find together, or suggest, regular opportunities for your students to practice, bringing mindful attention to daily activities like walking and eating, teaching parents or friends about mindfulness, or breaking automatic habits by, say, brushing teeth with a nondominant hand in the morning.

Much of the best teaching and learning comes not just from leading or following a guided practice, but in the discussion and reflection after the practice. The experience of mindfulness is inherently subjective, and thus observations and reflections about it cannot be right or wrong. Encourage discussion, help students put their insights to use in the real world outside of your office or classroom, and make connections to times that they can use mindfulness when feeling stressed, angry, afraid, mindless, or disconnected. Certainly ordinary homework is not most kids' favorite activity, but when the mindfulness homework is explained with as a smile as "Your homework is to do nothing," some kids might appreciate it. A beneficial type of peer pressure can support more reluctant individuals in engaging in practice. Creative means of expression, including reflective writing, poetry, artwork, and music, may engage kids who are hesitant to participate in discussions. Know your audience and adjust accordingly; utilize the chapters in this book that address your particular kids and context.

During this stage, as mindfulness is integrated through informal practice in daily life, the group or the therapy dyad becomes more familiar with mindfulness through common insights and shared frustrations. Insights create common language we can speak across other differences. We can begin to speak of "sitting with that," "allowing it to arise and pass," and "dropping in," all of which reinforce the lessons, serve as reminders, and fertilize the practice.

Living Mindfully

The final stage, which few kids we work with will experience, especially in the short time we have with them, is that of independent *living mindfully*. This is the stage I grandiosely imagined everyone reaching with my help when ego drove my teaching in the early years. Let go of this as a goal to reach, and yet never stop aiming for it. This is the stage in which the people we work with have a fairly consistent, integrated, formal and informal practice (something to which even we as mindfulness teachers continually aspire). And with practice we, and the youth we serve, can live this way more often, using mindfulness to skillfully see and respond to various situations. Some days we will be more skillful than others, and large doses of self-compassion will certainly help us through it all. Ideally at this stage, an individual can use mindfulness to be with his or her experience and then choose a wise or skillful action. This is where young people can use their awareness to see a range of choices in a challenging moment: "Do I drink or do I walk away?" "Can I focus on my breath, even for a moment, or will I give up on this test?" "At my most compassionate, will I stand by and watch that bully pick on a classmate?"

Looking at the chart you might notice that the base is wider than the tip, like the sail of a sailboat. The top, representing *Living Mindfully*, is small, whereas the base of *Self* and *System* are large. Though the parts are different sizes, they are all important and interrelated. Like a sailboat, we want to move toward a mindful life under natural power. In our journeys we, and the children in our lives, will encounter sunny days, storms, and doldrums, yet we can learn to skillfully navigate through them. We can use mindfulness to see the weather approaching on the horizon, and to skillfully respond to it, maintaining our equanimity and balance (at least most of the time) with whatever comes our way. And at some point, we, the adults, let go and hand over the ropes and tiller, so that the children with whom we work can learn to sail for themselves, internalizing the lessons of mindfulness, staying afloat and balanced in the face of whatever arises, and perhaps bringing a few others along for the ride. After all, as the saying goes, "Calm seas never a skilled sailor made."

Body Awareness: The First Foundation

To illustrate these five stages of teaching and learning in the model, I offer the example of mindfulness of the body. Mindfulness of the body is the first foundation of mindfulness, and one of the first practices taught in Jon Kabat-Zinn's (Kabat-Zinn, 1990) mindfulness-based stress reduction program. On one level we can use the body as an early warning system, an emotional barometer, and on another as resource to soothe a difficult emotion or feeling. Some mindfulness teachers speak of turning the mind into an ally; the same idea holds for our bodies. Body-based awareness practices give us information, and the tools to respond to that information. Our own body scans and check-ins tell us about what is happening within us, in the present moment. Our bodies can even indicate what we *think* may be coming on a moment-to-moment basis. Mindfulness can help us feel our bodies tighten or loosen, notice our heart skip a beat, or tune in to other precognitive signals that our bodies send about our emotions. Still other body practices serve as a vehicle for healing, calming, or relaxation; through breathing, awareness, yoga, and other body-based mindfulness exercises, we can respond to emotional situations.

Within a *system*, our bodies continue to give us information. When I worked in a particularly overcrowded, underfunded inner-city school, my body was signaling burnout to me well before the thought reached my mind. I often slept poorly the nights before I went in; had stomachaches the mornings I went in; and my muscles, fists especially, would clench as I entered the building and roamed the halls. Bringing mindfulness to my body, I was able to sense the effect the job was having on me even before it reached my consciousness. Body awareness allowed me care for my body and overall well-being by taking action, such as walking mindfully from the subway to the school, eating more healthfully on those days, and nurturing my body after work by getting to the gym or yoga class. Because I was burnt out, I didn't particularly look forward to going to work, but by attending to my body's messages and responding accordingly, the physical and mental burnout of the work began to fade.

My calmer demeanor in the chaotic school *system* attracted the attention of a few teachers who knew of my interest in meditation and mindfulness, and who wanted to bring more awareness to the students through yoga and simple mindfulness. Students also noticed and gravitated toward the safety of any staff member who demonstrated authentic presence and compassion. I now had an "in" and was able to collaborate with interested teachers on creating some programming in the classroom for the students, setting the stage to create a more mindful system in which we could effectively teach basic mindful *awareness* to the students. Together, we taught them and ourselves basic body awareness through body scans, and methods for identifying emotions in our bodies through scans and other short practices. These included the CALM scan of parts of the body—chest, arms, legs, and mind—and the check-in HALT to see if one is feeling hungry, angry, lonely, or tired. Scanning our bodies allowed us to skillfully respond to our experience?

Over time true *integration* began to occur. We encouraged students to notice how their bodies felt in different contexts, as they experienced or even just imagined different emotional states. We invited them to bring their reflections to the larger group or classroom for discussion, or to individual therapy where they could write, draw, or talk about the experience. When I worked one-on-one as a therapist, I tended to steer away from longer traditional body scans and found other ways to encourage kids to regularly find and identify emotions, thoughts, and triggers in their bodies, for example, by just taking turns naming our own physical experiences.

Did the majority of students reach a consistent level of practicing mindfulness independently, and truly *living* their practice? I don't know, as I eventually went on to work elsewhere. What I do know is that the seeds were planted for these teens to use their bodies as a way to check in on their physical, mental, and emotional health. From there, they learned to mindfully respond to and *use* their bodies proactively through diaphragmatic breathing, yoga stretching, mindful walking, and movement.

Your Role in Bringing Mindfulness to Youth

Take a moment and consider a child in your life, perhaps the one who inspired you to learn about teaching mindfulness. What might be the best way to begin with him or her? What way of introducing mindfulness will have the most impact for this child? Perhaps it's teaching a few short take-home practices to the child, or perhaps it's teaching mindfulness to the child's family, to create a mindful home. Maybe it's leading a mindful movement exercise in a classroom, or maybe the best way mindfulness can help this child is by deepening your own practice, so that you can be more compassionate and authentically present for him or her. Bringing mindfulness to others means far more than reading a meditation script or leading an exercise. Make a *practice* of considering all the possible ways mindfulness can help the child, beyond your directly instructing them.

We encourage you let go of outcomes and expectations about what teaching mindfulness looks like, and to open and return to your intentions. Consider these stages as loose guides; they are not rigid, and the reality is that we and our students bounce between and among them at any given time. Wherever we and our students are on the spectrum, from our own independent practice to our students' independent practice, mindfulness is being taught, and mindfulness is being learned. Over time, we recognize and develop our own strengths with teaching. Perhaps the best way some of us can teach is by example, whereas others are best at system-wide interventions. Still others may have the charisma to inspire home practice, and some may lead through creative expression, inspired by chapters in this book. Find the approaches that feel true to you, that honor your strengths; open to sharing your mindfulness in new ways.

Your best work may not occur in all the stages; you may be most effective at one or a few of them. When I offer workshops, I often joke that I spend more time teaching adults how to teach kids than I do teaching kids, but perhaps that is where I'm best and most needed right now. Someone else may pick up the lesson after you and inspire the children to deepen their practice, or the kids may find their own path. It is not entirely, or always, up to you. Rest in a job well done, with faith in your own work and that another teacher will come along when the time is right. Be happy, be grateful, whether today you are the one who plants the seeds, or today you are the one who appreciate the blossoms.

Most importantly, the best parenting advice is the same as the best mindfulness advice: *Never give up.* Don't give up on trying to bring mindfulness to the people in your life, especially your own mindful presence. Don't give up on your own practice. And don't give up on the youth you serve. Because what better way than mindfulness to teach resilience in an often uncompassionate and complicated world? Difficulties will inevitably arise no matter how hard we try to protect and shield our kids; they will get hurt, if they haven't been already. So although we can't always protect them, we can empower them to protect and heal themselves. Make bringing mindfulness practice to kids *your* practice. Just as in your own meditation practice, some days will be full of joy and inspiration, and other days you may feel frustration or boredom—but stick with the practice of teaching in the face of whatever arises, learn from the challenges, and keep moving forward. So with the simple goal of changing the world, one moment, one child, at a time, we offer you this book.

REFERENCES

Bögels, S. M., Hellemans, J., Van Deursen, S., Römer, M., & Van der Meulen, R. (2013). Mindful parenting in mental health care: Effects on parental and child psychopathology, parental stress, parenting, co-parenting and marital functioning. Retrieved from *www.livingmindfulness.nl/downloads/Bogels_Hellemans_MindfulParenting_2013.pdf.*

Flook, L., Goldberg, S. B., Pinger, L., Bonus, K., & Davidson, R. J. (2013). Mindfulness for teachers: A pilot study to assess effects on stress, burnout and teaching efficacy. *Mind, Brain and Education?: The Official Journal of the International Mind, Brain, and Education Society, 7*(3), 182–195.

Grepmair, L., Mietterlehner, F., Loew, T., Bachler, E., Rother, W., & Nickel, N. (2007). Promoting mindfulness in psychotherapists in training influences the treatment results of their patients: A randomized, double-blind, controlled study. *Psychotherapy and Psychosomatics, 76,* 332–338.

Hanh, Thich Nhat. (2011). *Planting seeds.* Berkeley CA: Parallax Press.

Kabat-Zinn, J. (1990). *Full catastrophe living.* New York: Bantam Doubleday Dell.

Kabat-Zinn, J. (2011). *Mindfulness for beginners.* Boulder, CO: Sounds True.

Saltzman, A. (2014). *A still quiet place.* Oakland, CA: New Harbinger.

Turkle, S. (2012, April 21). *The flight from conversation.* Retrieved March 29, 2015, from *www.nytimes.com/2012/04/22/opinion/sunday/the-flight-from-conversation.html?_r=0.*

PART I

BRINGING MINDFULNESS TO YOUTH

CHAPTER 1

Mindfulness with Elementary-School-Age Children

Translating Foundational Practices from the Clinic to the Classroom

Lindsey M. Knowles
Matthew S. Goodman
Randye J. Semple

The outward person is the swinging door;
the inner person is the still hinge.
    —MEISTER ECKHART (1260–1327)

In this chapter we explore how mindfulness may broadly benefit all children, not only those who may be struggling with anxiety or depression. We review some issues that are unique to working with children in clinics and schools, issues that are common to both settings, and offer suggestions for addressing those factors. We introduce two mindfulness programs for elementary-school-age children in the two distinct settings. The first is a clinic-based group program for treating children with mood and anxiety difficulties: *mindfulness-based cognitive therapy for children* (MBCT-C; Semple & Lee, 2011). The second is a similar model adapted for elementary school classrooms: *Mindfulness Matters!* (MM!; Semple, & Madni, 2013). We explore the common aims of both programs, and describe a few sample activities designed to help children achieve those aims.

A Unique Time

The period between the ages of 8 and 12 years is a unique developmental time. From the perspective of some therapists, these children are challenging in that they are "too old to play and too young to talk." Cognitively and emotionally, however, latency-age children are cultivating ways of being and interacting in the world that will persist into adulthood. According to Piaget's (1962) theory of cognitive development, children at this age are primarily in the stage of concrete operations, during which they are developing the ability to use rational logic and inductive reasoning. During this stage, children's thought processes begin to mature as they practice solving problems in a more reflective fashion. Specifically, they develop perspective taking and learn to use inductive reasoning. In viewing events from another person's perspective, children begin to eliminate previously held egocentric beliefs and start to build interpersonal, social, and cultural capabilities such as empathy, compassion, and altruism. They begin to use inductive reasoning, in which inferences are drawn from specific observations in order to make broader generalizations. Thus, 8- to 12-year-olds are at a critical stage; they are ready to develop social–emotional intelligence while opening to a greater understanding of how their inner and outer worlds function. By teaching children constructive ways to interact with themselves and the world, mindfulness training can be instrumental in shaping positive self-perceptions and expectations that carry into adulthood.

Mindful awareness influences how we relate to our own thoughts and feelings (Teasdale, 1999). "Decentering" is a term used to describe the (experientially acquired) insight that thoughts are "just" thoughts, rather than interpreting thoughts as evidence of reality. Decentering may improve a child's ability to consciously respond (rather than impulsively react) to both internal events (e.g., thoughts, emotions, body sensations), and external events (e.g., situations, interpersonal interactions). For example, before an exam, decentering lets a young student shift her attention from habituated anxious thoughts of not being "good enough" or "smart enough," which tend to interfere with attention and concentration, to focus on her breath, which helps her calm down and concentrate on responding to the exam questions. Decentering can be one result of cultivating mindfulness. Yet, for us, teaching mindfulness to children does not begin with decentering. Drawn from our work, we outline four foundational skills, three of which may precede the development of decentering. In our teaching, we aim to (1) cultivate present-focused awareness; (2) identify thoughts, feelings, and body sensations; and (3) differentiate judging from noting. Decentering may emerge as a result of developing these skills. Decentering also seems to strengthen the ability to see and expand what we call "choice points," which are simply moments in which choices can be made. Choices are only ever found in the present moment, so bringing mindful awareness to this moment enhances the mental clarity to see what choices are present. Seeing clearly offers opportunities to make more skillful choices and to make thoughtful, insightful, and more compassionate behavioral responses to the ever-changing vicissitudes of life. Learning to see choice points is the fourth aim of our programs.

Age-Appropriate Mindfulness

Three key points to consider when working with children are age-related (1) affective and cognitive development, (2) capacity for attention, and (3) interdependence within the family. Latency-age children are learning meta-cognitive awareness. *Metacognition* is awareness of one's own thinking processes. Children must learn to first identify and differentiate their internal experiences, and then label them as thoughts and emotions (Bailey, 2001). Systematically bringing attention to thoughts, feelings, body sensations, the breath, and other sensory experiences supports the development of metacognitive awareness. Concepts and activities must be explained in simple, "child-friendly" language. Handouts content and visuals need to be appealing and engage children's interest. Children have less attentional capacity than adults and are less able to engage in extended repetitive activities without becoming bored or restless. So we offer short activities focused on different sensory modes (e.g., sight, taste, sound, smell, hearing, touch, kinesthetics). Practice activities are shorter than in adult programs and offered with creative repetition and variation. Finally, because children are embedded in their families or systems of care, caregivers are integral to the child's home-based mindfulness practices. Caregivers participate in an introductory session before each program begins, review weekly summaries and handouts with their child, and attend a caregiver review session after the child completes the program.

Overview of Mindfulness in the Clinic and the Classroom

Mindful awareness activities can be used to develop essential social–emotional competencies and reduce childhood stress and anxiety. Clinical programs such as MBCT-C are aimed at applying mindfulness skills to reduce anxiety or depression, improve attention, and bolster social–emotional competencies. School-based programs such as MM! teach similar skills in the classroom, thereby offering a cost-efficient way to develop social–emotional resiliency in children who do not have significant emotional or behavioral problems.

Mindfulness-Based Cognitive Therapy for Children

MBCT-C is a group psychotherapy for children 8–12 years old who suffer anxieties sufficient to interfere with their daily functioning (Semple & Lee,

2011). It is modeled on two evidence-based adult programs: mindfulness-based stress reduction (MBSR; Kabat-Zinn, 1994) and mindfulness-based cognitive therapy (MBCT; Segal, Williams, & Teasdale, 2013). MBCT-C is tailored to suit the developmental and attentional abilities of children. It uses a variety of interventions aimed at reducing anxiety, enhancing attention, and bolstering social–emotional competencies. The course consists of weekly 90-minute sessions for 12 weeks. Groups are small—six to eight children— and facilitated by one or two therapists, so that each child receives appropriate individual attention. The therapist guides and participates in all activities and leads the group discussions. Activities include short breath meditations, experiential sensory-focused activities such as mindful eating, smelling, or touching, interspersed with movement activities (e.g., simple yoga postures). Adults are considered vital to the program (Lee, Semple, Rosa, & Miller, 2008). Caregivers gain opportunities to cultivate their own practices by engaging with their child's activities. Therapists conduct a parental orientation session before the program begins and a review session at the end of the program. Each includes a program overview, experiential activities, and information about home practices that parents can do with their child. A brief overview of MBCT-C that describes session-by-session themes, key points, and in-session practices is shown in Table 1.1.

Mindfulness Matters!

Adapted from MBCT-C, MM! (Semple et al., 2013) is a school-based mindfulness and social–emotional literacy curriculum for children in grades 3 through 6 (8–12 years of age). The curriculum is facilitated by teachers in the classroom and aimed at teaching children to cultivate mindful awareness in all aspects of their lives. MM! is a 12-week program consisting of two 45-minute lessons per week. Each lesson includes short activities that are taught, then practiced throughout the day. MM! aims to help children enhance present-focused awareness; bolster social–emotional resiliency; increase cognitive flexibility; make more skillful behavioral choices; promote adaptive changes in how they relate to thoughts, emotions, and body sensations; and cultivate acceptance of things that cannot be changed. A brief overview of the week-by-week themes, key points, aims, and activities is shown in Table 1.2.

Foundations of Mindfulness

Four Common Aims

Mindfulness can be defined as the regulation of attention to cultivate a present-moment awareness that is nonelaborative, curious, open, and accepting (Bishop et al., 2004). MBCT-C and MM! share four common aims: (1) cultivating present-focused awareness; (2) identifying thoughts, feelings

TABLE 1.1. Overview of Mindfulness-Based Cognitive Therapy for Children

Session and theme	Key points	In-session practices
1. Being on Autopilot	• We live much of our lives on autopilot. • Mindfulness exists, and it is a different, more helpful way of being in the world.	• Getting to Know You • Discovering Awareness in a Cup • What Mindfulness Means to Me • Taking Three Mindful Breaths
2. Being Mindful Is Simple, but It Is Not Easy!	• Living with awareness isn't easy, so why are we doing this anyway? • We give attention to the barriers to practice. • Understanding the importance of practice. • Bringing awareness to the breath and body.	• Taking Three Mindful Breaths • Raisin Mindfulness • Mindfully Moooving Slooowly • Taking Three Mindful Breaths
3. Who Am I?	• Thoughts arise in the present, but are often about the past or future. • Thoughts may not be accurate relative to the present reality. • Thoughts are not facts.	• Taking Three Mindful Breaths • Mindfulness of the Body • Hey, I Have Thoughts, Feelings, and Body Sensations! • Listening to the Sounds of Silence • Taking Three Mindful Breaths
4. A Taste of Mindfulness	• We have thoughts, feelings, and body sensations, but these are not who we are. • Thoughts, feelings, and body sensations are not exactly the same as the events they describe.	• Introduction to 3-Minute Breathing Space • Opening to One Orange • Mindful Yoga Movements • 3-Minute Breathing Space
5. Music to Our Ears	• Thoughts, feelings, and body sensations often color how we experience the world. • With our thoughts, we create individual and unique relationships and experiences. • Awareness holds it all.	• 3-Minute Breathing Space (at beginning and end of session) • Do You Hear What I Hear? • Mindfulness of the Body • 3-Minute Breathing Space

(continued)

TABLE 1.1. *(continued)*

Session and theme	Key points	In-session practices
6. Sound Expressions	• Practicing mindful awareness helps us recognize that thoughts, feelings, and body sensations influence how we express ourselves. • We can choose to express ourselves with mindful awareness.	• 3-Minute Breathing Space (at beginning and end of session) • Sounding Out Emotions—Mindfully • Mindful Yoga Movements • 3-Minute Breathing Space
7. Practice Looking	• Judging is not the same as noting. • If we simply observe experiences rather than judge them, the experience may change. • We can choose to observe or note our experiences instead of judge them.	• 3-Minute Breathing Space (at beginning and end of session) • Visualizing with Clarity • Mindful Yoga Movements • Seeing What Is in the Mind's Eye • 3-Minute Breathing Space
8. Strengthening the Muscle of Attention	• Judging often changes how we experience the world. • Becoming more aware of judgments may change how we relate to thoughts and feelings. • Discovering choice points.	• 3-Minute Breathing Space (at beginning and end of session) • Seeing through Illusions • Moving Mindfully • Seeing What Is Not There • 3-Minute Breathing Space
9. Touching the World with Mindfulness	• We have little control over most events that occur. • We do have choices in how we respond to events. • Choice points exist only in the present moment. • Bringing greater awareness to this moment, we may see more choice points.	• 3-Minute Breathing Space (at beginning and end of session) • Being in Touch • Mindfulness of the Body • 3-Minute Breathing Space
10. What the Nose Knows	• We often react to events by moving toward things we like or judge as "good" and moving away from things we don't like or judge as "bad." • Judging an experience may interfere with seeing clearly what is present in each moment. • We have choices in how we respond to events.	• 3-Minute Breathing Space (at beginning and end of session) • Judging Stinks! • Mindful Yoga Movements • 3-Minute Breathing Space

(continued)

TABLE 1.1. *(continued)*

Session and theme	Key points	In-session practices
11. Life Is Not a Rehearsal	• Mindfulness is available in everyday life. • We can practice mindful awareness using all our senses.	• 3-Minute Breathing Space (at beginning and end of session) • Thoughts Are Not Facts • Feelings Are Not Facts Either • Raisin Mindfulness • Mindfulness Is . . . • 3-Minute Breathing Space
12. Living with Presence, Compassion, and Awareness	• Mindful awareness can be helpful in our daily lives. • Bringing greater awareness to our lives is a personal choice. • Living with awareness requires commitment, compassion, and continued daily practice.	• 3-Minute Breathing Space (at beginning and end of session) • Exploring Everyday Mindfulness • Program Evaluation (optional) • 3-Minute Breathing Space • Graduation Ceremony • Graduation Party! • 3-Minute Breathing Space

Note. Adapted excerpt from Semple and Lee (2011). Copyright 2011 by New Harbinger Publications, Inc. Reprinted by permission.

(emotions), and body sensations; (3) differentiating judging from noting; and (4) identifying and acting skillfully upon choice points (moments in which mindful choices can be made). Decentering often develops along with these skills, enabling children to see more clearly and objectively and to act with awareness.

The Role of Decentering

When practicing mindful awareness, children often discover that thoughts and feelings are not permanent, nor do they necessarily reflect reality. Instead, children begin to experience these internal phenomena as transient events in the mind. Decentering develops slowly, with practice and patience. Rather than conveying these concepts to children didactically, we practice *experiencing* moments of nonjudgmental, present-focused awareness that promotes the development of decentering. For example, children may intentionally bring awareness to their thoughts and feelings following a disagreement with friends. Attending to the "upset" thoughts, feelings, and sensations with a stance of curiosity and openness grants opportunities for choices to be made. Children may choose to be more accepting of their own thoughts and

TABLE 1.2. Overview of Mindfulness Matters!

Week and theme	Key points and aims	Session activities
1. Introduction to Mindfulness	• We are often on "automatic pilot," functioning without full awareness of thoughts, feelings, and body sensations. • Mindfulness lets us step out of "automatic pilot" mode. • Bringing mindful awareness to everyday life calls for practice and patience.	• "Mindfulness is . . ." drawing activity • Mindful breathing • Describing experiences • Why breathe? • Exploring the breath
2. Mindful Movement	• Body sensations influence thoughts and emotions, just as thoughts and emotions are expressed in the body. • Each of us brings our own thoughts, beliefs, memories, expectations, and attitudes to the events in our lives. These influence the quality of our life experiences.	• Body scan • Learning about judgments • Mindful walking • Describing experiences • 3-Minute Breathing Space
3. Mindfulness of Taste	• Changes occur when an ordinary act is performed slowly with conscious awareness. • Eating is a complex sensory experience, but often done on "automatic pilot." • Bringing greater awareness to experiences can reduce distress, enhance enjoyment, and increase what we learn from them.	• 3-Minute Breathing Space • Mindful eating • Describing and charting experiences
4. Mindfulness of Smells	• Changes occur when ordinary actions are done slowly and with conscious attention. • The act of smelling and the process of judging what we smell are not the same. • Thoughts and feelings are part of our experiences.	• Mindful smelling • Differentiating describing from judging • Describing and charting experiences
5. Mindful Seeing	• Changes may occur when ordinary actions are done with openness and nonjudgmental awareness. • Bringing attention to sensory perceptions enhances awareness. • Becoming aware of how we judge what we see can enhance our enjoyment of what is present.	• Drawing what's in the mind's eye • Bringing mindfulness to seeing art • Describing and charting experiences

(continued)

TABLE 1.2. *(continued)*

Week and theme	Key points and aims	Session activities
6. Mindfulness of Touch and Hearing	• Changes occur when an everyday act is performed with nonjudgmental attention. • Sensory experiences and the act of judging those sensory experienced are different activities. • As we observe the judging, we may learn to accept all our experiences just as they are.	• Mindful touching • Mindful listening • Describing and charting experiences
7. Mindfulness of Happiness	• Feelings are constantly changing. • Thoughts, beliefs, and expectations influence how we experience the events in our lives. • Habituated responses can be changed when bringing mindful awareness to our experiences.	• The wonderful present • Describing and charting experiences • Charting other pleasant experiences
8. Mindfulness of Frustration and Anger	• Unrealistic beliefs and expectations can bring up feelings of frustration or anger. • Anger and frustration are usually accompanied by strong body sensations. • Mindfully observing the events, thoughts, and feelings that precede these emotions can help us learn to be better friends with these emotions. • We have *choices* in how we respond to our feelings.	• The impossible crossword • Distinguishing reactions from responses • Visualizations of frustration and anger • Practice seeing choice points
9. Mindfulness of Sadness and Loss	• Sadness is a strong feeling that is often avoided. • It is okay to feel sad and to express sadness. • Memories and expectations can color our interpretations of new experiences. • Bringing mindful awareness to sadness and loss can change the way we experience an event.	• Story: *Charlotte's Web* • Journaling with sadness • Describing and charting experiences • Finding choice points that may be helpful to others
10. Mindfulness of Jealousy and Embarrassment	• Jealousy stems from *wanting*. Embarrassment arises when we feel others have seen us do something wrong.	• Guided imagery: Jealousy • Journaling the jealousy scenario

(continued)

TABLE 1.2. *(continued)*

Week and Theme	Key points and aims	Session activities
10. Mindfulness of Jealousy and Embarrassment *(continued)*	• Thoughts can exacerbate or reduce feelings of jealousy or embarrassment. • The actual experience of getting what we want is often different from what we expect. • Mindfulness lets us accept and enjoy what we already have, and forgive others and ourselves.	• Guided imagery: Embarrassment • Describing and charting experiences • Seeing choice points that may be helpful to ourselves
11. Mindfulness of Worry and Anxiety	• Anxiety is sometimes helpful, but can also interfere with our ability to enjoy what is happening now. • Thoughts and body sensations that accompany anxiety are frequently neglected. • Worrying about the worst thing that might happen is almost never helpful.	• Guided visualization: Anxiety • Discerning thoughts and body sensations that accompany anxiety • Mindfully coping with stressful situations
12. Making the Most of Mindfulness	• Our experiences can be different when we observe them with mindful awareness. • Thoughts are "just thoughts." Emotions are "just emotions." • Mindfulness is accessible in everyday life. Every new moment is another invitation to be present.	• Thoughts are not facts • Feelings are not facts either • Poem: "Slow Dance" • "Mindfulness is . . ." drawing activity

feelings and be more compassionate of their friends. They may choose to let the thoughts and feelings go—as they inevitably will anyway. All thoughts and feelings can be experienced as transient, ever-changing internal events, to be explored with curiosity, acceptance, and self-compassion. Essentially, the practice of looking clearly at what is present—without judging what is seen—promotes a nonavoidant relationship with one's own thoughts and feelings. Decentering enhances clarity of mind, from which children discover opportunities to make more skillful behavioral choices. Together, we practice looking so that we may learn to see.

Activities to Cultivate Mindfulness with Children

Cultivating Present-Focused Awareness

We begin teaching mindfulness by guiding children through simple, present-focused activities. With repetition of these sensory-focused activities, children learn to attend to actions that are often performed with little awareness, such as breathing, walking, and eating. They learn that the mind wanders, especially during ordinary, everyday experiences. *Ordinary* does not mean dull or boring. Sensory-focused activities allow children to explore and rediscover the novelty and richness in each moment. We use the word *rediscover* here because, left to their own devices, children often dwell in the present moment. For some, the ordinariness of daily life is extraordinary. Mindfulness is watching a caterpillar inch across a leaf or a hummingbird hover over flowers—watching with wonder and delight. Unfortunately, the capacity to see the extraordinary within the ordinary can become buried. Attention becomes scattered with rapid thoughts flitting between worries about the future, ruminations about the past, and judgments of the present. For both children and adults, the quality of our attention defines our experiences in each moment. Through sensory-focused mindful awareness activities, we teach children to bring a nonelaborative, curious, open, and accepting attention to the present moment. Simple though this may sound, cultivating mindful awareness radically changes lives. As Kabat-Zinn (1990) observed, "It is remarkable how liberating it feels to be able to see that your thoughts are just thoughts and that they are not 'you' or 'reality'" (pp. 69–70).

As children learn to direct attention to the present moment, we remind them that it is completely natural and normal for the mind to wander. We invite children simply to note when they become aware of the mind's wandering, and then bring attention back to the present moment with kindness. Like training an exuberant puppy, patient repetition and a gentle hand are essential. Subsequently, children cultivate mindfulness by returning the wandering attention back to the present sensory-focused activity—over and over again.

Children develop an experiential understanding that their perceptual experiences influence how they interpret and respond to the world. We help them to recognize both pleasant and unpleasant experiences of which they may not have otherwise been aware. By bringing greater awareness to pleasant experiences, children enjoy them more fully, integrating the myriad sensations that contribute to the experience. On the other hand, bringing greater awareness to unpleasant experiences helps by creating an internal observational "early warning system" that is stable enough to recognize when erroneous interpretations or emotional reactions might be coloring their experiences—and to do so quickly enough to respond to difficult situations with greater wisdom and skill. Two introductory activities that help children grasp the usefulness of mindfulness and enhance their motivation to participate and practice mindful awareness are described next.

Activities: Present-Focused Awareness

Initially, practice activities are very brief. Snow globes can be used to illustrate chaos and clarity in the mind. When the globe is shaken and the snow is agitated, the figure inside the globe is obscured; as the snow quietly settles, the figure becomes visible. When their minds are clouded by busy thoughts or strong emotions, children can choose to stop for a moment—using the breath to give the mind a chance to settle—becoming calm and clear. The snow globe illustrates both the hectic activity and the clear calmness of the mind (Greenland, 2010). We hand each child a snow globe while it is still and clear. The children shake the snow globe vigorously until the snow clouds the water and obscures the figure inside the globe. This is the mind clouded by thoughts. While the snow globe is cloudy, we ask the children if their minds have ever felt this way—busy and hectic. Most children can relate to the experience of rapid thoughts and intense emotions. Watching carefully, they set down the globe, letting the mind settle with the snow, restoring calmness and clarity. Simply stopping for a moment to see what is present can loosen or release us from the clutches of hectic thoughts or strong emotions.

Another brief activity is "Listening to the Sounds of Silence," during which we listen for the space of silence between three slow bell tones. A moment of listening can clear the mind while cultivating mindfulness of sounds. "Listening to the Sounds of Silence" is a core activity used throughout both programs. We have found the small Tibetan *tingsha* cymbals to be particularly well suited for this activity because they produce a resonant, long-lasting tone; however, any bell will suffice. We invite the children to take a seated position that is comfortable, but with an erect posture. We might pretend that the head is like a balloon, gently straightening the spine as it floats toward the sky. Children can choose to close their eyes or gaze softly at a fixed point in front of them. We ask them to listen to each ring until they hear the silence, listening for the space between the sounds; we remind them, in soft voices, that it is normal for attention to wander. Whenever they notice that their minds have wandered, they are simply to note that their minds were "wandering" or "thinking" and bring their attention back to the sound—be it the sound of silence or the sound of the bells.

When first introducing the activity, three bell rings may seem inconsequential; however, these moments provide opportunities to see how quickly attention can settle—and how quickly it can become distracted. An important component of these introductory activities is to help children recognize the difficulties (shared by all of us) of holding our attention where we *will* it to be. We invite children to treat the wandering mind like the excited puppy that is best trained with gentleness, compassion, and patient repetition.

One teacher who participated in MM! noted the importance of practicing mindful awareness herself *before* ringing the bell. For her own benefit, she chose to sit at her desk, pick up the *tingsha* bells with slow and deliberate movements, suspend the cymbals by their string in the air until they were still, breathe three times, and then gently tap the bells together. Over time, the simple act of sitting at her desk and then moving slowly and deliberately toward the bells was enough to stop the usual classroom activities. Her students would also become still, better to be present with the first sounds of the bell. "Listening to the Sounds of Silence" began as a guided mindful aware-ness activity. Once her students became familiar with it, she repeated it a few times each day. She also invited the children to ring the bell whenever they felt a desire to quiet their own minds, or the classroom as whole, by bringing mindful attention to the sound of the bells.

Snow globes and bells provide concise visual and auditory introductions to the differences between ordinary attention and mindful awareness. The snow globe demonstrates the importance of allowing the mind time to settle. The bells invite the children to open to the richness of simple experience. They learn that a few moments of mindfulness can create a calm space around hectic thoughts or strong emotions. Both activities are used throughout the day to cultivate present-focused attention.

Cultivating Awareness of Thoughts, Feelings, and Body Sensations

After teaching mindfulness of the breath ("3-Minute Breathing Space"), we shift to sensory-focused activities that are aimed at enhancing awareness of thoughts, emotions, and body sensations as discrete, but related entities. Chil-dren strengthen attention by focusing on exploring an experience through a single sense while also observing and noting thoughts, feelings, and body sensations. In these activities, and the guided inquiries that follow each one, children discover the interdependence of thoughts, feelings, and body sensa-tions and how they might be related (or not related) to external events.

We perform many ordinary activities in our lives essentially on "auto-pilot"—habituated, dulled by repetition—often not fully aware of where we are or what we are doing. We rarely give conscious attention to all the information brought to us by the five senses (i.e., sight, sound, taste, smell, touch). We may continue on autopilot until an experience is so unpleasant or so unusual that it demands our full attention. How often do we observe the myriad colors in the tree growing outside of our door? Are we conscious of the songs of birds or the music of traffic sounds throughout the day? Do we really taste our breakfast, or is the mind so busy thinking about what may lie ahead that we are scarcely aware of what we eat? Wherever we go, the senses gather information. Sense perceptions occur only in the present moment, which makes mindfulness via the senses readily accessible. Becoming more aware of sense perceptions is one way to access mindfulness in everyday life.

Sense perceptions influence our thoughts and emotions, just as thoughts and emotions influence how we interpret what we perceive. Smelling smoke, we may think "There's a fire here!" and then become fearful, experience heart palpitations, shortness of breath, and muscle tension. Thoughts—often cata-strophic, particularly for anxious children—proliferate in an attempt to fig-ure out what might be causing the smell and what to do about it. Thoughts become more real than reality, distorting interpretations and influencing sub-sequent behaviors. We can be captured by strong thoughts or emotions so easily that we lose awareness of the information being brought to us by the senses or even awareness of our own body sensations. Mindfulness is a way of turning off mindless, autopilot that blurs experiences. Children learn to observe their internal and external worlds with an open, nonjudgmental, and compassionate attitude. One "mindful seeing" activity is described to illustrate how simple, sensory-focused activities enhance awareness. Most other sensory-focused activities follow a similar format.

Activity: Thoughts, Feelings, and Body Sensations

Sensory-focused activities include mindfulness of the breath, body sensations, and movements, as well as mindful hearing, tasting, smelling, seeing, and touching. After each activity, children are guided through an inquiry to explore and share experiences. The inquiry helps children (1) bring attention to their internal experiences; (2) differentiate thoughts, feelings, and body sensations; (3) explore how thoughts and feelings interact and how they influence felt experiences; (4) understand the subjective nature of their experiences; and (5) explore ways to integrate mindfulness into their lives.

Mindful seeing is simply the practice of seeing with mindful awareness. During this activity, children view two pieces of art. We invite them to explore the images as patterns of lines, shapes, colors, and textures, rather than seeing the entire piece as a whole. Children will sometimes slip into judgments (e.g., "That's a pretty picture") or inferences about what they see (e.g., "I see a horse") rather than simply describing what is seen. An occasional gentle reminder may be needed to remind children to simply *note* any thinking, and then bring their attention back to observing the picture. With a little practice, most children begin to understand how frequently they add expectations, beliefs, judgments, or evaluations to the experience of seeing. Creating stories or getting lost in memories derails the experience of looking with mindful awareness in the present. After they have observed an image for a few minutes, children share their observations while we chart them. The chart separates objective descriptions, thoughts, feelings, and body sensations, and then identifies subjective judgments about the image (see Table 1.3).

We engage in this process of observation and inquiry for each image and then pose questions to explore the subjective nature of experience. For example, we might ask children, "What did it feel like to be limited to sharing only objective observations?" This part of the activity can be difficult for some children who are accustomed to moving quickly beyond objective observations and body sensations to indulge in a habituated *thinking about* an experience. We invite the children to consider how these categories (objective descriptions, thoughts, feelings, body sensations, subjective judgments) relate to each other. We might point out habituated or reactive thoughts or feelings that redefine an experience. For example, we would invite an anxious child

TABLE 1.3. Mindful Seeing Activity: "Autumn Rhythm" (Jackson Pollock)

Objective descriptions	Thoughts	Feelings	Body sensations	Subjective judgments
White, black, and gold colors	"It's complicated."	Tense, energetic	Heart beating fast	"I like this painting—it makes me hyper."
Different shades of tan in the background	"It's messy looking but cool."	Happy	None noticed	"Awesome and cool."
Stringy, lots of black blobs	"My baby brother could have painted this."	Bored	Wrinkled nose	"It's stupid. I don't like it at all."
Bumpy looking and dripping	"I don't understand what it's supposed to be."	Confused	Tight in stomach	"It's ugly and weird."
Dark, paint in splatters and spots	"I wish I could have this picture in my room."	Wanting	Tapping fingers against my pencil	"It's kind of scary looking, but, really nice."

to explore ways in which the thought "I'm terrible at math" might influence what he or she sees during math class. We then ask the children to consider, "How was this way of seeing different from how you usually look at things?" In reflecting on how mindful seeing might be different from ordinary seeing, children explore ways to bring mindful seeing into everyday life.

Mindful seeing and the other sensory-focused activities offer children opportunities to explore present-focused awareness in different ways. Doing so, they cultivate awareness of the direct sensory experience (objective noting or describing) along with their internal responses to those stimuli (i.e., thoughts, feelings, and body sensations). They learn to differentiate thoughts that are *descriptive* (objective) from those that are *judgmental* (subjective). Once children have participated in these activities, they continue to foster mindfulness by bringing mindful awareness to activities such as eating, walking, brushing teeth, or doing chores. As Jon Kabat-Zinn reminds us, "The little things? The little moments? They aren't little."

Cultivating Awareness of Judging versus Noting

The third aim when facilitating mindfulness with children is differentiating between judging and noting (or describing) experiences. As children increase awareness of the inner world of thoughts, feelings, and body sensations, they may also recognize that judgments frequently attach to experiences.

Judgments end up being projected onto objects, situations, and even people. Mindful awareness helps children learn to observe the experience *as it is*, and notice that the judgment is not the same as the event. Adopting this observational stance is the foundation from which decentering emerges, which in turn can have a profound influence on thoughts, emotional states, speech, and behaviors.

A full range of emotions is ubiquitous to the human experience. Practicing mindful awareness offers children opportunities to experience emotions as "just" emotions, to observe them with compassion, and to open themselves to experiencing emotions just as they are. Some emotions will be "liked" more than others. Multiple emotions can arise simultaneously, blending together like colors on a paint palette. We teach children that there are no "good" or "bad" emotions; happiness and sadness, for example, are simply different experiences. Some emotions may be more comfortable, and some less so. By bringing nonjudgmental awareness to emotions, children experience their transience in a way that sometimes feels like surfing. To stay on the "surfboard" requires considerable attention, balance, and a willingness to follow the natural movement of the wave. Jumping from one wave to another to find a "better" wave or riding a wave after it has crested is not the best way to surf. Emotions can be experienced the same way; some are calm, some are turbulent. All are normal and "okay" to feel, but the main lesson learned is that emotions are transient and often have little relationship to actual events. Embracing the ebb and flow of emotions, particularly uncomfortable or unwanted ones, appears to increase a child's self-compassion and empathy for others. Practicing kindness to themselves, children become kinder toward others. Teaching acceptance and compassion early may provide a stable foundation for children as they move into what, for some, can be an emotionally turbulent adolescence or adulthood. Mindful smelling is a powerful activity that helps children recognize their habitual, often automatic, judgments while also practicing seeing those judgments as "just" judgments.

Activity: Judging versus Noting

The activity called "Judging Stinks!" demonstrates how quickly and automatically we react to events with judgment. Children learn that their expectations, beliefs, associations, memories, and even current emotional state can radically influence or change the quality of the experience itself. The therapist begins by passing around small containers that hold pungent scents such as camphor, vinegar, chocolate, coffee beans, cinnamon, ginger, or perfumes. Children are invited to explore each with their sense of smell. In silence, they observe and jot down the thoughts, feelings, and body sensations that arise in response to the scent, and write a few words to note how they might describe that scent to someone who has never smelled it before (e.g., a "Martian").

After six to eight different scents have been explored, the therapist leads a group inquiry while charting the responses (see Table 1.4).

Referring to the table, the therapist might observe that some children had different experiences of the same smell and then discuss what contributed to those differences. The group discussion can explore the nature and quality of differing experiences, consider ways in which thoughts and feelings influence the experience, and ponder how these subjective thoughts and feelings might subsequently affect behavioral responses.

It can be helpful to point out when some children physically move away from scents they don't like, whereas others move toward the ones they like. This observation can support a discussion about the general tendency we all share to move toward things we like and to move away from things that we don't like. Exploring the "judging" words, the therapist might ask if those ideas could help a Martian understand the scent. Children identify which items on the chart are related to memories or expectations (past or future) and which describe the experiences of that present moment. Differentiating judging from noting allows children to focus more on the actual experience without conflating it with their own beliefs or expectations about the way things "should" be. Interactive dialogue and charting during the inquiry offer the children guidance and practice in recognizing when they might be judging versus describing an experience. Practicing this throughout the day, children quickly learn how often these autopilot judgments influence their lives.

TABLE 1.4. Mindful Smelling Activity

	Description of scent	Thoughts	Feelings	Body sensations	Judgments
	Scent A (vinegar)				
Student 1	Bitter, strong, acidic	"I can't stand this anymore."	Uncomfortable, repulsed	Tingling in nose, pursed lips	"This is the *worst* smell ever!"
Student 2	Sour, sharp	"This reminds me of French fries."	Open, happy	Stomach growling	"I like this."
	Scent B (perfume)				
Student 1	Fruity, sweet, fresh	"This smells like a flower."	Excited	Eyebrows raised, warm feeling in chest	"I love this scent!"
Student 2	Musky and mossy	"This is like a spring day."	Cheerful	Soft and relaxed	"This is very nice."

Cultivating Awareness of Choice Points

Seeing clearly what is present allows children to decenter from their own thoughts. Decentering, like the snow settling in the globe, increases visibility of whatever choices might be available. This momentary "stepping back" allows a child to see what thoughts or emotions may be influencing his or her perceptions and interpretations of events. Decentering may promote more conscious decision making, inhibit socially inappropriate behaviors, encourage more empathic communication, and improve self-regulation of emotional distress (Scherer-Dickson, 2004). Decentering forms the foundation for the fourth and final aim: cultivating awareness of choice points.

Choice points are only ever found in the present moment. Choices can be made only in the moment between the triggering event and the child's *reaction* (automatic, unconscious) or *response* (considered, conscious) to that event. Mindful awareness of what choices might be available can lead to decisions that are less reactive and more reflective, skillful, and appropriate. Decentering grants opportunities to see the choice points. Children cultivate awareness of when they might react unthinkingly (are on autopilot), and then choose an appropriate response. One child described this clarity of seeing: "Mindfulness lets me see when I'm about to do something bad and just take three breaths instead."

We teach children that some things are controllable and others are not. Things over which we have little control include nearly all situations, events, and even interpersonal interactions in our lives. We have no control over the past or the future. However, we can choose *how we respond* to the many situations or events over which we have little or no control. We also teach children that they have choices about how to relate to their own thoughts and emotions. Children learn that they don't have control over what the school bully might say or do, but they do have control over how they respond to the bullying. They can choose to respond with anger, or indifference, or perhaps even with compassion for the unhappy bully. They can choose to fight back or choose to walk away. They do not have control when it comes to getting a second scoop of ice cream, but they can choose to respond with enjoyment while they eat the first scoop, or alternatively, eat it with irritability or frustration at not being allowed the second helping.

"Choosing to respond differently" might seem contradictory to the practice of acceptance that also underlies mindfulness practice. It is important to consider the relationship between acceptance and choice. Children are first taught simply to explore their internal landscape as a "neutral" observer. There is no attempt to change thoughts or feelings, just repeated practice in noting that thoughts and feelings do change, regardless of our wishes for them to stay or leave. Children learn quickly that the mind itself seems to have a mind of its own. Simply noting what is present is seeing clearly. In this clear space, more skillful choices may also be seen. Without distortions from habituated thoughts or emotions, opportunities to choose more appropriate behaviors become evident. Decentering supports the child in shifting from automatic reacting to conscious responding. Essentially, mindful awareness helps children separate the subjective from the objective, let go of the things they cannot change, and interact more skillfully with those things that can be changed.

Activity: Choice Points

An activity called "The Impossible Crossword" helps students bring greater awareness to the events that prompt anger or frustration. Children recognize where in their bodies they are feeling anger or frustration, how thoughts influence emotions, and ways that they can choose to respond differently. The teacher begins by passing out a difficult crossword puzzle and telling the class that they only have 3 minutes to complete it. After 3 minutes, the teacher stops the activity, then invites students to share their experiences while preparing a chart (see Table 1.5).

During the postactivity inquiry, the teacher explores any frustration or anger that may have arisen, and gently examines the associated thoughts. Simply bringing mindful awareness to thoughts that may be unrealistic expectations (or "shoulds") allows children to choose to respond in a different way to their own emotions. Thoughts such as "That wasn't fair" or "Mr. Jones should have given us more time" are commonly voiced. This activity also reinforces the message that although we often cannot control or change life events, we can choose to respond to them in ways that creates

TABLE 1.5. Choice Points Chart for "The Impossible Crossword"

	Event	Thoughts	Feelings	Body sensations	Choice point
Student 1	Trying to complete crossword puzzle.	"I can't do this!"	Frustrated	Tensed shoulders and jaw	"I can try, and even if I don't finish, I will be okay."
Student 2	Trying to complete crossword puzzle.	"Why is the teacher making it so hard?"	Confused, angry	Heart pounding, scowling forehead	"Take three deep breaths. Once I calm down, I can concentrate better."
Student 3	Trying to complete crossword puzzle.	"This is so easy! I'm so good at crossword puzzles."	Excited, eager	Smile on face, butterflies in chest	"Remind myself that I have only 3 minutes. Even if I don't finish this one, it will be still be fun."

less suffering for ourselves and others. The inquiry discussion highlights the distinction between *reactions* and *responses*. *Reactions* are unexamined, often habitual, autopilot thoughts, speech, and behaviors that may be inappropriate to the current situation. *Responses* are consciously chosen after bringing mindful awareness to relevant internal and external events. Responses tend to be more skillful, more appropriate to the situation, and less likely to lead to negative consequences. Brainstorming specific experiences and outcomes that illustrate reacting versus responding is helpful.

Cultivating present-focused attention; bringing greater awareness to thoughts, feelings, and body sensations; and differentiating between judging and noting can expand children's opportunities and ability to make more appropriate choices. Invariably, we are given many opportunities to make choices throughout each day. The practice discovering choice points supports the realization that we *can* choose to respond in ways that are more helpful to ourselves and others.

Special Considerations When Teaching Mindfulness to Children

Working with children provides each of us adult facilitators with unique opportunities to access our own "inner child," which can open us to a wealth of creativity, playfulness—and frequently our own vulnerabilities and childhood insecurities.

Embodying Mindfulness

Most mindfulness programs for adults or children recommend that the facilitator (therapist or teacher) cultivate his or her own personal mindfulness practice. Simply teaching mindfulness activities from a book without having experienced them oneself is like offering violin lessons without ever having played a violin. Teaching mindfulness requires the facilitator to embody mindfulness in his or her attitude, speech, and behaviors. When the adult embodies mindfulness, children learn these skills in unique and profound ways. Semple and Lee (2011) suggest that mindfulness is best exemplified by demonstrating its elements, such as acceptance, curiosity, and openness to experience, while avoiding criticism or judgmental attitudes and language. One useful approach, for example, is to invite participation rather than calling upon a specific child. Creating a safe, non-threatening ambience allows children to explore at their own pace and express themselves as they wish. Listening quietly and respectfully to each child encourages inward exploration and outward sharing in a safe and supportive environment. Practicing mindfulness is also likely to enhance the facilitator's well-being (Jennings, Snowberg, Coccia, & Greenberg, 2011), self-efficacy (Poulin, Mackenzie, Soloway, & Karayolas, 2008), and work motivation (Jennings, 2011).

Working in the Clinic

In MBCT-C, multiple adaptations have been made to meet the needs of children struggling with mood or anxiety problems. For example, groups are kept small: six to eight children with one therapist, or up to a dozen children with two therapists. Each once-weekly session lasts 90 minutes. Children of similar age may vary in their physical, cognitive, social, and emotional development. Keeping each group relatively homogeneous can be useful to maintain a developmentally appropriate pace of teaching. Once a group is established, it is important to create an environment with clear behavioral guidelines and to provide both structure and a safe space for playful exploration and discovery.

Working in the Classroom

School settings have their own unique challenges. First, it is important to understand that many school administrators and teachers will not be keen to add another teaching component to an already packed curriculum. Mindfulness is intended to further children's social–emotional development, which some may view as less essential than academic fundamentals such as the reading and math that will be measured by state exams. Addressing teacher concerns about time constraints is essential. MM! is offered as a 12-week after-school program that is conducted by a trained classroom teacher. Two 45-minute lessons each week teach activities that are then incorporated into the classroom in smaller segments throughout the regular school day. Inevitably, circumstances arise in which mindful awareness can be helpful to teacher and students alike, certainly before those statewide exams when teachers and students are often at their most anxious! A year after one MM! program, some children wrote their mindfulness teacher (spellings unchanged from original):

> "I know we were in your class last year, but we still want to thank you for teaching us how to be in the preasent momment and for teaching us how to be mindful. Ever since last year our grades have been going up because of you. Again thank you for makeing our lives better."

Concluding Thoughts

Teaching mindfulness to children can have a profound influence on their ability to focus, to cope with social and emotional demands, and to make proactive, healthy behavioral choices. Working with latency-age children offers unique opportunities, but also requires special considerations in the clinic and classroom. We believe it is important that facilitators have personal experiences of mindfulness, so that these teachings do not become another tool with which to "fix" a "broken" child or turn into another dull, intellectualized lesson. How much experience or personal practice is "enough" remains an open question. Although bringing in trained mindfulness facilitators or teaching mindfulness in after-school programs is effective, to sustain these practices in the schools, we must weave mindfulness into the threads of the ordinary classroom day, integrating mindful awareness practices into classroom activities as seems appropriate in the moment.

Every child has unique talents, skills, emotional needs, psychological vulnerabilities, and environmental stressors that influence how he or she responds to mindfulness training and subsequently uses these skills. Adults often tell children to pay attention—at home and at school—but rarely do we give them effective tools to do so. Technology and other shifts in our culture provide still more distractions that can interfere with cultivating self-awareness of thoughts, emotions, and body sensations and development of social–emotional resiliency.

We are just beginning to explore the long-term benefits that may accrue from cultivating mindful awareness skills in children. Research is emerging that supports the efficacy of teaching mindfulness to young people in both the clinic and the classroom, but there is virtually no research on the long-term effects of teaching mindfulness to children. Will these children grow up to be mindful adults? Is ongoing mindfulness practice necessary, and if so, how much practice is needed? How might learning these practices improve relationships with peers, siblings, parents, and other adults? Mindfulness is not a panacea to treat all ills, and some may see little or no benefit. We know little about the contraindications that might inform us about when *not* to teach these skills to children.

We do not know what we someday will know about teaching mindfulness to children. As we learn more, we adults can simply do our best to bring our own mindful attention to the complexities and uniqueness of each child we work with. Our personal mindfulness practices guide us in making conscious choices aimed at helping children cultivate skills to become healthy, emotionally resilient adults. In teaching children to bring mindful awareness to their lives, we hope to provide them with essential attentional and social–emotional skills that will free them to experience their lives with awareness, compassion, and joy.

ACKNOWLEDGMENTS

Research on Mindfulness Matters! was supported by NIH/NCRR/NCATS SC CTSI Grant No. UL1 RR024131 to Randye J. Semple, Principal Investigator. Contents of this chapter are solely the responsibility of the authors and do not necessarily represent the official views of the National Institutes of Health.

REFERENCES

Bailey, V. (2001). Cognitive–behavioural therapies for children and adolescents. *Advances in Psychiatric Treatment, 7,* 224–232.

Bishop, S. R., Lau, M., Shapiro, S., Carlson, L., Anderson, N. D., Carmody, J., et al. (2004). Mindfulness: A proposed operational definition. *Clinical Psychology: Science and Practice, 11,* 230–241.

Greenland, S. K. (2010). *The mindful child: How to help your kid manage stress and become happier, kinder, and more compassionate.* New York: Free Press.

Jennings, P. A. (2011). Promoting teachers' social and emotional competencies to support performance and reduce burnout. In A. Cohan & A. Honigsfeld (Eds.), *Breaking the mold of pre-service and in-service teacher education: Innovative and successful practices for the 21st century* (pp. 133–143). New York: Rowman & Littlefield.

Jennings, P. A., Snowberg, K. E., Coccia, M. A., & Greenberg, M. T. (2011). Improving classroom learning environments by cultivating awareness and resilience in education (CARE): Results of two pilot studies. *Journal of Classroom Interaction, 46,* 37–48.

Kabat-Zinn, J. (1990). *Full catastrophe living.* New York: Bantam Doubleday Dell.

Kabat-Zinn, J. (1994). *Wherever you go, there you are: Mindfulness meditation for everyday life.* New York: Hyperion.

Lee, J., Semple, R. J., Rosa, D., & Miller, L. (2008). Mindfulness-based cognitive therapy for children: Results of a pilot study. *Journal of Cognitive Psychotherapy, 22,* 15–28.

Piaget, J. (1962). The stages of the intellectual development of the child. *Bulletin of the Menninger Clinic, 26,* 120–128.

Poulin, P. A., Mackenzie, C. S., Soloway, G., & Karayolas, E. (2008). Mindfulness training as an evidence-based approach to reducing stress and promoting well-being among human services professionals. *International Journal of Health Promotion and Education, 46,* 35–43.

Scherer-Dickson, N. (2004). Current developments of metacognitive concepts and their clinical implications: Mindfulness-based cognitive therapy for depression. *Counselling Psychology Quarterly, 17,* 223–234.

Segal, Z. V., Williams, J. M. G., & Teasdale, J. D. (2013). *Mindfulness-based cognitive therapy for depression* (2nd ed.) New York: Guilford Press.

Semple, R. J., & Madni, L. (2013). *Mindfulness Matters!* Unpublished manuscript, University of Southern California, Los Angeles.

Semple, R. J., & Lee, J. (2011). *Mindfulness-based cognitive therapy for anxious children.* Oakland, CA: New Harbinger.

Teasdale, J. D. (1999). Metacognition, mindfulness and the modification of mood disorders. *Clinical Psychology and Psychotherapy, 6,* 146–155.

CHAPTER 2

Teaching Mindfulness
to Captive Teens in the Classroom

Richard Burnett

When some teaching colleagues and I created the Mindfulness in Schools Project, our ambition was to fuse two areas that we hold very close to our hearts: mindfulness practice, which had long been a central strand in our personal lives, and the art of classroom teaching. As schoolteachers we knew, through a combination of instinct and experience, that the method for instructing adults in mindfulness—the pedagogy of adult mindfulness-based stress reduction (MBSR; Kabat-Zinn, 2013) or mindfulness-based cognitive therapy (MBCT; Segal, Williams, & Teasdale, 2013)—would simply not work in a classroom of adolescents. The genius of MBSR and MBCT was that they were tried, tested, and had evolved through years of experience to become tailor-made for their target audience. But that method did not fit in the face of 25 adolescents in a classroom. So we wrote .b (pronounced "dot-b"), which is code for *stop* (the "." is like a red light), *breathe*, and *be* (b). The .b method was, in essence, our answer to the following question:

When 25 teenagers tumble into your classroom on a wet Tuesday morning, how are you going to interest them in mindfulness? It's 11:45, they are hungry, they are playing with their phones, and they would rather be somewhere else. They have walked in as they always do: joking and laughing, jostling and bustling, some texting or gaming, colorful bundles of chaotic energy. Chairs screech. A few sit down. Bags are plopped on desks. They are late because they have walked as slowly as they could from science, the preceding class—and no, not mindfully. These kids are not about to look up at you bright-eyed and bushy-tailed and say "Please teach us mindfulness,

Sir, for we know it will help us to be happy and flourish." No. It does not work like that. They have never heard of mindfulness, it does not sound that exciting, and if they knew that it involved periods of silence and stillness, you would lose them before you began.

How are you going to convince these young people that mindfulness is a life skill worth learning? You may know it is, but they do not, or at least not yet. .b was our response to the challenge we set ourselves, to write a brief course that could be taught in a standard school classroom and offer young people a taste of mindfulness in a way that was engaging, fun, memorable, and of immediate and practical use on the roller-coaster that is modern adolescence.

To put it another way, we wanted to write a course that would work with a "captive classroom" of teenagers. Teaching mindfulness to a dozen 16-year-olds who have chosen to be there is an entirely different context to teaching 25 or 30 14-year-olds who are there because it is required. You are teaching young people at an age when their first thought is, "Why should I? What's in it for me?"

Of course, this is why you came to teaching; situations like these make you feel alive. You love to connect with the abundant, tumbling energy of this rabble. Perhaps you have some experience teaching mindfulness to adults and also find it gratifying, but the experience takes place in an entirely different context. In most adult classes, it is likely that you have a dozen or so people who want to be there, or at the very least are there because their friends/family/doctors have suggested it. You can begin the first class with the well known practice of eating a single raisin mindfully, encouraging participants to put their full attention on the processes of chewing and tasting. Even if adults feel the playful urge to flick a raisin across the room, they will choose not to, and when you ask them to bring the raisin to their nostrils, they will not try to wedge it between their top lip and their nose. And silence. *Silence*. In your adult courses the participants do not need to be reminded just how nourishing silence can be; the silent passages of their MBSR course are a blessed refuge from the chaos of daily life.

However, in most classrooms silence often has negative or even punitive connotations. Pupils are quiet because they have been told to be quiet, or perhaps because trouble is brewing. We follow the line of researcher Helen Lees (2012) in calling this kind of silence "weak silence." In teaching and promoting mindfulness in schools, we are trying to extend the way in which both pupils and school staff think about and relate to silence such that they come to see it as something that can be chosen, cherished, and used as a nourishing resource. This is "strong silence," and with your average teenage class it can take some time to learn. In .b we try to "slide" the teenagers into these silences, starting with short practices that engage their curiosity and gradually building on these until it feels natural for them to be sitting quietly for 10 or even 15 minutes at a time.

Some might ask why we limit ourselves to teaching mindfulness to pupils in normal classrooms in the same way that we might teach them math, geography, or chemistry. I hear more radical thinkers suggesting that we should question the classic classroom pedagogy that defined 20th-century schools. "In the digital age, surely this is old-fashioned" they say. I have a lot of time for these thinkers and, in many respects, I am one of them. There is certainly a lot wrong with the current system, and technology has the potential to free up both teacher and pupil in many inspiring ways. However, in the meantime, we are going to assume that, for at least the next decade, kids will still go to school and sit on plastic chairs under fluorescent lights in square classrooms with whiteboards. We are going to assume they will continue to be more interested in their music, their media, and of course in each other than in listening to a grown-up try to teach them something they have never heard of. We reckon we probably have one, two, or if we are lucky, three lessons before they switch off completely if they have not connected with the practice. But, if we teachers can bring mindfulness to life for them in the classroom, then suddenly we have an opportunity to give thousands—dare we even dream—millions of young people a taste of mindfulness and how it might help them.

So how do we bring mindfulness to life for these less-than-willing "captives"?

First of all these kids need to know *why* they are going to be learning about this mindfulness thing. What exactly is the point? If we ask them to pay attention to the sensations in their little toes and they have no idea why, then they will giggle. If we ask them to pay attention to the sensations in their little toes because they know that with practice, this will actually change the shape of their brains and make them happier and better at basketball, they might give it a go and forgo the giggling fit.

Second, it has to be fun. I cannot stress this enough: We must be realistic about our intentions here. The primary objective is for pupils to have a positive experience of mindfulness. We are sowing seeds for their future. Yes, a few of the seeds we sow may end up transforming lives, but the most important point is that as many students as possible finish with a positive experience of mindfulness and some notion of how it might help them. So do not worry if you do not create legions of young meditators—but do worry if you bore them to tears! It all comes back to your objectives.

Third, a little "tough love" might sometimes be needed. Kids in classrooms mess around. We jokingly refer to the classroom mindfulness teacher as having "a raisin in one hand, whip in the other." While we advocate teaching from your own practice and embodying mindfulness, we understand that sometimes you have to stop Jimmy from poking Jenny with a pencil. Pupils will fool around, call out, go off topic, fidget, fall asleep, and so on. You need to be able to let go of every little preconception and feel comfortable to go with the flow and have fun. And, at the same time, if there are no ground rules, no boundaries, minimal emotional security, and a teacher without authority, then mindfulness is never going to come to life for anyone.

Fourth, get to know your pupils. This is important on a number of levels. You need to know the class well or at least be working with someone who does. If a child has experienced a recent loss or divorce in the family, then it is important to know this if you are going to manage the class in a way that is both fun and sensitive in the right places. It also helps to know the dynamic of the class: that is, who are the confident kids, the troublemakers, the class stars, the social leaders, the lowest on the pecking order, the teacher's pet, the quiet ones, the bullies, the bullied, and all those various roles in the social order. This knowledge can guide decisions about who sits where, who works with whom, who to ask to speak and who to quietly ignore, with what level of probing to respond to the pupils and with what degree and type of humor. In this way, as many pupils as possible remember their mindfulness classes for the right reasons, not the wrong ones.

What we certainly do not recommend is that you throw yourself in at the deep end with a captive class unless you are already a teacher in that school and know the kids well. If you have an existing rapport with a group of 20 or 30 kids, then it is possible, as long as you yourself are a well-sat mindfulness practitioner. If you are an adult mindfulness teacher who wants to try teaching in schools, we suggest starting small. It's far better to teach a new course all the way through once, with a handful of kids who want to learn, than begin in a captive classroom. If you are too ambitious and it goes wrong, then it becomes hard to recover with the kids as well as the administration. Slow and steady wins the day!

We are bound to say that teaching mindfulness to captive adolescent audiences without a clear and organized plan is extremely difficult. To improvise or "wing it" for a lesson or two may be possible, but to teach an extended course to a group of 20 or 30 teenagers without strong material behind you is beyond most mortals, even the most mindful among us. We cannot stress enough that teaching mindfulness in such a context is as much about the art of classroom teaching and classroom management as it is the art of mindfulness.

Frequently Asked Questions

The following material provides answers to frequently asked questions that my colleagues and I have garnered from our experiences of both success and failure in classrooms and schools over the years. We sincerely hope that these perspectives will support you in your ventures.

"How Do I Get a School Interested in Mindfulness?"

If you are a mindfulness teacher, we suggest that you start by offering mindfulness to the teachers and the parents. If teachers and parents can experience the benefits of regular practice, they will be keen to start helping the kids to learn. They may not want to sign up for a whole 8-week course, so we suggest a sample session for staff and/or parents. This could include a few practices from the course you plan to teach, so that they begin to understand what it is you might be doing with their kids, and what the effects can be.

If you are already teaching mindfulness to the kids, you may want to encourage fellow staff and parents to come and observe your lessons, depending on your school.

If you want to get an entire school on board, then there are also a few things to avoid. As with the kids themselves, we suggest you avoid being too messianic about mindfulness. Avoid talking about it as if it were morally superior to all other features of school life, and please do not suggest that it is an immediate solution to the school's problems. It isn't. Be modest at the outset in your claims for what it might do, emphasize that this is simply an awareness-raising exercise, and allow any more dramatic results to filter through and gradually speak for themselves.

"How Do I Prepare the Classroom?"

If you can, get to the classroom early so that you can arrange the desks, check the technology, remind yourself of the pupils' names and whatever other tasks need doing. Ideally, a short practice can help you settle. We understand, however, that sometimes none of this is possible, and you will walk into somebody else's classroom as their lesson ends and yours is set to begin!

The way the desks are arranged can have a very real impact on the class dynamic. If you are working with a small group, then of course arrange the chairs in a circle or a horseshoe. However, with a captive class of 20–30 kids, this might be a recipe for disaster! As soon as a group of teenagers face each other, the temptation for distraction grows exponentially, even more so if they are excited by the sheer novelty of sitting in this way. We strongly suggest keeping the desks apart from each other with each pupil facing forward. This arrangement helps them each to stay in their own "bubble."

Providing cushions for the seats of chairs, behind backs, and/or under (socked or bare) feet can be a pleasant addition because pupils like them and they can make the mindfulness session feel special and more comfortable. However, with captive audiences cushions can often cause more trouble than they're worth, because pupils start competing for them or throwing them around!

Place a single desk at the front of the class on which to perch yourself. If you are sitting down, you can't see what is happening at the back of the class; if you are standing up, it is much easier to lead the practices well and hold students' attention. Leaning or sitting on a desk is ideal. It is relaxed and authoritative; you can see everyone in your peripheral vision, even when leading practices; you can easily get up and wander around, if you need to do so.

"How Do I Lead the Practices?"

The core of any lesson is the practice. Here are reminders of the basics:

• Do the practice yourself. Do not just give instructions for the practice, *actually do it yourself.* If you are inviting students to drop their attention into their feet, drop your attention into your feet. If you are inviting them to notice the sensations of breathing, notice yours too. This focus helps you to embody the mindfulness you are teaching, to stay connected to the reality and experience of the instructions, and to role-model.

• Stay in touch, as much as you can, with your own reactions in real time. They are a valuable indicator to you of how the lesson is going and how the pupils may be feeling. If you yourself are starting to feel agitated or lost, bring some awareness to the lower half of your body to ground yourself, breathe, and pause. Remember, you are doing your best to actually embody presence, steadiness, calm, and acceptance, so take care of your own well-being too.

• Keep the instructions short and simple, with plenty of pauses, but with liveliness so that the pupils do not fall asleep (too easily). Use your voice as a subtle instrument to set the mood rather than barking instructions like a sergeant major.

• Use "*ing-ing*" verb forms. While in a classroom setting, it sometimes helps to begin a practice by giving the majority of your instructions as present participles—words ending with "-*ing*"—rather than using the imperative verb: for example, use *observing*, not *observe*; *noticing*, not *notice*; *exploring*, not *explore*; and so on.

• Use sensuous, experiential language. When you invite pupils to notice whatever they are experiencing, use words that prompt their inquiry into the felt "texture" of an experience: for example, *fizzing, tingling, flickering, itching, aching, warmth, coolness*, etc.

• Stay interested in the instructions you are giving. If you become bored with a routine set of instructions, the pupils will pick up on this. Try to keep things fresh, and vary things from time to time. Do not worry if you say something that sounds stupid; if you are "in" the practice, doing it yourself as you lead, then what you say will probably work. And if you think you have made a mistake, keep in mind that the pupils do not know how the practice is supposed to proceed, so go easy on yourself. And of course you can always rephrase or discuss what you feel was a mistaken notion after the practice.

• Ensure also that your attention includes everyone in the room, especially those farthest from you. Ensure that your voice is loud enough for all to hear clearly, without having to strain.

• Play with the balance between providing guidance and allowing silence. Silence is the eventual ideal, but often we need to give plenty of steady instructions to keep people focused, present, and awake, so maintain a lively tone and reasonable pace to ensure that pupils remain engaged.

• Accept that restlessness goes with being young. Particularly with a captive class, fidgeting and giggling will inevitably occur, especially in the early lessons. It is important that pupils do not feel trapped, intimidated, coerced, or in the wrong. If they are acting up, then you might incorporate that behavior into the practice and awareness with something like this: "If you are feeling fidgety/giggly/distracted, just notice how that feels in your body or mind." Be realistic with yourself and them about how much calm and focus to expect. Be patient and above all . . .

• *Never lose your sense of humor!* Enjoy and have fun in the lessons as best you can, and if it all seems to be going badly, then breathe into those sensations of discomfort and see it as an opportunity for your own practice!

• When leading practices, keep your eyes open, at least in the beginning. If you perch on the edge of your desk, you can give instructions while letting your gaze fall into a neutral space in front of you. You ought to be able to hold most of the class in your peripheral vision. An appropriate smile or "death stare" to the "badly behaved" pupil can speak a thousand words!

• Consider how to start and end the practices. Some teachers prefer to use a bowl or bell, the soft sound of which pupils may find calming in itself. But for others such objects have connotations of Eastern religion that you may wish to avoid, particularly if you want to emphasize the secular nature of the course. A less spiritually loaded alternative is to use chime bars or a triangle. Otherwise you can just use your voice.

"What Do I Do When a Pupil Falls Asleep?"

Students fall asleep frequently, and it is no big deal. Teaching mindfulness to adolescents makes you realize how tired a lot of our young people are. A few practical pointers:

• Do what you can to preempt this nodding off with advice on posture, such as sitting tall and with a sense of purpose.

• Keep your voice lively and varied. If you notice someone beginning to drift off, voice the next instruction a little more loudly in that direction and suggest that "If you feel yourself falling asleep, try sitting up nice and tall again, or breathing more strongly, or opening your eyes, and if that doesn't work, just stay with the sensations of falling asleep for as long as you can. What does 'getting sleepy' or 'falling asleep' feel like?"

• Leave them be, if one or two (or more!) of the pupils have fallen asleep quietly—it's much better not to disrupt the rest of the class by drawing attention to it.

You can use the noisy breathing or snoring of a sleeping student as an invitation for the rest of the kids to notice how their attention is grabbed and to bring it back mindfully to the sensations in their own bodies. If the noise carries on, and if you think you can do it discreetly, quietly make your way over to the pupil and rest your hand on a shoulder to wake him or her up.

• Make clear in the introduction or inquiry that falling asleep is totally normal and that they do not need to feel stupid or wrong; it just shows how tired and/or relaxed they are. (It may in fact be a welcome break for you—the tired pupils are sometimes the most likely to be disruptive!) Try to normalize falling asleep by saying something like: "I can't believe nobody fell asleep! Would anybody who did fall asleep be happy to share what he or she noticed?" [Turning toward a student with a barely raised hand] "What is the last instruction you remember? How did you feel when you came to?" Show that you are really interested in this phenomenon of sleep.

"What Do I Do When a Pupil Starts Giggling?"

Roll with it! Smile! This too is natural, and if the class notices you becoming flustered by a little giggling, then your authority will begin to seep away. As with sleep, you can use the giggling as an invitation to the rest of the students to notice how their attention is often grabbed by what is more immediate—in this case, that "someone's giggling"—and bring their attention back to the sensations of their feet on the floor, for example. Directing attention into the feet can calm the impulse to giggle.

Depending on your relationship with the pupil(s), a smile, disapproving glance, or a "calm down" gesture with the hand might help settle him or her.

If it proves to be a particularly contagious giggle and the mood of the classroom is completely lost, then with calm, patience, and good humor you can always simply stop the practice. Use the giggle eruption as the basis for an inquiry, perhaps exploring how we are not used to silence, that it can feel unusual, awkward, or difficult. Then change the gear of the lesson by getting students out of their seats for a mindful stretch, or something else active such as stamping their feet or hands in rhythm, before trying again.

"What Do I Do When a Pupil Is Really Messing Around?"

"Messing around" can mean many different things, and in some cases you may need to manage this the way you would manage any other serious classroom disruption, using the school's sanctions system if necessary. We would always suggest that if you don't actually teach in the school where you are leading mindfulness practice (e.g., if you have come in as an external mind-fulness teacher), then you should always have a classroom teacher present in support, because someone already working in the school will know the standard procedures for handling "misbehavior." Ideally you want to be able to manage things so that the difficult pupil(s) doesn't hijack your attention and energy, preventing you from teaching the rest of the class. Particular suggestions:

• "Sending out" a pupil may be an option, but check the school's policy on this. If a child is in your care, you do not want him or her wandering the school unsupervised.

• If some students are overtired and irritable, suggest that they put their heads on the desks and go to sleep. Explain that sleep is a positive use of silence.

• If some students are "hyper" and all your normal efforts to settle them have failed, suggest that they sit or stand at the back of the class and quietly doodle on a piece of paper or get on with some other work.

• With children who have attention-deficit/hyperactivity disorder (ADHD), use the same tactics that you would use in any school class. There is an excellent summary of these at *www.tes.co.uk/teaching-resource/50-Tips-for-Managing-ADD-ADHD-in-the-Classroom-6051439.*

• If you know there are more troublesome children in the class, then try preempting any disruptive behavior by deciding beforehand where they will sit for the lesson (e.g., in front of you, away from any fellow noisy pupils).

• Try keeping troublesome pupils behind after the lesson, giving them your time, *listening* to them and making an ally of them. Better yet, chat with them before class if you can make the time. Being curious as to how they feel about the course and perhaps reminding them why you are teaching these skills may help to win them over.

"What Do I Do If a Pupil Starts Crying?"

Crying is less likely to occur in a captive class than a volunteer one because you are not going into the depth that you would do with a smaller and more relational group. We cannot stress enough that a regular school classroom is not (or is very rarely) the forum in which pupils should be sharing intimacies and getting vulnerable. There are peer dynamics that will carry on as soon as the lesson ends, so be careful, as a teacher, that your questioning does not expose too many vulnerabilities for students to cope with once back in the corridors and out on the playground. Susan Kaiser-Greenland speaks about the classroom as being an inappropriate place to reveal "the soft underbelly of the child"—I wholeheartedly agree.

However, it can and does happen that tears emerge out of the stillness and silence of longer practices, and it helps to normalize the tears in that case. Reassure the pupil with a glance, a gesture, a quiet word, or by passing a tissue, but do not draw attention; attention is the last thing he or she probably wants. After the lesson, find a moment to check in and remind the student of the various supports that may be offered by the school or community.

"How Do I Get the Kids to Do Any Home Practice?"

Getting kids to do home practice is the Holy Grail of teaching mindfulness to schoolchildren, and if you work out how to do it please let us know! "You'll get back what you put in" is a message we stress. We know from research that the more home practice a pupil does, the greater the rewards in terms of his or her well-being, but although an appeal to your students' better nature will help, it is unlikely to be enough to win them over. On the other hand, if you are too strict about it, then "home practice" can end up feeling a lot like "homework," which easily can sour the experience. The home practice question is not easy, particularly with captive participants. Having said that, there are ways and means.

Leave time at the end of the lesson to set the home practice. If pupils see you cramming it in at the last minute, they will be less likely to value or understand it. Make sure they write it down in their homework diaries, school calendars, or whatever other system they have for recording their homework.

Make it easy for them to access the sound files by giving them CDs, or e-mailing them the files, or putting the files on the school intranet, or sending reminder texts.

And finally, try bribery! Promise them a reward (chocolate is always good) if they can come to the next lesson and show you that they have downloaded the sound file onto their phone or media player.

I would like to add an important footnote about what professionals in the United Kingdom refer to as *child protection*, and those in the United State refer to as *mandated reporting* and related issues. Although I have stressed already that mindfulness should not be used as therapy in a classroom, even simple practices may raise sensitive issues for young people. For students' sake and yours, be certain that you understand your region's policies about child abuse and neglect, as well as disclosure of imminent safety concerns. If a pupil discloses to you, or if you suspect, that he or she has serious problems such as depression, suicidal feelings, an urge to self-harm, are bullied or bullying, or are abusing drugs or alcohol, then you must take the steps appropriate to the ethics and laws relevant to your profession, including seeking supervision and reporting information to the appropriate agency. Under no circumstances should you become a pupil's sole confidant, offer to keep secrets, or to hold on to information that directly concerns his or her welfare.

Be aware, too, of your own professional limitations. If a child stays behind after a class and begins to disclose matters that are outside your training, consider whether you are qualified and/or experienced enough to offer him or her appropriate support or advice. Even if you are trained in psychotherapy, it may be outside of your training or role in the school. Tell the child that you would like to support him or her and are happy to listen to what he or she is saying, but that you will have to pass the information on to those who are responsible for students' care. Do not promise to keep any secrets.

This point leads to the next one, which is that if you swiftly need to make a referral for any pupil you think may be getting into difficulties or has mental health needs, do you know where you should go? To be able to refer appropriately, you need to be well informed about the school's support system, including lines of referral. Either do your homework if you come from outside the school, or as suggested, try to have a classroom teacher from the school, who knows the system, in your lessons.

None of this means that you should discourage pupils from asking for help or from establishing a positive rapport with you. Indeed, you should encourage students to ask for help, and they should feel comfortable seeking advice if they have problems; it is just a matter of you knowing what to do, where to go, and what your own limitations are if and when a student does ask for help.

And as a final word of advice, teach the teachers. We often find that after one of our training courses, those who are already experienced classroom teachers cannot wait to get into the class and teach mindfulness, whereas experienced adult mindfulness teachers unfamiliar with the lion's den of a teenage classroom feel a bit daunted. If you are in the latter group, fear not! One option I have already mentioned is to work with a smaller volunteer group. But the other is to approach a school and offer to teach their teachers mindfulness for their own health and well-being. Not only is this a good "way in" to a school, it is also potentially the most transformative and ultimately beneficial support you can offer. No school will really embrace mindfulness into its culture unless there is a corps of mindfulness practitioners at its heart, and perhaps your gifts are best employed in this more indirect manner. If later you feel that you can work directly with the kids, great, but rest assured that if you do a good job teaching the teachers, there will be more than one of them wanting to bring it to the kids, perhaps with your support.

I have mentioned more than once how important it is to remind teenagers *why* they are learning mindfulness. "What's the point?" they will rightly ask. Well, I'd like to conclude by asking the same question of ourselves: Why are we *teaching* mindfulness in schools? What's the point? What we are certainly *not* pretending to engineer is some utopian vision of all young people sitting quietly for half an hour every morning. No. We are always very clear about our objectives in teaching .b. Our ambition is:

For *all* pupils to learn about mindfulness.
For *most* to have enjoyed it.
For *many* to use it every once in a while.
For *a few* to practice daily.
And for as many as possible to *remember* it.

The last point is the crucial one. Even if we dare to dream that mindfulness might be taught in schools alongside reading, math, and sciences, let's be realistic about exactly what it is we are aiming to achieve. Our hope is for all kids to become aware that mindfulness exists, that there *is* this amazing life skill available that might help them in some way at some point. The key word is *possibilities*. We are not telling them how they should or should not use it. By giving them a genuine taste of mindfulness, we are simply raising their awareness of an innate faculty they already possess, one that can be deployed in lots of wonderful ways. They might use mindfulness right now to help them with stress before an exam, to cope with a conflict at home, or to perform at a higher level in sports or music. Or they might not use it for another 10 or 20 years, but then one day, perhaps when things begin to fall apart, they remember that there was this thing called *mindfulness*, and wonder whether it might help. They might ask someone about it, Google it, YouTube it, or investigate it in some other way that doesn't even exist yet—who knows? My experience is that for every one or two kids who immediately take to mindfulness in a big way, there are a dozen others who, in a quieter and subtler way, "get it" nonetheless. Now and again I receive an e-mail many years later from a pupil I can scarcely remember. "Hi," or sometimes "Hi, Sir," it might say. "Do you remember those lessons you gave us on mindfulness? Where can I find out more about that?" the young person asks. This warms the heart enough to sustain me through even the coldest, darkest, and wettest of those Friday afternoon lessons.

REFERENCES

Lees, H. (2012). *Silence in schools.* Staffordshire, UK: Trentham Books.
Kabat-Zinn, J. (2013). *Full catastrophe living: Using the wisdom of your body and mind to face stress, pain, and illness* (rev. ed.). New York: Bantam Books.
Segal, Z. V., Williams, J. M. G., & Teasdale, J. D. (2013). *Mindfulness-based cognitive therapy for depression* (2nd ed.). New York: Guilford Press.

Mindfulness
with Special-Needs Populations

Wynne Kinder
Christen Coscia

Carlos was in fourth grade when his *teacher's* parents started coming into his classroom. Each week they led the class in paying attention, listening, moving slowly, and relaxing. He struggled with the pace and seriousness of the sessions. He tried hiding in the back row, but he still couldn't get out of it. The teacher's parents showed the class drawings of brains, muscles, nervous systems, and people slouching or standing tall (the "posture cards").

But as the weeks passed, some parts of the class became tolerable, occasionally fun. Carlos got to try balancing himself in challenging ways, listening deeply to hard-to-hear sounds, feeling how his breath moved in and out and through his body (even under his arms and in his back) and he got to truly rest—so still that he could feel the weight of his own body lying on the floor.

Eight years later, Carlos found that his very own fourth-grade teacher (Wynne Kinder) and another, much funnier teacher from down the hall (Christen Coscia) had left the predictability of their classrooms to teach that very same program to seniors in an emotional support class at the high school. Carlos's past had returned, perhaps to haunt him, perhaps to help him, through a curriculum we call "Wellness Works."

Carlos didn't jump into the front row, ready to help or lead the group, as his previous teachers had hoped. Carlos was now a middle-row guy, who made a deal to participate in the program, in exchange for the privilege of wearing his hoodie. He did ask about the posture cards and about the original couple (Midge and Rick Kinder), who he remembered invented the program in his fourth-grade classroom. He answered one or two of the discussion questions and stayed for the entirety of each session. Getting through a whole period in any subject, we found out at the end of our first class with him, was a rarity for Carlos. But something connected with him, in him, which inspired his engagement. For the remainder of that spring semester, he stayed. And so did we.

Mindful Beginnings

Thirteen years ago, Wellness Works in Schools™ was born. In 2001, Kinder Associates created a mind–body health and wellness program, teaching mindful awareness and mindful movement to students in grades K–12. As classroom teachers, we knew firsthand the great need for the kind of skill building and self-regulation practices that this kind of approach offered. Although our program initially targeted stressed-out students and staff in an urban elementary school, it has expanded over the years into the wider Lancaster, Pennsylvania community, and been adapted for a broad range of students.

Over the years, we have evolved to working primarily with special-needs populations. In this chapter we will define "special needs" in a more traditional sense, as students who may "require a special setting or supports." We spend much of our time in school-based classrooms providing learning support and emotional support. Additionally we work in autistic and multiple-disability settings, during instructional time, and with a great many other special-needs populations who require accommodations and adaptations that are more specific to their needs, settings, and backgrounds. These groups include but are not limited to basic occupational skills; school-to-work programs; night school/summer school; life skills; high school credit recovery programs; high school mothers with babies; visual, auditory, sensory, social skills, and speech–language supports; developmental delays; traumatic brain injury (TBI); diagnostic kindergarten; homeless/transitional living; residential placement; house arrest support; alternative education; youth shelter care; incarceration; juvenile detention; probation; anger management groups; anti-bullying programs; sexual assault recovery; LGBTQ youth support; refugee support; "earn back recess" programs; after-school programs; trauma recovery for youth; and abused women shelter for teens.

Why Mindfulness for Special-Needs Populations?

"I find myself incorporating many of the [mindfulness] strategies within our daily routines because they not only relax the students, but the adults as well."

—Teacher, school-to-work program

With each of these populations, mindfulness has proven valuable for the students as well as for the teachers, support staff, and caregivers who give so selflessly each day. We have always promoted the "oxygen-mask-on-the-airplane" approach, advocating self-care first for our collaborating teachers, support staff, and administrators. This permission to care for oneself is particularly important for workers in special-needs settings. Because teacher and staff burnout is rampant, we consider it to be an essential part of our job to nurture the nurturers.

> "When she [sixth-grade female] is doing mindfulness, it is her best time of the day. We can see the best she's got. I think she can too."
> —Counselor, middle school learning support

Children and youth by nature live close to the moment. Perhaps the younger a human being is, the more this capacity shows through. For students with special needs or abilities outside the mainstream, individual processing time and unique circumstances can keep them closer to each moment in a way that the rest of us may find only fleetingly. This quality makes them ripe for mindfulness, and often we can follow their lead in a very organic and naturally unfolding way. So often students will chime in, "I have an idea . . ." and announce something relevant, creative, and innovative. They may think of an extension of what we are doing or envision another way of doing it that makes much more sense. With their permission and blessing, we have adopted many of our students' insights. Their judging minds do not get in the way of what they have to offer.

There is a raw curiosity and that lends itself well to the work that we are doing with young people each day. In fact, curiosity in the moment often wins out, even for the most defiant, angry, or shutdown students. Tapping into their natural curiosity is often a good start. We begin class with a unique sound and an intriguing tool, object, or some interesting and challenging movement sequence. We invite students to use all of their senses to be right here, right now, in this moment. We often find that they are already here, and it is we adults who frequently need the reminder and require the practice.

Perhaps engaging students in mindfulness practice provides them a welcome relief from the usual schoolwork, tasks, and everyday routines. For many it is a novel experience, different in so many respects from their ordinary daily processes, and therefore just what science says the teenage brain especially craves. For others, their dedicated teachers might have intuitively been tapping into mindfulness notions all along (whether formal or informal in its delivery). When it's time for our Wellness Works class, we hope we are just expanding upon and reinforcing students' natural foundation of moment-to-moment awareness. Some students may have already been asked to practice noticing how they feel, what they need, and what it's like to be in their unique classroom community. Everyone comes to this practice with their own base of knowledge and experience; we hope to meet them where they are and build on that.

Before Even Going into the Classroom

"I do not know of any program which works so quickly, with students, for them to begin to take control of their lives and begin developing an internal locus of control."

—Principal, middle school

As often as possible, we orient teachers and staff to our curriculum, goals, expectations, and requests in advance of our arrival. Their presence and participation, whatever that might look like, will play a major role in creating the learning environment that will foster growth. We simply ask for openness, a willingness to try when they are ready, and that they help us encourage students to follow only two rules: "Let us teach. Let others learn." Time and again we have learned that connecting ahead of time is beneficial for all. We often find that our approaches may be different, but our hopes and expectations are equally high. We are not always welcome, and at times confusion or feelings of discomfort arise for the classroom teacher as she tries to find her way with our practice. Modeling a "being-okay-with-whatever-is" attitude (although not easy to sustain) can be invaluable in setting a non-judgmental tone from the start.

Upon Arrival to the Classroom

Creating connection with the adults in the school and classroom is critical, especially when we are visiting on only a weekly basis over 2 or 3 months of the year. This connection-building begins in the office, with the administrative staff, the assistants who have their fingers on the pulse and tone of the school day so far, as well as the principal, counselors, and nurse. We try to arrive with time to spare, to listen, and to be present and respectful in the space of others. We consider ourselves there for the hard-working adults, as well as for the children.

One of us usually enters the classroom first. For some students, two adults at once (familiar or not) might be overwhelming. Staggered arrival also creates a subtle curiosity that can build learning readiness. Connection might look like walking in the door and before taking off my ("my" referring to whichever of us enters first) coat, before putting down my teaching bag, I find each student at his or her station and greet them, perhaps saying, "I just wanted to say hello and check in with you before I unpack, *before I do anything else*." This kind of greeting creates that felt sense of "I see you, I hear you, I feel you, and there is nothing in this moment more important than being with you." Once the second teacher has also entered and greeted the kids, we invite each student to come over to the rug, to our space, when they are ready.

Team Teaching Whenever We Can

We divide to connect. We have found that some students respond better to one teacher than the other, and so taking ego out of the situation and just accepting human nature helps everyone. It's important to notice those subtle cues coming from the students and act accordingly. We work with the teachers and support staff in a similar way, encouraging as much genuine connection as possible.

We always defer to a teacher as the decision maker in his or her own classroom space and ask permission before doing seemingly simple things like adjusting lights or desks, or asking for a student's help. Whenever possible, we partner with the classroom teacher and support staff. It is crucial for us to learn what we can about the tone of the day so far, particular students, or other details that may be important before we begin.

Play, Play, Play

We are strong advocates of a playful, open attitude. Playfulness might look like arriving in the classroom, tiptoeing and stepping on only the dark tiles as we move toward the teaching space. Play might look like dropping everything (all our stuff) and joining in on whatever the class is doing: joining Zumba with a dancer on the projection board, plopping down on the rug for the end of their read-aloud story, grabbing an empty chair and quietly sidling up to a student so that he or she can catch us up on what is going on—in essence, letting the students be the masters, teaching us.

Play also looks like students tapping their hands on their legs, first slowly then quickly. There may be no words. We just lead and they follow when they are ready: tapping toes, clapping hands and wiggling fingers, blinking quickly, blowing air and making noises like popping bubbles, or using all of the long-vowel sounds with extended exhales. We let them bring their attention to what we are doing when they are ready, on their own terms. And when we speak, we ask questions and invite their participation: "What if we do this? How about if we try this? How about this?" Play opens and relaxes the brain, opening the door to voluntary practice.

Meet Teachers Where They Are

> "Having time for my students to sit in my lap, having the time to truly connect with them and show my care of them, show that I want to do this with them, all with no academic or learning expectation is something that I consider one of the gifts of this mindful program."
> —Teacher, primary autistic support

For many teachers, just like their students, this class may be their first encounter with mindfulness practice. We keep that as our operating assumption and try to remember what it felt like for us to have outside consultants drop in on our autonomous classrooms when we were teachers—though, if memory serves, we are sure that none of them, back in the day, ever came in and told us to sit and relax and just be with our breath!

And so we gently invite teachers to step away from their paper piles, red pens, inbox of e-mails, manila folders, and endless to-do lists. We also invite them to take a break, to take care of themselves, to come and be students and to be with their students.

Much like our students, a teacher's participation may vary, or wax and wane, from class to class and week to week. Some will firmly resist all of our encouraging invitations for gentle self-care. Some will dive in headfirst on the first day and beam each time we show up. After a few weeks, one teacher announced, "The breathing ladies are here!!! Ahh, I feel better already. Get the lights!"

No matter what students' or teachers' engagement appears to be, we just keep showing up, ever-positive and ever-encouraging of whatever they need in that moment. We share with them how much we honor their work and skillful support. Whether they participate fully, or merely tolerate our being there, we always make time for positive reinforcement and true connection. We thank them all for their time and willingness to fit our program into their busy day.

Provide Consistency

Part of creating a safe space and keeping kids and staff engaged is consistency. We show up. We are very predictable in our schedule: weekly, same place, same time, same support, same T-shirts, and same jokes (some might say). We use a very predictable format that starts with attention practice, from auditory to multisensory to visual, and then move on to movement practice, from subtle to fine motor to gross motor. This predictability supports a sense of safety. Cultivating curiosity comes in small doses. Sudden surprise is not an intended element in our classes, especially with trauma survivors. One of our most important intentions in creating a sense of safety is to never trigger anyone, ever. Without knowing students' histories, we find it helpful to create opportunities for choice and to guide them to find and stay in their "comfort zone."

Students Teach Us How to Treat Them

We met Amanda during our weekly classes with the female shelter care unit at our local youth intervention center. She had been a little quiet but mostly amenable to what we were offering. One day after a month or so, we were leading a movement called "Open and Close." We reminded the girls to notice what they were feeling in their bodies and to make any changes or adjustments as they chose. Their options included stopping altogether, if they felt like that was best for them.

We moved slowly, modeling the movement at the front of the room and talking them through it. While most of the girls extended their arms out to their sides and then wrapped themselves up (as in a self-hug), Amanda stopped. She stared blankly, with her arms folded low across her waist. We could tell that she was processing something and perhaps not feeling the best.

One of us asked, "Are you okay? Does this movement not feel right for you?" Her response was quick and genuine. "No. I hate it, actually. First, when my arms are out you make me feel vulnerable, and then when I curled up and crossed, I felt like a victim." Silence.

The class came to a full stop. We quietly acknowledged her intuitive sense of awareness—noticing what she felt, really felt inside, moment to moment. We were also grateful to her for being brave enough to share her authentic experience. Her disclosure created an invaluable reminder for us to make our "invitational, choice-based language" as clear and as deliberate as possible. The element of choice needs to be repeated continuously throughout our instruction. This is important in all our classes, but especially in a predominately choice-less environment like the one in which we were working with Amanda. We continue to learn from students like Amanda exactly what we need to do in order to create the most mindful experience in the most healthful and helpful environment *for all*. Specific examples of the invitational, choice based language we use are provided in the next section.

Make the Plan, Work the Plan, and Let It Flow

We go in with a lesson plan, sequenced and comprehensive, based on where we've been with a group and where we want to go with them. We open the binder, begin to follow it, and remain flexible to mix it up in response to the students' needs, rather than our own, when it becomes clearly appropriate. We hold onto our initial objectives and adjust if our students would benefit. Our lessons are predictable enough in structure that by the end, we always close mindfully, with as much connection as possible, no matter what. Finding a way to help students end well, even if things started messily, creates a positive closure and sets them up for success, with positive associations for the next session.

Components of a Lesson

We typically follow a basic lesson structure, always hitting a few key points in some way and at some time:

• Choice—*sitting in chairs*: "Go ahead and get comfortable in your chair. You might want to try sitting tall, leaning back or not. Decide where you wish to place your hands, in your lap or on your legs. Your feet can be crossed or flat on the floor. You choose how sitting comfortably is for you. You have lots of choice here."

• Attention—*teacher's flashlight is utilized as a visual example of targeting one's attention*: "Notice how this light can move slowly, quickly, back and forth or all over the place. This light can be like our attention. Sometimes our attention can settle and focus. But there are times when our attention can feel like this—scattered, hard to make still. Raise your hand if yours has ever felt like that? Mine too. We're going to practice settling our attention, even just for a moment. Everybody's attention will get distracted; it simply drifts off. Notice when it does that and just try to bring it back . . . back to what we are doing."

• Sound—*a student rings the tone bar/chimes*: "We can practice using our minds by putting our attention on a sound. Just notice the sound and notice where your attention goes. Then try to return to the sound before it ends."

• Breath—*Hoberman sphere (breathing ball) gets passed from student to student*: "Here's our chance to move our attention to our bodies, to our breathing. When each of you have the breathing ball, just match the opening of the ball to your next in-breath and close it as you exhale. The rest of us will practice noticing when we begin to breathe in, opening our hands—like we're holding the ball too—with our inhale, and closing our hands as we breathe out. There is no need to control or change your breath; each of our movements will look different from everybody else's. That's okay. Whenever you are ready, move your attention to your breath and go ahead—breathe in and out."

• Movement—*practice using attention by noticing the sensations involved in small movements*: Try lifting your chin slowly, and notice what you feel in your neck and shoulders. Then slowly drop your chin—do any sensations change? Lift again and then drop. Check out how your body feels with this movement. Do a couple more ups and downs if you want to. Maybe try tilting your head side to side, slowly. Check in on your jaw. Where else does your attention go when you tilt your head? Your shoulders? Your upper back? Let the flashlight of your attention go to wherever you notice sensations. Now move based on what you feel. Maybe you lift, tilt, or turn your head or roll and rotate your shoulders. It is entirely up to you."

• Sensations while moving—*self-care and choice*: "If it feels like too much to do all of this movement, just ease off. Or if it feels like your body wants you to do more, make it more intense for you. It's up to you, what you do. Just notice what you feel in your body and make your next choice based on what you feel."

• Rest—*notice and make your own choice:* "Resting might seem easy for you or it could be really challenging. Either way, it's okay. We're just going to give it a shot. Notice if there is any part of the next few minutes that feels okay. Your eyes can be closed or open, or you can try long blinks, or maybe stare at the floor. It's up to you. The way you sit is also up to you. How can you rest best? Slide back and lean? Stretch your legs long, cross or uncross them. Arms too. Hands on belly, interlaced? Arms crossed or hanging down? See if getting still works for you. If not, try getting half of your body still; the other half can catch up later. Is breath moving in your body? Be a detective; use your flashlight to follow your moving breath. This is our last part of practice. If it has been a little rough for you so far, end well. This is what your brain and body will remember. End well."

Let Students Lead

During his fifth and sixth grade years, Toby was a "frequent flyer" in our after-school detention program. We first met him in his fourth-grade classroom as part of a small grant to provide programming across 5 weeks in regular education classrooms. Toby's resistance was evident, and his teacher's goal, by spring of that year, seemed to be to just get him out of the classroom (and to the hallway, another classroom, or the principal's office) as soon as possible. So that first year our connection was mixed and brief.

The next year came with a contract to provide skills training after school for students who had "earned" detention. We were there twice a week and so was Toby, when the principal or attending teacher would allow him stay.

After a few months and a few rough exits from the program, Toby seemed to figure out that we were going to continue to be in his life, given that his behavior did not change and his principal wasn't backing down. The principal was present on the day we saw a shift in Toby. We were working through a standing series of mindful movements when he asked to lead. Up until that moment, we had little trust in him to follow along, let alone to lead. But there was something in the air, maybe hope or a new optimism. With a simple nod, Toby came up to the front of the group of a dozen students, ranging from first to fifth graders.

He used some of our words, but mostly what we heard was his own flare: "Look up here, stand up tall, no—taller. Breathe in and open your arms like wings. Like this. Really wide, lean back and look up. Breathe out or whatever. Drop your arms and relax. Do it again. Okay, I'm done."

Toby finished and went directly to a chair in the back of the room, seemingly distant from the group.

Adults and students alike were all a little stunned, for our own various reasons. Toby had absorbed what we had been teaching all along. He had asked his fellow detention servers to focus, breathe, move, and repeat. He led the group in a relevant activity. He used school-appropriate language.

"Toby, can we borrow that for other classes at other schools? Our high school students would love it?" We expected a protective reaction and got the opposite: "Sure, Miss, just call it *Angel Wings*. And have them do it slowly."

This was also a reminder to us to remain open, lest our own prejudgments preclude the realization that kids may be absorbing more than we see.

Tangible Tools

"I love the fact that students are given tools to use. They enjoy all hands-on activities and will talk about specific tools and what they mean, such as the Slinky [students get to move them slow and fast, big and small, up and down], and then they ask if I could get some for my classroom prize box so that they can earn one to take home and try on their own."

—Teacher, intermediate emotional support

From drums and songs to Slinkies and balloons, an important part of nearly every class we teach involves some form of play with younger students and the use of tangible metaphors with older students. As often as possible this means getting something into our students' hands. By doing so, we are showing them that we believe they can do it, and we trust them to show us that they can.

We might have students explore the air moving out of big balloons as a way to connect with the air moving in their own breath. We may ask students to find their own way to create sound with a drum and watch to see what they produce. After they have experimented in their own way, they are empowered to lead the group. Feedback and variations might include requests such as "Can you speed up? Slow down? How about tapping very softly? And now maybe get really loud—make it a big finish."

The giggles and smiles tell us that students are having fun even as much learning is occurring. Students are initiating and inhibiting responses, waiting for their turns, mirroring the actions of others, encouraging their classmates with high fives and kind words, and leading their peers and teachers—all of which is creating community and enhancing a feeling of being okay on the inside, even if for only moment.

Communication in Practice

"When you greet our students, it is truly moving to see you look at them, hold their hands, and really wait until the students are connected with you. It is something that I just do not see often."

—Teacher, autistic support classroom

For our students with more complex needs, we have been told that the goal of any program should be communication. We considered this overall objective in terms of mindfulness. As best we can, we try to demonstrate mindful communication. Students know that our attention is in this moment with them. We are nowhere else. Connection is the core of our work and the foundation of our communication. We greet them and (when time allows) shake hands at the end as well. Handshakes are full of eye contact, slowing down, listening and reminiscing about the previous week or tapping into an individual detail ("So, did you get to go to the Lego movie this weekend?"). We often jot down notes to lead the connection the following week.

Invitational Approach

> "One of my favorite parts of Wellness Works is the way you use so much choice with my most stubborn students, and they eventually all get it and try what you are asking them to do. I can't believe they do it."
>
> —Teacher, middle school emotional support

One of the most critical parts of our program—allowing smoothness and ease in all our work with special-needs students and populations—is our use of an "invitational approach." We provide lots and lots of opportunities for choice. For us, this is a recent change in attitude toward participation and effort. Our eyes were opened when we trained with David Emerson in his trauma-sensitive yoga course in April 2013.

As teachers, we can think we aren't doing our job if we let students "get away with too much," make their own decisions, or know that they can opt out of an activity. We can get stuck in the "my-way-or-the-highway" attitude when, in reality, there is no highway, and we lose credibility with every empty threat. A stance of inviting students is against most of what we have learned as autonomous classroom leaders: "Don't give them choice because what if they don't follow?" is a more typical classroom stance. Yet when we don't meet their resistance with force or limited options, they have nothing to fight against and usually will try things out for themselves. We also encourage our students to "Notice what your body feels and make your choice based on that." At the very core of this model and a key component of our program is self-care.

The Power Is in the Return

One of the contexts where we offer mindfulness is in a diagnostic kindergarten classroom. The students are 5 and 6 years old, and their everyday lives in and out of the classroom prove to be quite challenging. One student in particular, whom we have gotten to know fairly well, is Marcus. He is a sweet boy with tousled curls and a body that wants to be on the move, though perhaps not always at the most opportune moments. He is resistant but curious about what we do.

One recent day, he began the session on his chair in the group. But unlike his classmates, he was bogged down by his daily gear. His winter coat was on and zipped to the top, and his full backpack was still securely strapped to his shoulders. He had trouble sitting on his chair with his cumbersome backpack in the way. The teacher and staff had tried to encourage him to put it away, in his cubby, but we could see his growing discomfort and knew that pressing him might make him bolt. So, one of us squatted down to his eye level to help him adjust it a bit so he could lean back on it like a pillow and told him if he could sit quietly with *ready hands* and *ready feet*, we would be okay with the backpack. The deal worked, and Marcus stayed.

Marcus was curious to ring the tone bar that we use to begin class. He would fidget and talk, call out and push back from the circle, wanting his turn to strike the tone. Then he would gather himself every time a student took his or her turn. We reinforced his efforts with a thumbs-up or a smile, for even that one tiny moment of stillness or quiet. At last came his turn, and with a bit of help he rang the tone bar, followed by an entirely new expression on his face: one of wonder, even delight.

Throughout class he came in and out of practice. Each time he left, we kept the flow of practice instead of calling him out or begging him back. He ran to the cubbies and lay on the floor, rolling around. When he returned to the circle, we smiled and guided him quietly back into the group activity. While he was present, we expected good things. Commands, pushing, and pressuring went nowhere with Marcus, and invitational language allowed him to return by choice, his pride—one of the only things he had—intact. On one occasion he did exit abruptly, but it was for a bathroom break. Rather than criticize his departure, we commended him for listening to his body and for being so quiet and considerate upon his return.

Working with Marcus, and many of our students, is like watching waves. Some days are smooth, with rolling highs and lows, whereas other days are tumultuous and rough. We cannot miss the parallel between Marcus's behavior and our own minds. One moment there is clear focus and then the next, our thoughts have wandered far away. What is true for us is also true for young Marcus: The important part is not the drifting off; the power is in the return. And so we just keep showing up. We keep returning. And Marcus does too.

Try It, then Take It and Run with It

After all of our plotting and planning, instructing, playing, resting, breathing, moving, and connecting, we often look at each other after a class and wonder, "Was that successful?" We debrief as co-leaders, calling attention to the glimmers of positive change for a child who has otherwise been mostly struggling. We share our curiosities aloud, our plans for the following class, including moments of challenge as well as those of laughter and levity. This is yet another benefit to our team-teaching approach, of having a community of teachers. But perhaps even more fulfilling than the checking in that we do with each other is the checking in that we get to do with students the next time we see them.

> Kevin had been in two of our sessions at the youth intervention center and on this day, we were about to begin our third class with his unit. Because the population at the facility is always changing, we begin the session by asking a question: "Who can tell our new residents why we are here, and what this class is about?" Kevin threw his hand up and said, "Miss, I kinda already told them." Curious as to know how he had explained mindfulness and the things we had been sharing and practicing, I said, "Wow—good for you, what did you say?" He responded at length: "I told them the same story you told us last week about your own kids. And how you were in your kitchen and heard they were fighting down in your basement. That in the time it took you to get to them, you had taken some deep breaths and you were able to respond, instead of react. So you didn't scream and yell; you just stayed calm. And that's what I told these guys: that you are showing us how to respond instead of just react, because when you respond, it turns out better."
>
> We sat so quiet, so still. The grin appeared on Kevin's face. He could read the awe and excitement over the connection he had made. We bumped fists, then told him to get out of the detention center and finish school so he could join our teaching team. That is the power of mindfulness and connection.

Evidence-Based Research

Cheryl Desmond, Professor, Educational Foundations, Millersville University, has published findings of two research studies on the effectiveness of a school-based program of mindful awareness (Wellness Works in Schools) on students in an urban, low-income public middle school in Lancaster, Pennsylvania:

- *Observational study of middle school special education students, 2008–2009.* The study examined six students' behavioral responses during a series of seven to nine lessons on mindful awareness practices from Wellness Works lessons. The findings "strongly support the positive effects of mindful awareness teaching on student cognitive, physical and social behavior" (Desmond, 2009, p. 9).
- *Randomized controlled study of sixth-grade students, 2009–2010.* This research project evaluated the effectiveness of the school-based program of mindful awareness on the self-regulation and the executive functions skills of 40 sixth-grade students in an urban middle school in Lancaster, Pennsylvania. The findings indicated that "treatment

students (participated in ten sessions) maintained or improved executive function skills while the skills of control students regressed" (Desmond & Hanich, 2010, p. 6)

Offering mindfulness in special education settings offers the possibility of growth in an individual and in the larger group. If we, as teachers, are not rigidly attached to expectations, outcomes and lesson plans there will often be a very natural unfolding of learning taking place. Instruction that is mindful, attentive, and fluid will best match the needs within the group. And isn't that precisely what mindfulness is about? Noticing. Notice what is happening, moment to moment, and notice what is called for in each moment. Gratefully, quite so often we are the ones who are learning from our students. They are mindfully leading us and themselves, one breath, one movement, one moment at a time.

REFERENCES

Desmond, C. (2009). *The effects of mindful awareness teaching practices of the wellness works in schools program on the cognitive, physical, and social behaviors of students in an urban, low income middle school.* Research report, Millersville University, PA.

Desmond, C., & Hanich, L. (2010). *The effects of mindful awareness teaching practices on the executive functions of students in an urban, low income middle school.* Research report, Millersville University, PA.

CHAPTER 4

Teaching Mindfulness across Differences

A Spectrum of Perspectives

Betsy Hanger

I teach mindfulness in the Los Angeles Unified School District as a volunteer trained by Mindful Schools. My students live in "at-risk" communities with families under stress. Caregivers may live with insecure immigration status and/or be unemployed, underemployed, or working multiple, low-paying jobs. Nearly 70% of my students identify as Mexican American, living in historically Latino neighborhoods in East Los Angeles. Others are part of more recent immigrant communities, including Armenian American, Korean American, and other Asian/Pacific Islanders. As a European American woman, my presence in these Los Angeles classrooms is often a novelty. Many of my students may not regularly encounter people with blue eyes or hear English spoken by an American-accented native speaker.

I am blessed to be the mother of two adult children who identify as queer. Their coming-out process catapulted me into activism around LGBTQ civil rights. During this process I have learned about my own "privilege" and the oppressions, visible and invisible, of others. I have learned about multigenerational trauma and its long-term effects on oppressed communities. I have observed that the celebration of differences and "outsider" status can be confusing and uncomfortable for some. I am still learning. Examining my own preconceptions about frequently hidden, often reviled communities has meant looking hard at my conditioning, deconstructing my Midwestern, Protestant, suburban upbringing, as well as my straight identity, and noticing my reflexive "othering" of fellow human beings. The Riddle Scale charts my own attitudes as I move beyond tolerance of differences, to celebration (Riddle, 1994).

Contemplative practices teach us that we are "both–and"—both unique *and* united in our humanity. Nevertheless, a decade of mindfulness practice has not eliminated "ouch" moments in my work with youth, who make me acutely aware of my errors. I am prodded "off the cushion" to become an ally and do social justice work. The resulting friends and colleagues educate and inspire me to continue deconstructing my hidden presumptions. My mistakes, but more my willingness to feel and grow from them, have become my practice. The embodiment of contemplative practices has been crucial for me to unlearn the layers of oppression that I've uncovered, both as recipient and as perpetrator.

This chapter proposes two realities: that mindfulness training with diverse populations requires special attention and intention, *and* that we share a common humanity. The experts cited in this chapter note many through-lines of connection that apply to all mindfulness teaching. Eschewing assumption and replacing it with curiosity and openness allows empathy to arise and community to be created.

In researching the material for this chapter, I reached out to dozens of people, primarily mindfulness educators, working in varied settings with many kinds of people. Some identify as people of color, sexual minorities, or as recent immigrants to North America; others are European American. They are all pioneers in mindfulness training in urban classrooms, juvenile halls, group homes, with pregnant teen mothers, and in public schools where most students are labeled *at risk*; their voices give this chapter its variety. Direct quotations, when taken from interviews, have been approved for publication and are cited as personal communication.

This chapter is comprised of four sections. The section on diversity contains a primer on privilege as well as observations from youth educators (whose first mention includes their identity descriptor). The next section, "Gleanings," provides descriptions of best practices that have worked in diverse settings. "Entering the System" offers skillful means to meet with some of the challenges we face when we are disconnected from the community we serve. The final section, "Celebrations," shares examples of successes to inspire us.

Diversity

A Primer on Privilege: Definitions

Many of us find that we stumble in spaces where differences in race, ethnicity, cultural background, or economic or educational privilege make us uncertain or uncomfortable. The following section aims to give us vocabulary to speak about this challenging subject with increasing fluency and comfort. For example, by asking a group of youth for their preferred gender pronouns, we normalize identities beyond the gender binary and acknowledge the existence of an often invisible minority. Learning to use gender-neutral pronouns— simply inserting *they* or *zie* into your usual conversation celebrates all youth in a respectful manner.

What Is Diversity and Why Does It Matter?

There is no "standard" or "normal" set of human attributes along the dimensions of race, ethnicity, gender, sexual orientation, socioeconomic status, education, age, physical or mental ability, religious beliefs, and political beliefs. Beyond simple recognition, we have a responsibility to respect the ways in which individuals and groups differ from ourselves and our expectations. That respect helps move us beyond tolerance toward embracing and celebrating the rich dimensions of diversity contained within each individual. This perspective parallels mindfulness practice, in which we also learn to examine what we fear, with the ultimate goal of embracing it that we might gain new insight (Christopher Willard, personal communication, 2014).

What Is Privilege and Why Does It Matter?

Privilege is "an institutional, rather than personal, set of benefits granted to people whose race resembles that of the people who are in power" (Kendall, 2006, p. 63). Structural, institutional racism and other forms of bigotry, which extend across and beyond just racial identity, are deep and persistent in our modern lives. Privilege is a crucial lens for understanding a society that is filled with inequalities and injustices. Despite many advances in legal, economic, political, and social arenas, the majority culture continues to impose itself. "Privilege and power work together to create both a system of disadvantage (institutionalized racism) and overadvantage (privilege)" (Elizabeth Berila, personal communication, June 2014).

When we hold these realities in mind, we become more skillful in sharing mindfulness. Mere consciousness of my privilege does not enable me to shake it off. Because I hold (unearned) privilege, I feel the imperative to actively engage those without it, and to educate myself and others who share it. Understanding the advantages of privilege allows me to be a better ally. Awareness, cultivated on or off the cushion, reinforces the moral necessity to stand up for social justice.

What Is Microaggression?

Sue et al. (2007) describe microaggressions as "brief and commonplace daily verbal, behavioral, or environmental indignities, whether intentional or unintentional, that communicate hostile, derogatory, or negative racial slights and insults toward people" (p. 271). Mindfulness can bring the "micro" into the light where it can be seen, felt, and responded to more skillfully. Yet even among those who can recognize their privilege, microaggression still occurs. We must continually practice being mindful about the speech and actions that have been unconsciously conditioned by the larger culture, and we must ask for and be open to feedback.

Privilege and marginalization can become complex aspects of identity. Beth Berila, who identifies as a white queer woman, offers an insightful example:

We are all complex human beings; we may be privileged in some ways and marginalized in others. For example: A working class heterosexual African American male student likely experiences some privilege because he is male and heterosexual. However, not only does he experience marginalization because of his racial identity and his class identity, but his very experience of privilege will be shaped by those aspects of his identity. Whereas he may receive male privilege in some moments, in other moments, he may be targeted as "threatening" because of how black masculinity is too often constructed by dominant culture, which is probably even more nuanced by his class location.

This complexity means that we need to nuance our understanding of power and privilege. But it also opens more points for mindful connection with one another, since many (though not all) of us experience marginalization in some arenas and privilege in others. Rather than "ranking" oppressions, we can use these connections as points of empathy, so that we connect through our commonality while also valuing and honoring our differences. (personal communication, June 2014)

How Mindfulness Can Work against Presumption

Mindfulness can help us cultivate awareness of our impact: how much "space" we take up in the room, what presumptions we bring. A trainer in mindfulness-based stress reduction (MBSR) at Kaiser Permanente in Oakland, California, who identifies as Chinese American and taught with Mindful Schools, describes the potential for "neutral openness":

When you enter a room with students who have a different background from yourself, you need to pay special attention. Working cross-culturally with race, age, class, gender, or language issues, you always need to be aware of the diversity of the class as a whole and with each individual. I invite students to share from their experience and how it applies to their family life. This allows them to speak from their perspective, giving them respect and the space to share from their reality. As a mindful instructor, I try to be in a neutral and open place moment to moment, allowing the young people to be seen for who they are. (Michele Ku, personal communication, March 2014)

Megan Cowan, the cofounder and program director of Mindful Schools, who identifies as white European, describes her mindful lens on diversity:

"Open" characterizes how we're meeting people: unbiased, unfiltered. Retreats sensitize us to the idea that we easily get caught in an assumption without realizing it, even when diversity is not an issue. Mindfulness is a fundamental human capacity. Walking into any room, I am always attempting to meet the universal qualities of being human. Everyone has emotions, but I don't know yours, or your life background. I'm looking for commonality, feeling into the situation with my heart, in stillness and in quiet, to let the group teach me who they are.

When you look and sound like someone wants you to look, it's an easier entry point for connection, but presence and open-mindedness are more important in these cases. It may take more time for those filters and biases to fall away because we automatically and blindly act on our backgrounds, our prior experience, and assumptions. Our defenses are highlighted when our unconscious expects something different. So we want to recognize that, and then let go of our assumptions. (personal communication, March 2014)

Skillful Ways of Working with Youth, from the Perspective of Diverse Teachers

Avoid Generalizations and Respect Individual Difference

Claire-Anne Touchstone, a dance teacher with the Los Angeles Unified School District, identifies as multiracial. Her doctoral research was on microaggression in multiracial communities.

A white teacher once told me: "I just want to let you know that black students need to have some freedom of expression. The Asian kids learn quickly and they can be quiet, but the black kids need to be able to banter with their teachers and jump around a lot." She had been taught that Standard English language learners from different cultures have distinct learning preferences, but had not absorbed the caveat that not all members of an ethnic group learn identically. This is what racial presumption looks like in the 21st century. (personal communication, March 2014)

Be Open about Differences

Pam Dunn is an African American educator and trainer with Mindful Schools:

When I'm with youth, I name the ways we're different before I bridge it. I'll say, "I don't know what you know about me, and I don't know about you." I lean into how I stand out, rather than as part of the group.

With adults, there can be an added disconnect with people who've done "diversity work." They don't want to question *anything* because they've heard "you can't ask." That's a funny invisibility. It feels much more impersonal than presumptions. If you want to know something about me, I need you to ask me. I don't want you to have to go to a white privilege workshop two states away to learn that I can't speak for my "group," but I will tell you how *I'm* doing. If I know you are asking *me* something, you win points by taking the risk to ask that. (personal communication, March 2014)

Honor the Roots of Mindfulness

Dzung Vo, pediatrician and adolescent medicine specialist at British Columbia Children's Hospital, in Vancouver, British Columbia, Canada, is a second-generation Vietnamese American Canadian who identifies as a person of color and a Vietnamese Buddhist. He explains:

My patients are going to find out about the Buddhist roots of mindfulness, even if I don't mention it, so why not? It's like trying to avoid "the elephant in the room." It's important to honor the roots of these practices. Otherwise, this risks cultural appropriation. When people discuss mindfulness as if they invented it, that makes the roots invisible. Mindfulness comes out of a historical tradition, culture, and people. Failing to mention it marginalizes the peoples that have given us this practice. (personal communication, 2014)

Cultivate Cultural Humility

In addition to his work at British Columbia Children's Hospital teaching mindfulness awareness and resilience skills for adolescents (MARS-A), Dzung Vo teaches First Nations/Native American youth living in high-risk environments in the inner city. In his words:

I am learning from them, not trying to change or hide anything in the curriculum, but increasingly framing it in the context of what they've taught me. I usually say outright that "I don't have the same experiences as you, and I want to learn from you. I didn't grow up in this neighborhood or live this history. I'm not here to lecture you." What we need is not cultural competence, but cultural humility.

First Nations youths' at-risk behavior is rooted in social determinants and multigenerational trauma. In Canada it's directly traced to the legacy of residential schools. We see poverty, multigenerational sexual abuse, alcoholism, and poor mental health. These can be directly traced to trauma. Many mindfulness practices are consistent with First Nations spiritual teachings. We talk about reconciling the past and present moments: How can we use the present moment to heal the past and the future? (personal communication, March 2014)

Learn Your Students' Concerns: Don't Presume

Christine de Guzman, a Philippine American, teaches in two elementary schools in the Sacramento, California, area. One is in a low-income neighborhood with public housing. The students live close-knit lives: the school is small, and most students go to the Boys and Girls Club after school. By asking, de Guzman learned that family dynamics preoccupy the students. So she frames mindfulness as an inner sanctuary: "Sometimes you just want to have a little time to yourself at home. Mindfulness is good even when people around you are stressed." In the more middle-class elementary school across town, her students report overscheduled lives; they worry about getting their homework done when they have a soccer game. They respond to a different message (personal communication, March 2014).

When a Group Is Very Diverse, Don't Lean on the Students of Color

Devin Berry, an African American mindfulness trainer, integrates youth leadership and contemplative work in many programs, such as the Mosaic Project and the East Bay Meditation Center.

Sometimes I work in private schools, diverse ethnically and racially, but the majority is middle-class and upper-class white kids. I peer-teach with a white woman, and my identity is advantageous. I tell the kids who I am: my background, how my color brought me to this practice. It's raw and honest. I don't leave out any mysteries. They connect with me because I'm real. Our differences are no longer an elephant in the room.

Often, a handful of students of color will be there. As I introduce myself, a few have been from my same neighborhood, so we feel a commonality. After class, I make a point to connect with them. But I know that I won't always be there; the students of color have to stay after I leave. So I won't put them on the spot or pull something out of them that won't feel comfortable after I leave. In subtle, easy ways—just a simple hand slap, or my voice may inflect a little differently with a different slang—by a bit of code switching, I acknowledge that we're working within the dominant culture. It's subtle but important. (personal communication, March 2014)

A "Bill of Responsibilities" for Mindfulness Trainers

I didn't always teach in public schools. My musical career was in historically white-majority private schools, weighted down by the codes of the dominant society. Professional development training on diversity was arranged infrequently and rarely led to change. Privilege saturated these schools in a way that did not welcome diverse "newcomers," be they faculty, staff, students, or their families. The more visible aspects of my identity seemed to prevent deeper conversations about difference, and I became acutely aware that I had segregated myself in bastions of privilege.

Distilled from many sources, the following "Bill of Responsibilities" has been created and refined by colleagues and students who identify in one or many ways as outside the dominant culture. Couched in mindful prose, it speaks in plain language, clarifying our students' right to respect, acknowledgment, and skillful communication. These statements appropriately place the onus of responsibility on the privilege holder. Allow these words to help you uncover unconscious attitudes and deep roots of oppression, which may enable you to act more skillfully on your heart's intentions.

1. Make space. The more space you relinquish, the more you show through your actions that you are committed to radical listening and empathy. Being quiet is a radical action for a person of privilege.
2. Don't ask me to represent the opinions of everyone else whom you think looks like me. I have the right to be an individual.
3. Don't assume anything about me, my life, or my family. Don't assume that my dad is not living with us, my brother is in jail, I like to play basketball, I can speak Spanish, my gender presentation matches my assigned identity, or my parents pressure me to get great grades. I am a person, not evidence of a statistic, not a stereotype.
4. Let me tell you about my hopes and ambitions; they may not be what you expect. Encourage me to pursue them.
5. Don't mention my identity, or your friends who share my identity, in the first 5 minutes you meet me.
6. Don't assume any of my identities invalidates my experiences of any other of my identities. I can hold multiple identities: a person of color (POC) *and* queer, someone who goes to public school *and* has very well-educated parents, who may hold privilege or can "pass" in some circumstances but not others.
7. Step up when you hear or see instances of racism, homophobia, gender bias, or any other prejudice. Discrimination is a problem for everyone, not just for me. Be an ally: an upstander, not a bystander.
8. Let me define oppression, racism, homophobia, privilege, and the intersections of these for myself. If I don't already know what these terms mean and you are well versed in the area, give me a foundation with which to work. Then let me work with and express those definitions without passing immediate judgment.
9. Talk the way you usually talk. Don't take up my rhythms, inflections, or energy to bring me closer to you, or fake appreciation for anything I might like: music, clothes, food, trends, games, heroes.
10. Ask your friends who share your identity how to be a better ally. Don't rely on me to correct you, fix your opinions, or make you better. It is not my responsibility to educate you on me. When I want to share my story with you, I will, on my own terms.
11. Be content if I don't feel like answering your questions about my

identity. It might not be about you. I might talk about my identity with people so often that I am just tired.

Oppression and microaggression are real. Learn about the discrimination that are faced on a daily basis by those who are different from you. You can start by downloading Peggy McIntosh's classic "White Privilege: Unpacking the Invisible Knapsack" (in McIntosh, 1988). Stay informed about school-based practices that empower diverse students to use mindfulness, but might not have that label (e.g., restorative justice, council process, nonviolent communication). Resources for further anti-bias education can be found at the end of this chapter.

English Language Learners and English as a Second Language Teachers

When teaching students who have partial bilingual skills, ask the experienced English as a second language (ESL) teacher in the classroom for feedback. For example, you might ask, "What can I do better—did you understand the concepts I taught?" If we respect teachers' layers of skill, they will partner with us.

Paige Leven, a bilingual ESL-trained seventh-grade social studies teacher who identifies as white, recommends these strategies to share mindfulness with students of varying English proficiency:

- When you pose a question for discussion, let students talk to a partner before they share with the group, so they have time to practice and prepare.
- Build the key vocabulary in multiple ways: Write it, act it out, bring in imagery to strengthen attention on the vocabulary.
- Encourage students to come up with their own images and connections; the cultural capital they bring into the classroom is powerful.
- Tap into their immediate knowledge; note what their classroom teacher is working on and refer to those ideas.
- Some students might go through a whole day without speaking English. So if a student doesn't seem confident, ask him or her the next time. Look for volunteers, but also for new voices. (personal communication, 2014)

When students contribute, thank them. Sometimes the first time a student speaks in class will be to lead a practice. Students' enthusiasm for speaking often grows after such an honor.

Use writing in your teaching. Andrea D'Asaro, a European American ESL teacher in Philadelphia who researches the intersection of mindfulness and ESL, teams with a senior ESL teacher to incorporate practices for the whole year. Inspired by the Learning to Breathe curriculum, she moves directly from mindful practice into writing, because it helps overcome students' concerns about language fluency: "As we observe our thoughts, we can move more easily into free writing; the practice works to build confidence and introspection" (D'Asaro, personal communication, 2014).

As adults who work with youth, if we carry racial, economic, educational, gender, or other kinds of privilege, we must be aware of their impact on ourselves and others. When we identify our missteps, increase our empathic sensibilities, and learn about being a good ally, our mindfulness practice deepens. Substituting openness for conditioned presumption becomes a moment-to-moment practice. Compassionate collaboration with people who don't share our backgrounds is a necessity for this growth, and a rich benefit as well.

Gleanings

This section includes anecdotes and advice about best practices from teachers working in a wide range of challenging settings.

Take It Slowly

Peter Levine [2009] and other developmental trauma psychologists have noted that the nervous system integrates new information through titration; when you adjust to a new medicine, you take low doses and increase very slowly. We should guide students into a state, then out of a state, then into it again. If children are holding trauma, "unmodulated attention" is not right for them. You need to recognize the symptoms of trauma responsibly. (Chris McKenna, personal communication, 2014)

Certainly not all diverse or at-risk students exhibit trauma, and it's invaluable to learn about how to work skillfully with those who do.

Set a Modest Goal So That Every Student Succeeds

We used to be unrealistic, promising "You'll gain self-control, you'll feel . . .," but we changed to: "There are things you can try to help yourself feel okay, even when you don't feel okay. Your mind is like a muscle; work with it. Notice what your attention does right now. Your trained attention helps you when you want to feel okay." This [kind of wording] allows every student to achieve some success. (Wynne Kinder, personal communication, 2014)

If we refrain from telling students what they're experiencing and don't oversell mindfulness training, students will find their own practices and become empowered.

Teaching Is Serving; Serving Is the Practice

How do you get clear in your intention? Where do you begin? You need to get your head and heart ready to go into an institution. This is called the "intervention before the intervention." Have a North Star, your ultimate guiding point. Be in line with your own intentions as you walk into a new setting.

The real value of working with youth, service as practice, is a different kind of paycheck. Alignment with service, with your North Star, changes everything. Alignment springs from the treasure in the middle: what we have to share.

What am I sharing? An invitation to freedom? Every person has value, no matter what they've done or been through? You must mine this for yourself before you're in the parking lot, ready to go in and teach.

When service becomes the practice, it's a hero's journey: completely personal and individual. An [experienced] mindfulness teacher can help to prepare you for work in the field. Getting ready can be a long process. But in the end, it's like going into the woods to shoot arrows. You stand straight, align your body to the target, pull back your bow, and let it fly.

I believe that we're capable of freedom beyond conditions. When I used to go to San Quentin Prison, if I was turned away at the gate, I got super frustrated. But I needed to check out the ecology of this system: It is full of frustration for everybody in it. I need to connect with the frustration of everybody in that system, and all the people exposed to it: the families of the prisoners, the guards, the corrections officers. Suddenly my frustration becomes *the* frustration. I can feel the dehumanizing feeling: Nobody escapes it, not even the oppressors in the institution. The more frustrating it is, the more I need to connect to the universality of that feeling state. Then I'm not making it about "my" frustration. It's the frustration of that whole world.

Wherever my heart is needed the most, I need to be. But I get to leave, and then come back: There's power to that. So, the more you try to keep me out, the more I'm coming in, to stand and deliver. (Vinny Ferraro, personal communication, April, 2014)

Allow Some Personal Choices

When there's resistance, and there is almost always a little, I remember we are not trained to probe that resistance: It could be cultural, religious, or economic. New students may still be working on their bravado, figuring out where they stand in the group. So they can choose to look out a window or sit wherever they choose in the room. When you give up that control, you don't lose control. The invitation to choose can be a huge ice breaker. (Wynne Kinder, personal communication, 2014)

Roll with It

Explain the practice posture vividly, with humor. Amy Saltzman notes:

Other than "staying in your space bubble," I do not normally ask students to sit in or maintain a particular position. Currently, my unspoken internal boundary is that participants can hum, whisper quietly to themselves, doodle, rock, fidget, wiggle . . . as long as it doesn't disrupt the class, either by distracting their classmates or pulling my attention. (blog post, March, 2014)

If I'm teaching in a chaotic classroom where the teacher resorts to tight-fisted, punitive "class management," these more flexible boundaries can invite more cooperation from the students. Many times, this is what the classroom teacher was seeking.

Patience Is Power

Wait while a student summons an answer, and ask everyone else to listen, mindfully waiting, with him or her. Ask students to notice how they feel while waiting. Remind them that patience is an act of generosity. This "slower" model can change a class atmosphere beyond the mindfulness lesson, as Roberts (2013) explains:

The meaning of patience today has reversed itself. . . . The virtue of patience was originally associated with forbearance or sufferance . . . about conforming oneself to the need to wait for things. But now that, generally, one need not wait for things, patience becomes an active and positive cognitive state. Where patience once indicated a lack of control, now it is a form of control over the tempo of contemporary life that otherwise controls us. Patience no longer connotes disempowerment—perhaps now patience is power.

Be Authentic

Doing some mindful movement, I directed the students into a forward bend. They're wearing uniforms—pants, skirts. One skeptical student said "I'm not going to! I'm wearing a skirt!" At the beginning of the next class, I apologized that we hadn't mentioned the movement portion ahead of time. It's really good to acknowledge when you've goofed. Teens are so unused to hearing an apology from an adult (Heidi Bornstein, personal communication, March 2014).

At the end of a lesson, I often ask, "What did you hear me say today? What might you practice again?" Sometimes the seemingly removed student has a profound response. This kind of experience has taught me not to scan the room anxiously or push too hard. I teach the ones who are making eye contact, who're raising a quiet hand, and remember that cultural norms around feeling invisible or disempowered to speak may be present. Or perhaps those who appear ambivalent may just be making up their own minds.

Be an Ally and Show Up for All Students

People of many identities, particularly sexual or gender identities, are or may feel invisible to outsiders. Students holding such identities often welcome our acknowledgment and advocacy. So I check if the school has a Gay Straight Alliance (GSA) or an equivalent group, and ask students how they observe "National Coming-Out Week" or the "Day of Silence." These simple actions could mean the world to a student—possibly invisible to you—who may be in agony and isolation. We never know who's going to turn out to be queer or otherwise feel different, so make no assumptions. I wear an "OUT for Safe Schools" badge every day, not just on the days of celebration and awareness.

Beyond being a queer ally, it's critical to show interest in the activities of all identity groups on campus that might wonder about your support. Small gestures, such as trying a new food at a multicultural bake sale, often mean more than you think. Connect the ethical tenets of mindfulness (e.g., compassion, generosity) to the cultural heroes of monthly celebrations, and weave these heroes into conversation throughout *all* months of the year. Students and staff deserve to know they have you as an ally.

Most importantly, show up for events. I once attended an after-school basketball game where I was shocked to realize that I was the only white adult face in the gym. Parents of the team members were surprised to see me. The team mentioned my attendance several times the next week, and their coach grew interested in the mindfulness elective I was offering to athletes and performers. This taught me to wonder about segregated spaces that I might be ignoring. Are there unspoken cultural and ethnic divisions that I could mindfully "disrupt" and thereby support? This is mindfulness is action.

Families, and Gratitude, Take Many Forms

Sol Riou teaches mindfulness in a school where 89% of students qualify for free or reduced lunch, with a diverse population of European American, Asian American, African American, Native American, and Mexican American students. Some students are homeless; many have single-parent families or are being raised by relatives. When she asks students about their caregivers, she knows their families might not have the same formation, so she uses the wording "who you go home to" rather than "parents." When she teaches gratitude practices, she welcomes everything. One boy surprised her by being grateful that his sister had been adopted away from the family; he felt she was better off financially and was at peace with their separation (personal communication, March 2014).

Working with Difficult Emotions

Many youth may never receive mental health services. Sometimes they will bring up a particularly vulnerable disclosure. If you find yourself the recipient of such a disclosure, Vinny Ferraro suggests following these steps, using your own words:

1. Acknowledge it. "Most of the time we're all just living a normal life, but we all go through difficult times, too." Most people are simply looking for some acknowledgment of what they've been through.
2. Respect this moment, this person's vulnerability. "Now that you've brought up something very difficult, let's just let it land in the room."
3. Normalize it, and if it's within your personal experience, make an authentic connection: "I know something about that feeling."
4. Create community by involving the others in the room (unless the young person brings up sexual abuse; see note at end of this section). "Does anyone else know something about how this feels?" *or* "Can you feel that in your hearts, can you feel your compassion arising?"
5. Invite them to receive what's in the room. Looking around the room, encourage the vulnerable person to do so, too. It may be hard for the person to come out of the feelings of isolation and loneliness; he or she may think, "No one knows what I'm going through." Perhaps say "See how many of us join you in knowing something about that hard feeling? See who's joining you in sharing this moment?"
6. Thank the person who shared the vulnerable feeling. "It's a gift that you've shared this. Thank you for being a leader." "Who feels closer to that person, knowing now what's been shared?" (The tension about sharing something so deep begins to transform as soon as hands start going up; let the empathy rise.) There's alchemy in this progression: normalize, respect, acknowledge. It shifts the scary or dirty secret into something powerful the vulnerable person can now share.
7. Now perhaps pull the atmosphere up a little, using a very kind tone. Acknowledge the sweetness of feeling compassion and move gently on. (personal communication, 2014)

Note: If a student brings up abuse, neglect, or something that requires mandatory reporting, don't move to points 4 or 5. Complete the process by letting others express compassion, as you model respect. Afterward, follow the legal and ethical guidelines of your institution, state, and profession, consulting with whomever necessary along the way.

Entering the System or Culture

Mindfulness training for youth is a relatively new undertaking. It's growing rapidly, thanks to skillful organizations providing training, excellent research, and media attention. Many providers are trained in a curriculum, but wonder how to bring their skills into a school district or community center. This section addresses a few of the systemic challenges in urban or public settings. For further ideas, attend conferences, participate in online list-serves, and keep in contact with mindfulness trainers who have experience in diverse settings. Many providers are forming collectives to pool resources, share contacts, and support one another through ongoing education about mindfulness, as well as issues of diversity, mental health, education, and different learning styles.

Is This for Everyone?

"Universal access" is part of the public school mandate in the United States. If we frame mindfulness training as providing universal access to some skills of self-regulation and self-compassion—time to reflect on purpose—public schools may be more open. For example, administrators may suppose that the child with attention-deficit/hyperactivity disorder (ADHD) might "need mindfulness" the most, and in this way, he or she could "get it" alongside peers. Rather than feeling singled out, as if the student needs to "get fixed," whole-class participation embeds the practice and extends the vocabulary of mindfulness to any other social–emotional learning already occurring.

Emphasize the Biophysical Foundations of Mindfulness

Defining mindfulness training as "mental health" may not be the most skill-ful way to navigate within diverse cultures. Chris McKenna observes:

Mental health services carry enormous negative stigma in almost all the immigrant communities I have worked with (primarily Central American, West African, Tibetan). At least some of this has to do with Western models of therapy that rely on Western constructs of "the self" to function. This is why biophysical/ somatic modalities are promising; they can accommodate a variety of cultural views. Overall, I think it's best to cast this training as stress reduction and inner life skills. Training some juvenile prison guards (mostly African American, first- or second-generation Latino, and Pacific Islander), we found that stress was a publicly acceptable thing to disclose and share, whereas "emotions" were not. Learning that "stress" and "emotion" are the same thing from a biological point of view was a breakthrough for this group. Kabat-Zinn's framing of "mindfulness as stress reduction" allows the best cross-cultural understanding. (personal communication, May 2014)

Anticipate Questions; Prepare Skillful, Secular Answers

If we are asked about "teaching religion," we need to be firmly secular, but also to demonstrate cultural understanding of the point of view of our questioners. In public school contexts, it's crucial to adhere to the separation of church and state, on which some questioners may need clarification. Devin Berry observes:

In the first class I taught at an East Oakland school, a couple of African American women devoted to their Pentecostal churches asked if we were teaching Buddhism. What were the differences between mindfulness, meditation, and prayer? I responded: "As I understand it, from my childhood, prayer is me talking to God. Mindfulness—and meditation, if you want to view it that way—is following the breath to see what's there, as we are present to the experience." (personal communication, March 2014)

One East Los Angeles elementary teacher, a devout Catholic, did research about the secular nature of the curriculum, before agreeing to go forward:

My first question was if mindfulness had anything to do with a religious practice that was not in accord with my personal religious beliefs. I found that [secular mindfulness] was a form of meditation, that there was no worship in it. Then I was able to be more relaxed about practicing the technique with my students. (Theresa Vazquez, personal communication, March 2014)

Presenting to Stakeholders

A good presentation to adult gatekeepers offers them a set of mindful experiences and steers away from promises to "fix" the students. Therapist Sarah McCarthy presented mindfulness to social workers from Teen Success Inc., whose clients are pregnant teens. She modified a set of questions from the adolescent curriculum of Mindful Schools. Framing the presentation around the adults' need for self-care and stress management, she said:

"Raise your hand if you've ever . . .

- said something you wish you could take back.
- felt like you're a pretty good multitasker, but sometimes you miss stuff.
- felt overwhelmed by all the things you have to get done in a day at work.
- felt preoccupied by thoughts about something that came up with a client.
- had a hard time sleeping because there's a lot on your mind.
- been in a bad mood but not felt sure about what emotion it is.
- spaced out at a meeting or conference."

Once there was some levity and connection in the room, she observed aloud:

These are all very normal aspects of daily life. Some take their toll on us, especially as service providers. Our emotions, levels of stress, thoughts are continually changing. Difficult emotions like anger, fear, worry, and stress actually release chemicals in our brain that can prevent us from thinking clearly and learning. Mindfulness helps stop these chemicals. It's also a tool you can use to notice thought patterns or mood states. (personal communication, 2014)

Growing a Program: One Model

The community of East Palo Alto hides in the shadows of Silicon Valley and was once the murder capital of the country. There is tension from cultural isolation and the contrast of poverty amidst much wealth nearby. The high school is small: 300 students, all low-income, many undocumented. At East Palo Alto Academy High School, Caren McDonald, chair of the English department, teaches mindfulness as half her course load. First she adapted the Still Quiet Place curriculum to settle her English students, just 5 minutes a day. Then she got permission from the administration to teach in all the freshman advisories once a week, and to create two elective courses. "Mindfulness Community" (grades 10 and 11) and "Mindfulness for Seniors" meet 3 days a week. Some students are directed into her electives by school staff, but many sign up voluntarily. When a visitor came from the Australian Department of Education to their school to research mindfulness, "students realized that people are paying attention to them, that mindfulness is a movement that's growing and they're part of it" (Caren McDonald, personal communication, March 2014).

Celebrations

Though working with different kinds of youth can be challenging, it is also filled with small triumphs and joyful epiphanies. The anecdotes below are offered by our colleagues as an inspiration: May your day-to-day resources outmatch the stresses you perceive, so that this crucial work can spread to even more overlooked but deserving communities.

Mindfulness Can Help with Bullying

In a Latino neighborhood a third-grade girl passes notes to two boys during mindfulness practice. Her mindfulness journal reveals that they pester her often, and she feels helpless. When she realizes how mindfulness lessons can help her stay strong against what she calls "the bully boys," she becomes more attentive. Then she advises her own mother how to use mindfulness to stay calm.

Mindfulness Can Empower Students with Trauma

In an impoverished neighborhood, over the summer, a student's sister and best friend were killed: one by a relative, the other run over by a car. Upon return to school the student asked his new third-grade teacher for the "lessons with the bell" to help him deal with the losses. His teacher did not feel prepared to lead the lessons, so the student led them in the new second-grade classroom. The previous year he did not seem to be paying attention to the mindfulness lessons, but clearly he absorbed a lot (Patrice Berlinski, personal communication, March 2014).

Mindfulness Can "Go Viral" in a School When Students Make It Their Own

In a large urban school that used character education as its social–emotional program, a colleague approached the mindfulness teacher. Could her mindfulness groups introduce a kindness practice during the schoolwide Kindness Month? The students responded eagerly: From the group of 60 advisory students who had the training, 40 middle school students volunteered to teach all the other advisories. They collaborated on the lesson plan; after defining mindfulness in their own words, they led an introductory practice using "Take Five"—one long breath, four normal breaths. They led their peers in two runs of "Take Five"; the second time included a silent repetition of "kind wishes" for themselves. The student leaders were really excited to get in front of their peers, to explain mindfulness, to ring the bell, and to share experientially what mindfulness is. By the end of the school week, the entire school—teachers and students alike—had experienced mindfulness woven into Kindness Month. The student leaders were proud to share the practices—to pique people's interest, then to be available as a resource (Becca Voss, personal communication, March 2014).

Mindfulness Can Make the Classroom a Community

I was sending kind thoughts with a small group of fifth graders, one with autism. He was upset, could not focus, and stammered. It was so hard for him to identify relationships or connect with emotions. He was unable to repeat any phrases; he just wanted to change the subject. A boy in the group chose to send him kind thoughts, then others began voicing their own phrases spontaneously. One said "I've liked you since first grade." His face softened instantly. When we wrote in the workbook about sending kind wishes, it was too much for him. He sobbed. I told him that it's good to feel; it's okay. He sat in his chair, assumed his mindful body, closed his eyes, and breathed until it was time to go. This is the miracle of mindfulness (Cheri Scarff, personal communication, April 2014).

Conclusion

Mindfulness practice can shine light on unseen and often difficult emotions. By revealing what is hidden, we are no longer as triggered by unseen forces.

Our fear does not as readily metastasize into hatred or aversion, from which we may act unconsciously. We often learn the most from our discomfort: What we avoid or dislike becomes our greatest teacher. When we accept and appreciate this experience, studying the process, we move toward freedom from those unseen forces, but it requires action off the cushion as well (Christopher Willard, personal communication, June 2014).

There is a clear parallel with this interior process when we work with those who are different from ourselves. The real consequences of bigotry—conscious and unconscious—can manifest in all of us. We may at first be wary or uncomfortable. But with open awareness, we appreciate the power of differences and the blessings of diversity. Mindfulness helps us overcome fear and distrust.

But it is not sufficient to practice diligently, set intentions to be open, and grow our awareness of privilege. True change requires courageous action. First we are obligated to reflect within ourselves and communicate within our communities. Mindfulness practice can inspire and empower us to stretch out of our comfort zones, into principled action. Only through wise action, constantly replacing presumption with open presence, will we transform mere awareness of diversity into connection, celebration, and social justice.

The teaching of mindfulness must evolve so that it can reach everyone. The stories of who "we" are, who "they" are—otherness as a distancing mechanism—*can* dissolve. Although we may never reach that complete freedom, we should never stop trying. We may never end hatred in our lifetime, and we must never stop trying. Only through action in the world, in collaboration with "others," can we hope to end bigotry. Our shared vision of freedom from suffering depends on it; the compassion and generosity practices that are crucial aspects of creating a strong, mindful community depend on it. The youth we teach, their elders with whom we partner, and the communities in which they live will be our best teachers.

ACKNOWLEDGMENTS

For interviews, inspiration, and much wisdom, I thank Rebecca Alleyne, MD, Patrice Berlinski, Beth Berila, PhD, Devin Berry, Jenny Betz, Heidi Bornstein, Claudia Chen, Megan Cowan, Andrea D'Asaro, Joyce Dorado, PhD, Pam Dunn, Vinny Ferraro, Connie Fourre, Baruch Golden, Argos Gonzalez, Christine de Guzman, Logan Henderson, Wynne Kinder, Michele Ku, Paige Leven, Rachel Lewin, Caren McDonald, Chris McKenna, Pragya Mathur, Renée Metty, Roger Nolan, Sol Riou, José Rodriguez, Amy Saltzman, MD, Cheri Scarff, Sofia Rose Smith, Oren Sofer, Peter Sutheim, Claire Anne Touchstone, EdD, Lisa Turetsky, Theresa Vazquez, Dzung Vo, MD, Becca Voss, Sarah Waxman, and Christopher Willard, PsyD.

ANNOTATED RESOURCES FOR ANTI-BIAS TRAINING

Gay, Lesbian and Straight Education Network (*www.glsen.org*).

Mindfulness teachers in schools can locate colleagues working for this diverse group of youth for trainings, conferences, education, advocacy.

Heise, S. (2013). Micro-aggressions have no place in school [Blog message]. Retrieved from *www.tolerance.org/blog/microaggressions-have-no-place-school*.

A personal view of microaggression. For a lively dialogue, see *www. microaggressions.com*.

Kivel, P. (2012). Guidelines for being strong white allies. Available at *www.beyond-whiteness.com/2012/02/20/paul-kivel-guidelines-for-being-strong-white-allies*.

A helpful introduction for trainers who identify as white.

Scott, T. (2013, July 5). Gender-neutral pronouns: They're here, get used to it [Video file]. Retrieved from *www.youtube.com/watch?v=46ehrFk-gLk*.

An amusing and well-researched plea for *they* as a singular pronoun.

Sparks, L. D., & Edwards, J. O. (2010). Anti-bias education for young children and ourselves. Retrieved from *www.naeyc.org/store/files/store/TOC/254.pdf*.

Very useful for PreK through elementary settings.

Teaching Tolerance (*www.tolerance.org*).

Activities and resources for schools working to reduce prejudice, improve intergroup relations and support equitable school experiences; a natural partner for anyone offering mindfulness in schools.

White Privilege Conference (*www.whiteprivilegeconference.com*).

A yearly gathering of over 1,500 youth and adults focused on skill building in a challenging atmosphere and working for equity and justice in "understanding, respecting and connecting."

REFERENCES

Berila, B. (2014, June 5). Towards an embodied social justice: Integrating mindfulness into anti-oppression pedagogy [Webinar]. Retrieved from *www. contemplativemind.org/archives/3004*.

Kendall, F. E. (2006). *Understanding white privilege: Creating pathways in authentic relationships across race*. New York: Routledge.

Levine, P. A. (2009). A summary of trauma and somatic experiencing [Video podcast]. Retrieved from *www.youtube.com/watch?v=ByalBx85iC8*.

McIntosh, P. (1988). White privilege and male privilege: A personal account of coming to see correspondences through work in women's studies (Working Paper 189). Wellesley, MA: Wellesley College Center for Research on Women.

McKenna, C. (2014, Spring). An interview with Chris McKenna. Retrieved from *www.tricycle.com/buddhist-life/interview-chris-mckenna*.

Riddle, D. (1994). *The Riddle Scale: Alone no more—developing a school support system for gay, lesbian and bisexual youth*. St. Paul: Minnesota State Department.

Roberts, J. L. (2013, November). The power of patience: Teaching students the value of deceleration and immersive attention. Retrieved from *www.youtube.com/watch?v=AnQVT_p6pxg*.

Saltzman, A. (2014). *A still quiet place: A mindfulness program for teaching children and adolescents to ease stress and difficult emotions*. Oakland, CA: New Harbinger Press.

Sue, D. W., Capodilupo, C. M., Torino, G. C., Bucceri, J. M., Holder, A. M. B., Nadal, K. L., et al. (2007, May–June). Racial microaggressions in everyday life: Implications for clinical practice. *American Psychologist, 62*(4), 271–286.

CHAPTER 5

Child Development
Attunement, Attachment, and Emerging Qualities

Lesley Grant

In order to teach mindfulness to children, we need to be able to empathize with their circumstances, points of view, and experiences. To this end, it's helpful to develop a refined understanding of child development and the child's unfolding sense of self. In particular, I find that it's important to attune to the naturally occurring qualities and capacities that constitute what I call the child's "innate nobility," or authentic goodness. These qualities include empathy, compassion, loving-kindness, attunement to others, patience, joy, equanimity, generosity, discerning awareness, and many others.

As children grow, these qualities and capacities are close to the surface and begin to emerge more fully during certain developmental stages. As teachers, therapists, and parents, we can support children in their development by attuning to these qualities as they begin to emerge. In large part, the ability to attune to a child's authentic goodness is based on our own receptivity and presence, mindfulness, and attunement to our authentic goodness. An understanding of child development adds another dimension to this process.

In mindfulness, these emergent qualities have a chance to arise spontaneously in moments when our minds stop busily pushing away what we don't like, holding onto what we do like, and dulling out to what we feel neutral about. Mindfulness supports this process by inclining the mind and heart toward the natural arising of these emerging qualities. Also, we can cultivate these qualities directly, for example, with loving-kindness or compassion practices.

In mindfulness, we practice returning to what's present now, however challenging or painful it might be. Whether rage, fear, anxiety, or embarrassment, moments of mindfulness allow us some freedom from difficult emotions and create some space in which loving-kindness, compassion, equanimity, joy, discernment, and other beneficent qualities can spontaneously arise. Older children who practice mindfulness have a similar experience at the appropriate developmental windows.

But children before the age of about 6 experience something different, what I call "premindfulness." In early childhood, children are in a period of unconscious imitation, and the presence and attunement of the adults in their lives have a profound effect on the maturation or veiling of their emerging qualities.

Roots of Mindfulness in the Parent–Child Attachment Relationship

When adults practice mindfulness, we generally turn inward to our own individual experience. Adults learn to apply mindfulness first to their inner lives and then to their relationships, including parenting. But children start out learning mindfulness in unconscious imitation of their parents' qualities of presence. Their relationship with their parents is the place where they learn attunement and lack of attunement; in other words, they imitate what they experience in their parents. Attunement is the essence of mindfulness, attunement with our own direct experience and the experience of others. Children unconsciously imitate the attunement they receive from their parents and develop an attachment style—secure, anxious, ambivalent/resistant, or disorganized—based on this experience. This unconscious imitation and resultant attachment style is the focus for premindfulness.

In his book *A Secure Base* (1988), John Bowlby discussed Mary Ainsworth's (1970) experiment commonly known as the "strange situation" and how it reflected the four distinct attachment styles. Each of these styles markedly influences the ways the infant responds to others, as well as the ways he or she regulates emotional experience. A full discussion of attachment styles is beyond the scope of this chapter, but what is relevant to our topic is the fact that the development of attachment style does not end in infancy.

Developmental theorist Gordon Neufeld (2010) expanded on Bowlby's (1988) theory by explaining the importance of the attachment relationship throughout early childhood, and the ways in which a secure base supports the child's maturation. The experience of a secure base in the early years is associated with success in many areas of adult life, including personal relationships and career success. Neufeld described how the attachment relationship evolves over time, comparing the stages of the development of a healthy attachment relationship to the roots of a tree. These roots of attachment support the secure base in early childhood from which the child's maturation can emerge.

Not all parent–child dyads succeed in developing through all of the stages in early childhood, according to Neufeld, and adults themselves may be underdeveloped and stuck at one of these stages. In a healthy parent–child attachment relationship, there are approximate developmental ages when the child matures through the following stages of attachment.

- Infancy: Sense-based attachment.
- Toddlerhood/2-year-old: Attachment through a sense of sameness.
- Three- to 4-year-old: Attachment through a sense of belonging and loyalty.
- Four-and-a-half-year-old: Attachment through special significance to another
- Five-year-old: Attachment through love/giving one's heart.
- Six-year-old: Attachment through being individually known and understood.

Each subsequent stage of attachment builds on the one before, deepening the secure attachment relationship between parent and child and fostering the child's maturation.

Understanding these stages of the attachment relationship is helpful in understanding early childhood development. Each of these stages influences the ways we can teach mindfulness to young children and what they learn through the process. In my experience, when children do not have a secure attachment relationship, some of the methods of premindfulness may be helpful in supporting them in opening to attach more fully with their parents and with other caregivers, teachers, or therapists. Specific premindfulness games and activities, designed for preschool children at each of these stages, enhance the development of their natural capacity to attach to others.

In his book *The Developing Mind*, Daniel Siegel (2012) refers to the importance of attachment in the development of a child's ability to regulate emotions: "Within the attachment relationship, the child's developing mind and the structure of the child's brain will be shaped in such a way that the ability to regulate emotion *in the future* is affected" (p. 321).

At Marin Mindfulness Institute we see that mindfulness practice helps adults who did not have an experience of a secure base in childhood to develop an inner experience of a secure base and then to offer the possibility of a secure base to their children. If parent and child both engage in mindfulness practice or, in the case of younger children, premindfulness practices, difficult attachment relationships can be healed. In order for parents to form a secure attachment with their children, they need to attune to them. Parents who didn't have secure attachments with their own parents are likely to have difficulty attuning to their children and are likely to pass on their own anxious, avoidant, ambivalent/resistant, or disorganized attachment style. To attune to a child, the parent needs, at the least, the quality of open, nonjudgmental attention, which the parent can cultivate with mindfulness.

If parents practice mindfulness before their children are born or during their children's infancy or early childhood, will the practice support their ability to attune to their children and develop a healthy attachment relationship with them? We believe so. In our parent mindfulness and inquiry groups, we teach parents mindfulness and related practices to nourish their ability to be attuned and compassionate toward their own experience as well as that of their children. In these groups, we've seen how parents can support each other in strengthening these abilities.

> One of the fathers in our parent group had experienced severe physical abuse as a young child. As the father of two preschool-age children, he struggled with violent impulses and often fell into verbal bouts of rage with his wife and children. During our parent mindfulness and inquiry group one week, he spoke about the benefits of the applied mindfulness dyadic practice we teach to parents. He told the group that his family was struggling financially and was about to lose their house. With their remaining resources, they made a last effort to stage the house and try to sell it. As a result, they were living in a newly staged house with their two young children, a very difficult thing to do.
>
> One morning Dad woke up and walked into the staged living room, which they had painted a beautiful mint green. Looking across the room, he saw his 3-year-old son drawing in large arcs with red crayon on the mint-green wall. The young father described feeling the heat in his face, the tension in his hands, and the tightness in his belly. He reported being mindful of the rage arising within him.
>
> Recognizing what we would call "the conditions" of the situation, looking at the staged room, he recognized that his young son had no awareness of tight finances or the staged house. He saw how little his son really was. The father went on to explain that he felt first shame for his rage and then compassion for himself in that moment, for his struggle to make a living and support his family. Then he felt compassion for the whole situation, for the financial problems and the prospect of losing the house, like so many other people across the country.
>
> Looking at his young son, he saw that his 3-year-old felt great joy drawing huge arcs with red crayon on the open green wall. The father reported going over to his son and telling him, "Crayons are for paper," then gently taking his son's small hands and guiding him over to the table with the paper. Then he got a sponge and some soapy water and helped his son try to clean the wall, a rather hopeless venture. They had to repaint, but for the father this was a transformational moment of insight as he realized that training in mindfulness could help him in moments of rage. He told the group that he felt mindfulness has the potential to help stop child abuse.

Mindfulness is not a magic or instant cure for a parent who has deeply rooted abusive impulses, but numerous parents in our programs have credited mindfulness and applied mindfulness with helping them attune to their children and work with the violent impulses in their own minds. This is a powerful application of these practices for families. As parents experience healing through mindfulness practice and begin to develop a stronger internal sense of a secure base, they can provide a greater level of attunement and thereby nourish a secure attachment experience for their children.

The preschool-age child mirrors the adults' quality of attention as well as their movements and ways of speaking. In addition, specially designed premindfulness practices can nourish children's attunement to their own internal sense experiences and the ways their bodies move in space. When children participate in premindfulness and loving-kindness practices during circle time, we notice an increase in group play and more harmonious play in larger groups.

When the children practice yoga and mindfulness together as a group, they seem to have both an increased awareness of their own bodies in space and an increased awareness of others. They're able to move and play in space in greater harmony, which enhances their attunement to one another and increases their interest in co-creating.

For example, the 4-year-old child is ripe to develop a sense of belonging and loyalty; with the support of attuned, mindful caregivers, he or she can develop a profound and healthy sense of belonging in his or her first peer group experiences in preschool. In turn, this early experience can establish the expectation for positive group experiences throughout life. Through premindfulness practices and early childhood partner yoga, children can extend their mindful attunement to their relationships with other children.

The Emergence of Generosity in the Young Child

As children mature in the development of their attachment relationships and in the experience of a secure base, the qualities of their innate nobility continue to emerge. A full discussion of the emerging qualities through the ages of childhood is beyond the scope of this chapter, but I do discuss a few key qualities, including the developmental age and the timing of their emergence. As children reach the developmental stage of belonging and loyalty, ideally between the ages of 3 and 4½, the quality of generosity is especially ripe to emerge within their attachment relationships, including their peer attachments.

Now this does not mean that children this age don't say, "Mine, mine, mine!" because they do! But it does mean that the entire realm of experience from having and possessing to giving spontaneously to others is ripe for development.

As children reach the stage that Neufeld (2010) referred to as belonging and loyalty, those with a secure attachment base feel the heartfelt wish to join in the work of the family and classroom. They want to be part of things. They want to belong to the family and peer group.

The Cree people traditionally celebrate a "walking-out" ceremony, which some still practice to this day. In this ceremony, a young child of 3½ to 4 is dressed in his or her best clothing, and the community of family and friends gathers around. The child is given beautiful things to eat and drink, and more drinks and food and blankets are piled around him or her. As the community gathers around the child, someone from the edge of the crowd will call out, "I'm thirsty, I'm thirsty," and the child will carefully carry a cup of something to drink, stepping through the crowd to give it to the person who called for a drink. Then someone else on the other side of the crowd will call out, "I'm hungry! I'm hungry!" and the child will carefully take a plate of food and walk over to deliver it to the person who is hungry. Yet another person in a different part of the crowd will call out, "I'm cold! I'm cold"—and the child will bring him or her a blanket. This ceremony is an example of celebrating and honoring the young child's naturally emerging quality of generosity.

In our parent–child cooperative program model, we have a water-serving practice for children in PreK. The child whose parent is participating in the cooperative that day has the special job of serving the water cups and food to his or her parent and to all the children in the group. Children as young as 2½ and 3 years move slowly and carefully through the room carrying the cups, learning to practice mindful walking, mindful carrying, and gracious offering. The child brings a quality of care for others to the serving of the water. Through this practice the child has an opportunity, common in some cultures but rare in Western culture, to extend special respect and care for his or her own parent.

By modeling careful, attentive service of food and drink to others, we can, to some extent, transmit mindful presence to young children. In fact, this kind of activity can help bring children back into balance after an upsetting experience. Doing something beneficial and imitating the mindful presence of adults is calming and soothing to them.

Example: The Emerging Quality of Generosity
after Premindfulness Practice

In one of the preschool cooperatives, we had a 3-year-old boy named Jack who had experienced a lot of violence between his parents. He was acting out in destructive, aggressive ways, grabbing toys from other children and pushing them. Teachers tried to comfort him and help him to integrate into the classroom, encouraging him to use words to express what he wished to have happen, but without much success.

Then a 5-year-old boy, Ethan, one of the oldest in the group, saw Jack and began to bring toys to him. Each time he brought Jack a toy, Ethan said, "Here you are, Jack. Here you are, Jack." Soon the other children began to bring toys to Jack as well: balls and trucks and small figures and clothes and dolls. These children had engaged in the premindfulness practice of water serving and were accustomed to mindful giving. As Jack sat wide-eyed in the middle of the room, the 11 other children in the class gradually piled nearly all the toys in the classroom around him. Suddenly Jack got up and started bringing toys back to the other children, saying, "Here you are, Susan. Here you are, Lucy. Here you are, Sarah. Here you are, Nathan."

This marked a turning point for Jack in the classroom. I said to the children, "That's generosity. How does it feel?" "It feels good," said several children. They stood there amid all the empty shelves, with Jack in the middle delivering toys to everyone. It felt as if the children had seen his suffering and comforted him by giving to him with their generosity. The actions and speech of the children became a healing for Jack.

When we recognize and attune to a child's emergent quality and bring our adult mindfulness to it, we encourage it. When children exemplify a quality and attune to it in others, just as these children attuned to the emerging quality of generosity in a member of their own class, we encourage the child to cultivate this quality spontaneously in daily life.

In a similar way, we can support the 4½- to 5-year-old's attachment impulse toward connecting in a meaningful way with parents and special friends by doing mindfulness movement dyads to cultivate a sense-based experience of empathy with others.

Using Premindfulness Imagery to Support Emotional Self-Regulation in the Young Child

Premindfulness can be nurtured and supported by a series of adapted Buddhist practices for children ages 3 to 6. At about age 6, children are able to develop calm and stability by returning their attention to an object of awareness, and they can begin to cultivate traditional mindfulness of sensations, emotions, and thoughts.

From the ages of 5 to 7, the prefrontal cortex strengthens its capacity to hold conflicting elements in mind simultaneously. Before this age, children typically do not have the capacity to embrace conflicting feelings, thoughts, and impulses at the same moment in time. When the child is feeling angry, for example, he feels only anger; when frightened, she only feels fear. The child does not have the neurological wiring yet to have a broader perspective or larger view. Adults caring for the child must provide the larger embracing perspective, the attuned presence that allows him or her to integrate difficult emotions with empathy and compassion.

Before the age of this developmental shift, however, preschool-age children do unconsciously imitate adults' qualities of presence, empathy, and compassion and can take in imagery that offers support for self-regulation and for embracing emotional experiences with empathy.

In a sense, young children are very "in the moment," which is one of the primary qualities of mindfulness, but they have not developed the capacity of mindfulness to embrace divergent aspects of experience, such as conflicting feelings, thoughts, and impulses.

Through play, children explore a soft, fluid sense of identity. They can be a kitty, a mom or dad, Superman or a pizza maker at a moment's notice.

Children personify and animate objects and often think in images. This affinity with imagery and their ability to identify with imagined objects can be engaged in simple imaginative games and practices that give children a felt sense, in imagination, of receiving and embracing their feelings in a friendly way.

By giving children specific stories, games, and images that represent facets of mindfulness, we take advantage of their imaginative capacities. Some of these are traditional images that have been taught to adults for hundreds of years, but we have adapted the way we present them to support children's capacity to unconsciously imitate the aspects of mindfulness that assist with self-regulation. We share this imagery—of a mountain, the ocean, the sky, and the sun—through games, stories, and songs. Each of the images has very specific experiential gestures that exemplify aspects of mindfulness. We teach these methods in detail to mental health professionals and educators in our professional trainings. The use of these practices requires that the adults teaching them embody these facets of mindfulness themselves.

Children in early childhood relate to these images of the mountain, ocean, sky, and sun in a direct way, by playing at "being" them. Because young children rest while in motion, rather than in stillness as adults do, we embed the images in yoga practice that includes moments of stillness.

Being Mountains

While ringing a bowl bell, we suggest that we are now mountains. In being mountains, we can be steady, stable, and present with everything that happens. A mountain is steady when it snows or rains as well as when the sun shines, and it supports the trees and flowers that grow on it. A spring flowing through the mountain is like our breath, coming and going in our bodies, while our bodies remain still. When children sit like a mountain while the bowl bell rings, they discover something about their capacity to be steady and present with whatever happens. The children experience this through unconscious imitation.

In the elementary and teen years, as children grow older, they can understand the mountain as a metaphor for a stable awareness that is occurring while other experiences are coming and going. Starting at the preschool age, we are planting seeds for later insight in mindfulness practice.

Being the Ocean

When we ring a bowl bell and suggest that we are the ocean, the children can feel their breath coming and going in their bodies and can recognize that this coming and going is like waves. We then ask the children to notice whether there is anything in their ocean. By asking them to describe these "picture thoughts," we create a playful opportunity for children to notice thoughts and images that appear in their minds. If a child says, "There is a shark," we can ask, "Does the shark have a color?" If the child says, "There is a fish," we can ask, "Does the fish have a color?" The child might respond, "It's a blue fish." We might ask, "Does the fish have a feeling?" The child may answer, "It's a sad fish." Then we might ask, "How does the blue, sad fish move?" and the child will show us with his or her body, by moving arms, legs, and torso while sitting on the mat.

By inviting the children's imagery, we are supporting them in recognizing their image or picture thoughts and affirming for them that this inner imagery is valuable. Through play, we are giving children an experience of recognizing their picture thoughts and joining them in experiencing the images in their minds. By asking about the image's color and feeling, we are modeling the process of recognition and investigation. When the teacher or therapist receives a child's imagery and describes it back to the child, and the group expresses in movement what the child has imagined, we are modeling a friendly allowing or welcoming toward what is arising. When we mirror the child's movements, we are also expressing empathy in our bodies.

Young children experience things through their entire bodies. With this reality in mind, we encourage the children to move, welcoming their capacity to fully embody their experience. In the preschool years the child's nervous system is set up to enjoy sameness, and children of this age like to be imitated. This kind of game offers them the experience of being seen and received.

When a child is done moving (the child is the one to determine when he or she is done), we invite the child to ring the bowl bell, and we all stop moving. We say to the children, "See if you can let the blue, sad fish swim through you, while you are sitting still. And you can give it some love." By doing this, we're giving the children the opportunity to play at emotional regulation using their own imagery. We are giving them a chance, in the form of the game, to experience creating a loving, spacious presence around the image of an emotion.

One of the important aspects of this game is the chance for children to practice self-regulation in a playful, friendly context, as opposed to the less friendly, imposed regulation they may be used to elsewhere. The experience of group empathy through movement and stillness, along with the soothing sound of the bowl bell, can often be healing.

Through this circle game and the practice of emotional regulation, children develop a sense of their own agency, but it doesn't end there. The experience is then naturally and spontaneously applied outside of the game, in their daily lives, when emotions arise. They apply what they've learned through play, without the prompting of adults, because it's the nature of a young child to play and then apply that play to life. This is what children do when they play house and then help their parents cook real food or play doctor's office and then are more at ease when they go to the doctor.

Through this game, we've created a friendly atmosphere for verbally acknowledging feelings. Prior to this, a child might have heard about feelings only in moments of distress. Since young children have a sense-based associative memory, we are associating the calm, soothing feelings evoked in the game with the child's own pictorial representation of the feeling. Then, when the child is in a situation where he or she feels a difficult emotion, the child's associative memory references the soothing experience of sitting with the teacher or therapist, ringing the bowl bell, and being joined in sending love to her own pictorial representations of the feeling—the sad blue fish, the angry red fish, the scared gray shark. There's a sense that it's safe to acknowledge and receive nurturing attention and to self-soothe when feelings come up.

Example: Sam and the Anger Fish

Sam, age 3½, had a lot of aggression and impulse control issues. At that time, our program was associated with a private elementary school, and administrators at the school were concerned about Sam entering kindergarten because of the level of aggression and impulsiveness he exhibited. He was the kind of child who would need the teacher to continually monitor his actions to make sure he didn't harm other children.

One day, several days after playing the ocean game, Sam—now 4½ — was making a puppet show with another child using small figures. The other child, a 3½-year-old, began knocking down the figures. I sat down next to Sam, ready to put my body in between him and the other boy (because Sam's usual response would have been to strike out in anger). Instead Sam looked at me and said, "My anger fish is here." I looked at Sam, and I could see the feeling on his face. As I took a breath with him, his face remained tense and angry. "Oh," I said, "What's it like?" Sam shed a few tears and then said, "Anger fish wants to drink up all the water!"

Now think about that for a moment: "Anger fish wants to drink up all the water!" Isn't that what anger does in our minds? When we're very angry, the emotion takes up all the clarity of our minds. It takes up our ability to think and speak clearly and act in a calm, spacious way. Sam, having experienced that calm, spacious feeling in the ocean game, called it "the water." He had the experience that the anger was taking over his mind and explained that in a child's way as a picture: "Anger fish wants to drink up all the water!"

More tears began to flow from Sam's eyes. I put my arm around him and the other boy, who had now come closer. After Sam had a chance to cycle through his feelings a bit, I said, "But can the anger fish drink up the whole ocean?" Sam looked at me and said, "No! I'm bigger than the anger fish!" He had experienced anger, but his awareness was bigger than his anger. This was a moment of insight for this little boy. At 4½ years old, the child for whom impulsive anger was a big problem that often got him in trouble with adults and peers was able to experience his anger in a different way, as a fish in the sea. Sam was then able to tell the other child clearly and calmly what he was trying to do with the puppets in the puppet show he was making.

How different this kind of insight is from simply hearing an adult say, "You are angry." That's how we commonly speak in our language. We say, "You are angry," "You are sad," "You are scared." Many adults have learned to speak that way in their attempts to express empathy to preschool-age children.

Example: Empathy for a Child's Feelings

A young mother in our parent mindfulness and inquiry group told a story about her 3½-year-old daughter. "Jennifer often gets very angry and frustrated," she said, "and I had learned to say to her, 'Oh, Jennifer, you're so angry,' or 'Oh, Jennifer, you're so frustrated.' But when I would do that, Jennifer would become even angrier and go into a full tantrum. I couldn't understand what I was doing wrong."

This mother was trying to convey empathy toward her daughter, but her daughter clearly wasn't receiving her words that way. "Then yesterday," she reported, "when I said to Jennifer 'Oh, you're so angry,' Jennifer screamed, 'I am not angry! I'm *Jennifer*!' Then I understood. She thought I was saying she *was* the anger."

Children are very literal at that age. How much more helpful it is to a young child to have an inner understanding of anger or sadness or fear as something that moves through her rather than to think that she *is* that feeling!

With the ocean game, we are also teaching something else, something very simple that we would not be able to explain to a young child. We are teaching not only acceptance and allowing, but also nonidentification with emotions. In doing so, we're helping the child learn to self-soothe much more effectively than we could do through explanation.

As children grow older, the ocean becomes a metaphor for the aspect of mindfulness that recognizes that feelings and thoughts are temporary events in our minds that come and go. Ultimately, that recognition offers an experience of some freedom and ease.

Being the Sky

When we ring a bowl bell and suggest to children that we can be the sky, we are teaching a sense of allowance and spaciousness. Children have told me that they feel calm and happy when they are the sky. There is joy in "becoming" the sky. Children easily relax and open into that experience. As children practice in later years, the sky becomes a metaphor for an open, spacious mind that allows sensations, thoughts, and feelings to arise without a feeling of clinging to them.

Being the Sun

When we ring the bowl bell and suggest to children that we can be the sun and fill ourselves with sunlight, it is natural for them to feel a sense of warmth, loving-kindness, and caring for themselves and others. When we invite children to be the sun and to notice who they would like to shine upon, we hear a variety of answers: "A dog," or "Mommy," or "Grandpa," or "My friend." Children never ask, "What does that mean?" Young children know what it means to shine love upon someone.

As children approach their teen years, the sun also becomes a metaphor for awareness. By starting with the sun as a metaphor for loving-kindness, we help bring the experience of a friendly mind to the practice of awareness itself.

For older children and adults, these four elemental images of mountain, ocean, sky and sun can be understood on various levels. Premindfulness practice with this imagery in early childhood invites children to nourish certain capacities that develop in later mindfulness practice.

> An 8-year-old in our elementary school group who began with these four practices, and many others we teach in early childhood, described in our children's group a time when her teacher at school became very angry at her and told her she would have to go to the principal's office for talking out of turn in class.
>
> She said, "I was mindful of my breath moving up in me and down in me, like in a bamboo. It felt like no one could knock me down. I did mindful breathing. I was so scared, and it calmed me down. Then I let my mind be like the sun, and I felt really relaxed. Then I let my mind be like a mountain and I felt really steady."
>
> She went on to say that the teacher did not send her to the principal's office after all. From the teacher's perspective, the child calmed down. From the child's perspective, she was actively using imagery to guide herself into mindfulness and a friendly, soothing state of mind, in the middle of a difficult moment in her life.

Transitioning to Mindfulness

According to Neufeld (2010), the next developmental stage in the attachment relationship, occurring around age 6, is the desire to be individually known and understood. Around this time, the development of the prefrontal cortex allows the child to hold conflicting emotions, thoughts, images, and impulses in mind at the same time. Neufeld dubbed the prefrontal cortex "the mixing bowl of the brain," using this image to illustrate the capacity to hold conflicting elements simultaneously.

Neufeld considers this "mixing bowl of the brain" to be the basis of morality. In other words, until a child can hold his or her own conflicting feelings and impulses *and* a sense of another's perspective and feelings in mind at the same time, he or she can't really have a moral sense.

This shift has important implications for learning mindfulness. Once children can hold two thoughts, images, feelings, or impulses at the same time, they can also begin to develop the capacity to return to an object in the mind or to the breath or to a sound, smell, or taste. In addition to various games and songs, one of the ways we train children in mindfulness from the age of 6 onward is to invite them to return their mind to an object of awareness until the mind settles and gains some stability, and then to expand that awareness to include a broader field of experience.

Example: Exploring Mindfulness of Motivations

Once children in early elementary school have learned the basics of mindfulness of sensations, feelings, and thoughts, we invite them to explore mindfulness of motivations. For example, we might help a child imagine that he is on the playground and a friend has fallen down and hurt herself. The teacher asks him to run inside and get the first-aid kit. The child runs inside and sees a huge plate of chocolate chip cookies on the counter for a child's birthday, and just above the cookies on the shelf is the first-aid kit. There are lots of cookies, the child is told.

After describing this scenario, we ask the children to notice what kinds of thoughts and images come into their mind about what they might do. Six- to 8-year-old children have given a number of responses to this exercise. Some have said, "I would eat a cookie, because no one would know." Others have said, "I wouldn't eat one because I wouldn't want to get in trouble." Still others have shared more involved thought processes, such as, "I would want to eat a cookie, but I wouldn't, because I would be afraid that someone wouldn't get one if I ate one. I would also worry that my friend wouldn't get help while I ate the cookie, and I wouldn't want the teacher to see me eating the cookie, so it would take longer to bring the first-aid kit to my friend."

As the children share the various feelings, motivations, and thoughts they discover in exercises like this, the teacher receives the responses nonjudgmentally and notes the mindfulness of thoughts, feelings, and motivations in what each child says. As the children explore their thoughts and feelings through a number of different exercises, they grow more comfortable with recognizing the entire range of their motivations ("positive" and "negative"), and develop an understanding that everyone has many different thoughts, feelings, and motivations. At the same time, they begin to understand more fully that they can make choices about how they act on their motivations.

The Emerging Quality of Compassion in 6- to 8-Year-Olds

Once we have explored motivations, we engage the children in reflective exercises that invite them to notice their motivations for benefiting others. We ask them to think about who they would want to help if they could—including people and animals—even if they have no idea how they would help. We also ask them to list three to five things that they really like to do and can do.

They might say, for example, "I like to draw," "I know how to sew," "I can write stories," or "I like making lemonade and cookies."

We then ask the group of children to brainstorm ways they might apply what they can do and like to do to helping people or animals. Children have come up with ideas as simple as "I'd like to pet the dog down the street every day. It looks lonely. But first I have to ask the neighbor if it's okay." Or, "I want to pick up trash in the woods so the deer won't eat it and become sick."

> At age 8, one of our students saw photos of child slavery—young children carrying large, concrete blocks on their backs—and decided that she needed to do something to help. She started a lemonade stand called Make-a-Stand Lemonade. With her parents' help, through Twitter and by traveling into different communities, she inspired kids from all over the world to make lemonade stands. They raised over a million dollars, which they donated to nonprofits, such as UNICEF and Not for Sale, to help rescue and rehabilitate children who are victims of child slavery.
>
> We saw some deep healing happen through this project. One of the other children in our elementary school children's mindfulness group was a young girl who had been diagnosed with selective mutism. She spoke at home but had a very difficult time speaking in school or among groups of children. This girl joined with the other children in squeezing lemons and making a lemonade stand on our corner as part of the Make-a-Stand Lemonade project. When children began shouting, "Free kids from child slavery!" on the street corner to draw the attention of passing drivers, the girl with selective mutism began shouting along with the others. She was so moved, so concerned about children she would never meet, that somehow she found her voice. Perhaps she recognized that her voice would be heard, and that what she says and does really matter.
>
> When we support children's beneficent motivations and give them opportunities to act on them, we often spark the empathy and compassion of adults around them as well. The 8-year-old who started Make-a-Stand touched the hearts of tens of thousands of people, and a feature length film, *#Stand With Me*, was made about her project. Our elementary school group was in the film.
>
> Other children did equally meaningful small projects such as planting organic seeds and gathering trash from the forests in our area. Whatever the project, they drew about it, wrote about it, and came back and shared their experiences with the group. As each child spoke about his or her project, the other children listened for the emerging qualities. In response to a teacher reading a list of qualities to the group, children raised their hands when they recognized specific qualities in a child's description of his or her project. The qualities listed included empathy, compassion, courage, perseverance, honesty, integrity, and many others. Each child also chose one of those qualities that he or she wished to further develop and received a sticker with that word on it to put in his or her mindfulness journal.

Children are very practical and naturally want to act on the empathy and compassion that arise in mindfulness practice. Compassionate action that extends from their own motivations feels quite different from joining a service project designed by the school.

The Emerging Quality of Discerning Awareness

As children approach the developmental age of 8 to 9, the faculty of discernment becomes stronger. Parents of children at this age often first notice this quality as criticism. A 9-year-old girl might say, "Mom, are you really going to wear that?" Teachers often notice that children at this age are not just going along as they were before, but are questioning what they're learning. They may develop negative views about certain teachers or notice things about their friends that they don't like.

Along with criticism of others, there is often a lot of internal criticism of themselves. Children of this age often feel that they are different or alone. They question their place in their group of friends: "Do they really like me?" In later elementary school, children may suddenly awaken to the contexts they live in and begin to look critically at their place in the world. They may be self-conscious if their families are different in some way—poor, wealthy, more or less educated, of a minority race or religion—and they're likely to notice such things about others.

At the same time, children of this age have a number of wonderful emerging qualities. With increased discerning awareness comes increased metacognition, the ability to witness their own thoughts, feelings, motivations, and actions and to begin to reflect on them. This capacity tends to arrive earlier for girls than for boys and develops more fully in the preteen and teen years.

In mindfulness practice with children ages 9 and up, we teach the acronym *RAIN*, a variation on Michelle McDonald's acronym familiar to many adult practitioners: **R**ecognize, **A**llow, become **I**nterested or **I**nvestigate, and **N**ature or **N**on-Indentification—understanding the ephemeral nature of our direct, moment-to-moment experience of sensations, feelings, and thoughts. Nine-year-olds are beginning to have the discernment to work with their emotional experience in a conscious way. They're excited by this ability to explore the working of their own minds. We still use imagery to guide them into mindfulness, but they're also able to relate to their experiences more directly, as they develop the capacity for discerning awareness.

This discernment is directed both inward and outward. One 9-year-old I knew suddenly noticed that most of the people who did certain kinds of jobs in her community had a certain skin color, and from there she became interested in social justice issues.

Mindfulness and loving-kindness practice at this important developmental juncture can help a child feel accompanied by her own friendly mind, and sharing with others about inner life experiences can help the child deal with what may be experienced as a growing sense of aloneness and difference.

Example: An Applied Mindfulness Empathy Practice

Applying mindfulness practices in dyads can be wonderful for 8- and 9-year-olds. Younger children can do movement-based partner dyads, such as partner yoga stretches, which help children develop empathy for their partners' sensations. For children in middle elementary school, partner exercises that include discussion of their experiences can help reassure them that they're not alone—that others have similar experiences.

A partnered walking meditation is an example of this kind of dyadic exercise. One partner closes his or her eyes and the other partner leads, while they both practice mindfulness of the sensations, feelings, and thoughts associated with leading and following. This practice is an opportunity to develop care and empathy and a sense of responsibility for another. For the child who is following, it's also an opportunity to experience the sensations, feelings, and thoughts associated with both fear and trust.

As they approach the age of 9, children are also ready for more verbal partner practices, including mindful listening and mindful speech. One example is a compassion practice we do in which we ask children to reflect on a recent difficult experience with a friend. (The following exercise is not appropriate for situations where a child is being bullied. Mindfulness exercises can be applied to working with bullying, but these exercises are beyond the scope of this chapter.)

The children are invited to close their eyes and remember key aspects of the experience. They focus on three domains: The first is their own sensations, feelings, and thoughts; the second is the conditions in which the experience took place, such as where they were, who else was there, and the cultural context (e.g., the understanding that it's not okay to yell in the library); the third domain is what the child imagines the other person was feeling and thinking, the experience of the other person. Both children have an opportunity to share their experience of the three domains with one another, and to send "caring about" or compassion to all three domains when a bowl bell is rung. They send compassion by sending an imagined color that, for them, represents compassion. Children then reflect on any insights they may have gained about any of the three domains and share their reflections with their partner, if they wish. This process may include gaining a new perspective. One 6-year-old said with surprise, after doing this dyadic practice, "Oh, I realized that *I* started the fight with my friend. I had thought that *he* started it!" Children sometimes have insights about the need to ask for help from an adult or the need to take action in a given situation. Many children say something like, "Oh, I just feel so much better about the whole thing!"

Mindfulness with Teens

Through these methods and many others tailored to each stage of development, we support children in their developing sense of self and help them to recognize, strengthen, and mature their naturally emerging qualities. This process continues and deepens in the teen years. At Marin Mindfulness Institute, teens practice mindfulness and apply it to relationships with others, learning what we call *mindful interview skills* and *mindful leadership skills.* In a program they help to run, "Inspire Café: Voices of Mindful Youth," they lead adults and children in mindfulness and loving-kindness practices and bring mindful presence to the process of interviewing peers about what inspires them and then sharing these interviews with others. In addition to conducting interviews, Inspire Café offers youth poetry, music, dance, and social action projects.

At the adolescent stage of development, children have a lot of curiosity about how their awareness works and a lot of interest in relationships with others. We include study of brain science related to mindfulness and offer practices that encourage teens to explore their own hearts, minds, and motivations in creative ways. Mindfulness helps teens balance their naturally strong emotions and impulsivity.

As adolescence is also a time of innovation, teens often find new ways to share applied mindfulness practice with their peers, younger children, and adults. After growing up with mindfulness since preschool, some of our teenage students have led mindfulness practice in clubs at their local high school. Mindfulness helps teens to focus and make the most of emerging qualities of innovation, creative inspiration, and passionate engagement. Through Inspire Café, we empower them to apply their mindfulness to relationships and touch the hearts of adults and older children.

Throughout their development, children and teens at Marin Mindfulness Institute learn to embrace both their own inner experiences and the tender hearts of others with care, compassion, and inspiration.

REFERENCES

Ainsworth, M. D., & Bell, S. M. (1970). Attachment, exploration, and separation: Illustrated by the behavior of one-year-olds in a strange situation. *Child Development, 41,* 49–67.
Bowlby, J. (1988). *A secure base.* New York: Basic Books.
Neufeld, G. (2010, October). *Transformative parenting workshop.* Marin County, CA.
Siegel, D. (2012). *The developing mind: How relationships and the brain interact to shape who we are* (2nd ed.). New York: Guilford Press.

CHAPTER 6

"Right Now, We're *Not* Meditating"

Working with Youth Who Challenge Us

JoAnna Harper

In 2003, following a weeklong meditation retreat in Northern California, I was driving through the hills of the East Bay, feeling inspired, connected, and blissed out, thinking about how I would love to share my practice and newfound inner peace with my own children and those in our larger community. I had never taught anything before and doubted my qualifications, but in that moment it all came together, in a way that nothing else had before. *I wanted to teach young people.* I began plotting, calling friends and colleagues, ordering "spirituality-for-kids" books, and set a date. My intention was for children from ages 7 to 11 to gather every Friday night in the spirit of the Ojai Foundation Council tradition in which I had recently trained (see *http:// ojaifoundation.org*). I will speak about this practice more in depth later in this chapter in the section called Fostering Connection and a Safe Emotional Space.

In our meetings, we would do simple meditations, practice listening and sharing from the heart, and open our minds to new spiritual traditions. Each Friday I would introduce something new—shamanism, Ifa (based on the teachings of the indigenous faith of the Yoruba people of Nigeria), Buddhism, Hinduism, Christianity, Judaism, paganism, and others—and celebrate the corresponding holidays for an immersive experience of food, prayer, meditation, and fire ceremonies. We took peace walks with Thich Nhat Hanh, collected money for the homeless as a practice of generosity, held a memorial for one of our own that had died, and brought in guest teachers to offer practices and wisdom. Together we created a true spiritual community, often up to 30 kids strong, no parents allowed. This was a place where the kids felt safe enough to be more vulnerable, connected, and authentically themselves, than anywhere else. A trustworthy adult (me) held the circle while they expressed themselves and held each other. They learned to listen deeply, to feel cared for, to hold their bodies in stillness and feel their emotions, and to speak from a place without shame and therefore without limits.

The children and I learned to do this together. I did not know of anyone else conducting these kinds of groups when I started in 2004. Although I had had many spiritual teachers, I had no mentors or predecessors to look toward to guide me in teaching children about their own spirituality and mindfulness. and never ended up even cracking the "spirituality-for-kids" books. What I did have was a dedicated mindfulness practice of my own and a deep desire to be a stable, informative, fun, and curious presence for these kids. The group ended up branching into two paths: one for teens who needed their own space to share age-appropriate issues, and the other for the younger children. Ten years later, teens still call me to "circle up," even as many enter adulthood.

Two years into the Children's Circle (as we called ourselves), my friend and teacher, Noah Levine, asked me if I wanted to lead a similar group at Camp Gonzales Juvenile Detention facility in Los Angeles. As a tattooed woman of color, he may have imagined I would go over well with this predominantly black and Latino gang-populated facility. Due to his reputation as someone who had taught meditation in juvenile detention facilities, Noah was called in to speak to the youth and he asked me to lead with him. Very fortunately for Camp Gonzales, at the time, an organization called New Visions was helping the youth transition from the juvenile justice system back in to the general population. Through their funding and program, I was able to continue working with the youth on a weekly basis for the next two years. My job was to lead the court-ordered anger management class; I created a program which was a combination of meditation, yoga, emotional skill building, and discussion groups. I had never worked with this population, but I figured I could either worry and tell myself I didn't know what I was doing or I could offer all that I had learned over the years of working with the Children's Circle. I would discover if my experience and my desire to serve would allow the mystery to unfold and allow space for something to emerge. One of the best personal lessons I have learned, as both a parent and professional, is that these kids do not have to be my friends. I am there to offer what I have as a grown woman, a mentor, and an elder. I do not have to show up as anyone other than myself, or give any more than the best I have to offer. When I began on my teaching journey, I had neither the intention nor desire to work with "at-risk," "troubled," "challenging," or other adjectives we place on youth, yet almost 8 years later, with experience in dozens of different facilities—alternative or continuation high schools, gang intervention centers, juvenile detention centers, and foster care facilities—there is nowhere else in my work where I feel more alive and where my skills are more needed. Though it might seem hard to believe, the years of working with "typical" kids informed my teaching with this population more than I can say. They *truly* feel no different to me; I can see the innocence, joy, and curiosity just below the surface that takes only a little encouragement and care to draw out. Many times I have walked into a room of tough, shutdown, and disinterested faces, yet within an hour, they look like different people, literally transformed. By the time they left our circle these kids were calm and had laughter in their eyes. One young man that I am working with now told me that the class gives him hope, and he now believes that he can have a better life.

The reason for the quotation marks around the descriptors of these kids is to suggest the questionable value and potential inaccuracy/harm of these labels, whatever side of privilege they show up on. The truth of the matter is that these young human beings are the product of many causes and conditions arising at once, including neighborhood, parents (or lack of), unemployment, abuse, culture, skin color, historical legacy, poverty, or privilege, and they are the living product of these conditions. Ultimately, we want these kids to feel that they belong, that they are good enough, and that they too deserve to be happy, healthy, and cared for like anyone else. This livelihood has become for me a path of personal transformation that I never expected, certainly not during my own turbulent teenage years. It is an honor to work with these young people, and I dedicate these following pages to them and to you, who work with them.

Guiding Principles

I would like to offer three guiding principles in working with young people that have helped me and others remain centered, clear-headed, and clear-hearted. These also happen to be the guiding principles of my personal practice. When these principles are at the forefront of my teaching, the concept of "difficult" or "resistant" kids is eradicated and a shift of perspective takes place. This shift allows everyone and everything to have its place, and to be free of the judgments that others have placed upon them.

Understanding Others and Ourselves

The first principle is to *understand* the group. As teachers, it is our responsibility and our privilege to know the people with whom we are working. This means knowing how they view their world and ours, knowing their home and family life, their gang affiliation, how many foster homes they have been through, if their mom is a crackhead or their dad incarcerated, if they themselves have their own children, or have an addiction, if they had a candy bar and Coke for breakfast, if they have a diagnosed learning or behavior issue, if they have ever held a dying friend in their arms, or if they themselves have ever been shot. Many of these kids are living with past or current trauma in their family, neighborhood, or in their school. All of this makes connecting, let alone communicating or calming, far more complicated than with kids who have not experienced such severe trauma.

As adults, it helps to be mindful of the fact that the hormonal and brain development of a young person is different from our own, often still in a state of constant change. Adolescents are full of sexual energy, while their still-developing brains make them feel like they own the world. At the same time their wisdom filters are not quite developed, their crazy new bodies are unfamiliar to them, and they struggle to feel socially accepted and held by their "tribe." Holding all this in mind gives us necessary sympathy and patience, which in turn gives them the space they need to address issues that are literally out of their control.

To do our work and to do it well, we must see clearly the truth of the lives of the kids in front of us. We cannot assume that they are "just being difficult" or "don't want to be there"; often it is far more complicated than those simple phrases suggest. Of course, many may not want to be there, in which case coming to our own acceptance around this basic reality will be far easier than trying to force their acceptance. Do not try to fight what is not fightable.

When we know what their lives look like; when we know where their pain, numbness, defensiveness, aggression, sadness, or inability to focus comes from; it is far easier to set and maintain the intention to understand and be compassionate rather than distance ourselves, as society has done, by using labels such as *challenging* or *resistant*. For us as facilitators the thought or idea of *resistance can only be present when we lack the acceptance of what is*. What *is*, is that a *behavior* is showing up as a result of the pain; when we can see behind the wall of the behavior, we can address the tenderness and fear instead of the resulting behavior.

I know, some of you are reading this thinking, "Yeah, but she doesn't know so-and-so. . . ." In fact I *do* know so-and-so and I still would suggest that when we can see the truth of these children, generally in some form of pain or loss, we can dance with them rather than struggle against them. Fundamentally, mindfulness is about turning toward the difficult in each kid, ourselves, and the world and working *with* it, rather than against it. We seek to be in the difficulty together, rather than imposing an agenda on our students. We have the exquisite opportunity to see these kids as nobody else does, to be *with* them in ways that others are not. This is a unique gift to us, and a new experience for children who have lived under the weight of impossible expectations and circumstances from family, schools, the state, and society.

As much as we need to know and understand these kids, we also need to know and understand *ourselves*. We must learn to recognize not just those parts we know as strengths, but also our blind and distorted spots. What are your prejudgments as to how or why these kids are the way they are? Investigate your own feelings and biases about social issues that oppress or disenfranchise groups and individuals, and learn to recognize them as they arise. Is there some anger or ill will that needs to be worked with first? What is your own and your family's history with oppression?

On a more personal note, is there an agenda with your own ego or perhaps your own history? Many of us feel the need to save these kids who perhaps are stand-ins for troubled childhood friends, relatives, or even our childhood selves. This work is deeply personal, and it is essential to remain mindful of your intentions. Are you trying to heal a childhood wound and hoping to process it through working with these kids? When our own healing is the agenda, who is the beneficiary? I know many, myself included, who have made this error; it has taken decades of therapy and mindfulness practice to be able to be present for others with a healed and healthy heart. Healer: Definitely heal thyself first! Good intentions aside, when there is an agenda, or a residue from the past, going on within us, we can easily lose sight of what and who is in front of us in the here and now. Know why you are choosing the work you do and know what you are bringing to this work: your baggage and your toolbox. A good mentor, supervisor, or teacher can help tremendously, but only if you remember to ask for help!

If this practice has changed your life and relationships, share it. If you love seeing kids transform from lost and alone to feeling hopeful and connected, then come with the intention to meet these kids right where they are. One of the greatest outcomes of a mindfulness practice is that we can see ourselves more clearly, and the "shoulds" begin to drop away; "I should be in a great mood every time I meet with these kids," "I hope they like me," "I know I can help them if only they'd sit still and listen." These are a few of the sentiments my internal dialogue continually shared with me when I first started this work. And if you have nurturing mother energy, are a wonderful storyteller or poet, are a strong male elder, have a humor that lifts a room— that is what you need to bring fully to these kids. Share yourself and allow them to share themselves. Ultimately, understanding self and other together is the alchemy that allows for the unfolding of a powerful group experience.

Modeling

The second teaching principle is to *model* the behaviors we would like to see in these young people, many of whom have not had consistent role models in their lives. The type of presence we convey is what we can expect to see in return. I have found the most powerful qualities to communicate are honesty and authenticity/sincerity. When I am honest and authentic, it gives others permission to be the same. When I am caring and kind, they tend to follow. When I share from my heart, they have the opportunity to care for me just as I am caring for them. It is magical to enter a room of what society judges the toughest and most dangerous kids and have them ask how I'm feeling, or how my kids are doing. It is beautiful to share the experience of caring and being cared for within the appropriate boundaries. They are not taking care of me or my feelings, and they are expressing genuine, mutual care and concern, invited through my modeling.

When I first started in this work, I met a woman who worked at a foster care facility where I was holding a mindfulness class. In my new role, I saw her as the Pied Piper; the kids adored her and did whatever she asked. I inquired about her secret, and she told me to "start off hard and firm with them, and then soften as they get to know you. If you start off soft, you're screwed." I have followed her advice ever since, with great success. As you come to know your kids, you will know intuitively the skillful action to take, recognizing the moment to be flexible and the moment to stand firm, but a clear tone from the beginning lays the foundation for these positive developments.

Consistency is also important to model. If you say you are going to do something, do your best to do it. If you cannot follow through, share your reasons, even if they are not good ones. This transparency not only helps you to practice and model communication and humility, it asks them to show up consistently for themselves and each other in the same way. When you show up, you can then ask them why they did *not* show up, and you can allow them the space to feel safe enough to explore the answer. These kids need to know that their teachers are not just being "flakes" or ignoring or avoiding the effect they have on others.

And finally, especially when teaching a practice as difficult as mindfulness, model diligence. Many of these kids have experienced numerous adults as giving up on them over and over, and consequently have learned to give up on themselves, their passions, and their dreams. I have found that sticking with them, *not* giving up and remaining available, yields powerful benefits. They learn that not only do they deserve care and compassion, but that they can show up with strength and courage for themselves and others.

Our Own Practice

The third and most important practice for teaching challenging kids is our own mindfulness practice. There is a common belief that parents and educators can buy some books or attend a weekend workshop and learn how to teach kids to be mindful, hoping that a few techniques and a bell will lead to better behavior and ease suffering all around. This is well intentioned but not how it works. With *mindfulness* as a popular catchphrase these days, it can seem like something that is easy enough for anybody to do or teach. For those with an existing practice, you know that nothing can replace sitting and doing the work of bringing attention to your internal experience through mindful awareness. Your personal practice will be invaluable to your teaching. More importantly, a grounded practice will ensure that the kids will be less likely to press your buttons or throw you off balance. As we learn early in mindfulness practice, wanting things to be different from the way they are is the core cause of our suffering. This wanting for things to be different, the way *we* want, pulls us away from present-time awareness and reality. This is important to remember when we are faced with a child, a parent, a teacher, or even an institution that we feel is "difficult" and think should be different, especially when we hold a curriculum in our hands to prove it. Moments like this are opportune times to engage our own practice and check our agenda, in contrast to what that moment and the group are truly calling for.

A few years back I was teaching at a juvenile detention facility in Los Angeles that housed older offenders, 18 and 19 years old, usually on their way to federal prison. I was alone with about 12 boys in a trailer way out in the middle a field. A kid that had been coming to this class voluntarily for a few weeks started talking out of turn, interrupting others when they shared. Such behavior was not unusual for this particular kid, and to be honest, I was aware of tension in my body whenever I saw him walk in the room because the class never went as smoothly (according to my definition) when he was there. Still, this time his presence felt more aggressive and provocative than usual. I let him know, calmly and directly, that he was breaking our respect agreement of not speaking when others are speaking and that I needed him to check himself. Of course, this was the point where I also needed to "check in" with myself, because his 6-foot frame was suddenly standing up and in my face. (Remember, I'm alone with 12 young men.) Internally, my whole world slowed; I felt my fear transform into anger as my body temperature rose. I was scared and I was pissed, and I had to choose if I was going to show these feelings externally. Instead, I opted for a little bit of fierce kindness. I knew this young man usually enjoyed the group but that today was not a good day for him. I choose not to let my own fear or anger dominate because there was so much this kid could learn from having a different experience of conflict than what he had known. Of course, this all blazed through my body and mind in seconds; my own mindfulness practice allowed me to model for these kids and show up in a way that would be a learning experience for everyone. It was risky, because at this point I had no idea whether he was going to hit me, hit someone else, or worse. But instead of doing what was expected—calling for backup to cuff him and throw him in solitary—I gave him a choice. I made him part of the solution by respectfully asking if he wanted to be here and if he wanted to talk about what was really going on. As it turned out, he *did* want to be there and he *did* share his pain and he *was* really grateful. He came back to group again and again until he left camp. He was always a bit edgy but never like that again. By accessing my own mindfulness, I used my understanding, my modeling, and my practice all in one incident.

Teaching mindfulness can often mean accepting conditions as they are. It is crucial to cultivate self-understanding: to know our triggers, our habitual reactions in certain situations, and the ways to skillfully respond while in the presence of others. At times we may feel doubt or confusion. That is okay. Confusion and self-doubt are real. Can we make contact with these uncomfortable states and allow them to be present? If we can radically accept our own humanity with some humility, we are already ahead of the game. Yet all of this takes *practice*. It is up to us. It is not so much about what we do or even how we do it; it is about our presence. We need a solid and grounded foundation upon which to build and teach.

Through our own practice we build insight and acceptance, creating an invaluable tool for dealing with our own compassion fatigue. We also build empathy for our many devoted colleagues, from caseworkers to cops, serving youth and struggling with burnout. Our own practice, along with support from others who are also practicing, rejuvenates and grounds us in ways that nothing else can. That calm and inspiration are contagious in our work communities. We learn not just to give skillfully, but also to receive skillfully.

The more consistent and solid our own practice as we enter a challenging situation with challenging kids, the less effort will be needed when thorny situations arise. The habit becomes one of skillful response, rather than reaction through fear or frustration. We become infused by our practice, breath by breath, to the point that it is there when we need it without even realizing it. The kids will trust you if you walk your talk.

One of the best compliments I ever received was from an 18-year-old student at a continuation high school in Los Angeles, who said, "The reason I like going to your meditation class is because I just like hanging out with you, because I can talk to you about anything and I don't feel judged." He added that it made him feel peaceful and positive. What better compliment, and what better presence, could we seek to cultivate?

Once I shifted my core intention to one of connection and support, to seeing these kids as they are, as the flower of multiple causes and conditions, the result was a whole lot of mindfulness all around. We are mirroring and even infecting them with the contagion of mindfulness, showing them what mindfulness looks like, and watching their own practice blossom.

Ideas and Suggestions for Practice

Before walking in the door, take a moment, clear your head, and set the intention to be present, to see clearly, and to offer what is needed for them, not you. I tend to have an idea of a few concepts to get across for that day and multiple ideas of how to do so through modeling, story, formal meditation practices, games, and discussion. Prepare to be flexible; it is always skillful to have a plan in mind, but if you walk in to the room and are planning on doing a forgiveness practice and you learn of a community tragedy, or have to process a conflict between two rival members of the group, it might not be your day for forgiveness. What may be needed at that moment is a safe place to process what the kids are experiencing.

If you are not the primary teacher or caregiver, check in with that person to see if there is anything you need to know that might be relevant to your time with the kids on a given day. This can include topics they are discussing in class or in therapy groups (e.g., racial issues, identity, culture, social justice, history), personal or gang issues between kids, tender topics, triggers, and other important dynamics of the group that might be invisible to an outsider, and that often change day to day.

There are differing philosophies, even in this book, as to whether it is best to have a familiar adult present or not. I find it best if the teacher or care providers are *not* in the room during the sessions, though others may disagree. This can be a hard issue to navigate, depending on where you are teaching, and may not always be possible. For the most part, even if the kids get along with their teachers or care providers, there is emotional and mental self-censoring that can happen, and that hinders intimacy and honesty. The kids may need to discuss their relationship with these people, and it helps to have a safe and neutral adult with whom to do this. We have the privileged position in an institution or organization that our primary and perhaps only loyalty is to the kids themselves. Hopefully the adults can understand this, and appreciate the fact that mindfulness may ultimately help their relationships with the kids.

I did once have a teacher ask if he could join the group; he could see the great impact on the kids and wanted to meditate too. I could see the look of dread on the kid's faces, because they saw our class as "their" time. I turned the teacher away. The kids were stunned and grateful that I advocated for them, maintaining the safety of their space. To an outsider, this refusal may sound harsh, especially since often the teachers are the organizers of these types of activities, and it may not always be practical. Honesty, humor, and good intentions always help lighten the blow. This teacher clearly cared greatly for the kids and was generous enough to give the kids what they needed without taking it personally. But such a request from a teacher or caregiver may also be an opportunity, as you can always offer interested adults local resources, or better yet, offer a staff-only meditation group. You also can and should invite them into the kids' classes on an occasional basis, but only with the kids' permission.

Space

Create a sacred space. The details of what creates such a space are up to you and your group and can be personal, creative, and beautiful. It is likely that your space may be limited or very institutional looking. The actual physical space is not so important; it is intentions with which we fill it that make a space sacred. I recommend the use of a circle for seating, so that nobody can hide in the back and everyone is on equal footing rather than having one person in power standing at the front of the room. Looking at the faces of others in the circle is an opportunity to work with vulnerability and distraction, which can show up as silliness, shyness, or intimidation, any of which is wonderful material to address.

In some groups it may be possible to have candles and flowers (not usually allowed in institutions) in the center of the circle, or to have the kids create a centerpiece of their liking. I have had kids contribute artwork, poetry, their cell phones, photographs, or whatever they feel best represents them as a group. Leaving the space as is also works, as long as there is an intentional understanding that "when we sit together in this way, we have entered our formal time together." If the lighting can be adjusted, low light can feel peaceful. Part of creating the sacred space includes an invitation for group members to leave whatever they want to leave, emotionally or mentally, outside of the space. The opportunity to create their own space is empowering, as many of these kids maybe never have had, their own space or thought of space in an intentional way.

Language and Speech

Be mindful of language. I recommend caution in using any spiritual or "New Age" concepts or words. The more your communication can be rooted in language that is simple, clear, and relevant, the better. This is why the first principle—to understand to whom we are talking—is so important. I am not suggesting that you start talking in any kind of slang, unless this is already how you talk. Use language that is helpful and makes sense to the kids in each particular group. A mistake I once made served as a growing moment for me. Years back I was leading a group at a gang intervention facility in Los Angeles, and I said that "nobody can save us except ourselves" to a group of ex-gang bangers recovering from addictions. They also happened to be predominately Catholic, with a strong faith and belief that God's salvation was the only reason they were alive today. One young man was very vocal in his mistrust of my teaching and of me. I felt awful and apologized for any disrespect that I had exhibited. Yet, at that moment, just the right teaching story came to mind, and I was able to offer it to the group.

> "A pious man, after hearing flood warnings on the radio, decides to stay in his house and pray, saying to himself, 'I will trust God and if I am in danger, then God will send a divine miracle to save me.' His neighbors drive by, yelling to him to jump in the car and get away safely, but he declines, 'I'm fine, God will take care of me.' The water begins to rise, and soon he is forced to the upper floors of his house. A police boat passes by, telling him to grab a life preserver and jump in the boat, but

again he says, 'No, thanks, God will save me!' By afternoon the water has risen and he is now on the roof. A helicopter flies over and drops a rope down, but the man waves them off, shouting 'No thanks, God will save me.' Finally the waters wash him away and he drowns. He arrives in heaven and standing in front of God, he asks, 'God, I've been nothing but faithful, why didn't you save me?' And God replies, 'I sent you an evacuation warning, a car, police boat, and a helicopter. What more do you want?'"

The story and its message were understood. No matter who has got your back, you still need to take care of your business. Still, that particular student never returned to the class. The experience was humbling and ever since, I make even more of an effort to understand who I am talking to, where they're coming from, and to find the best medium to communicate what I have to offer. This lesson is also a reminder of the power of teaching through story. Especially for young people, poetry, song lyrics, or inspirational quotes can illustrate abstract concepts and spark discussion, that just a lecture cannot.

When starting a new group, it helps to clearly set expectations and guidelines around respect and acceptable language and behavior in the first session. Do not hesitate to be stern or clear. Standards and expectations are set high at first so that mutual care and respect can create a strong and safe group. In terms of expectations or rules regarding types of acceptable speech, I establish norms of no gossip, no slander, and no aggressive or sexualized conversations or behavior—unless these are specific topics we are addressing and how they affect those around us as a group exercise.

Fostering Connection and a Safe Emotional Space

Teens tend to judge how they are doing by the relationships around them, far less than from an introspective perspective. Belonging and acceptance can feel, and perhaps are, tantamount to survival. The cultivation of qualities that enhance relationship, including warmth, empathy, curiosity, acceptance, self-attunement, and emotional intelligence, are relevant and immediately useful to how kids engage with the world and find value in themselves.

I was trained in council facilitation at the Ojai Foundation, and I use this model with most of my groups. Council is a modern practice derived from many ancient forms of communicating in a circle. Sometimes referred to as "Listening Circles," council utilizes a center, a circle, and a talking piece to create an intentional space in which to share our stories. Four core principles of council are (1) listening from the heart, (2) speaking from the heart, (3) being lean with our sharing, and (4) spontaneity with our sharing.

The practice of deep listening without judgment fosters an atmosphere of respect for ourselves and for others. Council gives room for flexibility and creativity that allows a group to explore different aspects of mindfulness and communication. The core tenets of listening from a place of openness and presence and speaking from a place of honesty and vulnerability, allows everyone the possibility of success through simply trying. There may be sessions when we formally practice mindfulness meditation for only 5 minutes, but we continually guide the awareness back to stay present with each other while observing our internal experience. Because relationships are critical to these kids, if they can safely practice wise listening and speaking, they will feel empowered to explore these tools in other aspects of their lives. As the kids become curious about what others have to say, and experience compassion for each other, a sense of ownership develops; this in turn generates more cooperation and involvement.

The council practice of listening and speaking from the heart creates a very good jumping-off point for working with the thoughts, emotions, and sensations that arise as we speak or listen to others speak. With no "cross talk" allowed, we sit with whatever arises in us as another is sharing. This is truly a rare practice when most are used to just jumping in and cutting off another person. While listening and speaking, encourage the kids to check in periodically and share their internal experience. We create a safe space and invite everyone to try out new ways of being. For some, maybe their reputation in their real life will not allow vulnerability or experimentation; they can try it on here. Plenty of kind encouragement and acknowledgment when they show up in any way that is uncomfortable or unfamiliar to them keeps them coming back for more. Highlight their strengths and allow them to be successful. To find more information on the council process, see the references at the end of the chapter.

Reflecting the Positive: A Corrective Experience

The more we can reflect back to these kids their strengths, the more they can see the good in themselves. Many kids have only ever heard how bad they are and begin to see themselves in this light; eventually, through their words and actions, they end up fulfilling the prophesy that was placed on them from a very young age. I worked with a young man whose fifth-grade teacher told him he was stupid. He is now 19 and remembers that moment vividly. Without intending to, he had given that teacher the power to control the rest of his educational life. When he shared this experience and understood what it meant, he was heartbroken to realize that things could have been so different had he had a different experience.

We can make a point of finding the positive spin on what the kids share. Another young man came to group feeling guilty about breaking a promise to himself not to drink. Instead of getting in to how bad drinking is for him or the benefits of abstinence, I made sure that he knew how positive even contemplating quitting at his age is. I did not let him off the hook or condone his drinking, but instead celebrated his wisdom and insight into what could bring him health and happiness. This kid who never smiled suddenly lit up with a smile to melt hearts; instead of beating himself up, he felt good about himself. I often include exercises that ask kids to share what they like about themselves, their best qualities, and what they think others like about them. This can be very hard for them, as it is for most people, because they have mostly felt and been told that they are "bad" in some way. Cultivating a change of mindset in this way can take time, but is well worth it. I like the practice of "If You Really Knew Me" for this. "If You Really Knew Me" is a personal sharing practice, made popular by an MTV series of the same name, originated by Challenge Day. With one participant saying three times, "If you really knew me you'd know that . . . ." it allows the speaker to explore how they see themselves, what they want others to know about them, and where they feel they fall short. It allows participants to learn about their peers and to see commonalities in those around them. The emphasis is on the word REALLY, to avoid communicating from a shallow level. I always start first to set the tone and model the depth of the practice. More about this can be found at *www.challengeday.org/mtv/downloads/IYRKM_IntroGuide.pdf.*

Some Favorite Practices for This Population

Before initiating other mindfulness practices, a forgiveness practice can be helpful to clear some emotional baggage. Forgiveness practice involves forgiving ourselves for hurting ourselves, forgiving ourselves for hurting others, and forgiving others for hurting us. For kids who have been told for years how bad they are and are tightly bound by the guilt of past actions, it can be hard to feel deserving of the good in life. What these kids need to move forward is an ability to forgive themselves and others for instilling these negative messages. Over years, such messages can harden into core beliefs, so that kids wonder why bother hoping for happiness, if it will just be taken away. This process of forgiveness, a vital component in many spiritual traditions, does not have to be flowery or soft. We can offer a basic understanding of forgiveness as letting go of past suffering and betrayal, a release of the burden of pain and hate that we carry. We can emphasize that forgiveness does not mean allowing perpetrators or abusers to harm then again, or to invite these people back into their lives, but rather it is to free the kids' own hearts and minds from the pain that hatred creates. Often this means letting go of a long-held idea of what the future should look like. For instance, many gang members have a hard time leaving their gangs because they had made promises of "forever" at 12 years old, and they feel that they are betraying their younger selves and their neighborhoods for not upholding this promise of what their future was supposed to look like. The forgiveness practice allows us to let go of past ideas and hurts so that we can see the present for what it is instead of what the past is holding us to.

According to Jack Kornfield (2008), forgiveness (1) is not weak or naïve, (2) does not happen quickly, (3) does not forget or condone, and (4) does not mean that we have to continue to relate to those who have done us harm. I use forgiveness practices from my meditation lineage, but you can do some research and find what works for your group and your particular kids.

Because this practice can be triggering for some kids, I suggest consulting with trauma experts if you have particularly vulnerable kids in your group. Such a consultation can also help you cope with any surprise moments of high activation or arousal. I have yet to have any real fallout from such intimate practices, but safety is of foremost importance, especially for kids whose lives have felt so unsafe. If you are uncertain, seek supervision and wait until you feel ready. When I first started working with this population, a therapist said to me, "Be sure to put them back together before you leave or the staff will be the ones left cleaning up the mess." So take your time and do what works for you and your group, and the larger community of other staff as well.

Another valuable practice is "empathy dyads." I'll assign partners who tell each other, one at a time, about their family, their childhood, or another topic for about 3 minutes. This practice is not a dialogue. The listeners are present to and focused on the speakers, and the speakers are heard, uninterrupted, possibly for the first time in their lives. Back in the group, the kids share three things that they learned about the other person. This is a powerful practice for this population because it creates, and allows kids to practice, intimate connection; the kids come to see what they have in common, rather than their differences. In one juvenile detention facility, I paired two boys who, unbeknown to me, were rivals. Through sharing stories about their families and childhoods, they discovered more similarities between them than differences. They came back to the circle saying that they understood each other much better and actually have some compassion for their "enemy." We can even ask them specifically to listen for three things they have in common. Going back to a group again and again creates the opportunity for us all to build on these newfound realizations and walk through the door of empathy and compassion.

Perhaps the best part about teaching mindfulness to these kids is that they keep us honest, they keep us on our toes, and the work never becomes boring or rote. I love this! There are an abundance of practices, techniques, games, stories, and connections to explore, as well as mistakes to make and ultimately learn from. Teaching this population can offer the biggest joys and most challenging lessons that a teacher can hope encounter. By having a template that holds us, such as the three guiding principles of understanding, modeling, and practice, we then have space and freedom to move around. When we go in to this kind of work, heart work, there may be tough experiences to endure, but ultimately, the look of joy and belonging that we hope to, and often do, see on a kid's face is enough to keep us returning day after day. Many days I have wanted to quit, yet every time I leave the room I have been in with these kids, I remember the warmth and purpose that I feel; I remember why I am there. Know that they need you, and appreciate the true privilege of their presence.

One of my favorite stories beautifully illustrates a different kind of approach to working with the kids who challenge us personally and who challenge our larger society:

> In the Babemba tribe of South Africa, when a person acts irresponsibly or unjustly, he [or she] is placed in the center of the village, alone and unfettered. All work ceases, and every man, woman and child in the village gathers in a large circle around the accused individual. Then each person in the tribe speaks to the accused, one at a time, each recalling the good things the person in the center of the circle has done in his lifetime. Every incident, every experience that can be recalled with any detail and accuracy, is recounted. All his positive attributes, good deeds, strengths, and kindnesses are recited carefully and at length. The tribal ceremony often lasts for several days. At the end, the tribal circle is broken, a joyous celebration takes place, and the person is symbolically and literally welcomed back into the tribe. (Kornfield, 2008, p. 42)

REFERENCES

Kornfield, J. (2008). *The art of forgiveness, lovingkindness, and peace.* New York: Bantam Books.

Zimmerman, J., & Coyle, V. (1996). *The way of council.* Las Vegas: Bramble Books.

CHAPTER 7

Mindfulness-Based Substance Abuse Treatment with Probation-Involved Youth

Sam Himelstein

Substance abuse and dependence have been long-standing social issues, especially among underserved and disenfranchised communities (Daniel et al., 2009). In 2004, more than 300,000 inmates were held in state and federal facilities for drug charges (Mumola & Karberg, 2006). The illicit use of drugs in 2007 alone was estimated to cost taxpayers more than $193 billion (National Drug Intelligence Center, 2011), and current residential substance abuse rehabilitation centers offer, at best, mild statistics for offenders maintaining sobriety after their release. Furthermore, trends in recent data suggest that young people generally perceive less risk of, and use more, marijuana than in past years (Johnston, O'Malley, Bachman, & Schulenberg, 2012). Suffice it to say that substance use is an important social issue, and as young people experiment with more drugs, they are at higher risk to become addicts as they age.

An onslaught of substance abuse treatments has been directed at youth involved in the justice system, including 12-step interventions, harm reduction models, motivational interviewing, and family system approaches. Research on these models show mixed results at best, with family approaches showing the most promise, but with frustratingly high relapse rates (Liddle et al., 2001). Sadly, many young people in the justice system are targeted and blamed for their substance use in the absence of contextualizing the larger picture of their lives, including the oppression they encounter and their personal and historical trauma. It seems clear that the use of substances is a way to cope with the pain and suffering inherent in their realities. Clearly, these young people need treatment that is both effective and culturally competent. One such intervention that can be adapted within other existing therapeutic models is mindfulness.

In my work I have found that mindfulness is not only a powerful means of achieving personal insight, emotional regulation, and reduction in substance use, but also a method by which young people can empower themselves and their communities, contemplate their relationships with others, and catalyze the development of kindness, compassion, and forgiveness.

Mindfulness, as a useful adjunct, is not a "silver bullet" intervention that can "cure" probation-involved youth of their substance-abusing habits. On the contrary, many conditions and causes, such as oppression, contribute to substance abuse and cannot all be dissolved by practicing mindfulness. Mindfulness is, however, a method for personal transformation through which young people can be empowered to make more positive choices in their lives, and which they can share with their communities.

A Brief Overview of Research on Mindfulness for the Treatment of Substance Abuse

Over the past four decades, various clinical applications of mindfulness have been researched with diverse populations and are now backed by empirical evidence (Baer, 2006; Shapiro & Carlson, 2009). Mindfulness, often described as the practice of attuning one's attention and awareness in particular ways—being aware of mental, emotional, or physical phenomena in the present moment, with a nonjudgmental attitude—can be developed both through formal mindfulness meditation (i.e., the intentional act of training one's mind and heart), and the informal practice of mindfulness (i.e., bringing the stated qualities into any moment or activity throughout the day).

Because at its root mindfulness has philosophical ties to approaching the challenges of craving, aversion, and delusion (Nanomoli & Bodhi, 1995), it is an ideal practice for young people dealing with substance abuse, which is fundamentally a disorder of craving, aversion, and delusion. The conceptual explanation for why mindfulness may be useful in reducing substance use is that mindfulness practice enhances awareness of craving for a substance in the moment, enhances the ability to consciously choose an action in response to the craving, and after consistent practice may offer insight into why someone might choose to use substances in the first place (e.g., gaining insight on using drugs to avoid trauma symptoms). Given these attributes, researchers and clinicians are interested in mindfulness as it applies to the treatment of substance abuse and dependence.

Research on mindfulness-based substance abuse treatment remains small but promising. A growing body of research is being conducted on mindfulness-based relapse prevention (MBRP; Bowen, Chawla, & Marlatt, 2011), an intervention built upon mindfulness-based stress reduction (MBSR; Kabat-Zinn, 1990) and mindfulness-based cognitive therapy (MBCT; Segal, Williams, & Teasdale, 2002), and the findings suggest that MBRP may reduce both substance use and relapse (Bowen et al., 2009). Research on mindfulness and substance use among adolescents is even more limited than that with adult populations. However, I conducted a study evaluating a mindfulness-based substance abuse program that I co-created with incarcerated youth (Himelstein & Saul, 2013). Although the data are preliminary, the results are hopeful, with youth who participated in the program showing significant reductions in impulsivity (a strong factor in reacting to substance use craving) while seeing increased risks in drug use after the intervention (Himelstein, 2011). In more recent research that my colleagues and I conducted, incarcerated youth described mindfulness as a method for preventing both substance relapse and overall recidivism (Himelstein, Saul, Garcia-Romeu, & Pinedo, 2014). Mindfulness as an intervention for substance abusing adolescents merits clearly further research and consideration.

What research in the field of mindfulness and substance use has rarely reviewed is the impact of the clinician or facilitator on the therapeutic process. In recent work (Himelstein, 2013) I cover building authentic relationships, working with resistance, group facilitation processes, and other topics. In this chapter, my goal is to briefly present the necessary components of developing authentic relationships with group participants, teaching mindfulness, and facilitating mindfulness-based substance abuse groups. I do not intend for this chapter to be read as the "end all, be all" of a comprehensive approach, but rather to provide the gist of the type of style I employ with the young people I serve. Readers interested in this style may find useful my past (Himelstein, 2013) and recent (Himelstein & Saul, 2015) publications.

Relational Mindfulness

As has been suggested elsewhere, mindfulness can be employed at many levels of psychotherapy substance abuse treatment (Germer, Siegel, & Fulton, 2005; Hick & Bien, 2008; Himelstein, 2013; Shapiro & Carlson, 2009). Probably the second most referenced application of mindfulness in therapy is the clinician's own personal mindfulness practice. This application is important to the development of clinical skills, given its ability to transcend paradigms of therapy (e.g., a therapist from either a cognitive or dynamic orientation can benefit from being aware of his or her own emotions, thoughts, and impulses in session). This use of mindfulness emphasizes the therapist's commitment to self-awareness, personal growth, the development of presence, and mindful awareness of personal emotions, uncomfortable feelings, and countertransference. Mindfulness training for the therapist emphasizes the sharpening of the therapist's awareness as the tool with which therapy is practiced. Being more present to young people and modeling self-care are vital in developing authentic relationships and what I see as receptive learning environments (i.e., environments in which youth are more open to interventions and curriculum).

One element that most mindfulness and therapy texts have in common is the importance of personal practice among clinicians. Elements that are often not included in mindfulness and therapy texts involve the development of personal qualities that both enhance mindfulness practice and therapeutic relationship. Qualities such as authenticity, compassion, kindness, and connecting with other human beings can be practiced, improved upon, and ultimately affect the quality of therapy that is provided. In this sense, the practices become not only *intra*personal mindfulness practices (i.e., practicing them for personal improvement), but also *inter*personal mindfulness practices because they directly relate to the quality of the therapeutic relationship and contribute to a receptive learning environment. There are three basic qualities that I have found extremely useful in developing relationships with substance-abusing young people: authenticity, connecting on a human level, and taking a radical stance on behavioral change.

Authenticity

One of the most important factors in developing trusting relationships with challenging adolescents—whether justice-involved, substance abusing or not—is the degree to which you are authentic. That is, it is important for you to be comfortable with yourself, be fairly stable in your identity and ego strength, and not be overly concerned with being liked by your clients. For example, there would be no need to adopt slang or dialect your clients use if that's not authentic for you. Doing so would be not only inauthentic, but also many adolescents who already have a keen sense of inauthenticity would observe such behavior as disrespectful; you would thereby unwittingly create an artificial barrier between you and your client from the start. Substance-abusing adolescents are much more likely to respect a clinician who is comfortable with him- or herself and does not use language outside his or her normal subcultural vernacular to create a relationship. I worked for many years with a clinician whom most of our incarcerated adolescents clients would classify as "nerdy." Everything from his body language to his speech could have been, and sometimes was, described as nerdy. He was never incarcerated and came from a different background from the majority of our clients. He had never struggled with major substance abuse and could not relate to that story. However, he demonstrated his comfort with himself and was authentic as a person and clinician. Because of these qualities, our incarcerated adolescent clients (many of whom came from tough backgrounds) absolutely adored him. They admired and respected that he did not try to pose as someone or something he was not. They gravitated toward his quirky sense of humor and the fact that he was not afraid to make fun of himself. His authenticity not only let youth feel safe and trusting, but also modeled that it was okay for the youth to be themselves as well—which is an area in which many young people struggle. Without such authenticity, the beautiful relationships he created might never have occurred.

When working with your kids, you may have had experiences that are similar to theirs, or you may have had drastically different experiences. The important point is that you *own* your experience as yours, because when you do that, you can truly listen and witness the experience of the young people with whom you work. Authenticity begets authenticity, and when working with substance-abusing adolescents (really, with any substance-abusing population), it is important to be authentic so they can to tell their story authentically and be open to intervention.

Connecting on a Human Level

Another ingredient in the development of an authentic relationship is the explicit intention to connect on a human level. Often professionals can get trapped in the idea that what every young person needs is a solution to a problem. In the world of working with adolescents "in the system," this "solution" often takes the form of either implicitly believing or explicitly telling an adolescent that there is some problem in his or her behavior that needs to be changed. The issue with presenting such a stance is that it automatically aligns you against authentic connection with the young person because he or she will most likely feel judged. It is therefore important to enter the relationship by making the explicit treatment objective to connect with the client on a human-to-human level. Establishing this basic human connection can be cultivated in many ways; simply examine your own authentic relationships and delineate the experiences that led to their development. Young people are no different. Next I briefly discuss two qualities that I have found very useful in building such connections: curiosity and skillful self-disclosure.

Curiosity

Most adolescents, like people of any age, appreciate when someone takes a genuine interest in them. When I'm authentically curious about and interested in the youth I work with, I see and *experience* the benefits in our relationship. When they talk about themselves and share their stories, I *listen*. When they honor me by sharing their opinions and experiences with drug use, I ask detailed questions—not to be nosy, and not always just to collect clinical information, but to demonstrate that I'm present and listening. I give my clients permission to talk about serious issues, such as substance abuse and addiction, and I give them permission to talk about what interests them in life (sports, music, etc.). This openness creates an atmosphere in which I can be authentically curious about their experience, yet not appear too nosy or come on too strong. I have had many clients who initially had nothing to say to me during session, and when I told them that their silence was okay and that we could simply play cards, I ended up getting full life stories. Because of my curiosity, my authentic intention to want to get to know the person in front of me, I have been able to build an authentic relationship that forms the foundation of an effective treatment.

Furthermore, young people of different cultural backgrounds often are not listened to in a serious way; their opinions and perspectives are ignored, marginalized, or minimized. If you can be genuinely curious about their lives and listen to their stories from a place of presence and authenticity, you right a persistent wrong in our culture and correct an injustice. The young people are seen, heard, and authentically "taken into account" by you. This corrective process alone contributes to an authentic relationship and is healing in its own right.

Skillful Self-Disclosure

Self-disclosure in therapeutic settings may be encouraged or discouraged depending on your theoretical orientation. In my observations as a supervisor, it appears that most graduate schools of psychotherapy discourage their students from disclosing personal information. Often, this position comes from a desire to ensure mutual safety. There is typically a concern that any information disclosed might be manipulated in some way and used against the therapist. For those working with substance-abusing, adolescent, and justice-system-involved populations, this fear is often amplified to the nth degree. I believe, however, that self-disclosure is a necessary process in building an authentic relationship with young individuals. They need to know that you are *real*—that you have real preferences, real faults, and are not a robot. That realness, which comes from skillful self-disclosure, is a prerequisite for most adolescents to open up and disclose their personal information to you. Therapists and facilitators who elude the question in some way (e.g., "Let's examine why you'd like to know that information about me") are often met with blank faces and rolling eyes. Young people know when you're uncomfortable disclosing something; simply stating that you're uncomfortable disclosing would go much farther toward an authentic connection than using the bob-and-weave method. If you disclose nothing about yourself, even with good reason, you will most likely bump up against or create barriers, and treatment will stall.

The key to self-disclosure with young people is that is must always be skillful, with right intention and action. *Skillful self-disclosure* occurs when a therapist asks him- or herself (and/or a supportive supervisor) whether or not the disclosure would be in the best interest of the young person, and sincerely reflects on the answer. When this questioning occurs, the therapist puts him- or herself into a contemplative state of mind from which he or she can wisely discern if the disclosure will be skillful. I have worked with many clients with whom I have *chosen* to disclose that I have a history of substance abuse; I chose these disclosures because I felt they would contribute to building relationships. And they did. I have also worked with many clients to whom I have never disclosed my substance-abusing past because I thought it would negatively impact the relationship. I always do my best to consider how what I'm about to say may impact my relationship with my client. That process of consciously considering the possible impact is what constitutes skillful self-disclosure.

Often when I do disclose, my young clients don't pry too much (contrary to popular belief). They just want to know a little about me and then go back into their own story. When I felt it was appropriate and told my clients that I had a history of alcohol and marijuana use, 9 times out of 10 they simply smiled and went back into their own stories. I felt subjectively that in those moments, they were relating to me; this interpersonal relating is a pillar of developing real relationships. I know there are probably some readers still concerned with that 10th client who *does* continue to pry and ask questions or use information in a manipulative fashion. In those situations, I rely on my authentic subjective experience (therapist mindfulness) to intervene appropriately. Below is an example of interactions I've had with some clients who've tried to pry after my self-disclosure:

CLIENT: I don't need this therapy shit. You're just some other dude who's gonna tell me what to do and what not to do.

THERAPIST: What makes you think that? Have you had some negative experiences in substance counseling before?

CLIENT: Yeah, everyone always tells me that I should just quit, but they don't know me—I'm done with this bullshit.

THERAPIST: Well, *we've* never been in therapy, and I can tell you that that's not my style. I'm *not* here to change you or tell you what to do. I just want to connect. If I can help you, that'd be great. If not, I just want us to get to know each other.

CLIENT: So you think you can help me? What? Have you smoked weed before? Have you been where I'm at?

[Here, I have been asked a direct question that requires a decision about self-disclosure. I weigh the options, and because my intuition tells me it feels right, I decide to disclose.]

THERAPIST: Yeah, actually I have. I used to smoke a lot of weed.

CLIENT: Oh. Usually, all the other therapists just dodge that question with a bullshit answer.

THERAPIST: Like I said, I want to connect. I don't think bullshit answers contribute to that process.

CLIENT: So hold up. You're out here telling me that you used to smoke weed, and that it's not cool for me to smoke weed. You did drugs, so why isn't it okay for me to do drugs?!

THERAPIST: Well, I never said it wasn't okay for you to do drugs. Like I said before, I'm not interested in telling you what to do and what not to do. I'm here to connect with you and hopefully help in some way. I'm more interested in why you use so much weed rather than trying to get you to stop.

I have had the above interaction in many different ways, with many different clients many times throughout my career. The overwhelming response to the last statement is an emotional sigh of relief. When young people understand that I'm not trying to change them, ironically they are more open to a relationship and, in turn, to change. This *must* be an authentic stance, however (which I'll describe below). Notice that it was my willingness to disclose that brought about the "clarifying" process that occurred in the vignette. It is in those clarifying moments that I experience my relationship with my clients growing the most. Over time they feel safer to disclose their story and are more open to deepening their own self-awareness.

Radical Stance on Behavioral Change

The third quality that contributes to an authentic relationship is highlighted in the preceding dialogue. It is the notion that when one attempts to "change" a young person before he or she is ready to embark on a transformative journey authentically, resistance occurs. Rather than focusing on the behavioral outcomes of reduced recidivism, substance use, and relapse, I focus on building real relationships and the development of self-awareness. I take this approach because if I were to focus on behavioral outcomes, I would automatically align myself with every system the young person has faced up until this point: parents, teachers, the judge, the police, probation officers, and sometimes other therapists. Such an alignment creates an uphill battle that is not worth the effort to me. I find it ironic that if you ask anyone on the street if anyone has the power to "change" another human being, the most common answer is that people have to change from within. In spite of that commonly shared wisdom, the research and clinical intervention paradigms remain focused on behavioral outcome measures. Furthermore, I have found that when employing this radical stance on behavioral change (e.g., focusing on connection and self-awareness and not pushing change), youth tend to change *more*.

I have had many justice-involved youth, both in individual and group settings, literally thank me for not trying to change them and tell me that *this* approach was what motivated them to change more. It is an ironic truth that if we focus more on connection and self-awareness (as in the above interaction), there will be more room for the identified patient to explore the possibilities of personal growth and transformation. This stance does not come without disclaimers, however. The following three disclaimers are imperative when employing such a philosophy on behavioral outcome.

Disclaimer 1: Use Common Sense

If an adolescent discloses to me in session that he or she really has a drinking problem and wants to cut that habit down, I am not about to respond with, "Well, it's not my philosophy to force change; I focus more on self-awareness and connection. So you're on your own with that." Such a response would be both preposterous and unethical. Of course, if a young person wants to reduce his or her substance use, I am absolutely present to that desire, and I have the tools to help. I have had many willing clients and have been honored to be a part of their transformations. Not all youth are resistant to drug treatment, or to any treatment. The radical stance on change is applicable only to those who are resistant in some way, not to young people who want to change their habits.

Disclaimer 2: Authenticity Is a Must

If the radical stance is employed, it must be authentic. That is, it's never a good idea to manipulate someone for our own interest. If we believe that holding a radical stance on behavioral change will result in more change, and then employ that stance to get to the change, *we perpetuate this problem*. It is of the highest importance for us to believe that the young person sitting in front of us is capable of choice. If we manipulate clients or misuse the radical stance, we take that choice away from them. If we are authentic in the philosophy, there is room for clients to feel valued, respected, and responsible— which leads to a real, authentic connection that fosters more transformation, but on the young person's terms.

Disclaimer 3: You Can Still Confront High-Risk Behavior

Just because we employ this radical stance on behavioral change, does *not* mean that we cannot or should not confront our clients on their high-risk behaviors. When they describe dangerous behaviors, such a stance does not mean simply sitting back and think, "Oh well, it's their life—they're choosing this." What's important to understand is that the medium of that confrontation is different from how many of us have been trained.

    I once had a client who overdosed on "spice" (i.e., a synthetic marijuana that many probation youth smoke because it doesn't show up on ordinary urine tests). He had a heart attack and was fortunately revived by the paramedics, who informed him his heart stopped for almost 60 seconds. In session when he recounted the incident, it would've been easy for me to engage thinking such as "What were you thinking? Don't you know you could've died?" Of course he knew that, and he's probably been told that by all sorts of people in his life by now, so my telling him that might not be the most skillful intervention in that moment. Rather than metaphorically point the finger at him, I engaged him through the medium of our authentic relationship (at this point he'd been in therapy for approximately 6 months):

CLIENT: Bro', I got something I need to tell you.

THERAPIST: Oh yeah, what's up?

CLIENT: Man . . . last week I was smoking spice again. That shit got me hella high! Bro', I passed out—I don't know what happened. I just felt a big pain in my chest and then woke up in the ambulance. My friends told me I started freakin' out and then just dropped. They called the police and dragged me out to the road and just left me there. Fucking friends, huh?

[At this point I have the option of confronting such behavior. But it makes no sense for me to chastise him. He is obviously in a vulnerable space, yet feels comfortable disclosing this experience with me. I practice in-the-moment mindfulness and ask myself what I really feel in this moment. Genuine concern arises, and I decide to disclose this.]

THERAPIST: Wow. (*pause*) I really appreciate your telling me that. You know, what comes up for me is that I'm concerned and afraid for you. I've only known you for 6 months or so, and we've built something good here. It would be such a sad day if I came in next week and found out you'd overdosed and died.

CLIENT: Yeah, it would. (*pause*)

THERAPIST: What's that like for you to hear that from me? To hear that I really am concerned about you?

CLIENT: Well, no one besides my mom really talks to me like that. So it's a little weird, but it's good. I appreciate it.

The client and I discussed his feelings about my authentic concern for him and how his actions affect others in his life (including his mother). This is an intervention I often use; *it highlights the relationship and confronts the client on his or her high-risk behavior, without sacrificing the stance on change.* It also contributes not only to deepening the relationship, but also to the continual processing of the relationship. This processing, in turn, translates into strong interpersonal communication skills as the client consistently discusses how he feels about people in his life (e.g., his mother) and, in some cases, speaks directly to that person (e.g., therapist).

The radical stance on behavioral change, connection on a human level, and the practice of authenticity are all qualities that clinicians, teachers, mentors, and healers can foster to deepen self-awareness and promote well-being in those with whom they work. They are also qualities that directly translate into relating with young people (or any population) and directly contribute to the building of a receptive learning environment where mindfulness (or any curriculum or intervention) might occur. This relational approach to mindfulness is the base from which all interpersonal work stems. Focusing on developing these qualities in relation to working with young people will enhance your ability to teach mindfulness and mindfulness meditation.

Teaching Mindfulness to Substance-Using Adolescents

Once a therapeutic relationship is established, the opportunity to teach that young person formal meditation may arise. Reaching this point is truly a privilege because it suggests that your client or student trusts you enough to learn from you. In a study I conducted with colleagues (Himelstein et al., 2014), we interviewed incarcerated adolescent substance abusers about their experience with mindfulness and inquired about specific approaches to learning and practicing meditation. Although there are many practices that constitute mindfulness meditation (e.g., mindfulness of the breath, noting, body scans), the method of teaching such practices has been fairly consistent over the past 2,500 years. For this reason, my colleagues and I were not interested in adapting such techniques, but rather interested in the context in which such techniques could best be employed. From our thematic analysis of the data we gathered, a number of concepts useful in teaching mindfulness to marginalized substance-abusing young people emerged. Although we collected data from young people who were incarcerated and participating in substance abuse treatment, these concepts apply to most youth, as well as to the general population. The data represent one approach to teaching young people, who had little to no prior experience with meditating, meditation. This endeavor includes defining mindfulness, starting with short meditations, using easy-to-understand and tangible techniques, using metaphor, not being attached to formal meditation logistics (e.g., eyes closed or certain postures), and empowering young people to lead meditations for themselves and their peers.

Defining Mindfulness

Defining mindfulness is an important aspect of teaching young people mindfulness meditation. I believe it is important for these youngsters to be able to express what mindfulness means to them. In order for that to happen, it is important to (1) convey a brief and simple definition of what mindfulness is, and (2) clarify any potential misconceptions about meditation. I usually attempt a very concise, "one-liner" definition to make sure the young people I work with can remember it. And although I certainly have used Jon Kabat-Zinn's (1990) well-known "paying attention, on purpose, in the present moment with a non-judgmental attitude" definition, I contextualize the wording to reflect the person, or group, sitting in front of me. I prefer to keep the definitions simple; for example, "Meditation is being present to your internal thoughts, emotions, and sensations, with a calm mind." Remember, this is just an introductory definition; discussions of components such as acceptance and nonjudgment can come later. If I'm lucky enough to have an ongoing relationship with this young person, I can always elaborate on the definition. The key concept is to come up with a one-liner definition, practice it, test it with young people, and refine it based on your experience with your clients. (See Himelstein, 2013, for exercises on developing this language.)

The second key concept is to clarify any misconceptions the young person may have about mindfulness or meditation. In one of my interviews, a young person stated the following when initially thinking about meditation:

"When I grew up I never think meditation could help. I ain't gonna lie, I thought that people who did meditation was weird. But I kind of figured out the real deal of meditation. It helps me a lot, to make my own decisions, be a bigger man. Feel me? Do what you gotta do." (in Himelstein et al., 2014, p. 564)

Another participant discussed how initial conversations about mindfulness could be used as mediums to clarify what mindfulness and meditation were:

"I don't know, maybe tryin' to explain to cats that meditation isn't like some shit for hippies . . . 'cause when you first asked me, I was kinda like 'what the fuck? I don't want to do this,' but then I was like 'I don't know, maybe I should.' Because like, that's what you kind of think of, like a monk or something. And I don't want to be a fucking monk. You know?" (in Himelstein et al., 2014, p. 564)

Thus, when defining mindfulness, there is a golden opportunity to present a simple and concise definition that normalizes the practice.

Starting with Short Meditations

Alongside a clear definition of mindfulness, it is important to not overwhelm beginners with meditations that are too long. The intention is to facilitate a short experience and then process that experience with the young person. Over time, longer meditations can be offered. Generally, starting with 3–5 minutes and a few minutes for processing afterward is a suitable amount of time. This is not to suggest that you will never be able to facilitate long meditations with young people. On the contrary, I have led group and individual meditations upward of 45 minutes, but we need to meet our clients where they're at. When I facilitate mindfulness-based substance abuse groups with justice-involved youth, I often clarify in the initial meeting an intention to practice meditation for longer periods of time in each group, so youth know what to expect.

Easy-to-Understand and Tangible Techniques

One of the more powerful themes we identified in our research was that all of our participants oriented toward either easy-to-understand or tangible techniques when first learning meditation. *Easy-to-understand* techniques are meditation methods for which the instruction has little to no ambiguity. For example, counting the breath to 10 and starting back again at 1 was very easy for young people to understand. They reported feeling more concentrated and focused after practicing this meditation (Himelstein et al., 2014), and those positive experiences reinforced their "buy-in" to meditation practice. In contrast, basic mindfulness of the breath (without counting), although indicated by all of our participants as a beneficial exercise, was described as sometimes confusing and ambiguous as a beginning meditation.

Tangible techniques consisted of the body scan and deep breathing practices. Young people described these practices as easy to follow, because their focus was on the body, and because they experienced positive, present-moment consequences as a result (i.e., usually relaxation and stress reduction) (Himelstein et al., 2014). Thus, starting with these meditations can frequently gain buy-in from young people. I have practiced many forms of mindfulness meditation with young people, and starting with a tangible practice often helps them solidify the experience in their memory. Especially for marginalized, justice-involved youth, tools that decrease stress and anxiety are often welcomed.

Use of Metaphor

One tool all of us who work with young people should utilize is metaphor, regardless of whether we facilitate mindfulness or substance abuse groups. Metaphors enable an understanding of abstract concepts on a deeper level than a lecture can provide. That is, sometimes the simple definition of mindfulness, although more easily remembered, is not understood on the gut level as a metaphor.

Recently, I have described that in my work at the Mind Body Awareness (MBA) Project, we illustrate mindfulness with the "lion/dog mind metaphor" (Himelstein, 2013). Our instructors ask youth what would happen if they were waving a bone in a dog's face and then tossed it a few yards away. "The dog would get the bone," the young people always respond. Then we ask, "What if we were waving that same bone in front of a lion? And threw it a few yards away? What would the lion do?" Eight out of 10 times the youth emphatically say, "He'd eat you!" We then facilitate a discussion about how the bone completely permeates the dog's reality; this reality, for the dog, is nothing but the bone. Therefore, wherever the bone goes, the dog's mind follows. But the lion has the ability to see beyond just the bone, and that's why she didn't follow it. The lion can see a person beyond the bone, holding and waving the bone. She has the ability (speaking metaphorically, of course) to choose whether or not to follow the bone or the person. In a state of mindfulness, we can observe thoughts, emotions, and sensations from a place of balance and not necessarily react to them. We are the lion, not the dog. This metaphor often resonates with young people.

Consider different metaphors that relate to the particular practices and particular population you teach. Metaphor can be implemented on many levels: to define mindfulness (as above), discuss the practice of meditation (e.g., relating it to "physical training" for the mind), and even incorporated into meditations themselves (e.g., relating the mind to a sword, and the breath sharpening that sword on every inhalation and every exhalation). As we sit with young people and get to know them and the lives they live, we can listen in a way that could point toward the appropriate metaphor that will resonate with them.

Nonattachment to Formal Meditation Logistics

It is important to avoid any kind of attachment to formal meditation logistics when working with young people. That is, there is no need to demand closed eyes or a completely straight-back, cross-legged posture. Those of us who are daily practitioners know that although these conditions can help, they are not necessary for practicing mindfulness. Although sitting up straight may enhance attention at times, remember that the kids are just starting this practice and that the form they use can be built upon in time. I had one client who didn't want to close his eyes or sit up straight because it activated his trauma. I worked with him over a number of months, and as he became more comfortable with me, progressing through the healing of his trauma, he felt more comfortable closing his eyes. By the end of our therapy relationship, he found pride in practicing the "nonmoving" meditation, where he'd sit with his eyes closed and not move his body for the entire meditation. I believe he was able to get to this point because I didn't push him into formal logistics before he was ready.

Empowering Young People to Lead Meditations

One final note: I would encourage us to empower young people in leadership positions whenever possible, especially those who have been disempowered by their families or the wider culture. One way to do this is to have them lead meditations. Of course, prior training is important, but after a few sessions it can be very powerful for everyone if one of the young people takes the lead with the practices. I have done this in one-on-one settings as well, but I believe it has the greatest impact in the group setting. When a young person is empowered to teach others by facilitating the meditation, the likelihood that he or she will remember the experience as a positive one and connect more with meditation as a practice is increased. Furthermore, this shows *all* the members of the group that the facilitators trust the young people enough to relinquish leadership to them. This trust conveys, on a deep level, a respect for them and a belief that they can be leaders with something to offer—qualities too often overlooked in our society.

Concluding Thoughts

In this chapter I have described my own experiences of using mindfulness with challenging, substance-abusing young people often involved in the justice system. This one chapter cannot do justice to the breadth and depth of mindfulness-based substance abuse treatment, but hopefully it offers some inspiration. My colleague and I (Himelstein & Saul, 2015) have plans to release an in-depth mindfulness-based substance abuse treatment curriculum for a group format that expands on the basic concepts in this chapter. Working with young people who use substances is a profoundly complex practice. We hold in our awareness that mindfulness is an equally powerful intervention, and that the practice of true "relational mindfulness," in which we authentically connect with another, is powerful in creating a container in which healing can occur.

The method for presenting and the choice of mindfulness exercise may enhance the young person's buy-in (at least initially) with the practice. What I believe to be most important when embarking on such a journey with a young person is the established personal practice and the openness of the adult, and the open receptive environment the adult fosters. It is in your client's best interest for you to deeply examine your own thoughts, biases, and values regarding substance use and any of your client's behaviors. Such self-awareness will guide you in this challenging work to practice from your own truth.

REFERENCES

Baer, R. A. (Ed.). (2006). *Mindfulness-based treatment approaches: Clinician's guide to evidence base and applications.* Burlington, MA: Academic Press.
Bowen, S., Chawla, N., Collins, S., Witkiewitz, K., Hsu, S., Grow, J., et al. (2009).

Mindfulness-based relapse prevention for substance use disorders: A pilot efficacy trial. *Substance Abuse, 30,* 205–305.

Bowen, S., Chawla, N., & Marlatt, G. A. (2011). *Mindfulness-based relapse prevention for addictive behaviors: A clinician's guide.* New York: Guilford Press.

Daniel, J. Z., Hickman, M., Macleod, J., Wiles, N., Lingford-Hughs, A., Farrell, M., et al. (2009). Is socioeconomic status in early life associated with drug use?: A systematic review of the evidence. *Drug and Alcohol Review, 28,* 142–153.

Germer, C. K., Siegel, R. D., & Fulton, P. R. (Eds.). (2005). *Mindfulness and psychotherapy.* New York: Guilford Press.

Hick, S. F., & Bien, T. (Eds.). (2008). *Mindfulness and the therapeutic relationship.* New York: Guilford Press.

Himelstein, S. (2011). Mindfulness-based substance abuse treatment for incarcerated youth: A mixed method pilot study. *International Journal of Transpersonal Studies, 30,* 1–10.

Himelstein, S. (2013). *A mindfulness-based approach to working with high-risk adolescents.* New York: Routledge.

Himelstein, S., & Saul, S. (2015). *Mindfulness-based substance abuse treatment for adolescents: A 12-session curriculum.* New York: Routledge.

Himelstein, S., Saul, S., Garcia-Romeu, A., & Pinedo, D. (2014). Mindfulness training as an intervention for substance user incarcerated adolescents: A pilot grounded theory study. *Substance Use and Misuse, 49*(5), 560–570.

Johnston, L. D., O'Malley, P. M., Bachman, J. G., & Schulenberg, J. E. (2012, December 19). The rise in teen marijuana use stalls, synthetic marijuana use levels, and use of "bath salts" is very low. Retrieved July 25, 2013, from *www. monitoringthefuture.org.*

Kabat-Zinn, J. (1990). *Full catastrophe living: Using the wisdom of your body and mind to face stress, pain, and illness.* New York: Delta.

Liddle, H. A., Dakof, G. A., Parker, K., Diamond, G. S., Barrett, K., & Tejada, M. (2001). Multidimensional family therapy for adolescent drug abuse: Results of a randomized clinical trial. *American Journal of Drug and Alcohol Abuse, 27,* 651–688.

Mumola, C. J., & Karberg, J. C. (2006, October). Drug use and dependence, state and federal prisoners, 2004. *Bureau of Justice Statistics, Special Report, NCJ213530.*

Nanomoli, B., & Bodhi, B. (Trans.). (1995). *The middle length discourses of the Buddha.* Boston: Wisdom.

National Drug Intelligence Center. (2011). *The economic impact of illicit drug use on American society* (Product No. 2011-Q0317-002). Washington, DC: Author.

Segal, Z. V., Williams, M. G., & Teasdale, J. D. (2002). *Mindfulness-based cognitive therapy for depression: A new approach to preventing relapse.* New York: Guilford Press.

Shapiro, S. L., & Carlson, L. E. (2009). *The art and science of mindfulness: Integrating mindfulness into psychology and the helping professions.* Washington, DC: American Psychological Association.

CHAPTER 8

Cultivating Rootedness and Connectedness in a Digital Age

Ozum Ucok-Sayrak
Gregory Kramer

We are plants which—whether we like to admit it to ourselves or not—
must with our roots rise out of the earth in order to bloom in the ether
and to bear fruit.
        —JOHANN PETER HEBEL (cited in Heidegger, 1959/1966, p. 47)

This chapter explores the ground of "rootedness" in human beings (or "the
loss of rootedness"; Heidegger, 1959, pp. 48–49) and the movement of relatedness that emerges out of such ground. We present and discuss various intra-
and interpersonal wisdom practices to facilitate the cultivation of rootedness,
relatedness, well-being, and compassion. Before delving into further specifics,
however, we wish to share the following narrative.

    Anny, a young female student in a college-level class on Human Com-
munication reflects on her realization of the disconnection between herself
and her everyday experiences and surroundings in response to a "mindful
activity" assignment. She states that she "disappears into" her mind and does
not feel the water as she takes a shower, for instance. She explains that the
only way she notices that the water is too hot is when she sees that her skin
has turned to red. She had to rewash her hair more than once because she
could not remember whether she had already done so. Furthermore, Anny
reports that similar habits of getting lost in her thinking and disconnect-
ing from her surroundings manifest in her relationships as well. Because she
"zones out" and disconnects from her surroundings, she repeats the stories
she just told because she cannot remember telling them in the first place.

After doing this assignment, Anny realized that she seems to never, or rarely, be present to where she is physically.

We invite you to pause for a moment before you continue reading further, and notice how you respond to what you just read above. The mindful activity assignment is simple; the instructions are as follows:

> "Pick a routine daily activity you do, such as brushing your teeth, taking a shower, walking, driving, eating, getting up from bed or going to sleep, and bring your attention to it. Allow yourself to be *in* your experience fully, attending to the motions, images, physical sensations, sounds, and tastes associated with it as well as any thoughts that run through your mind. The point is to be present to what you are doing, rather than thinking of other things (such as the next thing to do, plans for the day, etc.). If you notice that there are many thoughts in your mind that distract you, notice the thoughts as thoughts, bring attention to your breath, and come back to what are doing. You might get distracted many times, each time come back to breathing and the activity."

Anny, the student in the preceding narrative, picked showering and wrote about her realization of being out of touch with her experience, which she characterized as "frightening." Anny is not alone; we have heard many similar stories of hair getting rewashed, or other mindless repetitions, because the person engaged in the task was not attending to his or her experience.

So why start a chapter on human communication and rootedness with an anecdote about hygiene, typically a solitary act? Anny observed that her experience of losing touch with her surroundings (the here) and the present moment (the now) by "zoning out" and "disappearing into my mind" was not limited to showering but also extended to her interpersonal interactions—powerful realization. We invite you to take a moment to notice if any of this sounds familiar: tuning out as you listen to someone, not being present to others, or even yourself, disappearing into the stories of your mind, realizing too late that you have missed the whole point of a conversation. The quality of your presence in your body–mind—*intra*personal connectedness—has direct implications on your *inter*personal connectedness and communication. This chapter focuses on this relation between the intra- and the interpersonal realms, the interior and the exterior, as it informs our discussion of a new ground for rootedness in the digital age. We elaborate further on this point in the next section.

Purpose of the Chapter

In this chapter, we first share our observations and experiences on connectedness in the lives of college-age young adults and teenagers in contemporary

American society. The contexts that inform our writing include the college classroom, using observations from basic communication courses such as Oral Communication and Public Speaking, and our experiences teaching interpersonal mindfulness to teens and adults in workshops or retreats. Our discussion is not limited to exchanges in the classroom but also addresses how teenagers and college students relate to others in everyday life. Despite being more interconnected via social media and the Internet than in any previous time in human history, today's youth express deep and persistent feelings of disconnection, isolation, and loneliness (Price, 2011; Turkle, 2011; Konrath, 2013; Zajonc, 2006).

Second, we bring in philosopher Martin Heidegger's (1959/1966) discussion of the "rootlessness" and "homelessness" of the modern person, and explore the need for a renewed sense of rootedness supported by a kind of direct connection with ourselves, others, and our surroundings through the full presence in body and mind that is not mediated via technology (and available to us 24/7). We refer to this type of connection as "clear awareness" and mindfulness, and the interactions that thereby arise as "mindful communication." Heidegger's discussion of "meditative thinking" and "releasement towards things" enrich and inform our exploration of a new ground for rootedness in the digital age.

Third, we describe specific mindfulness practices to illustrate the implications of experiencing a direct connection to one's body–mind and to one's surroundings in cultivating purposeful attentiveness and in fully inhabiting the spaces in which we exist and work together toward creating and caring for the "local home" (Fritz, 2013, p. 156). Growing roots through intentional wisdom practices and inhabiting our lives and the places in which we live and work naturally lead to caring for this local home, which in turn provide us with new ground to move beyond a sense of homelessness and toward connection.

One of us (Gregory Kramer) has developed and teaches a relational meditation practice called Insight Dialogue (ID), which gets to the roots of separation and ruptured communication not by teaching communication or even relationship skills, but rather by offering an interpersonal practice of cultivating mindfulness and presence *in the midst of interpersonal interaction*. ID is not framed here as primarily a communication practice, although bringing mindfulness to communication naturally yields benefits in attentive listening and careful speech. Rather, ID is usually taught as a meditation for cultivating clear awareness and tranquility, which are then applied to directly experiencing the mind's dynamic processes. The meditative practices combine with the power of relationship to provide safety while helping to challenge, interest, and focus the mind. In this way, practitioners are able to see into the mind's entanglements *and* the fading away of those entanglements. We offer a discussion of ID as an interpersonal practice that emerges from attending to one's body–mind (i.e., rooted in the *intra*personal), while simultaneously attending to the relational experience (i.e., rooted in the *inter*personal) as it is happening. ID accesses the root of separation by enabling acute sensitivity to the physical sensations, emotions, and thoughts that occur during the continual dance between separation and nonseparation, social rupture and wholeness in the course of social interaction.

In the final part of the chapter, we discuss the implications of mindful communication and ID—and of simply slowing down while relating to others—for young people generally, as well as the potential impact on their communication with others across generations.

On "Being Connected" and the Need for Roots

"Being connected" is a common term found in everyday talk, frequently used by young adults in the popular discourse around cell/mobile phones and the Internet. Most of our students enter "wired" classrooms or workshops with earbuds in place or tapping on their smartphones. These young adults highly value "being connected" to others through mediated communication such as text messaging, instant messaging, social networking, and e-mailing. And, when it is time to connect in the room with each other and the instructor in real time and place, many appear distracted and unprepared for the task in front of them, not yet ready to be present and focused *here*, now. One might ask when the time to be present and focused arrives for those who are seduced into this ongoing flow of digital connectivity. Can they ever step out of this habitual process to discern when to connect through the technological devices and when to let go?

In his Memorial Address over half a century ago, Heidegger (1959/1966, pp. 53–54) stated that "suddenly and unaware we find ourselves so firmly shackled to these technical devices that we fall into bondage to them." Heidegger had significant insight about the future when he warned us about the dangers of the technological age. A recent *New York Times* article from November 1, 2013, highlighted the increasing attention to mindfulness related workshops and seminars in the business world in the United States, describing an event titled "Disconnect to Connect" in San Francisco that examined "how we can live with technology without it swallowing us whole" (Hochman, 2013).

A recent example of the "bondage" to technical devices that Heidegger (1959) states above took place in the classroom a few weeks ago. Despite the course policy against the use of cell phones, laptops and other technical devices in the classroom (unless explicitly permitted), I (Ozum Ucok-Sayrak) noticed one student at the back corner of the class who was engaged in texting for some period of time. After a few minutes, I walked close to him and invited him to join the discussion by asking him a question. To my surprise (and with no shame), he responded as he still continued texting! It wasn't until I reflected to the others in class, acknowledging right in that moment that this was really happening, that he stopped. In my 18 years of teaching experience, this was the first time that I had observed an incident like this one. After this, I announced a new policy in class following a dialogue with a colleague who has been implementing it: Students will be marked absent on that day if they are observed to be texting in the classroom during class time (and this extends to the use of other technical devices). I find this policy meaningful in the sense that one's *presence is absent* in class (and I would extend this to other contexts as well) when engaged with technical devices unrelated to the topic.

In his address Heidegger (1959/1966) asked whether we are "defense-less and perplexed victim[s] at the mercy of the irresistible superior power of technology?"—so many decades before the Internet and social media existed. Still, Heidegger wrote about the "homelessness" and "rootlessness" of human beings who either wandered off from their local home or stayed but got "chained to" the radio, television, and magazines that drove them further away from their immediate surroundings as well as their customs and con-ventions. Heidegger's insights have been revived by communication scholars in more recent years, including Arnett's (1994) discussion of the "existential homelessness" that is encouraged by the lack of "common centers" and moral stories that guide people. "Without a guiding story or a place to call home a sense of rootlessness can pervade one's life. The need for roots that sustain lives of human beings through a sense of connectedness is essential for all human beings" (Holba, 2008, p. 494).

The question then is, where do human beings turn for a renewed sense of rootedness, and how do we adults cultivate this in ourselves and in the young people in our lives?

Distinguishing between two kinds of thinking, calculative and medita-tive—"each justified and needed in its own way"—Heidegger (1959/1966, p. 46) warned that only by relearning to think meditatively could we reclaim a new ground for a new kind of rootedness and overcome the dangers of the modern technological age that reduce us and the world to a resource in service of technology and industry. He further explained that calculative thinking plans, computes, and investigates new opportunities but never stops to contemplate the meaning that underlies all action. In contrast, meditative thinking allows us to discern, to see what is nearest and thus can be hardest to perceive. It "demands of us that we engage ourselves with what at first sight does not go together at all" (Heidegger, 1959/1966, p. 53). Regarding our relation with technology, for instance, we can let technological devices enter our lives and we can use them without allowing them to control and take over our lives. (Referring back to the mindful activity assignment dis-cussed in the introduction, this could be referred to as practicing a "mindful use of technology.") Thus, through meditative thinking, we can relate to things beyond just the technical, calculative mode and discern their meaning and place in our lives. Heidegger refers to this capacity, which says "yes" and at the same time "no," as a "releasement toward things" that allows us to "dwell in the world" (p. 54) at a level beyond just the technical mode of planning, organizing, calculating, etc.

In the next section, we explore meditative thinking in connection with specific contemplative practices that contribute to "keeping awake for releasement" (Heidegger, 1959/1966, p. 61) and cultivating new ground for a renewed sense of rootedness.

A New Ground for "Rootedness" in the Digital Age?

Our experiences and observations with our students and workshop/retreat participants led us to introduce a transition activity before we formally start the class or begin the deeper work of the retreat. This activity can be seen as a step toward (re)learning to fully inhabit one's lived experience in any given moment and to dwell in the world in a way that one's attention is not constantly hijacked. We introduce this activity as a "checking-in" or "arriving" process and state that although we talk about being connected all the time, we're actually usually self- and media-absorbed. We share that there is a way of being with others, and in the world, that is less separated and more intimate, and that this mode of being fully connected is available to us at all times. Then we guide students to sit in their chairs in a comfortable yet straight posture and pause together for a few minutes in silence, feeling their feet on the floor, their breath entering and leaving their bodies, and the sensation of their entire bodies at they sit quietly. Depending on the day or the workshop, we might continue to direct their attention to hearing sounds as simply sounds, rather than interpreting or judging them, and to noticing their thoughts without "feeding" them further. Thus, we begin "class" by connecting with our bodies, minds, and the surroundings, acknowledging the state of body–mind in that moment with a nonjudging attitude: "This is how things are now." Noticing the body and releasing judgment and desire in the mind toward how we want things to be different, and opening to the present moment allows for a new, fresh space to emerge. A major shift in the mood and energy of the class tends to occur after this short pause. Students report noticing how busy their minds are after a few minutes of the "arriving" exercise, and feeling more connected to their bodies and their surroundings. Most appear more alert, awake, and ready to work, whether it is an academic class or a mindfulness workshop. Purposefully making space to be present and "keep awake for releasement," opening to and inhabiting the present moment, allows one to connect directly to one's phenomenological experience and to grow roots, so to speak. As one student said, "I don't jump toward things now. I think, accept, and then move forward."

Furthermore, reconnecting with the body–mind and with the surroundings affects the ways in which we inhabit a space: Now we bring increased attentiveness and purposefulness to the task at hand. Remembering our intentions to inhabit a space (e.g., the classroom, an academic department, the workplace) by bringing our full presence of body–mind to meet the work in front of us can be connected to an "ethic of care" (Fritz, 2013, p. 156) through which we "protect and promote the good of place" (Fritz, 2013, p. 154) and create a "local home." Recently, I (Ozum Ucok-Sayrak) introduced a discussion in class regarding the difference between seeing the classroom as a local home where we engage in "conversation about ideas" (Arnett, 1992) versus a place we come and go to earn grades and to get the "job" done. The students grew alert and engaged as we discussed creating a productive learning environment "an enlarged space" (Fritz, 2013, p. 168), through the ways in which we engage in attentive, responsive communication practices that center around our purposes. Thus, as we learn to be purposefully attentive to the state of body–mind and our surroundings, and as we "keep awake for releasement" as we mindfully pause, we also recognize that we don't just arrive and leave without affecting the spaces we inhabit. Rather, we are responsible for "caring for the local home" (Fritz, 2013, p. 156) and enlarging it.

The last 10 years have seen an upsurge of interest in mindfulness practices, particularly in the methodical development of relaxed, present-centered attention. A key feature of mindfulness, distinguishing it from simple directed attention, is the component of what might be called *self-awareness*, or knowing that one is aware. Multiple initiatives, some discussed in this book, have sought to introduce mindfulness to young people in classroom situations. However, because traditional mindfulness practices have mostly been intrapersonal practices, although they may be offered in highly relational ways, their application to communication, or indeed to overtly social or relational settings, has been indirect. We hope our work is able to bridge personal and interpersonal practices in a meaningful way. We discuss this topic in more detail in the section on contemplative knowing and contemplative relation in the upcoming pages.

A Brief History of Introducing Mindfulness-Based Activities in the Communication Classroom

The ideas for the mindful activity assignment introduced in the opening of this chapter and the checking-in activity discussed in the prior section, both intrapersonal practices, arose in response to a common experience of most of my (Ozum Ucok-Sayrak) students in the basic communication classes that I teach (on oral communication and public speaking). When they stand up to give a speech in front of an audience, most of the students lose touch with themselves, their bodies, and their surroundings due to stress, anxiety, or nervousness. They act like they are trapped in someone else's body; they appear to feel victimized and want to just get done with the speech. Furthermore, this disconnection from their bodies and their present-moment experiences is limited not only to giving a speech but also reveals itself in various other aspects of communication, such as listening, interviewing, and relating to others.

In terms of communication, the practical consequences of disconnection from one's body and the present moment include (1) hearing (physical reception of sounds by the ear) but not listening (actively making sense of and understanding the other); (2) speaking automatically and without awareness of what one is saying (leading to regrets about what was said, or not said); (3) attempting to relate without really being present; and (4) in general, living one's life without paying attention, on autopilot. When we do not truly listen to others, we miss information and damage relationships. When we speak without awareness and attention, we weaken the message and risk losing connection with the audience; in an interview we might misunderstand a question or comment and sabotage a job opportunity. Beyond the practical consequences, when we fail to attend to our everyday experiences, we miss the opportunity of participating in the beautiful, joyful, and significant experiences that give meaning to life.

Some years ago, I (Ozum Ucok-Sayrak) was observing and working with my students in a public speaking class. As they rehearsed their speeches, they displayed anxiety and fear. Most of them rushed to the stage, hurried through the speech, and then dashed back to their seats to avoid this painful process of exposure. They looked like victims of a required course whose primary objective was to get the speech over with as quickly as possible. They never allowed themselves to truly explore other aspects of the experience, including walking to the stage, greeting the audience, relating to the audience, sharing the information and connecting with others through eye contact and physical delivery. The anxiety of standing in front of a group to give a speech can be so overwhelming that being present to that situation may seem impossible. Most students lose awareness of breathing, speaking, and moving. They appear disconnected from themselves, their bodies, the audience, and the larger experience.

After observing my students and offering feedback for a time, I stopped the class. I'd had no previous plan to do what I did, though I had recently returned from a contemplative retreat, which no doubt influenced this action. Then, for a few minutes, I guided the students in attending to their breathing and suggested that by tuning into their breathing, they could relax their minds and bodies. After breathing in and out while actively staying present to the movement of each breath in their bodies for a couple of minutes, I demonstrated a mindful walking practice wherein one walks slowly and attends to the experience of walking itself (Goldstein, 1987; Nhat Hanh, 1992).

In this first class in which I spontaneously used intrapersonal mindfulness-based practices, I simply emphasized being present to each step as they rose from their chairs and walked to the podium, highlighting the goal of walking as slowly as possible as they took conscious breaths and relaxed with each step. Because my instructions were unfamiliar to them, the students giggled and glanced at each other and me with expressions of curiosity and uncertainty—yet, they were willing to try it. Despite the strangeness (to them) of what they were doing, their moods (calmer, more peaceful and interested) and the way they carried themselves (grounded, exploring, connected with their bodies) communicated a sense of subtle yet shared understanding. The students had walked to the podium more slowly and attentively than they had before, *releasing the idea* of just getting done with the whole thing. As a whole group, we slowly started to reconnect with and inhabit our bodies as well as the classroom space, taking the tiny steps towards creating a "local home" (Fritz, 2013, p. 157). Even if the urge to just get to the stage and get through the rehearsal was still visible in their bodies, a sense of curiosity to explore this new "technique" was now present as well. After this experience, I continued to integrate mindfulness-based practices into my teaching in a more systematic way.

Taking time in class to slow down or pause to check in with the body–mind as a way to cultivate awareness of self and other has become a major aspect of my pedagogy. Pausing enables mindfulness and supports exploration through contemplation and silence—and these, in turn, stimulate critical thinking and "conversation about ideas" (Arnett, 1992). My students now engage in exercises and assignments that are designed to cultivate attentiveness to their inner experiences along with observations of the outer world. These practices foster a classroom culture of inquiry and reflection. We provide further information and examples of contemplative knowing in the next section.

Contemplative Knowing and Contemplative Relation

A contemplative way of knowing invites the knower to participate in and connect with the material he or she is exploring. Hart (2008, p. 2) refers to contemplative knowing as "knowledge by presence . . . which involves looking not only at the outer data but also opening into our selves." Thus, contemplative knowing is a more participatory and intimate—less detached—form of knowing than "objective knowing."

A simple example from a recent class on intercultural communication that illustrates contemplative knowing, or "knowledge by presence," involves taking time in class to ponder the significance of studying intercultural communication. Rather than starting with the list of reasons conveniently provided by the textbook, we pause for a few minutes in silence to connect with ourselves as each of us asks, "Why is this topic important for my life?" Listening to what emerges from this calmer and more aware state, including ideas, images, feelings, memories, and stories, offers content for vibrant and rich discussions that are deeply connected to the lives of these young adults. Some make connections to their future careers in nursing, education, or business, stating that they need to be able to communicate effectively with a wide variety of people coming from diverse backgrounds. Some relate the topic to globalization and the increased need to understand the expanded world in which we all live. Their comments are mostly creative, relevant, and stimulating. After this discussion, we consider the points in the list in the textbook and realize that they resonate with us. As Hart (2007, p. 6) puts it, "Challenge, curiosity, rich sensory experience, and juicy information wakes us up by producing an echo or resonance within us." It is through such influence that young people realize the connectedness of information to their lives and themselves, of self and others, of inside and outside. Zajonc (2006) describes contemplative inquiry as an epistemology (theory of knowledge) of participation, connection, and intimacy (familiarity), rather than one of separation. He suggests that "knowing itself remains partial and deformed if we do not develop and practice an epistemology of love rather than an epistemology of separation" (2006, pp. 1–2).

A fine example that clearly articulates the implications of "an epistemology of love" comes from a student in an Interpersonal Communication class in response to the mindful observations assignment. The instructions are simple. Students spend 5–10 minutes simply "people watching." However, the difference from an ordinary people-watching experience comes with this added instruction: "As you watch others, you will also be engaged in a kind of 'internal' watching wherein you observe your own mind: the judgments that come up, the likes and dislikes, attractions and avoidances, stories, images, memories, ideas, etc. Thus, you will be 'minding the mind'" (Ting Toomey & Chung, 2011, p. 168). "As a final step, after taking a few fresh breaths to clear the mind, see if you can release the thoughts, ideas, labels, stories, etc., and observe again. Notice if there is any difference in these ways of seeing/receiving/relating." This exercise allows students to take the first tentative steps from intra- to interpersonal mindfulness practice.

Most students describe their surprise at how many judgments pop up about others, as they had considered themselves to be nonjudgmental people. They also report a new awareness of the ways that judgments and labels create a sense of separation. One student wrote in her journal that she was shocked to notice the way she immediately labeled and judged others solely based on their appearance. After clearing her mind and observing again, she noticed that "these girls I'm judging so harshly are real people." She described feeling a sense of encouragement and hope from this process, as she recognized that she was now more open to accept these girls just as they are.

This experience can be related to a mode of contact that Buber (1958) referred to as I–Thou, wherein the subject–object orientation is transformed into a "dialogic" meeting of persons, and the participants are no longer the object of each other's perception. Stewart (2003, p. xi) quotes Buber in describing this experience as "imagining the real of the other," whereby one becomes aware of the other person, as well as oneself, as a whole (Stewart, 2003, p. vi).

Practicing mindfulness and intentionally cultivating tranquility may, at first glance, seem alien to education or even disconnected from communication. However, as illustrated by some of the examples provided in this chapter, meeting oneself and others with nonjudgmental awareness and openness and experiencing life as an emergent flow has a direct impact on the clarity of mind we bring to learning. Practicing these qualities builds and stabilizes our capacity to express ourselves clearly and to understand and relate to others with intelligence and compassion (also see Hart, 2004, 2008). In the next section, we expand our discussion to explore interpersonal contemplative practice.

Insight Dialogue as Contemplative Practice

Interpersonal mindfulness practices hold a special place in communication and contemplation. Learning occurs as the student makes contact with the world: with the conceptual representations of the subject matter, with direct physical experiences, and so on. Crucially, learning happens upon contact with the world of other people. Learning is a relational process, so as mindfulness in relationship grows, the learning process is enhanced. In-the-moment awareness, in or out of the classroom, includes noticing one's thoughts as new information is presented, noticing one's resistance or biases to material being presented, and bringing open attentiveness to relational transactions. At the same time, calm concentration helps to steady the mind to remain attentive over the course of an inquiry. Relational cultivation of awareness and calm, and the resultant sense of intimacy with present-moment experience are precisely the domains of ID.

Mindfulness and calm *while engaged with others* is an essential feature of ID. A nonjudgmental attitude, interpersonal sensitivity, and a moment-by-moment flexibility of mind are all natural outcomes of ID. From these qualities flow enhanced relationship and communication. To understand how this is the case, and to connect it with the communicative outcomes, it is essential to understand the practice.

An ID session usually begins with a period of silent meditation practice. During this time, practitioners are establishing mindfulness and tranquility in a more or less traditional fashion, such as by observing the breath rising and falling, maintaining mindfulness of bodily sensations, or perhaps simply noticing when awareness is and is not present as thoughts and feelings come and go. Following this, people are invited into small groups, most often dyads, and sit facing each other, still in silence. Practice instructions are offered by a teacher, usually including an emphasis on one of the practice guidelines discussed below, and a contemplation topic is offered as a topic for the dialogue. A bell is rung to invite participants into mutual meditation practice, with eyes open and speaking and listening as part of the practice. Sometimes meditators are asked to take turns speaking and listening; more often it is a free flow of investigation, mindfully, of present moment experience using the framework of the guidelines and contemplation topic. Bells are used throughout to start and stop practice, returning participants to silence and internal mindfulness. During longer teachings, practitioners will have a series of partners, and slowly ease and safety grow along with the tranquility of practice and recognition of the shared human experience.

There are six guidelines in ID (Kramer, 2007), and each functions as a reminder of how we can meet the moment of interpersonal contact with mindfulness, calm, and open flexibility. Each guideline has a simple, action element, such as "pause" to observe feelings and actions, as well as a subtler, deeper layer. For the pause guideline, these layers are mindfulness and a nonclinging quality of mind. In the following material we list the guidelines, then examine how they work together and can be combined with topics for reflection that serve to integrate inquiry into the human condition with in-the-moment observed experience. It is from this integration that we see the emergence of qualities such as a nonjudgmental attitude and kindness toward, and caring for, others. The six guidelines are:

1. Pause
2. Relax
3. Open
4. Trust emergence
5. Listen deeply
6. Speak the truth

Pause

To pause means to stop long enough to pay attention to the experience in the here and now. In other words, the pause is a mindful moment. It also refers to a nonclinging state of mind and it practices letting go of the mind's current fixation.

Relax

At a superficial level, this guideline refers to bodily relaxation, which can be a helpful entryway into the deeper layers of practice involved in relaxing the mind. What relaxation is to the body, acceptance is to the mind, so *relax* also refers to an attitude of receptivity, of nonresistance. This attitude ripens into tranquility and concentration.

Open

This is the key instruction that opens mindfulness practice into relation. It also incorporates mindfulness of the other's experience, as well as mindfulness of the self and other at the same time. In this way the instruction to open invites an investigation of the flow of connection and disconnection as they unfold in the moment.

Trust Emergence

The instruction to *trust emergence* refers to attending to the impermanence of this moment of experience—that is, to notice the rapid micro changes constantly unfolding in one's sensations, thoughts, and emotions. Noticing change leads to a flexible and therefore steady mindfulness because one learns to easily shift attention as conditions change. *Trusting emergence* also encompasses what some Zen schools, such as the Kwan Um school (Sahn, 1999) refer to as "don't-know mind." One rests in the changing moment, not grasping at any idea, emotion, or sensory event, but dwelling in the emergent quality of moment-by-moment experience.

Listen Deeply

This guideline has a superficial meaning of paying attention to another or others. When developed as meditation practice, however, it involves a profound, continuous receptivity to arising experience with the particular other. One learns to listen to voice, gesture, vocal tone, and so on, with attention beyond just the ears; importantly, one learns the attitude of receptivity.

Speak the Truth

This guideline is initially understood as speaking without falsehood, speaking with kindness, using economy of speech, and so on. As practice ripens— and this is particularly important for teenagers who are just developing their lifelong communication styles—*speaking the truth* invites a deep inquiry as to what is actually, deeply true in this moment of experience. The mindfulness practice must be strong enough to allow one to know what one is thinking and feeling, and to consciously decide whether these thoughts and feelings are "true," in the sense that they are worthy of expression. So, there is the mindfulness of knowing one's subjective truth, but also the mindfulness of discerning whether a given thought or feeling is precisely what is meant, and whether it needs to be spoken now. Even beyond all the refinements of speaking the truth, just taking the step from automatic to mindful speech is a significant move.

Practicing within these guidelines, the mind becomes calmer and clearer. Once participants have developed the ability to speak and listen more deeply, thereby enabling a focused reflection, facilitators offer contemplations on the shared human experience, suggesting topics ranging from aging and doubt to generosity and freedom. These practices are, for many young people, the first time they have seriously contemplated such substantial topics. Moreover, it is likely the first time they have heard others' thoughts and feelings on life's central issues and problems, and the first time they have been deeply heard by others. Such experiences can fundamentally deepen feelings of relatedness, happiness, engagement, and meaning in life.

When sharing mindful relationship practice with teens and young adults, it can be helpful to develop individual, silent mindfulness practices first, such as those described throughout the examples we shared. Teaching relational practice to youth also requires attending to their need for a strong sense of trust. As adults, it is essential that we provide a safe container for practice. It further helps for the instructor to meet the kids on their own terms, using their words, their metaphors, speaking their language. Consider playful elements, such as how the pause is used when talking really fast. And even in levity, it remains wise to maintain seriousness about confidentiality and mutual respect. Above all, the teacher must embody the practice in action, speaking truth with pauses, relaxation, and openness, while trusting emergence and listening deeply.

It may help to bring students into the practice gradually; in our culture, pausing can be a radical act. Young practitioners are particularly sensitive to the judgments and perceived judgments of their peers; thus posing and trying on roles are a substantial part of their social personas. So, when beginning to offer even the simple instruction to *pause*, care is given to invite—but not force—participants to examine just how it might feel to face another person physically and look at him or her without the distraction—and the cover—of other tasks. Bart Van Melik, an ID teacher who offers mindfulness-based practices to at-risk youth, reports that at first the kids hated the pause instruction. They were impatient and found the dyad setup awkward. Finding a partner was "weird" and the urge to respond, even when directed to take turns listening and speaking, was strong. In fact, any social discipline was difficult. But with highly structured practice as a protection, and supported by preparatory discussions on mutual respect and confidentiality, even the most seemingly unwilling students have been willing to enter into the practice.

Because ID is designed to include topics to discuss while practicing pausing, relaxing, and so on, it lends itself well to carefully chosen contemplations. For example, one group was given the theme of judgments on a day designated as Antibullying Day. A sequence of three contemplations was offered over the course of about 40 minutes. While learning to pause, the students were first invited to observe their own judgments of people in public spaces, including teachers, people in hallways, and so on. The second contemplation focused on judgments they might have of family members. The sequence closed with a contemplation of judgments about themselves. In addition to the guideline to pause, the students were also taught to relax, which they reported as helpful, especially while engaged so closely with their classmates. Following this sequence of judgment contemplations, there were some touching observations. After a young woman named Ella had shared her feelings of hating her body, another woman present, Justine, who was known to be verbally aggressive, shared with this with the group: "I thought I was the only one who was so judgmental about myself. I'm sorry, Ella, that there are also parts of your body you don't like." The others, listening attentively, gave a sigh of recognition. In that moment, mindfulness and relational connection were very strong. This shift echoed and endured in later classes.

In the beginning, we see improvement in the students' ability to listen to one another. Over time, the kids learn to pause in a larger group, and as they take a moment, everyone becomes silent with them. These are the first signs of a larger shift. When we begin, there are never moments of silence as people are always asking and answering questions. But over time, with practices of pausing and relaxing, there is more space. There is more trust. But the kids stay with what they are comfortable—they do not stretch beyond where they should be. We rarely offer the guidelines to open and to trust emergence because we feel that they are too challenging for many teens and there is so much benefit in just working with the opening practices of pausing and relaxing. Participants seem to improve at using language to express emotion, and they begin to trust themselves more, even if it is just trusting their own breath or physical balance.

And the practice carries over to their home lives, as well. One teen returned to group to share, "I paused with my little sister; I didn't finish her sentences." A student who had recently been suspended reported this: "Today I did the meditation stuff. There was this other kid who kept pushing me. Every time he pushed me, I could feel myself clench my fist. I wanted to hit him. But I didn't. I kept pausing. I didn't hit him. I felt really strong. I didn't hit him." With practice and time, students' self-regulation improves. Some of the students report insight into how their parents get upset and why they discipline them. Outside of class, students appear more settled, calm, and comfortable. One school principal observed, "After the ID practice, I notice there is a more peaceful interaction in the halls."

Introducing young people to exercises from the relational mindfulness practice of ID can yield a wide range of benefits. Some may experience greater calm and less social anxiety; some may become aware of their minds in a new way. As one student put it, "I found out that I am not my thoughts!" Through practice, the young people learn to recognize the stress inherent in maintaining a crafted social identity, and they find a way of being with others that is more authentic and therefore more peaceful. As one result of speaking their truth and being heard, and of listening to others without judgment and with care, these meditators, within and across generations, may experience a quality of nonseparation that heals the disconnection that haunts our youth. This felt experience, in turn, heals the sense of disconnection that haunts not just our youth, but also many people worldwide today. From such experiences of mindfulness, the capacity for relatedness and meaningful communication radically expands.

Perhaps we can follow Heidegger's (1959/1966) observations and extend our aspirations for this work even beyond meaningful or mindful communication. The capacity he called "releasement toward things" echoes the original roots of mindfulness practices as found in the Buddhist tradition. An attitude of releasement—of neither rejecting nor grasping at one's hungers for self-reification and constant stimulation (including smartphones and other technological devices)—can radically shift the quality of our lives. The nonattached, nonrejecting attitude can extend the benefits of our intra- and interpersonal mindfulness practices from daily instrumental goals such as improved communication or reduced stress, to encompass a balanced shift in the stability of our well-being and compassion. The impact on ourselves, on others, and on the quality of our relatedness spontaneously follows.

Conclusion

This chapter offers a discussion of intra- and interpersonal mindfulness practices as an invitation to explore the capacity of young people, at the onset of forming their sense of who they are in the world, to recognize and soften the attachments, fears, and hungers that usually drive the formation of self in problematic ways. Intrapersonal mindfulness practices offer young adults a means with which to establish greater awareness, ease, and effectiveness as they communicate with others and navigate the world. Interpersonal mindfulness practices such as ID take this practice a step further, by providing young people with a window into their own minds and emotions in the very moment of interpersonal contact. Such practices also offer a rare opportunity to move beyond entrenched cultural norms of guardedness and reactivity. Greater compassion and relatedness are the observable results of these practices, as seen in the words of these young adults themselves. Furthermore, growing roots through intentional wisdom practices, and inhabiting our lives and the places in which we live and work, lead to creating and caring for the "local home" (Fritz, 2013), and in turn provide us with new ground to move beyond inner homelessness.

Interpersonal mindfulness practices are presently not so common in classrooms, teacher training, or even among professionals in the mindfulness movement. Many programs teach students to mindfully observe how they respond or react while in interpersonal situations, but the more intensive practices for cultivating mindfulness are almost exclusively individual. To realize the promise of explicitly relational practices of awareness and calm, especially with youth, a cultural shift is necessary within the community of mindfulness practitioners and facilitators. Understanding the value of individual mindfulness practices has been a necessary first step. Once practitioners and facilitators see these as a foundation for relational practices, and experience for themselves the value of training and practice in this area, they will continue to cultivate a wider culture of relatedness and connection. In such a culture, intra- and interpersonal practices would be skillfully adapted to the learning needs of the individuals and groups. This cultural shift would move through the teachers and mindfulness professionals to the teens and young adults they serve. Perhaps we can hope that from this shift, we will witness a welcomed improvement in intergenerational communication across the divide.

REFERENCES

Arnett, R. C. (1992). *Dialogic education: Conversation about ideas and between persons.* Carbondale, IL: Southern Illinois University Press.

Arnett, R. C. (1994). Existential homelessness: A contemporary case for dialogue. In R. Anderson, K. Cissna, & R. C. Arnett (Eds.), *The reach of dialogue: Confirmation, voice and community* (pp. 229–246). Cresskill, NJ: Hampton Press,.

Buber, M. (1958). *I and thou* (R. G. Smith, Trans.). New York: Charles Scribner's Sons.

Fritz, J. M. (2013). *Professional civility: Communicative virtue at work.* New York: Peter Lang.

Goldstein, J. (1987). *The experience of insight.* Boston: Shambhala.

Hart, T. (2004). Opening the contemplative mind in the classroom. *Journal of Transformative Education, 2*(1), 28–46.

Hart, T. (2007). Reciprocal revelation: Toward a pedagogy of interiority. *Journal of Cognitive Affective Learning, 3*(2), 1–10.

Hart, T. (2008). Interiority and education: Exploring the neurophenomenology of contemplation and its potential role in learning. *Journal of Transformative Education, 6*(4), 235–250.

Heidegger, M. (1966). *Discourse on thinking* (J. Anderson & E. Hans Freund, Trans.). New York: Harper & Row. (Original work published 1959)

Hochman, D. (2013, November 1). Mindfulness: Getting its share of attention. Retrieved from *www.nytimes.com/2013/11/03/fashion/mindfulness-and-meditation-are-capturing-attention.html?pagewanted=all&_r=1&*.

Holba, A. (2008). Revisiting Martin Buber's I–it: A rhetorical strategy. *Human Communication, 11*(4), 489–504.

Konrath, S. (2013). The empathy paradox: Increasing disconnection in the age of increasing connection. In R. Luppicini (Ed.), *Handbook of research on technoself: Identity in a technological society* (pp. 204–228). Hershey, PA: IGI Global.

Kramer, G. (2007). *Insight dialogue: The interpersonal path to freedom.* Boston: Shambhala.

Nhat Hanh, T. (1992). *Peace is every step: The path of mindfulness in everyday life.* New York: Bantam Dell.

Price, M. (2011). Alone in the crowd. *Monitor on Psychology, 42*(6), 26.

Sahn, S. (1999). *Only don't know.* Boston: Shambhala.

Stewart, J. (2003). Foreword. In R. Anderson, K. N. Cissna, & R. C. Arnett (Eds.), *The reach of dialogue: Confirmation, voice and community* (p. xii). Cresskill, NJ: Hampton Press.

Ting Toomey, S., & Chung, L. (2011). *Understanding intercultural communication* (2nd ed.). New York: Oxford University Press.

Turkle, S. (2011). *Alone together: Why we expect more from technology and less from each other.* New York: Basic Books.

Zajonc, A. (2006). Cognitive–affective connections in teaching and learning: The relationship between love and knowledge. *Journal of Cognitive Affective Learning, 3*(1), 1–9.

CHAPTER 9

Mindful Parenting

A Mindfulness Course for Parents in Mental Health Treatment

Susan Bögels

Parenting is one of the most all-consuming high-responsibility tasks of a lifetime. Yet parents do it with love, joy, pride, and a deep sense of fulfillment. In fact, raising children, and having grandchildren, may be the most fulfilling "job" that we ever have, and for many, being a good father or a good mother is our highest ambition in life. If we are asked how we would want to be remembered at our funeral, being a good parent (and grandparent) tends to top the list.

Yet this strong desire and cultural pressure to be the best parent possible may, in itself, be a source of stress. Many challenges and obstacles along the way make parenting stressful. To start with, the sudden transition in adult life from taking care of our own lives to giving birth and taking care of other lives as well demands an enormous change in how we divide our time, attention, energy, and resources. Life will never be the same again after children. In taking care of children, organizing family life, and balancing that with our careers and social lives, we often forget to care for ourselves. Depleted inner resources can result in irritable or depressed mood, fatigue, somatic complaints, and eventually in mental or physical disorders that begin to interfere with the quality of our parenting.

Children's as well as parents' mental health issues represent an added challenge that can make parenting even more stressful. These are the families for whom the Mindful Parenting course described in this chapter was developed, though it can be adapted for any family. A child who becomes stressed or oppositional when confronted with a new situation, who cannot play or organize school work independently, who cannot be left alone with siblings because of aggressive behavior, who cannot sleep through the night, or who presents any number of challenges can add an extra challenge to parenting. A parent's own symptoms may also add stress to the parenting task. The parent suffering from depression may experience parenting as too heavy a burden and label him- or herself a "bad parent"; the parent suffering with anxiety may become overly concerned about or overprotective with the child; the parent coping with posttraumatic stress disorder (PTSD) may struggle to break free of his or her own past or childhood; and a parent with problems in executive functioning may parent the child impulsively or inconsistently.

Even without mental health issues in the family, parents from all walks of modern life encounter many sources of stress. Children constantly change in their developmental trajectory, continually challenging parents to adapt to these ongoing transformations: a baby who starts to walk and talk, an adolescent who no longer obeys the family rules, the young adult leaving home. Even when the children are long grown up, parents experience a strong sense of responsibility for their safety and well-being, and may worry at times when their adult children meet new challenges on their own, such as traveling, joining the military, or confronting their own health issues. Stress may also arise from unexpected family changes such as divorce or separation, illness or death. The stress and mourning that accompany most divorces negatively influences parenting and parental attention temporarily, and in prolonged divorces, the negative impact on parenting is also prolonged. Nowadays, about one out of two children in the United States and United Kingdom will live in a single-parent family at some time before they become 18, and the lack of support of another parent who is co-responsible for the parenting task can be a source of stress (Cairney, Boyle, Offord, & Racine, 2003). Stepparents and stepchildren can be a source of support and joy, but they may also add stress to parenting, due to the complexities of navigating boundaries and loyalties.

Marital problems and problems in the co-parental relationship are another source of parent stress. As reliance on community has decreased in Western, individualistic cultures, marital relationships have become increasingly important as a source of social connectedness and support. With this shift, the expectations and responsibilities placed on marital relationships have become greater, as have the stresses, and these stresses have been found to negatively affect parenting by both mothers and fathers. The cultural shifts in the "modern" West defy our evolutionary history of raising children in community; it is not said for nothing that "It takes a village to raise a child."

Why Mindful Parenting Can Help with Parenting Stress

Under stressful conditions, parenting skills may collapse, not only in the experience of most parents, but in the findings of researchers as well (for a review, see Bögels, Lehtonen, & Restifo, 2010). Parents may have learned skills from parenting courses, books, or even popular television programs featuring a range of experts, often with a range of opinions and theories. However, when overwhelmed with stress or emotion, parents of all backgrounds resort to shouting, threatening, and even hitting their children, as the amygdala flares and the more primitive "emotion mind" sets in. All of the courses and knowledge about how a good parent "should" handle difficulties may ultimately have the effect of increasing parental shame and feelings of helplessness in these moments.

When stressed, most parents are unable to access and apply skills they have learned. In addition, psychopathology may also hinder the benefits of such courses (see Maliken & Katz, 2013, for a recent review of how parent psychopathology and related parental emotion regulation problems affect parenting and its outcomes). To illustrate, the parent management training program is an effective training program for parents of children with attention-deficit/hyperactivity disorder (ADHD), decreasing children's behavior problems (Fabiano et al., 2009; Van der Oord, Prins, Oosterlaan, & Emmelkamp, 2008). However, children of parents who themselves have ADHD as well do not benefit as much as children with neurotypical parents from such parent training (e.g., Sonuga-Barke, Daley, & Thompson, 2002). Interestingly, precisely in families in which child and parent share symptoms of psychopathology, such as inattentive or impulsive behavior, children are at the highest risk of developing mental health disorders such as ADHD (Sonuga-Barke, 2010). In a similar vein, children of depressed mothers are found to benefit less from parent training (Forehand, Furey, & McMahon, 1984; Owens et al., 2003; Webster-Stratton, 1990; Reyno & McGrath, 2006). Also, parents with marital problems may benefit less from parent training (Reisinger, Frangia, & Hoffman, 1976; Webster-Stratton, 1985). This evidence clearly indicates the need for a type of parent training in which parents' own stress, suffering, and symptoms of psychopathology have an important place in the process of improving family functioning.

What Is Mindful Parenting?

Mindful Parenting offers a new approach to parenting in high-stress situations. The approach is beneficial for a broad audience, not just those families with psychopathology. In Mindful Parenting training, parents' particular unique stresses are the primary focus, rather than the problem behavior of the child or "identified patient." Clearly, the behavior of the child can be the major source of stress in the family, but the resulting stress in the parent is what the program aims to address.

Mindfulness is a type of awareness that has garnered much attention and research in recent years. It involves staying present in the moment, focusing on the reality of particular circumstances, and accepting that reality for what it is. Bringing mindfulness to parenting, children, and family life ("Mindful Parenting") is one of the newer applications of mindfulness. Note, however, that Myla and Jon Kabat-Zinn published their book *Everyday Blessings: The Inner Work of Mindful Parenting* in 1997, and several similar books have been published since. The Kabat-Zinns define mindful parenting as

> the ongoing process of intentionally bringing moment-to-moment, non-judgmental awareness as best one can to the unfolding of one's own lived experience, including parenting. Cultivating mindfulness in parenting starts with self-awareness. It grows to include (1) recognizing and keeping in mind each child's unique nature, temperament, and needs; (2) developing the capacity to listen with full attention when interacting with one's children; (3) holding in awareness with kindness and sensitivity, to whatever degree possible, both one's child and one's own feelings, thoughts, intentions, expectations, and desires; (4) bringing greater compassion and non-judgmental acceptance to oneself and one's children; (5) recognizing one's own reactive impulses in relationship to one's children and their behavior. (Kabat-Zinn & Kabat-Zinn, personal communication, 2012)

This chapter is about Mindful Parenting in the context of mental health: that is, when parents seek help with their parenting because they or their child has a mental health issue. First, a short outline of the aims of the program is given. Then the eight sessions of the course and the follow-up session are described, with some examples of typical practices. Next, the effects of the program, based on empirical research, are outlined. Finally, directions for further research and applications are discussed. Facilitators who want to set up Mindful Parenting courses are referred to the book *Mindful Parenting: A Guide for Mental Health Practitioners* (Bögels & Restifo, 2014) for the full protocol.

Aims of the Program

In Mindful Parenting, parents learn to use the skills of mindfulness for themselves and apply them to parenting their children. Most parents come to the course seeking help with parenting: They hope to reduce their stress, improve the relationship with their child, parent more effectively or less impulsively, and help their child become calmer calm and better behaved. As facilitators, we try to hold the paradox of acknowledging these legitimate and worthwhile goals while remaining open to whatever experience parents have; we try to balance being with the reality of what is, with the parents' desire for things to be different.

We know from the research and from direct participant feedback that many parents and children *do* change as a result of this course. And based on the research, we believe that the program can help bring about these changes. The aims of the program are reflected in the ways this program has helped parents. Mindful Parenting has helped parents:

- Respond less reactively to parenting stress.
- Take better care of themselves.
- Develop more empathy and compassion for themselves and their child.
- Tolerate difficult emotions in themselves and their child.
- Become more accepting of themselves and their child.
- Recognize patterns from their own upbringing as they arise in the here-and-now relationship with their child.
- Resolve conflict more effectively with their child.
- Develop a stronger bond with their child.
- More fully experience both the joys and challenges of parenting.
- Relate in a new way to parental suffering to see that although not all problems will change fully, or may not change at all, parents' attitude toward these problems may indeed change.

Summary of the Eight Sessions and Follow-Up

Mindful Parenting is based on an adaptation of mindfulness-based stress reduction (MBSR) and mindfulness-based cognitive therapy (MBCT). We introduce all of the formal meditation practices—the body scan; mindfulness of the breath, body, sounds, thoughts, and emotions; choice-less awareness; mindful seeing and mindful walking; and yoga—in roughly the same progression. As in MBCT, we introduce mindfulness of everyday activities from the beginning, but with an emphasis on day-to-day parenting and family activities. For example, we ask parents to do a routine activity with their child with full awareness, such as bathing the child or asking how his or her school day school went. In addition, we weave short self-compassion practices throughout the 8 weeks.

The program also aims to help parents recognize patterns in their relationship with their child that may originate from their own childhoods. Especially when under stress or other intense emotions, parents tend to respond in automatic ways. In these reactive parenting behaviors parents may recognize behaviors of their own parents that they have internalized, or behavior patterns of themselves when they were children. We include exercises to help parents reconnect emotionally with their child after a difficult conflict, first by taking care of their own emotional state, and then, when calm, taking the perspective of their child. Finally, we help parents become aware of their own personal limits and boundaries, using mindfulness and self-compassion, in order to help them set effective and appropriate limits with their children that match their values.

Session 1: Automatic Parenting

The first session starts with a short, guided meditation inviting parents to explore their intentions in this course. Parents then share what came up during the meditation in pairs. Mindful listening and mindful speaking are emphasized in this dyadic sharing, and the various reasons to participate fully in the course are discussed. As parents meet each other, they often recognize similarities in each other. In this way, the universality of suffering and the challenges around parenting are felt and experienced. Next, parents are guided in a mindful eating exercise using a raisin (Kabat-Zinn, 1990) as well as a longer practice in body awareness known as the "body scan." These are followed by an inquiry and discussion of experiences. From these discussions important themes are distilled: for example, judging versus nonjudging, the doing versus being mode, and pushing away versus being with negative experiences.

The central theme of the first session is becoming aware of parenting on automatic pilot during daily interactions with children and under stress. We explore parents' reactions to a typical parenting stressor. The facilitator asks everyone to sit comfortably, close their eyes, and imagine the following situation as if it were happening to them:

"It's 8:20 in the morning. The children have to be at school at 8:30. You've already gotten a warning from the principal that your daughter has been late too often. Your daughter is taking her time, doing her hair and changing her clothes again. 'Come on now, hurry up or we'll be late' you say, several times, but she does not come down from her room. You walk into your child's room, urging her to come, but she throws herself on the floor, screaming, 'I'm not going to school!'

"Imagine this situation as vividly as you can, as if it's happening to you now. Notice what you feel in your body, what emotions come up, what thoughts run through your mind, and what you feel like doing in that moment."

Group members open their eyes and begin a discussion. On a whiteboard or flip chart, the facilitator draws four columns of categories and lists the various responses in each of the columns, starting with physical sensations and ending with action tendencies, stressing that the point here is not about what they eventually will do, but what their *first action tendency* would be (see Table 9.1). The facilitator then explains that many of the physical signals that indicate an adrenaline response are signs of stress. Under stress, we take a shortcut in our brain, bypassing our frontal cortex, with which we think, plan, and organize. The shorter route ensures that we can quickly react with a fight, flight, or freeze response. This automatic, evolutionary-based survival response is useful when there is real danger; for example, if your child is crossing the road while a truck is barreling down the road. However, in the situation described, is real danger present? How often do parents experience this kind of morning stress? For many parents, morning battles are an almost daily occurrence, and the action tendencies they exhibit are usually not helpful in getting the child to school on time. Meditation and mindful awareness help parents to better recognize these early signs of stress in their bodies. They can take a breathing space and engage in a short meditation, which helps them stay out of the stressful, habitual survival pattern. In this way, space is created between bodily responses and action, offering parents a moment of choice in how to deal with a situation.

The raisin meditation primes parents for the second goal of mindful parenting: parenting more intentionally and mindfully. Just as eating a raisin mindfully, as if you have never eaten a raisin before, may open you to the full and rich experience, being mindful with your child and with yourself as a parent may open you to the full and rich experience of this child at this very moment, and what it's like to be a parent of this child.

As homework, parents are invited to observe their child as a raisin, as if they have never seen this child before. The home practices are explained in more detail in a later section.

TABLE 9.1. Examples of Typical Responses of Parents in Situations of Parenting Stress

Physical sensations	Emotions	Thoughts	Action tendencies
Heart pounding	Angry	"She does this to hurt me!"	Drag her in the car
Short, high breath	Worried	"I'm a bad mother."	Yelling
Tense muscles	Sad	"Why me?"	Threatening
Sweating	Irritated	"What will they think of me?"	Leaving without her
Red in the face		"Why is it always me who has to bring the children to school?"	Going back to bed
Stomach knot			

Session 2: Beginner's Mind Parenting

The second session starts with a guided body scan, followed by an inquiry. Also, to demonstrate the central theme of Session 2, "beginner's mind," a seeing meditation is done. Parents are invited to look around the room and out the windows without labeling what they see ("tree," "car"). A simple meditation using awareness of breath as an anchor of attention is then introduced.

The central theme of Session 2 is observing a child with what Sunryu Suzuki (1970) calls "beginner's mind." Parents share their experience of the home practice they were asked to do between the first two sessions of observing their child with beginner's mind. They often discover positive qualities in their child, which they had overlooked in the focus on the difficulties. For example:

> Mary observed her son of 10 years, who was diagnosed with ADHD, with beginner's mind. She looked at him while he was reading. She saw that his whole body was moving; he often laughed and talked out loud while he was reading. She could feel how he enjoyed what he read. She described through tears the way she usually experienced the very same behavior as something difficult, or problematic, whereas she now could see in the movement his enjoyment of reading.

Alternatively, some parents discover just how difficult it is to view their child with beginner's mind, as they become aware of their own as well as others' judgments and preconceptions of their child. We discuss how we can become biased toward the negative in our children, especially when they have been diagnosed (e.g., with autism or ADHD) or when we have given them a label ("chaotic," "short-tempered," "shy"), and the way we view our children in the context of that diagnosis or label that creates a self-fulfilling prophecy.

A second theme is the attitude of kindness, which we invite parents to embody in their experience as parents, especially when they find themselves under stress. The facilitator tells a morning stress story, now from the perspective of a friend, and asks participants to imagine this story as if it's happening to them:

> "You've just dropped off your child at school when you see a friend running frantically onto the schoolyard, dragging her child by the hand. When the friend returns, she says, 'Oh, my god, you wouldn't believe what a morning I had! First my daughter refused to get dressed because her favorite shirt wasn't clean, then she threw a temper tantrum right before we left because her hair was not just right, screaming she would not go to school anymore. Then I just completely lost it: I started screaming that if she didn't get up off the floor right now I was going to school without her, and finally I just dragged her out of the house, while my

other two children were watching the scene from the car. It was horrible. It's a miracle we got here in one piece.'"

As in Session 1, we ask parents to list their physical sensations, emotions, thoughts, and action tendencies as they listen. We explore the way we often have difficulty being kind to ourselves in challenging parent moments, whereas we naturally feel kindness and sympathy toward another struggling parent.

Session 3: Reconnecting with the Body as a Parent

Session 3 opens with a longer sitting mindfulness meditation, using both the breath and body as anchors of awareness. This is followed by an inquiry about possible feelings of physical pain and discomfort, as well as positive feelings, in line with the central theme of this session. We also introduce gentle yoga practices and the 3-Minute Breathing Space (Segal, Williams, & Teasdale, 2012).

The central theme of this session is awareness of the body while parenting, whether pleasurable sensations or stress or fatigue is the focus. We explore how we tend to ignore our bodies' signals and our own physical boundaries and limits, and why this oversight happens especially when parenting (e.g., forgetting to eat, go to the toilet, or rest when busy with children). Returning to the body, again and again, and taking care of the body is the foundational skill that we practice and emphasize.

The facilitator asks parents to imagine a stressful parenting situation in order to practice self-compassion. This practice is based on Neff (2011) and Germer (personal communication, November 2012):

"Sit comfortably, letting your eyes close. Imagine a difficult or stressful parenting interaction that you feel did not go well. Imagine the situation as vividly as possible, as if it were happening right now. Who is there? What are they saying or doing? What are you saying or doing? When you have a clear picture, bring your attention to this moment check in: How are you feeling right now? Notice whatever comes up. Are there bodily sensations, emotions, thoughts, tensions? Say to yourself, 'Whatever it is I'm feeling, it is okay; let me feel it.' Just notice whatever comes up . . . are there critical or judgmental thoughts? Feelings of sadness, anger, guilt? Tension in the body? [Allow a couple of minutes.]

"And now, seeing if you can bring an attitude of kindness and compassion for yourself, the way you would toward a friend. Recognizing this is a moment of suffering for you. Comforting yourself, for example, by saying to yourself 'This is really hard' or 'My dear [name], you try so hard to be a good parent, but sometimes it's so hard.' If you like, experiment with comforting yourself physically by placing both hands over your heart, feeling the warmth of your hands on your chest. Or hug yourself by placing your arms around your shoulders. Or try stroking yourself wherever it feels comfortable for you, arms, face . . .

"And now, can you remind yourself that all parents struggle, make mistakes, or feel they failed their children at times? Perhaps remembering other parents who struggle or regret things they've done? Remind yourself that making mistakes is part of being human; it connects us with all other parents who struggle to do their best and yet make so many mistakes or even fail along the way."

Session 4: Responding Rather Than Reacting to Parenting Stress

The session begins with a sitting meditation in which, along with a focus on the breath and body, a new focus on sounds and thoughts is introduced. Also, standing yoga is introduced in this session.

We discuss the way that our thinking is often the main source of stress, and that becoming aware of thoughts fits well in this session as parents explore how the thinking mind adds to stress. The first step in responding to parenting stress is to become aware of it, in the body, as we have practiced in the last three sessions. In this session we address our automatic reaction to grasp at what we like and push away what we do not like, and the importance of accepting stress rather than pushing it away, while emphasizing that acceptance of what is present does not mean liking it. We explore the variety of automatic reactions that occurs when the fight–flight–freeze stress response is triggered. We also explore how our thoughts can exacerbate our stress reactions. For example:

> John shared an experience in which he came home, exhausted, and found his daughter in front of the TV instead of studying for an important test the next day. He could feel his heart pounding, and he felt anxious and angry. Thoughts that ran through his mind were: "She will never pass the test. She will never become independent. She does this to hurt me." His automatic reaction was to yell at her.

Mindful awareness and the breathing space can help us sidestep our automatic reactions, to pause and respond more intentionally to our daily stresses.

To explore the effects of taking a breathing space on sidestepping our automatic reactions, we do an imagination practice in which parents imagine a stressful parenting moment as vivid as possible, followed by doing a 3-Minute Breathing Space. In this practice, participants spend three minutes checking in with their experience in thoughts, feelings and sensations, then shifting awareness to the breath, and lastly to the body as a whole (Segal, Williams, & Teasdale, 2002). Then we ask them to imagine entering a large mansion, opening the door and entering into a wide corridor with many doors. We ask them to imagine that behind every door there is a way of dealing with the stressful situation. We ask them to open a door, look at what possibility is offered, try it out, and move to other doors, trying out other possibilities, even if they appear crazy or wrong. In this way, participants more fully explore all possibilities and come to know and trust their own intuitive wisdom.

Session 5: Parenting Patterns and Schemas

Session 5 begins with a sitting meditation on breath, body, sounds, thoughts, and a new focus on emotions. This new element complements the theme of this session, as intense emotions often emerge from old patterns and schemas that have been activated by present-moment triggers. In addition, a simple walking meditation inside the room is introduced.

Insight into the ways that our childhood experiences affect our parenting is the central theme of Session 5. Parents investigate reactive parenting patterns with their child and look for parallels with their own parents. Participants learn to recognize their own angry or vulnerable child states and the punitive or demanding parent states that may arise during emotionally intense interactions with their own child. As a response, we practice bringing self-compassion and acceptance to our inner child when these difficult emotional states are triggered.

Session 6: Conflict and Parenting

Session 6 starts with a sitting meditation in which "choice-less awareness" is the new focus. This practice involves attention to present moment phenomena as they arise in our awareness. Parents are also guided in a walking meditation outside, which dovetails with the central theme of Session 6, rupture and repair, as after a fight it may be wise to first take a walk, or do a walking meditation, before returning to the conflict.

In this session, we explore parent–child conflicts in the discussion, which we reframe as opportunities for growth and closeness with their children. Mindfulness creates the space to simultaneously hold their own perspective and the perspective of their child. After practicing self-compassion for their own emotional states, we now ask parents to extend a sense of compassion to their child's emotional experience. We invite parents to practice holding their emotional experience and their child's simultaneously, to turn toward their child after a difficult conflict from this new place, again and again, in order to emotionally repair the relationship.

Session 7: Love and Limits

The seventh session has two main themes. First, we extend the compassion practice by introducing formal loving-kindness practice as a means to cultivate our inherent capacity for kindness and love. The main message is that no matter what the difficulties have been, parents have what it takes to love and care for their children. They can cultivate this love even further with the intentional practice of a loving-kindness meditation.

The second theme of Session 7 is limit setting as a form of "ruthless compassion," since limit setting is actually a way of showing love to children. Parents have learned more about their own limits as they practiced feeling them in their bodies. Now we apply this to setting limits with their children—for example, becoming aware of when a child approaches or crosses the parent's personal boundaries and limits, and responding intentionally from a place of awareness. Setting limits is further explained as another form of self-care, while providing the child with the much-needed structure in order to thrive. In discussion we explore obstacles to limit setting with an emphasis on parents' own childhoods or the particular challenges of working with their own child.

Session 8: A Mindful Path through Parenting

Just as in the first session, we begin again with the body scan. Parents reflect on what the experience of following a Mindful Parenting course has been like for them, what they have invested, what they have learned, and what (if anything) has changed for them. Commonly, parents have struggled to find time to practice, have faced frustrations and perhaps felt a lack of progress, and have sat through difficult emotions. Some have had moments of insight, changed their perspective on their children, or have even made changes in their lives. In this way, their children have also been deeply affected by this process as well. To facilitate this reflection, participants bring in an object, picture, drawing, poem, or song that symbolizes their own personal journeys, and share their process of the past 8 weeks with the group. Parents also make a personal plan and commitment to continue with meditation and Mindful Parenting over the next 8 weeks until the group meets for the last time.

Follow-Up Session, 8 Weeks Later: Each Time, Beginning Anew . . .

Parents reflect on how they have continued with the process of Mindful Parenting in the absence of the group. How have they been taking care of themselves? What difficulties have they confronted? The main theme of the follow-up session is that they can renew their intentions to bring mindfulness into their parenting again and again. Just as they can always come back to the breath when they become distracted, they can always come back to the present-moment experience with their children and see them with beginner's mind. We then discuss what formal and informal practices parents wish to maintain in order to nourish themselves, their parenting, and their children. We end with wishing each other well.

The core Mindful Parenting themes and practices, per session, are summarized in Table 9.2, and explained in detail in Bögels and Restifo (2014).

Home Practice

The practice in between sessions, or "home practice," takes place when parents experience and practice many of the new skills that they are learning. Each week we devote a part of the session to dyadic sharing about home practice and then bring observations to the larger group. We encourage parents to make notes in their workbooks and to bring them to each session to help recall their experiences and to discuss the home practice concretely.

Parents are expected to reserve about an hour, 6 days a week, for homework. They receive a workbook in which the homework is explained, and several texts and registration forms are included per session (Bögels & Restifo, 2014). The homework consists of

- Reading the handouts.
- Doing the Mindful Parenting practices.
- Doing the formal meditations.
- Doing the informal meditations.

The Mindful Parenting exercises include recording parental savoring moments, parental stress moments, observing the child with beginner's mind, and practicing a breathing space using the "difficult behavior" of the child as a meditation bell or reminder. Formal meditations include the body scan, walking meditation, sitting meditation, and yoga. Informal practices are mindfulness exercises that do not require extra time because they are intertwined with daily life, such as giving attention to a routine parenting activity (e.g., dressing the child).

It is very common that parents struggle to find the time to practice during the week, so exploring informal mindfulness is important. There is often overt resistance to practice, due to lack of time or other challenges, and as a facilitator we encourage you to meet this resistance with openness. The home practice includes both longer meditation practice as well as shorter practices throughout the day, such as being mindful of daily routines or doing the 3-Minute Breathing Space.

Facilitators embody an accepting stance of whatever parents bring to the session. For example, many parents report at the end of the course that the 3-Minute Breathing Space is the most useful practice for them, so if this is all they have been able to do during the week, they should be commended. At the same time, parents are invited to see if they can make a little more space

TABLE 9.2. Themes and Practices of Each Session

Session no./title	Themes	In-session formal practice	In-session Mindful Parenting exercises	Home practice
1. Automatic Pilot Parenting	• Rationale (nonreactive parenting) • Automatic pilot • Doing versus being mode	• Body scan • Raisin exercise	• Morning stress exercise	• Body scan • Observe child as you did raisin, as if seeing it for the first time • Do a routine activity mindfully (dishes, chores, etc.) • Mindful first bite
2. Beginner's Mind Parenting	• Seeing child with beginner's mind • Attitude of kindness • Obstacles to practice • Spaciousness • Expectations and interpretation	• Body scan • Sitting meditation: breath • Seeing meditation	• Examining morning stress from the perspective of a friend • Gratitude practice	• Body scan • Sitting meditation: breath • Mindful routine activity with your child • Savoring pleasant parenting moments calendar
3. Reconnecting with the Body as a Parent	• Body sensations • Awareness of pleasant events • Watching the body during parenting stress • Recognizing messages from body about limits • Self-compassion when we're stressed	• Yoga (lying) • Sitting meditation: breath and body • 3-Minute Breathing Space	• Exploring bodily reactions to parenting stress • Imagination parenting stress: self-compassion	• Yoga (lying) • Sitting meditation: breath and body • Stressful (parenting) moments calendar • 3-Minute Breathing Space • Mindful activity with child
4. Responding versus Reacting to Parenting Stress	• Awareness and acceptance of parenting stress • Grasping and pushing away • How thoughts exacerbate stress • Responding rather than reacting to stress	• Sitting meditation: breath, body, sounds and thoughts • Yoga (standing) • 3-Minute Breathing Space	• Fight–flight–freeze dance • Imagination parenting stress + 3-Minute Breathing Space + doors	• Yoga (standing) • Sitting meditation: breath, body, sounds and thoughts • 3-Minute Breathing Space under stress • Parenting stress calendar with 3-Minute Breathing Space • Writing short autobiography

Session				
5. Parenting Patterns and Schemas	• Recognizing patterns from own childhood • Being with strong emotions • Awareness of angry and vulnerable child modes, and punitive and demanding parent modes	• Sitting meditation: breath, body, sounds and thoughts, emotions • Walking meditation inside	• Parenting pattern recognition • Holding strong emotions with kindness and self-compassion	• Sitting meditation: breath, body, sounds and thoughts, emotions • Walking meditation • 3-Minute Breathing Space when your child is behaving • Parental stress calendar + schema mode recognition
6. Conflict and Parenting	• Perspective taking, joint attention • Rupture and repair • Tuning in to your child's emotional states	• Sitting meditation: choiceless awareness • Walking meditation outside	• Imagination: parent–child conflict + perspective, rupture, + repair	• Own 40-minute meditation • Rupture and repair practice • Breathing space when you . . . • Mindfulness day
7. Love and Limits	• Compassion and loving kindness • Befriending yourself and your (inner) child • Awareness of limits as a parent • Mindful limit setting	• Loving-kindness • Self-compassion	• Imagination: limits • Role play: limits • What do I need?	• Own 40-minute practice • Bring in symbolic object • Write narrative • Mindful limit setting • Loving-kindness
8. A Mindful Path through Parenting	• Review of personal growth • Intentions for future practice • How can I care for myself (and my child)?	• Body scan • Loving-kindness	• Sharing process through symbolic objects or narrative • Gratitude practice	• Own practice
Follow-Up Session: Each Time, Beginning Anew	• Experiences, obstacles, and renewed intentions for practicing	• Body scan • Stone meditation	• Mountain meditation • Wishing well	• Own practice

Note. From Bögels and Restifo (2014). Copyright 2014 by Springer Science + Business Media. Reprinted by permission.

for the formal meditations, in order to experience how this level of practice may affect them. At the end of each session, time is reserved to review the home practices for the following week so that everyone understands them and to stress their importance.

The Role of the Facilitator

Facilitators are usually mindfulness teachers who have a background in working with children and families in mental health care. We emphasize the importance for facilitators to have experience with the formal meditation and yoga practices as well as with the mindful parenting assignments themselves. It is essential that facilitators incorporate these practices into their own (family) life before offering them to others. The stance we embody as mindful parenting facilitators may be different than how many of us have been originally trained in mental health fields, especially when working with parents and children. As child and family therapists, we are used to leading groups as the "professional"— the therapist with the presumed expertise. But as mindful parenting facilitators, we lead the group, but we are also present as parents who struggle to parent well, as opposed to professionals who have all the answers. It can be a very different experience to simply be with parents in their struggles, without trying to help them "fix" their problems or their child. This stance does not mean we have to give up everything we have in our training as psychologist, teacher, or child development worker. But it is important to be aware that our relationship to the parents and children may be radically different in this context. We relate firstly as other human beings who also struggle to bring mindful awareness and compassion to ourselves and our task as parents, partners, friends, or colleagues. This is why having our own mindfulness practice is so important. When we comment or ask questions of participants in order to help them clarify their experience, we do so not only from our professional expertise but also from our personal experience, with a spirit of journeying together. We do not have the answers, but we can help by joining together in investigation and sharing our own struggles with the practice and our own suffering as human beings.

We can also disclose more of our own personal experience as a way of embodying universal suffering and helping others to understand their experience. When I started leading Mindful Parenting groups, I had my own parenting stressors, raising four children from two different relationships, including one stepchild. I could use my experience as a personal test of how Mindful Parenting can help in dealing with the stress of parenting in general, and in dealing specifically with stepparent, stepchild, and ex-partner situations. Often I felt comfortable disclosing my own experiences as an example. But most importantly, being mindfully present with my own parenting stress and suffering helped me to be present with the parenting stress of other parents in the group.

Effects of the Mindful Parenting Course

We sought to evaluate the interest in, as well as the possible effects of, the Mindful Parenting course (see Bögels, Hellemans, Van Deursen, Römer, & van der Meulen, 2014, for a full report of the study). Parents had different motivations for attending the Mindful Parenting courses, and they experienced very different outcomes. Therefore, we measured possible effects on a wide range of measures. First, we assessed their children's internalizing problems: that is, when children direct emotions and feelings inward, resulting in anxiety, depression, somatic symptoms, and social withdrawal. We also assessed their externalizing problems ("acting out"), wherein their emotional problems are directed outward into aggressive or rule-breaking behaviors. Second, we assessed parents' internalizing and externalizing patterns. Third, we assessed various aspects of parenting and family functioning: parental stress; the parenting styles of autonomy, encouragement, overprotection, acceptance, and rejection; co-parenting styles of supporting versus undermining each other in the presence of their child; degree of marital conflicts; and degree of marital satisfaction.

Participants in the study were 86 parents (89% mothers), mostly white, and their educational level was high, on average. They took the Mindful Parenting course in 10 different groups of 8–12 parents. In 64 (81%) families, parents experienced problems with at least one of the children. These children were labeled the target children; 40% were girls, and their mean age was 10.7 (4.6). The children were diagnosed with ADHD (47%), autistic spectrum disorder (21%), anxiety disorder or depression (12%), oppositional defiant disorder (ODD) or conduct disorder (4%), learning disorder (3%), or schizophrenia (1%). A parent–child relational problem was classified in 58% of the families. In the other families (19%), parents' own mental health problems, which currently interfered or had interfered with their parenting, were the reason they attended the course.

We used a quasi-experimental design to examine the possible effects of the course. Those parents who had to wait before joining a Mindful Parenting group completed wait-list assessments. Parents were assessed immediately before and immediately after the 8-week Mindful Parenting course. A follow-up assessment took place 8 weeks after the end of the course. Only one family (1%) dropped out of treatment, which means the participating parent missed four or more sessions.

What did we find? Parents reported no improvements during the wait-list period, except for a decrease in parental externalizing symptoms. After Mindful Parenting, parents indicated that their target children's internalizing and externalizing problems were significantly and substantially reduced. At pretest, 59% of the children had subclinical or clinical levels of internalizing symptoms and 63%, of externalizing symptoms, whereas at follow-up these were, respectively, 39% and 43%. Also, significant and substantial reductions in parents' own internalizing and (further) reduction in externalizing problems occurred. Perhaps more importantly with respect to parenting, parents reported significantly and substantially reduced parental stress and significant improvements on their parenting. That is, they reported encouraging the autonomy of their children more and being less overprotective, less rejecting, and somewhat more accepting of their children. Also, they reported that they were improved in their co-parenting, in the sense of fewer conflicts in the presence of their child. Their improvement remained or further improvement occurred in the 8 weeks after the end of the course. Parents reported no changes in the quality of their marriages.

Participants also completed an evaluation form assessing their experience with the Mindful Parenting program. The vast majority (over 90%) felt the training gave them something of enduring value, that it changed their lives and their parenting, and that they had become more aware of parenting issues. Also, the vast majority (95%) intended to remain aware in daily life, and 88% intended to keep meditating. Most parents practiced less than advised: one to four times a week, rather than daily. Parents overall rated the course highly.

Based on this study, we concluded that the Mindful Parenting course is feasible, as only one (1%) of the participants did not finish the course. Moreover, the Mindful Parenting course was shown to be effective on a wide range of measures. It is interesting that changes were as pronounced on parental psychopathology as on child psychopathology, particularly because the vast majority of parents were referred because of their child's disorder, rather than their own. This improvement in parental psychopathology is consistent with the aim of the Mindful Parenting intervention: that is, becoming aware, in a nonjudgmental way, of (parenting) stress and anxiety, (parenting) sadness, and (parenting) anger before acting upon these emotions; practicing focused and nonbiased attention; cultivating nonreactivity; and practicing self-care. The ample research on mindfulness would suggest that practice would affect internalizing psychopathology symptoms as well as externalizing psychopathology symptoms, such as aggressive behavior, in parents.

The improvements parents reported regarding their parenting styles are also remarkable, given that the focus of the course was not to change parenting styles. The reduction in parental stress is important because such stress is found to negatively affect parenting (Crnic, Gaze, & Hoffman, 2005). The improvements in co-parenting are promising, given what we know about the negative effects of unsupportive co-parenting and conflict in the presence of the child, on child psychopathology (e.g., Cummings, 1994; Majdandzic, Vente, Feinman, Aktar, & Bögels, 2012).

Discussion

Mindful Parenting appears to be a promising intervention for parents of children with psychopathology, parents with their own psychopathology that hinders parenting, and for parent–child relationship difficulties and severe parental stress. The very low dropout rate shows that Mindful Parenting is "feasible" in mental health care contexts. The intervention reduces internalizing and externalizing symptoms in children and parents, reduces parenting stress, increases in autonomy, encouraging, and accepting parenting styles, reduces parental rejection and overprotection, and improves co-parenting. The effects of the Mindful Parenting course continue to exist or are even stronger 8 weeks after completion of the intervention.

The Mindful Parenting course had no measurable effect on the marital relationship. One possible explanation for this is that most parents participated in the course without a partner. Participating with or without the partner is an important topic for discussion and further exploration. Of our participants, a significant proportion was divorced. Participating in the course with the ex-partner (the biological parent of the child) may be problematic. Also, the inclusion of any new partner is not always appropriate, because the partner may not be involved in parenting. In our groups, most parents participate alone, not only because they are divorced or single, but also because their partner is providing child care or they want to do the course on their own. Because the couples are a minority in our groups, divorced or single parents do not feel marginalized. Nevertheless, couples taking the course together report finding it very enriching to do so. It would be interesting to assess whether effects on the partner relationship occur in a Mindful Parenting course for couples only. However, the aim of the course is to affect stress in parenting rather than in the partner relationship.

Our own research into Mindful Parenting involved a quasi-experimental design, in which those parents who had to wait for the start of a group completed a wait-list measurement. The effects of Mindful Parenting have yet to be investigated in comparison with a randomized wait-list control group, and, more important, with another effective parent training method. In that context, it is important to check whether there are differences in parents for whom Mindful Parenting works better and for whom another parent training works better. As discussed in the introduction, traditional parent training for parents who themselves suffer from ADHD or depression appears less effective. Since mindfulness is found to be effective in people with attention problems and hyperactivity (Mitchell, Zylowska, & Kollins, 2015)and in depression (Segal et al., 2012), it is possible that these parents would benefit more from Mindful Parenting than from other parent training, such as parent management training.

The Mindful Parenting training described here can be used or adapted to a range of settings or populations. An adapted form (e.g., with shorter or fewer sessions) could also be helpful for parents outside of a mental health care context, for preventing or reducing parental stress, for improving the quality of parenting, or for even simply enjoying parenting more fully. More research is needed on the positive effects of Mindful Parenting, such as whether parents enjoy their parenting and their child more after the training.

Research is also needed into the effect of Mindful Parenting on objective parameters of the quality of the parent–child relationship and parenting, such as by observations of the parent–child interaction, particularly under stress or when conflicts arise. This kind of research would help determine whether parents indeed have learned to pause before acting, even for a split second, and whether this pausing helps deescalate negative parent–child interactions as they arise. We often receive feedback on the case level about this important shift, and so we end with an example.

> Jill followed the Mindful Parenting course because of problems with her adopted adolescent daughter, who often lied to her and was diagnosed with ODD. Halfway through the course, Jill brought a cake to the meeting that was made by her daughter. She explained how her daughter had noted changes in her mother's behavior and in their relationship, and the daughter wanted to show her gratitude by baking this cake for all of us. While eating the delicious cake, we could all sense why we are doing this: We were savoring the fruits of Mindful Parenting!

REFERENCES

Bögels, S. M., Lehtonen, A., & Restifo, K. (2010). Mindful Parenting in mental health care. *Mindfulness, 1*, 107–120.

Bögels, S. M., Hellemans, J., Van Deursen, S., Römer, M., & Van der Meulen, R. (2014). Mindful Parenting in mental health care: Effects on parental and child psychopathology, parental stress, parenting, co-parenting and marital functioning. *Mindfulness, 5*(5), 536–551

Bögels, S. M., & Restifo, K. (2014). *Mindful Parenting: A guide for mental health practitioners*. New York: Springer.

Cairney, J., Boyle, M., Offord, D. R., & Racine, Y. (2003). Stress, social support, and depression in single and married mothers. *Social Psychiatry and Psychiatric Epidemiology, 38*, 442–449.

Crnic, K. A., Gaze, C., & Hoffman, C. (2005). Cumulative parenting stress across the preschool period: Relations to maternal parenting and child behaviour at age 5. *Infant and Child Development, 14*, 117–132.

Cummings, E. M. (1994). Marital conflict and children's functioning. *Social Development, 3*, 16–36.

Fabiano, G. A., Pelham, W. E., Jr., Coles, E. K., Gnagy, E. M., Chronis-Tuscano, A., & O'Connor, B. C. (2009). A meta-analysis of behavioral treatments for attention-deficit/hyperactivity disorder. *Clinical Psychology Review, 29*, 129–140.

Forehand, R., Furey, W. M., & McMahon, R. J. (1984). The role of maternal distress in a parent training program to modify child non-compliance. *Behavioural Psychotherapy, 12*, 93–108.

Kabat-Zinn, J. (1990). *Full catastrophe living*. New York: Bantam Doubleday Dell.

Kabat-Zinn, M., & Kabat-Zinn, J. (1997). *Everyday blessings: The inner work of Mindful Parenting*. New York: Hyperion.

Majdandzic, M., Vente, W., Feinman, M., Aktar, E., & Bögels, S. M. (2012).

Coparenting and parental and child anxiety: A review. *Clinical Child and Family Psychology Review, 15*, 28–42.

Maliken, A. C., & Katz, L. F. (2013). Exploring the impact of parental psychopathology and emotion regulation on evidence-based parenting interventions: A transdiagnostic approach to improving treatment effectiveness. *Clinical Child and Family Psychology Review, 16*, 173–186.

Mitchell, J. T., Zylowska., L., & Kollins, S. (2015). Mindfulness meditation training for attention-deficit/hyperactivity disorder in adulthood: Current empirical support, treatment overview, and future directions. *Cognitive and Behavioral Practice, 22*, 172–191.

Neff, K. (2011). *Self-compassion.* New York: William Morrow.

Owens, E. B., Hinshaw, S. P., Kraemer, H. C., Arnold, L. E., Abikoff, H. B., Cantwell, D. P., et al. (2003). Which treatment for whom for ADHD?: Moderators of treatment response in the MTA. *Journal of Consulting and Clinical Psychology, 71*, 540–552.

Reisinger, J. J., Frangia, G. W., & Hoffman, E. H. (1976). Toddler management training: Generalization and marital status. *Journal of Behavior Therapy and Experimental Psychiatry, 7*, 335–340.

Reyno, S. M., & McGrath, P. J. (2006). Predictors of parent training efficacy for child externalizing behavior problems: A meta-analytic review. *Journal of Child Psychology and Psychiatry, 47*, 99–111.

Segal, Z. V., Williams, J. M. G., & Teasdale, J. D. (2012). *Mindfulness-based cognitive therapy for depression.* New York: Guilford Press.

Sonuga-Barke, E. J. S., Daley, D., & Thompson, M. (2002). Does maternal ADHD reduce the effectiveness of parent training for preschool children's ADHD? *Journal of the American Academy of Child and Adolescent Psychiatry, 41*, 696–702.

Sonuga-Barke, E. J., & Halperin, J. M. (2010) Developmental phenotypes and causal pathways in attention deficit/hyperactivity disorder: Potential targets for early intervention? *Journal of Psychological Psychiatry, 51*(4), 368–389.

Suzuki, S. (1970). *Zen mind, beginner's mind.* New York: Weatherhill.

Van der Oord, S., Prins, P. J., Oosterlaan, J., & Emmelkamp, P. M. (2008). Efficacy of methylphenidate, psychosocial treatments, and their combination in school-aged children with ADHD: A meta-analysis. *Clinical Psychology Review, 28*, 783–800.

Webster-Stratton, C. (1985). Predictors of treatment outcome in parent training for conduct disordered children. *Behavior Therapy, 16*, 223–243.

Webster-Stratton, C. (1990). Long-term follow-up of families with young conduct problem children: From preschool to grade school. *Journal of Clinical Child Psychology, 19*, 144–149.

PART II

BRINGING
MINDFULNESS
TO LIFE

CHAPTER 10

Yoga
Reaching Heart and Mind through the Body

Jennifer Cohen Harper

Ten years ago I had recently moved back to New York City, was finishing graduate school, practicing lots of yoga, and teaching a kindergarten class in Harlem, where the kids were in an extended day program that basically kept them in school until 6 P.M. Although I'd worked with kids in tough settings before, and in situations where the kids had experienced trauma, the overall energy of this class was a new experience for me.

These kids had lots of energy, but their energy had a frenetic quality to it. They were scattered and struggled to be still long enough for even a story. When they did get still, they often fell asleep. They were kids, with big playful kid energy, quick to get excited, but also very quick to get very frustrated and to judge themselves harshly.

During this time, my own yoga practice was becoming a lifeline for me, both personally and at work, and sharing some yoga with my students was natural and happened without a plan or a curriculum. I was doing whatever I could to engage my young students, and to help both them and myself get through the day as well as possible. One of the first yoga-inspired activities I remember teaching was having them stand up to say the alphabet, raising their arms overhead and taking a big breath, then saying the letter as their arms came down. It was a simple little thing to do (and probably a bit much on the arms!), but the kids loved it. Some were serious, taking big, *big* breaths, and some were silly and wiggly, adding in jumps and banging their arms down against their bodies—but they were all *there*, with me in the room, in their bodies, and something felt different.

I think that standing up, breathing fully, and moving their bodies helped these kids, but in retrospect, I think there may have been another element to it that helped shift how they felt about me. I believe that by giving them that small experience, they felt like I might have understood how they were feeling, and that how they were feeling mattered. They kept looking at me when they embellished with a jump or a big movement of their body, waiting to get in trouble, but I was so happy that they were feeling and enjoying the process. I wanted them to feel good, not just do exactly as I said. Perhaps this was a way of being with an adult that many of them had never experienced.

Another activity I shared with this class was a cooling breath that the kids called "air conditioner breathing." If you have been in a school with no air conditioning on a hot day, you know how everyone struggles. This breathing practice is so simple; you just roll your tongue into a tube (or curl it to the roof of your mouth), and breathe in through your mouth. As the air passes over your tongue, it's cooled off, and that air cools your whole body. When I taught the kids in my class this kind of breathing, they were insanely excited. They were doing it all day, showing other kids, and walking around in the hallways with their rolled tongues sticking out. It was another moment when I felt like the activity was great, but the added bonus was that the kids and I felt like a team. They knew I was on their side, thinking about what they were experiencing and caring about making that experience better.

Once it occurred to me to start integrating yoga more fully into my class, I looked for more experienced yoga teachers to come in and share the practices with the kids, but with a little encouragement I realized that I had so much to share with them myself. I started to make yoga a regular part of our day, and it changed the entire dynamic of the room. It also changed how I thought about the kids. Instead of feeling like I had to manage them and corral them, I was paying attention to how they felt, and allowing those feelings to be important. It was a whole different way of being in relationship with children.

Since then, I've taught thousands of students and teachers yoga, and I'm still amazed by how the practice can shift both big people and little people's daily experience of life; how it can create connections between the body and the mind, but also how it can create connections between people in a community. As everyone starts to feel better, everyone has a little more space for compassion and kindness, for thoughtfulness and "heartfulness." Kids feel ready to learn, teachers feel ready to teach, and the classroom can fulfill its potential as a place of exploration, learning, and growth.

Why Yoga in the Classroom?

Classrooms are often high-stress environments for both teachers and students. Teachers are navigating the needs of large numbers of students, while facing tremendous pressure to deliver content and improve test results. Students are struggling with the academic challenges of school, as well as the significant social and emotional hurdles that growing up throws in their path. In the most challenging situations, classrooms are full of stress, anxiety, and fear, and these intense emotions make it harder for kids to thrive. School becomes a place of judgment and competition, instead of exploration and creativity. But even in the best classrooms, the challenges are many and the expectations are high, which naturally leads to a significant amount of anxiety and stress for both teachers and students.

Despite the numerous challenges of the education system, learning is the natural state of being for young people. When children's physical and emotional needs are met, their innate curiosity will surface, and the classroom can be a joyful and engaging place. As yoga has become more common in our society, its capacity to reduce the negative impact of stress and improve wellness has been experienced by increasing numbers of people, including many teachers. These benefits are now well documented in both popular and scientific literature. Sharing the practice of yoga with children in school is a low-cost way to facilitate substantial gains in student well-being and achievement, while also supporting a culture of compassion (for each other and for ourselves).

Yoga offers a powerful tool for addressing some of the most common challenges in the classroom. Even simple yoga-based activities, taught in small increments of 5–15 minutes a day, can improve the classroom climate, reduce impulsive behavior, and increase students' capacity for focus. Adding yoga to the day helps both teachers and students feel physically and emotionally better, supporting an environment conducive to learning.

Making Yoga Work in Schools: Accessibility and Relevance

In my work with children in classrooms and after-school programs, I've found many benefits to the physical postures of yoga, but the really extraordinary benefits happen when the practice is taught in its fullness. In order to make sharing this path more accessible for teachers and children, I created Little Flower Yoga, an organization dedicated to making the tools of yoga and mindfulness available to all children and teens. I created a structure for this process that incorporates the following five elements:

- *Connect:* "Connect activities" help children tune in and make sense of their experiences. They are practices that are used to develop mindful awareness of both the external world and the internal emotional state.
- *Breathe:* The breath is one of the most powerful tools for self-regulation. "Breathe activities" help children learn to reduce anxiety, stabilize energy, and create a sense of safety and peace in the body.

- *Move:* "Move activities" are based on yoga postures that help children maintain a state of alert engagement, where hyperactive behavior is minimized yet children still feel strong and energetic.
- *Focus:* "Focus activities" provide opportunities for kids to apply their focus in a step-by-step way, noticing when the mind wanders and practicing bringing it back, allowing for progressive improvement and experiences of success.
- *Relax:* The final element, relaxing, gives children tools that facilitate rest, relaxation, and restoration. Exhaustion is common in kids, and we know that being tired makes everything else much harder. These activities teach children ways to rejuvenate themselves, even when they aren't sleeping.

These five elements provide a structure for school-based yoga programs that can help you share the full potential of yoga to contribute to stability and balance in your group of kids. In the following material you will find examples of activities within each of these elements, along with a discussion of how they can be used in your classroom. Before you share these activities with your students, it would be helpful to keep the following in mind:

1. *Students only benefit from practices that engage them.* It's critical in this work that you pay close attention to your students, and make every effort to share practices that are relevant to their lives (and know them well enough to show them how the practices are relevant). When you are connected to your kids and stay connected to them during teaching, you'll quickly notice if what you are offering doesn't match their needs. At that point it's important that you either address this situation and reengage them in the activity, or that you choose another practice that is a better fit in the moment.

2. *Engaged students are often chatty students.* Yoga doesn't have to be quiet in order to be effective. If your students are engaged in what you are offering, it's completely natural for them to want to share their experience, ask questions, and hear about others' experiences. This interaction is something to encourage. Leave time in your work for discussions, especially when you are offering something for the first time. It's helpful to think about each activity not as something to just do and move on from, but something to experience and explore from multiple perspectives and in multiple ways. Don't expect your experience of yoga with kids to look *anything* like an adult yoga class (and if it does, I'd be a bit worried).

3. *Participation needs to be a choice.* In this work, kids can't benefit from a practice if they are doing it under duress. In fact, for many kids, feeling forced or pressured to do something will only ensure that they *never* do it voluntarily. In addition, one of the things we are trying to support by sharing yoga and mindfulness with students is a greater awareness of, and connection to, their own internal experience, and the ability to know what is safe for

them and meets their own needs. It's important that you tell your students often that they can choose to sit quietly instead if something hurts or otherwise doesn't feel right for them (or offer them an alternative, such as a gentle pose with which they are comfortable). Not only can they make this choice, but you should even let them know that you are impressed with their capacity to meet their own needs. Although allowing participation to be a choice can be nerve-wracking for a teacher, it will always provide you with valuable information. If lots of kids are choosing not to participate, you may need to reevaluate your connection with them and think about how you are making the practices relevant and engaging for them.

   4. *You'll be better able to share a practice when you've actually experienced it.* Please take time to try these practices yourself before you share them with your students. It makes a big difference in how you present the practices and in how you discuss them when you have internalized the experience. Plus, the kids can always tell!

Practices for the Classroom

Yoga in your classroom does not have to take a long time, and it doesn't have to involve yoga mats. The activities that follow can be taught and practiced either sitting at a desk or standing alongside it. Most can be experienced in as little as 3–5 minutes. As you read through the following ideas and activities, keep in mind that you don't need to do everything at once in order for the experience to be meaningful. Try practicing the activities yourself and consider sharing what resonates with you.

   Thinking about the activities in the following categories has been helpful for me, and so I have divided them into these categories in the material that follows:

- Activities that can be incorporated each day to build a foundation of engaged awareness.
- Practices that can be used during the transitions of the day to support a continuous flow of energy and experience.
- Strategies for reducing test-taking anxiety.

   Because consistency is important in building long-term resilience, I recommend that you start small, committing to just one or two practices and implementing them regularly in your class, then adding more once those feel natural and supportive, rather then trying a wide variety of things all at once.

   If you are interested in teaching longer yoga practices to your students—for example, putting together full 30- to 60-minute yoga classes—my recommendation would be to seek out additional support materials and consider an in-person training. Some resources are listed at the end of this chapter; in addition, be aware that a wide variety of children's yoga trainings are available all over the world.

Everyday Practices

These activities are foundational and can be practiced for short periods of time everyday. Please remember to practice them yourself, noticing what arises and how you are feeling, before offering them to your students. Then, when offering them to your students, approach them with these practices as an exploration and an experiment, with a sense of playfulness and curiosity.

Layers of Sound: A Connect Activity

This practice is a wonderful way to help your students connect both with what's happening in their environment and with themselves. It creates a centering and grounding energy that facilitates learning, and helps teach students to filter the wide array of stimuli around them all of the time.

1. First find a still and comfortable position with your body. It may be helpful to close your eyes for this activity. If it doesn't feel comfortable to close your eyes, let them rest on the desk right in front of you.

2. Now that you are still and comfortable, take a breath or two to help you get ready for what's going to come next.

3. Imagine opening your ears as wide as you can make them, and imagine stretching your hearing way out beyond the room you are sitting in, and maybe even the building that room is in, all the way to the outdoors. Listen carefully and find the farthest-away sounds that you can hear.

4. When you start hearing sounds, don't worry about identifying them or figuring out what is making them. Just notice each sound exactly as it is. [Allow a few minutes of silence here.]

5. Now that you have heard the farthest-away sounds you can find, bring your hearing in a little bit closer and find the sounds that are in this building. Again, don't worry about figuring out what is making the sounds; just listen to them.

6. Next we are going to bring our hearing even closer to find the sounds that are in this room. Reach your hearing into each corner of the room and see what sounds you can find.

7. After you have found all of the sounds in the room, we are going to bring our hearing to the closest place of all: our own bodies.

8. Pull your hearing all the way into your body. Pull your hearing out of the room and turn it to the sounds that you can find your own body making. Listen carefully. Your body might have a lot to say!

9. After a few moments of listening to your own body, gently open your eyes.

Take a few minutes to talk with your students about what they heard and how they felt, especially when doing this activity for the first time.

Anchor Breath: A Breathe Activity

The anchor breath is a simple but powerful way to help your students soothe their nervous systems and reconnect to their present-moment experience. It offers them a tool that they can use at any time, especially when things seem a little rocky or out of control. The most important part of this practice is that you encourage your students to keep breathing through their noses.

1. Talk with your class about what an anchor is, about how an anchor keeps a ship steady even when it's windy or there are rough seas.
2. Ask your kids if they ever have times in their lives when they feel a little like they are ships getting tossed around in big waves; if there are ever times when they feel like they could use something to help them feel steadier.
3. Explain that the breath is something that we always have with us, and that we can use to help us feel calmer, steadier, and more peaceful even when things around us are crazy.
4. Ask the students to sit up tall and to keep their bodies as still as possible.
5. Have them start to breathe in and out through their noses, taking full breaths all the way into the belly.
6. After a few rounds of breathing in and out, remind them that their breath is their anchor, and that if they notice their minds wandering or their feelings getting crazy, they have the choice to turn their attention to the sound and feeling of their own breath.
7. Many students find that placing one hand on their heart and one on their belly during this practice enhances the sense of being calmly supported.

Tree Pose Sequence: A Move Activity

A simple movement routine that you can practice with your students at their desks can be a powerful ally in your quest to keep your kids alert and focused. These postures are all modified so that they can be practiced right in a chair, or standing next to it, with no need for a mat. Practicing the full sequence doesn't take long, but once you are familiar with it, feel free to practice the poses individually. If you would like to see a short video demonstration of this sequence, visit *www.littlefloweryoga.com/tree-pose-exploration* and for illustrations of individual poses, see my book, *Little Flower Yoga for Kids: A Yoga and Mindfulness Program to Help Your Child Improve Attention and Emotional Balance* (Harper, 2013).

    1. Start by sitting at the very front edge of your chair, with your feet flat on the ground, and your hands on your knees. Roll your shoulders a few times, and then sit a little taller in your chair.

    2. Take a full breath in and draw your shoulders together in your back while lifting your chest and looking up into a modified version of cow pose. (In the traditional version of cow pose, you would be on hands and knees, with your belly dropping towards the group, back arched, chest and head lifting up, and shoulders moving towards each other.)

    As you exhale, round your back and look toward your belly button. Repeat three times.

    3. Inhale and reach both of your arms overhead. Twist to the right side while keeping both feet flat on the floor. Hold the right side of the seat with your left hand and the back of the seat with your right hand. If your left hip is lifting off of the seat, you've gone too far. Hold this twist for three breaths, using each inhale to sit up a little bit taller, and each exhale to twist just a little bit farther. After three breaths, inhale, lift your arms back to center, and twist to the left.

    4. With both feet flat on the ground, reach your arms out in front of you, press your feet down and stand up. Drop your arms to your sides with your palms facing forward, stand up a little taller, and take a full breath in and out for mountain pose. (This is a strong standing pose, with your feet together, or about hip width apart, your body engaged and strong, but your shoulders and face relaxed.)

    5. Now lift your arms overhead, relax your shoulders, and gently side-stretch to the right. Keep pressing your left foot down as you reach to the right, and after a breath or two, inhale back to the center and exhale to the other side. Lift back up and relax your arms down by your sides.

    6. Now we are going to practice balancing in tree pose. Start by finding a spot straight ahead of you on which to fix your focus. Stare at it throughout the whole pose. Shift your weight onto your left foot and slowly lift your right leg off of the ground. Bring the sole of your right foot onto the inside of your left calf (optionally, you can bring it to the inside of your thigh, but avoid placing it on your knee). Keep looking at your focus point, and bring your arms overhead. Hold for three breaths, and then slowly lower down and practice on the other side.

    7. When you are finished with your tree pose, come back to standing and bend your knees slightly; on an exhalation, fold forward from your hips. Let your body relax and even move around a little, swinging from side to side and nodding your head. Then roll up slowly to stand.

    8. Lift your arms straight out in front of you, bend your knees, and take five counts to slowly lower back into your chair.

Single-Pointed Focus: A Focus Activity

When we practice developing focus with our students, it's very important that we get clear on what it is that we are asking of them. It's unrealistic to think that kids (or adults) can maintain exclusive attention on schoolwork for an extended period of time, without getting distracted or otherwise having their focus pulled from the task at hand. The important skill for our students to learn is to quickly *notice* that their mind has wandered and learn to bring it back. This is something that we all can practice in many simple ways, and, through practice, get better at. Try the following activity regularly as a way to help your students strengthen this important life skill.

1. Choose something to be the object of your students' focus (in this case, I use a visual object, but it could also be a sound or the breath). This is an important choice. A candle flame works so well for an adult practice because it is, at once, constant and ever changing. A candle flame has a small amount of movement that keeps drawing you in, but it doesn't change so much that it inspires thoughts or ideas. Try to choose something with similar qualities for your practice with your students: a sand timer, a jar filled with water and glitter that you can shake, a battery-operated flickering candle (try putting it inside a brown paper bag), or even leaves blowing on trees outside the classroom window would work.

2. Arrange your group in such a way that everyone can see the object (or even better, have individual objects that they can each have on their desks; electric flickering tea lights are very inexpensive and are great for this). Tell your students to sit up tall and take a few full breaths to prepare.

3. Set a timer for 2 minutes. (This is a good amount of time to start with, but you can try more or less depending on your group.)

4. Offer the following suggestions to your students:

"Fix your gaze on the object you've chosen and let it fill up your mind.

"Now, here is the most important part of this practice: When your mind wanders away from your object, try to notice right away and then bring it back. Noticing your mind wandering and practicing bringing it back are the true purposes of this activity. Keep practicing until your timer goes off.

"When the timer goes off, close your eyes and try to keep the object you have been gazing at fixed in your mind. Take a few full breaths, and when you are ready, open your eyes."

5. Make sure to emphasize to the kids that the point is to notice their mind wandering and to bring it back, not to try to stay glued to the object. Every time the mind wanders, it's a chance to practice and make it stronger. (You can relate this effort to one rep in physical exercise—an analogy that often helps kids understand the idea better.)

Legs Up the Wall Chair Variation: A Relax Activity

Incorporating rest into the school day isn't very popular after kindergarten, but we all know that when students (and people, in general) are well rested, they are kinder, more capable of self-regulation, better able to learn and store new material, and better able to recall previously learned information. In this example, we are going to use a restorative yoga pose to increase the benefits of some quiet time for your students. Other effective practices include resting on the desk and listening to some gentle music or doing a simple body scan.

1. In this practice, the students are going to lie down on the ground with their legs propped up on their chairs. It's a very restful experience, and well worth the effort. If you have access to mats, that is great, but if not, kids are often okay with this if they have a sweatshirt or something similar to put down under them, or even just a thin notebook to put their head on. If it's not going to feel comfortable to do this, don't force it! Find another way to rest, allowing students to stay in their chairs. Offer the following suggestions to your students:

"Recline on your backs with your feet facing the chair and your hips close to the chair. Lift up your legs and put them on the chair so that your calves are resting flat on the chair, with your knees bent at about 90 degrees.
"Let your arms rest at your sides with your palms facing up.
"Take a few full breaths to settle in, and make any adjustments that you need to be comfortable. Rest here for as long as feels good."

It's always nice to dim the lights if that is possible, and if there is a lot of distracting background noise happening, consider playing some gentle music.

Transitions

Children often struggle with transitions, but the time between things is full of possibility. If you can learn to both manage and maximize your transitions, you will find that your day can flow more smoothly, with less abruptness and more intention. In addition, when you make transitions mindful, you have a built-in reminder to practice in a way that doesn't take any time at all away from other instruction.

Moving from Chair to Standing

We ask our kids to stand up many times in a day (hopefully!) and paying a bit more attention to *how* we do that can help them build strength and focus. It can also help with classroom management in a gentle way. Often when a teacher says "Stand up," the kids hear something more like "Stand up, jump a bit, maybe run around, and talk to each other." Being more deliberate in the transition can help keep your group on the same page. Instead of saying "Stand up," try something like this:

> "Put both of your feet flat on the floor, sit up tall and reach your arms straight out in front of you. Pull your belly button in just a bit. Now press both of your feet down and take 5 full seconds to slowly stand up, and when you get there, reach your arms overhead. Take a full breath in, and as your breathe out, lower your arms."

Changing Subjects

If you are an elementary school teacher, your kids are probably with you for most of the day, and you might not have much transition time or space between subjects and activities. Creating a routine of mindfulness in these transition spaces can give your students a chance to both internalize what they have just done and to mentally prepare for what is to come. It doesn't have to be complicated! Anchor breath or a single-pointed focus practice could work, but it's also a great time to have your students get comfortable in their chairs, with both feet on the floor and backs straight, if possible, and just give them 2 or 3 minutes of quiet time to close their eyes and take what I call a *mind wander break*. There is no goal or instruction, just time to go inside and let the mind drift where is needs to go. Bring them back gently, with a chime or a bell rung a few seconds before you ask them to move on.

Changing Rooms

Moving from place to place offers a great opportunity to practice a walking meditation. Instead of asking your students to just be quiet in the halls, try engaging them by turning their attention to the sensations of movement in their bodies. Start by inviting your students to stand up deliberately, as in the example above. Then encourage your kids to do the following:

> "Notice how your feet feel as you shift their weight forward and back, then side to side. Let's take a slow walk to the library. Do your best to notice how your feet feel as you walk. What is the sensation like in your heels? In your toes? After a few moments, start to notice what walking feels like in the rest of your body. What happens in your legs and hips when you walk? What about your arms? Can you feel walking in your neck and your face? If your mind starts to wander while you are taking your walk, that's no problem. Just notice where it is wandering to and then gently bring it back to how your body is feeling during your walk. When we get to the library, come back to mountain pose for one full breath and consider sending a thank you to your feet."

Reducing Testing Anxiety

As the use of standardized testing in school has grown, so has the stress it puts on our kids. Many students experience tremendous anxiety both in the time leading up to an exam and during the exam itself. In addition to reducing children's quality of life and enjoyment of their education, this anxiety also disrupts their ability to learn the information they need and their capacity to do well on their exams *even if they know the material.*

Below are two short activities that can help students manage the anxiety associated with testing, both in advance of and during the exam. Like any other practice, it's a good idea to familiarize students with the activity *before* the anxiety arises. Introduce these activities when things are going well, and give your kids a chance to practice them during mildly stressful experiences, like a quiz or before a presentation, so that they can internalize them before a big exam.

If the activities in the "Everyday Practices" section of this chapter are resonating with your students, you can also use some of these while preparing for and during an exam. For example, the layers-of-sound activity is a good one to use in the 2 or 3 minutes before a test starts, and you can encourage students to use an anchor breath activity as a way to reconnect and refocus at intervals throughout the test, particularly if they are feeling overwhelmed.

Body Break

Often kids need to move their bodies in order to get keep their minds engaged, but this is challenging in a school environment where students are often asked to stay relatively still for extended periods of time, and if they move around, they might get in trouble. Offering students this simple practice to do any time during class or during an exam can help them meet the need to engage their body in a subtle way that doesn't disturb anyone else. Explain to your students:

1. "Sit toward the front of your chair and put your feet flat on the ground.

2. "Place your hands flat on the desk in front of you with your palms down.

3. "Roll your shoulders a few times to relax them, and if it feels good, turn your head from side to side or make a few circles with your head.

4. "Push your right foot strongly down into the ground for 3–5 seconds. Then do the same with your left foot.

5. "Now push your right hand down on to the desk for a few seconds, and then do the same with your left.

6. "Do this for several rounds: right foot, left foot, right hand, left hand. After a few rounds you can give your brain a little extra stimulation by changing the order and engaging your left foot, then right foot, then left hand, and right hand.

7. "When you are ready to stop, push both hands and feet down strongly at the same time for a few seconds and let your entire body relax."

"I Can Do This"

This meditation is accessible and engaging for children who have trouble keeping their body still; for many students this becomes one of their most relied upon tools in everyday life. It is an active meditation that combines vocalization with movement of fingers and reinforces your students' personal power and capacity for self-determination. Before you begin, it's a great idea to ask your students to bring into their mind something that is challenging for them and to hold it there throughout the practice. You can practice it out loud during class, and then encourage students to practice silently if they need a boost during an exam.

1. "Connect each of your fingers to your thumb on both hands at once, while reciting the words '*I can do this.*'

2. "Press your thumb and first finger together saying '*I,*' thumb and middle finger together saying '*can,*' thumb and ring finger together saying '*do,*' and thumb and pinky together saying '*this.*'

3. "Put enough pressure on your fingers to really feel the connection they are making. Once you get the rhythm of the practice, close your eyes and keep going.

4. "Begin slowly, using both hands simultaneously, and as you feel more comfortable, go a bit faster. You can start saying '*I can do this*' in a regular voice, and each round get a little louder; then lower your voice each round until it becomes a whisper, and repeat the mantra silently to yourselves."

Let your students know that they can do this practice any time on their own, even if they aren't in a place where they can say the words out loud.

Engaging the Full Education Community

It is entirely likely that when you begin to bring yoga into your school, the reception will be positive. Many teachers, administrators, and parents are familiar with yoga, both from personal practice and increasingly from the research on its benefits making its way into the popular media. But although yoga has become much more widely practiced and accepted over the past decade, you may still encounter some resistance. Helping the kids, your administration, and the parents feel good about bringing yoga into classrooms is an important part of creating an effective and sustainable program, and if you can make these people your allies, then the work you are doing can grow. It's very important to be thoughtful about your approach to each of these groups, and to consider what both their fears and their needs might be.

The Students

The kids will usually be your most willing audience if you are approaching them with a genuine desire to share something meaningful and useful. In large part, engaging your students will be a product of the quality of your relationship with them; your cultivation of an environment of respect, compassion, and trust will allow their natural curiosity and enthusiasm to emerge. Meet that curiosity and enthusiasm with practices relevant to their needs in the moment, and they will engage with you.

The Administrators

Administrators are under the same tremendous pressure that teachers are, and they are accountable for everything that happens in their school. When you introduce something that is unfamiliar, it's natural for them to have concerns. One issue you will certainly have to consider is that some people express concern about a connection between yoga and religion. Yoga is not a religion, but I think that the larger issue at hand is making sure that the entire school community feels safe and welcomed by what you are offering.

When discussing yoga with your administration, my recommendation is to focus on sharing the benefits of the practice established by research, connecting them with administrators at schools that have a flourishing yoga program, and reassuring them that you will keep things completely secular. In your teaching, I recommend using English terms instead of their Sanskrit versions, and staying away from practices that might make the community uncomfortable, such as chanting *om* or closing a practice by saying *namaste*. Although you may be able to argue that neither of these practices is inherently religious, you also would have to admit that they aren't essential to students' experiences, and they have the potential to make parents and administrators nervous.

Another potential concern of administrators is that yoga will take time that could be better spent delivering academic content. In this situation, you want to focus on the ways that yoga can support efforts to make classrooms more effective learning environments, and can help the students become more receptive and engaged learners. You gain instruction time when you reduce the amount of time you spend dealing with behavioral challenges. You can teach content more effectively and thoroughly when your kids are calm and better able to focus. You can improve test scores when anxiety is mini-mized and kids can access what they have learned. Let's meet our students' internal needs so that they are ready to learn and can retain and use what they are taught.

The Parents

Parents want what is best for their children, and if they are questioning what is being done in your classroom, it's a great thing because it means they are engaged! This is what we want, although it can be hard not to become frustrated as the teacher. Parents may have some of the same concerns about perceived religious connotations of yoga as administrators do, and you can address them the same way, reassuring parents that what you are offering their children is a skill-building practice that is aimed only at helping them be more connected with themselves, not with any higher power.

Parents always welcome transparency, and if questions arise, you might want to consider inviting the questioning parent into class to see what you are offering the kids. It can also be helpful to send some written descriptions of activities home, both to help parents better understand what you are teach-ing, and to give them a resource to support their child. Integrating yoga and mindfulness into your classroom will be a wonderful gift to your students, but the impact will be enhanced if you can encourage them to practice at home, teach the practices to their families, and encourage parents to support a home practice.

Your Personal Practice

Although you may be reading this book in order to support your students, it is tremendously important that you take your own personal practice just as seriously. Your personal practice will make you a more compelling teacher of yoga and mindfulness, and it will also help you be a better teacher in many other ways. When you are living a mindful life, you can be fully present for your students, responsive to their subtle (and sometimes not so subtle) needs, and capable of handling challenging situations with compassion and skill. When you are nourishing yourself and committed to your practice, you'll be better able to see clearly and navigate your own emotions in the classroom. Rich teaching and learning happen when you can model mindful behavior in challenging moments.

Teaching is hard. So is being a student. You and your kids are in this together. Bringing yoga into your classroom and into your lives is a way to create a more compassionate and supportive community, make the challenges of the journey feel less overwhelming, infuse your daily routine with wellness, and strengthen both your own and your students' capacity for teaching and learning. Yoga is a powerful tool, and one that I hope makes your challenging job more sustainable and joyful.

RECOMMENDED RESOURCES

Devi, N. J. (2000). *The healing path of yoga: Time-honored wisdom and scientifically proven methods that alleviate stress, open your heart, and enrich your life*. New York: Three Rivers Press.

Flynn, L. (2011). *Yoga 4 classrooms card deck*. Dover, NH: Yoga 4 Classrooms.

Harper, J. C. (2013). *Little Flower Yoga for kids: A yoga and mindfulness program to help your child improve attention and emotional balance*. Los Angeles: New Harbinger.

Rechtschaffen, D. (2014). *The way of mindful education: Cultivating well-being in teachers and students*. New York: Norton.

CHAPTER 11

Movement and Dance
Creativity and Embodied Mindfulness

Suzi Tortora

Ten-year-old Suri bursts into her dance/movement psychotherapy session, runs immediately to the large physioball, straddles it, and begins to bounce vigorously. "I'm hot pink today!" she enthusiastically exclaims. As I watch her flying up and down into the air, using all the strength in her legs to bounce as high as she can, I have to agree. I ask if she would like music to match her hot pink feeling—the color we associate with feeling super fast inside—and provide a few music selections from my playlist. She chooses the most upbeat rhythmic song, and immediately I start to feel her enthusiastic energy pulsing through my body as well. Embodying the feeling tone of the child's energy is a core aspect of the dance/movement psychotherapy approach that is the focus of this chapter. As you read this chapter, you too can get a sense of this experiential way of working by noticing your own thoughts, feelings, and body sensations as you read the vignettes.

"Mom, Dr. Suzi—you do it too," Suri gleefully directs. We follow suit, embodying her joyful, bouncy spirit on our own physioballs as best as we can. No verbal explanation is needed, for our conversation is in the immediate moment through our shared action dialogue. The song ends and we pause, and we take a few "zip-up breaths": We glide our hands up our bodies, one along the front and the other along the back, as if zipping up a sweater, as we simultaneously breathe in slowly and deeply, followed by an exhale as our arms come down to our sides while maintaining a tall, central "zipped-up" sensation. "Do you have more hot pink in you, Suri?" I ask. She maintains her poise for a moment longer and exclaims, "Oh, yes, I am not done yet!" I put the music on a continuous loop and we begin again,

bouncing together, following Suri's movements throughout the song, pausing at the end of each song cycle to take zip-up breaths and check in with her
energy level and mood. When the music begins again, we add deep breaths
each time we push off the ground as our bodies lengthen and extend up off
the ball. During our pause in the third round, approximately 10 minutes
into our session, Suri states, "Okay, now I am ready for orange. I've gotten
enough super fast out of me for now."

We choose a song that reflects the orange speed of the Speed Spiral™
chart, associated with a fast, yet not-as-fast inner tempo, and adjust our
bouncing bodies accordingly. Suri's nonverbal actions reflect this calmer
state; her bounce is lower, her feet stay on the ground, and her arms reach
up with elbows bent to the height of her head rather than the full extension
she reached previously.

After two rounds of orange, Suri pauses, now wanting to talk instead
of jump. She reports that she is very excited about her school trip tomorrow, her playdate with her best friend on Friday, and how well she stayed in
control when she got angry at Mom for making her walk home from the bus
stop after school today. We discuss her growing ability to stop her impulsive
behaviors and to respond from a more reflective stance.

Now we explore the last two colors of the Speed Spiral: green, representing medium; and purple, representing a slow, calm-to-meditative inner
tempo. During these two dance and movement explorations we play an
improvisational game, in which we each take turns adding dance moves
to an impromptu dance. After additional new steps, we repeat the ever-
expanding sequence, testing our ability to remember all the elements of the
dance choreography. At the end of the session Suri reflects on how much
calmer she feels, stating, "I came in so excited, but it was too much! Now I
am still excited but in a calm way!"

How can *excited* and *calm* belong in the same sentence, let alone be physically felt at the same time? Yet, having experienced Suri's transformation
through our "dance-play" (Tortora, 2006, 2010b), I completely agree with
her. Paying close attention to my own reactions, bodily sensations, and feelings in the immediate moment as I am working with a child is central to my
approach. Suri is verbalizing her awareness of her *felt experience*, a term used in
dance movement psychotherapy (also known as dance/movement therapy and
referred to as DMT in this chapter) to encompass the simultaneously emotional and embodied nature of our actions. DMT is a therapeutic approach
within the creative arts therapies that include art, drama, psychodrama, and
poetry therapy. Creative arts therapies emphasize the use of the creative process as a core tool in the psychotherapeutic methodology. Using the arts as a
form of expression and healing is perfect for children, who generally thrive
when given the opportunity to creatively share who they are.

DMT is a compatible methodology to implement mindful body and
mind awareness strategies. Both DMT and mindfulness awareness encourage open observation, quiet listening and the nonjudgmental investigation

of sensations, thoughts, perceptions, and feelings in the present moment. In mindfulness meditation the focus is to observe where one's mind goes naturally (Willard, 2010). Mindfulness DMT activities provide a body- and action-based approach to focus one's attention and build concentration skills on a primary, kinesthetic level. In DMT the mover is asked to observe and listen to his or her body's actions and sensations as they naturally unfold.

"Now I am excited in a calm way" demonstrates Suri's ability to reflect on the path we took to gain this awareness. Her ability to lead us through this transformation during the session is at the heart of my Ways of Seeing methodology (Tortora, 2006, 2010b). In Ways of Seeing, my psychotherapeutic dance/movement theoretical framework and the title of my training program for practitioners, and Dancing Dialogue, my wellness creative dance program for all ages, both parents and children learn new ways to experience, understand, think about, and "see" themselves and each other. Feelings are explored through a creative process that includes physical discoveries using dance, movement, breath and body awareness, relaxation, music and art making, in addition to verbal processing. Through these methods participants actively explore their personal life experiences from a place of wonderment and acceptance. In mindfulness awareness attention is deliberately placed on an object or sensation to create a broad floodlight of illumination on the investigation process (Olendzki, 2010). This "spacious stance of awareness enables the activity of the mind to come, go and fade away without interference" (Kaiser Greenland, 2012, p. 5). In the Ways of Seeing mindfulness approach, the body and movement become the focus of attention, thereby creating a concrete, kinesthetic method for children to investigate their experiences and to become aware of, respond to, and express themselves from a place of thoughtful, compassionate action.

Emphasis on the body and embodied experience are at the core of these and other similar programs. These programs were developed from the principles of DMT, neuroscience research, infant mental health research, and knowledge of early childhood development. The premise of Ways of Seeing/Dancing Dialogue is the presence of a circular continuum between the mind, body, and emotions (Tortora, 2013, 2015). *Mind* refers to our thoughts, ideas, self-talk, and perceptions. *Body* relates to felt-sense experiences, involving kinesthetic and multisensory levels, including how it feels to inhabit and move in our bodies. Body sensations occur within a spectrum from very actively and energetically moving the whole body or one body part to complete stillness. Emotions are at first physical sensations that we then explain to ourselves on an expressive feeling level; they influence our overall feeling state. Discoveries and insights about the self can occur at any point along this circular continuum, for every thought has a corresponding emotional response and bodily sensation.

Often we register one element along this continuum without connecting to others equally present. This oversight is especially evident with children who tend to be kinetic, physical, concrete learners. These children respond to stimuli in their environment, or from within themselves, but often without an in-depth inner awareness about what is motivating their behaviors. Through mindfulness DMT activities, children begin to make connections between their thoughts, actions, and feelings while developing their emotional regulatory capacity. Physically exploring their feelings allows children to consciously experience feelings for which they may, at first, not have words. They may enter at any point of the circular cycle of attending to their thoughts, body sensations, and emotional feelings through a process involving: embodying the action; followed by attending to that action; and then pausing to reflect more fully about their experience, creating an action–attend–pause sequence. Encouraging children to show their thoughts and feelings through physical activity (while attuning and staying aware of their actions during the action–attend phase) enables them to go more deeply into an embodied exploration of their thoughts, sensations, and feelings. During the pause phase, the children stop and describe their experience verbally and/or through drawings and then reenter their physical explorations. Through this process children learn to train their attention from a place of increased understanding about how their actions, thoughts, and feelings work together. They develop the ability to attend to their inner experiences and *pause* rather then immediately reacting from impulse.

Suri first came to see me due to her "out-of-control" behaviors. Though her high energy, inventive thinking style, and fun play schemes attracted positive attention from her peers, her strong-willed nature was sometimes experienced as bossy. At home she could quickly shift from bubbly to defiant and was prone to tantrums when she felt misunderstood. These tantrums often escalated to full-blown violent outbursts, during which Suri became verbally and physically volatile. When she first came for treatment, Suri felt defensive about her out-of-control behavior, stating that her anger was justified.

Not Simply a Body Language Dictionary

In my first session with Suri and her mother Kendra, I listened intently to the specific words they each chose to describe Suri's behavior. Simultaneously, I intently observed *how* they explained their experience. By paying particular attention to their verbal tone, phrasing, word choice, and emphasis, I carefully observed the quality of their nonverbal dialogue.

Attending to the gestures and actions as clients describe their experience of each other is the key to my approach and a core DMT principle. In DMT, we believe that every action has a potential meaning. It is our job to look behind, under, over, and through these nonverbal expressions to glean their deeper meaning. This is not simply a "body language" approach; there is no dictionary in which you can look up the meaning of a particular body action. Our personal gestures are not one-size-fits-all. Following the Laban Movement Analysis (LMA) method in which all dance/movement therapists are trained, we consider the specific details of *how* a person is gesturing and moving (Bartenieff & Lewis 1980; Laban, 1976). We call these details "movement qualities." There are four movement quality categories: time, force, flow, and space. Everyone has his or her own way of combining these qualities even in the same action. That is what makes us unique. Just like we each have our own handwriting signature, we also have our own movement signature. How we uniquely cluster these qualitative elements, and which elements we use most, define our movement signature. Learning how to see these qualities is central to being able to respond in the moment from a place of mindful awareness. These four qualities, known as *effort qualities* in the LMA system, create the feeling tone of the action, setting the mood in the immediate moment. Understanding these effort qualities provides a whole toolbox of ways to connect to everyone in your life and to better understand yourself.

Without even knowing it, you already pay attention to these qualitative differences in your friends and your family, and even the salesperson at the grocery store. Not only do you pay attention to these qualities in others, your own actions can be unconscious *re*actions to the subtle details of their actions.

Actually, we are born with the capacity to imitate and connect. Meltzoff and his colleagues discovered that babies are able to imitate facial and manual gestures of adults who are playing with them as early as 42 minutes after birth! (Meltzoff & Moore, 1977; Meltzoff & Brooks, 2007) call this active intermodal mapping (AIM), for it reveals that babies are already able to take in information from one domain, for example, visually, and translate it to another domain, physical enactment, in a moment's time. In essence, babies are wired to associate their own actions with actions they observe from others. And, the most amazing part of this is that this nonverbal way of communicating happens in a split second and is going on all the time with all of us. It is the subtle details within our body actions that create and express our feelings and the feelings we pick up in others. As trained Laban movement analysts like to say, *we simply bring to conscious awareness what we are all unconsciously doing, all the time*—sounding rather like mindfulness teachers.

Think about waiting in the kitchen for your son to come home from school after taking an important exam. You're sitting at the table trying to read the newspaper, but you can't really concentrate, as worries about your child's day keep popping up in your mind. You feel jumpy inside; you notice that you're tapping your fingers on the table and you don't even remember when you started to do it. You try to take a deep breath and may even shake your body out, but you still feel that tension in your stomach. Suddenly you hear the front door open and you jump up. This is where the nonverbal dialogue between us and someone else begins. I call it the Dancing Dialogue. Even the way your child enters at the doorway is a tip-off about how he is feeling. And your immediate unspoken connection to him through his body actions is evident even before you see his facial expression.

Your son bursts into the room throwing his backpack on the chair in one sweeping action and runs directly up to you giving you a big, strong hug. You see this behavior, and you instantaneously feel it inside and interpret his meaning without missing a beat. Without even purposely thinking about it, you simply know that his quick entrance (time quality), the carefree sweeping action of his backpack (flow quality), his run directly toward you (space quality), and his strong hug (force quality) mean that he aced his test, and that knife cutting in your stomach immediately shifts into an excited fluttering as you return his hug with a strong squeeze.

But wait one moment! This whole scene could have a completely different interpretation with another child and parent pair. That quick entrance, tossed backpack, and the race toward you could also indicate despair and defeat. The sharp stabbing in your stomach turns into a flash of tension through your whole body as you embrace your son. How do you know which interpretation is accurate? Here is where the uniqueness of our personal movement signatures, your intimate knowledge of your child, and the open-minded approach to nonverbal interpretation come into play. That quick rush into the room for the first child expresses excitement but for the second is anxiety. The sweeping throw of the backpack exudes a carefree attitude in the first scenario and defeated abandonment in the second. Running directly toward you and receiving a strong hug shouts out triumph for the first child, but conveys a need for comfort in the second. The different interpretations are directly related to the way the movement qualities are clustered together, coupled within the context of each mover's own experiences. In LMA, nonverbal movement interpretation never occurs in isolation but always within relationship to the particulars of each individual in the immediate environment. Here is where skill in staying attuned to yourself and your child in the moment, a core mindfulness concept, comes into play. Maintaining this attunement may at first seem like a daunting task, for it can be very difficult to stop the rush of thoughts and ideas, especially when you are dealing with those you love.

The Self as an Open Vessel

In DMT we attune to the whole self by imagining the body as a container able to receive, hold, and release information freely and safely, as needed. This posture enables us to be open to and mindful of the underlying meaning of the mover. We first take several clear deep breaths to get in touch with our physical sensations. Next we clear our minds of thoughts and associations by imagining sweeping them through and out of the whole body. We then visualize and sense the body as a clear open vessel ready to receive. In this receptive stance we simultaneously observe the nonverbal qualities of the movers with whom we are working, while noticing our mental thoughts and associations, the emotions that arise, and the physical sensations that pass through the body. In essence, we place ourselves in a mindful state of being, present in the immediate moment, watching, feeling, and listening to both ourselves and the other person.

Let's return to the first session I had with Suri and Kendra to put these descriptions into action. As *you* read this section, place yourself in a mindful stance, aware of your own thoughts, feelings, and sensations while reading the passage.

We begin our conversation sitting on the floor. As Kendra shares her experience of Suri's tantrums, Suri curls her body into a ball and hugs her knees, rocking forward and backward in a short, quick, pulsing rhythm. Her facial expression is sad as she stares intently at her mother. Kendra sits tall and erect with her hands held on her lap, as if she were at once holding herself and pulling away. Looking directly at Suri with an expression of deep concern in her eyes, her mouth is tense, as if her words were being held momentarily before they slip out. Her voice trails up and down, pausing and creating an up-and-down seesaw phrasing quality. During one of these pauses, Suri suddenly flings her arms and legs open wide, as if throwing herself to the ground, and then catches herself by extending her arms and pressing her palms into the floor. Leaning forward toward her mother, she interjects, "You promised you would be at the bus, but you weren't and I had to walk home! You weren't there!" I feel intense anguish in my own body, as if my stomach were kicked, and I suddenly find myself taking a deeper breath. Kendra responds by pulling her body back and up even more, as she tries to explain that she was delayed by a necessary phone call, but actually met Suri on her way home. I experience despair and weightiness in my whole being. In this open-vessel receptive state, as I watch Suri lean toward her mother while holding herself up on the floor and pleading, "You weren't there," the awareness that Suri is adopted sweeps through my mind. Simultaneously, I feel Kendra's exasperation regarding how hard she is working to juggle taking care of her children and her household while also managing her own business. The fleeting thought "There is just not enough time in the day" appears as I resonate with Kendra's erect stance, seeming to be holding it all together with determination.

Accepting each of their statements and postures as their personal truths, without passing judgment, I shape my own body stance to create a soft, supportive container; I take a deep, calming breath and look directly at them, one at a time. I hold my gaze with each of them for a moment as a way to nonverbally tell them, "I see you, I am listening, I will hold your needs within me." Taking this time to silently acknowledge them both is important. As popular wisdom asserts, "It is not what you say but what you do that matters" and "What we don't say is as important as what we do say." Becoming more consciously aware of how our own and others' nonverbal actions *speak* can effectively enhance communication.

I look directly at Suri with a warm expression and simply state, "Suri, I wonder if you were getting excited to see Mom and became very disappointed when she wasn't there as you first got off the bus." I then turn to Kendra and say, "Sometimes no matter how caringly we prepare, a last-minute surprise can change our plans in an instant. I bet you really wanted to be at the bus stop on time to pick up Suri." Both Suri and Kendra nod their heads yes as their bodies visibly relax. Even the air in the room seems to feel lighter. Using simple language affirms each of their experiences and is the first step to their feeling safe enough to share their deeper feelings. I suggest that we create a dance that depicts how we are feeling right now, and Suri jumps up. "Yes, let's dance!" she shouts joyfully. We each take a turn adding dance moves to create a playful "dancing sentence" that renews their loving connection. Suri starts with a joyful full-body bouncing action. As she gazes at Kendra in a loving way, she slightly modifies the speed of her bounce to support her mom's ability to follow her more accurately. Kendra goes next, adding a diagonal stretch with each arm reaching toward her daughter. Suri giggles with delight. When it is my turn, I step forward, bringing us closer together in our circle. We reach our arms up, creating a *V* for *victory* gesture and a full-body triumphant stance, as we jump up in unison.

The Brain–Mind–Heart Connection

DMT developed the concept of attending to body sensations from a state of receptive listening as a way to attune and provide caring support to the people with whom we work. This approach was developed in the 1940s, but would take almost 40 years for science to catch up. In the 1980s and 1990s Esther Thelen, a psychologist studying the role of movement in early childhood development, discovered that it is not the brain that directs the body but rather the body that directs the mind (Thelen & Smith, 1994). We learn about ourselves and the world around us through our experience of moving. In the 1990s more exciting research found that our actions and experiences stimulate the types of connections our brain cells make (Siegel, 1999, 2007, 2010). What we do affects how we think and who we become.

Even more interestingly, scientists in Parma, Italy, discovered that when we watch someone physically doing something, we are actually mapping these same neural connections in our own brains. They learned that our actions and experiences play a role in our ability to respond empathically toward others. The brain cell activity that provides a neurological explanation for our human ability to experience empathy is called the "mirror neuron system" (Gallese, 2009; Gallese, Eagle, & Migone, 2007; Iacoboni, 2011). It has been a hot research topic since the 1990s, sometimes referred to as the "decade of the brain." The invention of many new methods of studying the brain has enabled scientists to better understand how our mind, body, and emotions are all connected, both within ourselves and between each other.

This early research has led to a fascinating burst of interest in how images, imagination, and multisensory stimuli (including music, dance, and art) all contribute to how we think, feel, heal, and even how we create a sense of community. Iacoboni, one of the pioneers of this new area of neuroscience states: "Mirror neurons seem to be a bridge between our thinking, feeling, and actions—and between people. This may be the neurological basis for human connectedness, which we urgently need in the world today" (in Freeman, 2013, p. 2). In short, we are hardwired to connect. The specific way we cluster our actions together communicates our deepest thoughts and feelings and plays a key role in how we feel and connect to others. Connection is at the heart of collaboration. Collaboration is the heart of communities that are supportive, loving, and kind. If we are lucky, this sense of loving, kind community support actually begins at the beginning of our lives, through our early experiences with our parents.

Creative Expression versus Mayhem

The neuroscientist Stephen Porges (2004, 2011) has contributed significantly to our understanding of how our early *experiences* of social connection are linked to our sense of emotional, physical, and personal safety on a neurological level. Porges has spent decades studying the fight–flight–freeze mechanisms of the autonomic nervous system as they relate to the development of primary attachment, social engagement, and positive social behavior. He found that our ability to feel relaxed and safe on a neurological level develops through the intimate relationships that are established in early infancy with our parents and other significant people who care for us. Our automatic nervous system circuitry instinctively, and out-of-conscious awareness, detects safety, danger, or life threatening situations. Porges's term "neuroception" (2004, 2011), formed from the two words *neurology* and *perception*, highlights his concept that the autonomic nervous system must perceive a sense of safety to support optimal social interactions. Neuroception is distinguished from perception to emphasize that this attentive awareness of social safety is instinctive and spontaneous, not a cognitive thought-out process (Porges, 2009). Our ability to feel safe or not is a *somatic* (body-based) phenomenon (Ogden, Minton & Pain, 2006).

I have worked for over 30 years with babies and children, including those who are typically developing and those with a variety of challenges, such as attention-deficit/hyperactivity disorder (ADHD), sensory processing disorder, Tourette syndrome, autism and Asperger syndrome, and those who are medically ill. Regardless of their condition, these children all share a common need: to feel safe enough to calm down and share their deepest feelings. As Porges (2004, 2011) has pointed out, we all share this need. Learning how to use movement and dance activities to create a neuroceptively safe environment for children starts by attentively watching and learning each child's nonverbal gestures and actions that signify comfort or distress. These movement cues comprise the child's nonverbal signature. Once this is clear, I modify my own actions to dialogue within the child's comfort zone, as indicated by his or her nonverbal vocabulary, and I create movement-based activities that enable the child to explore and expand this vocabulary. Approaching the child's movement vocabulary from a state of mindful, attentive listening enables me, as the DMT therapist, to create an atmosphere of care and respect rather then immediate judgment and punitive behavioral correction.

I have spent years watching children enter my dance space with so much pent-up energy that they need to literally bounce off the walls and run in circles. I enable them to do this while I attentively watch and even join them, which turns this potentially disorganizing activity into a communicative act. During this dancing movement dialogue, together we determine places to slow down, speed up, and pause, spontaneously creating organization and purpose to the child's embodied actions. Dancing and moving in this way facilitates mindful awareness on a felt-sense level. In the moving moments, the child experiences his or her mind–body–emotional connection in ways that enhance self-awareness and knowledge. A core focus of the Ways of Seeing/Dancing Dialogue program is to create an emotionally and physically safe environment that enables children to use dance and movement activities to express what is driving them. Supporting children's freedom of expression without total mayhem is a learned skill. Anyone who has ever tried to lead a group of children knows that total chaos is inevitable when children are free to move however they want.

There are many reasons pandemonium can occur during creative movement activities. The top three on my list point to the overabundance of sedentary activities children now engage in, the follow-the-leader tendency of children, and the power of movement to stimulate all the senses. With less recess time and heightened academic pressures even in the earliest grades, children are spending more and more time in sedentary positions during school. Instructional activities continue for many children after school. In addition, most children spend a startling amount of time staring at screen media—both an intellectually and physically passive focus. Young children need to engage in physical activities that encourage them to interact and problem-solve with their peers as a way to stimulate development on five key levels: social, intellectual, physical, emotional, and communicative.

We are wired to connect with others, and children naturally follow each other, especially when they latch onto another child who looks like he or she is doing something fun. And moving around wildly, particularly if the children have been sitting for a long time, definitely starts out as good-natured fun for most children. Even though children today are engaging in more sedentary activities, it is very difficult to keep them sitting quietly. More significantly, lively movement activities can be overstimulating or provocative. Dance and movement-based activities are very powerful, stimulating all the child's senses. Some children, especially those with ADHD, rev up rather than slow down when tired. Controlling physical impulses or transforming them into meaningful expressions and monitoring when to verbalize thoughts are skills children learn through practice and experience. This is where the mirror neuron system, body and emotional regulation, and neuroception intersect with the experience of the moving body in a potentially powerful way through mindful-based dance and movement activities. Helping children discover the balance between self-expression and control occurs by providing enough guidance such that the dance and movement activities have some structure without choreographing exactly what the children must do. Letting the children participate in how the structure of the activity is organized and giving them room to explore their own ideas within the activity keep them focused and eager to be involved and fuels their creativity.

Zipping Up, Bubbles, Speed Spiral™, and More: Dance/Movement Activities That Promote Mindful Awareness

It's 3:30 Friday afternoon. The kindergarten–first graders burst into my studio to begin a Dancing Dialogue class. A lively song with a strong beat fills the air, and they immediately take flight. Some skip, others hop, and still others race to the back of the room and roll around on the floor. Duets and trios naturally evolve as friends join the class. They shout out "This is medium speed" as they become more deeply engaged in their own dance-step combinations. The song changes, and now a melodic waltz takes over; the kids immediately shift gears, gliding and sliding across the room. Pirouetting couples appear, while others, like a flock of birds, soar and dip through the air. "Slow speed" they shout out.

They know the routine. They know how to respond to the tempo suggestions by listening to their bodies and sensing how the changing tempos make them feel. Many of these children began dancing with me when they were less than 2 years old, in dance classes with their parents. In those classes parents learn how to identify their own reactions to their babies, quiet down their assumptions, and watch their babies' emerging actions as communications. Following their babies' leads, they attune to these actions, creating spontaneous, improvised dances based on each baby's budding movement vocabulary. As parents get to know the deeper meaning of their babies' moves, their relationships strengthen, and each baby's unique expressivity blossoms.

Between ages of 3 and 4, toddlers start to share their own expressive nature through dance. In one recent parent–toddler class, a superhero dance theme emerges as the boys leap, run, jump, climb, and roll on an imaginary pirate ship. A verbal and physical "roughhouse" tussle arises as they suddenly realize that they are *all* good-guy superheroes, and no one is willing to become a bad guy. In an attempt to resolve the conflict, their parents begin to reprimand and direct their play. I step in and ask everyone to take a moment to breathe and zip up. Immediately the boys quiet down as they get in touch with their embodied sensations and are able to discuss their dilemma, coming up with a bad-guy turn-taking system that satisfies everyone.

From age 4 the children enter Dancing Dialogue creative dance classes without their parents. In these classes they further develop their sense of self as expressive movers through numerous dance and body awareness activities. Following a mindful awareness approach, the children listen to their bodies as a way of communicating with their minds; in the process, they discover their emotions. The children enter mindful awareness through attention to their moving bodies. Throughout all the activities, the children sense their immediate thoughts and images, sensations and feelings, while they move and then discuss their experience when we pause the action. These embodied responses are shared with their partners or the whole group. They feel their body sensations and attend to their emotional reactions through a creative process that includes responding to music and stories as well as their own storytelling, artwork, and art making. The curriculum emphasizes supporting children to develop a healthy self and body image; learn the importance of listening to and believing in their inner selves; feel confident in sharing their thoughts and needs; and listen respectively and with compassion to each other. The children learn that dancing is a way of speaking without words. Any movement they contribute to the dance is a meaningful contribution and a form of communication.

With this experience in their background, many of the children in my Friday dance class of kindergarten–first graders are very animated, self-expressive movers. About 10–15 minutes into their own explorations, I gather the children together for a whole-group activity. I never start class expecting them to focus immediately as one group. Rather, when they first enter I give them time to transition from their school day, connect to how they are feeling in the immediate moment, and regroup with their friends in small clusters. This opening exploration gives me time to assess the mood of individual children and the group as a whole. Though I have a general idea of the activities I have planned for that day, how these activities will actually unfold is completely dependent on the students' presenting moods and interests.

We gather in a circle in the center of the room and the children zip up their center. *Zipping up* is an activity I designed many years ago specifically to help children center their energy and align their bodies by creating tactile awareness of their vertical core. In this activity they place one hand at their tailbone and the other hand in the corresponding location in the front of their torso. Taking a deep, slow breath, the children slide their hands up their centers and elongate their torsos as if they are pulling up a zipper. Keeping their torsos tall as they exhale, they spread their arms open, out, and down, placing them at their side, or if sitting, on the chair or floor. Maintaining erect torsos and placing their hands down, rather then concaving their bodies and plopping their hands down, is an essential aspect of this activity. The felt experience of internal body space that comes with this action, combined with slow and deep breaths, develops body awareness and has a naturally calming effect.

Asking the children to follow the gentle, resonating speed of a musical instrument, such as a rain stick or tone bar chime, as they zip up deepens the quieting effect of this activity and develops their concentration. To further develop preschool- and elementary-age children's concentration and body attunement, I ask them to roll down their body centers, vertebra by vertebra, toward the ground to the speed of the seeds moving in the rain stick or the resonating sound of the tone bar. The heightened focusing component of this activity is that the children must follow the slow sound of the instrument, arriving in a crouched position only when they no longer hear the music. They return to standing with the same instruction.

Once the children have established the felt sense of their cores, they extend their arms out to draw "bubbles" around their bodies. A bubble, known in the LMA world as the *kinesphere*, is the personal space around each of us that is an arm's distance away from our centers. Defining our personal bubble space is an important skill in learning how to actively engage with others. This ability draws on our proprioceptive senses—the multisensory system that enables us to detect where our bodies are in space and to define our somatic boundaries. Managing how we move our limbs and bodies supports personal body coordination and our ability to move safely and in coordination with others. This important physical skill also has implications for how well we are able to communicate and engage with others.

In class children draw imaginary bubbles at varying distances around themselves, depending on how much physical space they actually have. Tight bubbles are drawn when they are sitting or standing close to each other, and wide arm-length bubbles are drawn if they have lots of room. There are many ways to develop this activity for any age group. I have adapted this activity even with 2-year-olds and their parents. The salient component for all ages is that each person's bubble is separate and does not touch another person's bubble. Children decorate the inside of their bubbles with anything they want. Often it is rainbows and hearts for girls, and superheroes and "boy toys" for boys. Next the children test their bubbles with each other by maintaining their extended arm lengths as they approach classmates, one by one, and step away when they are about to touch. Once everyone has tested their bubbles in this more subdued action, more vigorous dance activities begin.

It is amazing how effective this activity is. Actively moving through space stimulates our vestibular sense. Located in the inner ear, this sense has many properties, including visual–motor coordination, balance, and the ability to sense our bodies moving through space. It is the proprioceptive and vestibular senses working together that enable us to move without falling or bumping into things or people. Physically learning how to move with others in the same space in an aware, mindful manner is a natural step toward being respectful and becoming sensitive to others emotionally, physically, and thoughtfully. Sensing their classmates' personal space is a concrete way children learn to respect and dialogue with each other's presence and self-expression.

One dance game the children particularly like is the color-coded Speed Spiral that Suri used to shift her over-the-top energy to a calmer, more organized and focused state in the opening vignette. I developed the Speed Spiral to provide children with a concrete way to identify their energy level and to improve their ability to regulate that energy from very active or out of control to calm and peaceful. I have observed that many children, especially those with ADHD, sensory processing disorders, or autism spectrum disorders, have a very difficult time shifting through decelerating levels of activity. Very often these children become more disorganized and dysregulated with increased fatigue or upset. Once they get into a "superfast" tempo, children often cannot modulate their behaviors, but rather rev up their activity levels until they collapse. This depleted state is their attempt at feeling calm and meditative. The Speed Spiral is an effective tool to help all children explore the felt experience of accelerating and decelerating their energy in an organized way. Experiencing the shift step by step, from superfast to fast to medium to slow, is fun and rewarding for all children. For children who have difficulty with focus and regulation, this activity is often the first to begin the process of rebuilding their confidence. An amazing shift happens once these children begin to actually feel themselves moving their bodies with more purposeful volition. This felt body experience opens their ability to reflect on what it feels like when they are not in control. Their relief and pride are evident as they begin to feel more capable. As is evident in Suri's story, experiencing the mind–body–emotion circular continuum strengthens a child's full awareness of his or her actions in the present moment.

Using a drum or a selection of music is a simple way to guide children's dance explorations as they move from slow, to medium, to fast and superfast. Once the children are able to differentiate the different tempos clearly, I let them take turns leading each other with the drumbeat. As the children move through the space in tune to the music, they explore changing direction from forward to backward to side to side; levels of space from high to medium and low; and adjusting to the melody and syncopated rhythmic changes of the music. At times I ask them to partner and play "follow the leader" by mirroring their classmates' actions to learn about their classmates' feelings in that moment of dance expression. In DMT "mirroring" is defined as following the exact actions as well as the emotional feeling tone of the actions; it supports true embodiment rather then simply a mimicking of actions. Mimicking creates a negative experience of being copied to make fun of a child. To add more mindful awareness, I intermittently stop the music, have children listen to their body sensations, and ask them to describe what is going on for them in that moment from a mind–body–emotion perspective. Other times in this paused mode, I ask them to zip up as a way to demonstrate their skill in controlling their bodies in an instant.

To further develop their focusing ability and awareness of each other (and their confidence), I have them create a balancing pose. First they master balancing on one leg with the other leg extended to the front, side, or back, or placing the foot of the extended leg on the inner thigh of the standing leg. In this skill children learn how to sense the relationship between stability and mobility, which relates to being steady and centered yet flexible. I explain to the children that the trick to balancing is to first focus their eyes on a specific place in front of them. Once their eyes are focused forward, they direct their attention to the sensation of shifting their body weight over whatever body parts they choose to hold steady. Then the other body parts can be extended in a spatial range that enables them to maintain whole-body balance. Once the children are able to do this, I lead them through a sequence of balancing poses that requires them to shift their body weight, mobilizing different parts of their bodies through space while maintaining their balance. The children take turns leading and teaching each other their balancing poses. Elementary-age children enjoy having contests to see who can hold their poses the longest, and they even playfully distract their balancing peers—thereby providing an opportunity for their classmates to practice sustained concentration despite interruptions.

Conclusion: Adding Dance and Movement to Mindful Awareness Practices for Children

Ways of Seeing/Dancing Dialogue programs are different from typical dance classes in their overall focus, their tone, and their perspective of mindful awareness. The mindful dance, movement, and body awareness activities in these programs open children's perceptions to the connection between their embodied experiences and their behaviors. Through focusing on embodied experience, the programs bring conscious awareness to each child's nonverbal expression on sensory, kinesthetic, somatic, and emotional levels. Feelings (e.g., anxiety, agitation, love, overwhelm, distraction, fear, joy, compassion) are often initially experienced outside of conscious awareness. With mindful movement, these feelings are felt and expressed through embodied experience. Children explore the mind–body–emotion connection through the core curricular components of attuned attention, reflective awareness, and conscious embodied engagement. The children listen to their body-based felt sense in a way that speaks to their minds and helps them attune to their underlying emotions. Over time, the children build mental–somatic–emotional awareness; as they become more aware of the relationships between their thoughts, feelings, and behaviors, their self-regulatory capacities improve.

By using simple statements like "Dancing is a way of talking without words," "The body speaks to the mind," and "Any action can be a dancing move," the children learn how to attend to their feelings as they are felt and expressed through their actions. The tone of the classes is distinct from typical dance classes, which focus on learning specific dance techniques. Drawing on individual interests, each child contributes his or her own dance moves. The children try on each other's moves with respect, regarding the movements as each child's unique, personal expression. In this process of cooperative learning, the children build relationship and collaboration skills as they express their classmates' creative dance contributions.

Ways of Seeing/Dancing Dialogue activities provide an active, experientially based learning environment that supports the five concepts of social–emotional learning put forth by the educational advocacy organization Collaborative for Academic, Social, and Emotional Learning (2013). The five concepts are self-regulation of emotions and behaviors, self-awareness, social awareness, responsive decision making, and relationship skills developed through teamwork. The key components of Ways of Seeing/Dancing Dialogue facilitate active social–emotional learning. These key components are attending to feelings as they are felt through body actions; understanding the body is an expressive tool; learning to balance on and off center; developing strength and flexibility; responding to the expressive and rhythmic components of music; and attuning to each other by working in partnership. It is this shared learning experience that fosters the core tenets of mindfulness awareness practice: balance, flexibility, and attunement to self and others.

As Susan Kaiser Greenland states in Inner Kids, her mindful awareness program for children, mindfulness is the process of bringing awareness to what is happening in, to, and around us in the present moment (Kaiser Greenland, 2010). This awareness is emphasized in the Inner Kids new ABCs of Attention, Balance, and Compassion, taught through specific activities involving eight strategies: stopping, focusing, choosing, quieting, seeing, reframing, caring, and connecting (Kaiser Greenland, personal correspondence, 2012).

Movement and dance provide another medium in which children can actively explore these strategies through dancing, moving, observing, pausing, respecting their own and their peers' self-expressive actions, and interactive dance-play. These processes teach children how to redirect emotional energy into thoughtful self-expressions that they share with others. Children learn how their nonverbal style conveys their feelings within the context of creative dance arts exploration. Rather than reacting impulsively, they make connections between their thoughts, actions, and feelings and build their capacity to reflect on their inner experiences and outer behaviors. This awareness extends to others as the children use their bodies to actively explore each other's feelings from a place of curiosity, acceptance, kindness, and compassion. Ultimately, they learn how to listen to and quiet their minds and bodies through active and fun movement exploration.

REFERENCES

Bartenieff, I., & Lewis, D. (1980). *Body movement: Coping with the environment*. New York: Gordon & Breach.

Collaborative for Academic, Social, and Emotional Learning (CASEL). (2013). Skills-competencies. Retrieved June 25, 2013, from *http://casel.org/why-it-matters/what-is-sel/skills-competencies*.

Freeman, J. (2013, May 8). The neuroscience at the heart of learning and leading. Retrieved from *www.forbes.com/sites/ashoka/2013/05/08/the-neuroscience-at-the-heart-of-learning-and-leading*.

Gallese, V. (2009). Mirror neurons, embodied simulation, and the neural basis of social identification. *Psychoanalytic Dialogues, 19*(5), 519–536.

Gallese, V., Eagle, M., & Migone, P. (2007). Intentional attunement: Mirror neurons and the underpinnings of interpersonal relations. *Journal of the American Psychological Association, 55*(1), 131–176.

Iacoboni, M. (2011). *The Oxford handbook of social neuroscience*. New York: Oxford University Press.

Kaiser Greenland, S. (2010). *The mindful child: How to help your kid manage stress and become kinder, happier and more compassionate*. New York: Free Press.

Kaiser Greenland, S. (2012). *Zero to Three handout: Overview* [Inner Kids manuals]. Los Angeles: Zero to Three Training Institute.

Laban, R. (1976). *The language of movement*. Boston: Plays.

Meltzoff, A. N., & Brooks, R. (2007). Intersubjectivity before language: Three windows on preverbal sharing. In S. Bråten (Ed.), *On being moved: From mirror neurons to empathy* (pp. 149–174). Philadelphia: John Benjamins.

Meltzoff, A. N., & Moore, M. K. (1977). Imitation of facial and manual gestures by human neonates. *Science, 198*(4312), 75–78.

Ogden, P., Minton, K., & Pain, C. (2006). *Trauma and the body: A sensorimotor approach to psychotherapy*. New York: Norton.

Olendzki, A. (2010). *Unlimited mind: The radically experiential psychology of Buddhism*. Somerville, MA: Wisdom.

Porges, S. (2004). Neuroception: A subconscious system for detecting threats and safety. *Zero to Three, 24*(5), 19–24.

Porges, S. (2011). *The polyvagal theory: Neurophysiological foundations of emotions, attachment, communication, and self-regulation*. New York: Norton.

Siegel, D. (1999). *The developing mind*. New York: Guilford Press.

Siegel, D. (2007). *The mindful brain: Reflection and attunement in the cultivation of well-being*. New York: Norton.

Siegel, D. (2010). *The mindful therapist: A clinician's guide to mindsight and neural integration*. New York: Norton.

Thelen, E., & Smith, L. (1994). *A dynamic systems approach to the development of cognition and action.* Cambridge, MA: MIT Press.

Tortora, S. (2006). *The Dancing Dialogue: Using the communicative power of movement with young children.* Baltimore, MD: Brookes.

Tortora, S. (2010a). Ways of seeing: An early childhood integrative approach for parents and babies. *Clinical Social Work Journal, 38,* 37–50.

Tortora, S. (2010b). From the dance studio to the classroom: Translating the clinical dance movement psychotherapy experience into a school context. In V. Karkou (Ed.), *Art therapies in schools: Research and practice* (pp. 27–42). London: Jessica Kingsley.

Tortora, S. (2013). The essential role of the body in the parent–infant relationship: Nonverbal analysis of attachment. In J. Bettmann & D. Friedman (Eds.), *Attachment-based clinical social work with children and adolescents* (pp. 141–164). New York: Springer.

Tortora, S. (2015). The importance of being seen: Winnicott, dance movement psychotherapy and the embodied experience. In M. Spelman & F. Thomson-Salo (Eds.), *The Winnicott tradition: Lines of development—evolution of theory and practice over the decades* (pp. 259–272). London: Karnac Books.

Willard, C. (2010). *Child's mind.* Berkeley, CA: Parallax.

CHAPTER 12

Mindfulness in Sports

Amy Saltzman

Standing at the chalk box, she dips her hands in the cool smooth fluff, forms it into cakes and let's them sift through her construction worker's calloused hands. The metal and wood structure of the uneven bars taunts her with images of ghost gymnasts accomplishing her goals.

The bars giggle as she mounts, clanking and rattling with her motion. She pushes her body away from the upper bar, and directs it in a pendulum's arc toward the lower bar. At the instant of contact her oyster body snaps shut, its treasure inside. With her nose to her knees, and the bar imbedded in her hinged hips, she circles and snaps open again, stretching to crucify herself on the upper bar. Thud. Her landing mocks her efforts. Again and again she mounts. Each time her pendulum body swings and falls in a dull, tick-tock monotony.

The wine-colored bruises on her hips ache and throb, yet she chalks her blistered hands again. Echoes in her mind of an old coach's wise words about plateaus soothe her frustrations.

Once more she swings and falls. Perhaps tomorrow the chalk clouds she claps from her hands will have a silver lining.

The passage above was written in 1981, when I was a junior in high school, long before I had ever heard the term *mindfulness*. Yet it demonstrates that, unbeknown to me, gymnastics was my first mindfulness practice. Beneath the poetic language, the story conveys an athlete's moment-to-moment awareness of her physical sensations, thoughts, and feelings.

Since my days as a young athlete, I have gone through many changes; the most relevant has been the deliberate cultivation of a long-standing mindfulness practice. In this chapter we explore intentionally supporting young athletes through training their minds and hearts, as well as their bodies. This type of mind–heart training is an essential, and all too often overlooked, component of athletic performance.

My view is informed by many factors. As a young gymnast with minimal natural talent and unwavering commitment, I was coached by many competent and one truly exceptional gymnastics coach. At the age of 13, after suffering from multiple dislocations, I chose to have surgery on my right, and then my left, shoulder.

As a teen I was also privileged to support other athletes in different capacities. Throughout junior high and high school I coached very young, mostly adorable, gymnasts in the afternoons and on the weekends. Additionally, every day, during most of my junior year of high school, on my way from school to practice, I visited a friend and fellow gymnast who had been paralyzed in a fall from the high bar, in a rehabilitation hospital.

In college I earned a spot as a walk-on varsity gymnast at Stanford. After a series of injuries, fear set in and I chose to leave gymnastics. I subsequently became a competitive cyclist. In 1988 I was struck by a car while riding; fortunately, I had relatively minor injuries. Ultimately, it was this event that synchronistically led me to formal mindfulness practice.

In 1990, upon entering my third year of medical school, I became a devoted recreational athlete, running, cycling, developing a yoga practice, and, at the age of 40, I mindfully learned to snowboard.

I am currently a parent of two young athletes, one who is competing at the national level in cycling, and the other who recently chose to stop playing highly competitive soccer to pursue her love of the creative arts. Over the years I have had the privilege of sharing mindfulness with many young athletes from very young soccer players to Division 1 varsity athletes.

Most importantly, for the last 25 years, I have participated in weekly coaching with my mentor and transformational life coach, Georgina Lindsey. More than anything else this extraordinary, long-standing relationship has taught me that it is the skill, rigor, and compassion of a truly excellent coach that nurtures the best and truest in his or her players.

The Still Quiet Place

When I work with young athletes, I begin by helping them discover what I fondly refer to as the *Still Quiet Place* within. I invite them to follow the rhythm of their breath, *feeling* the in-breath, the stillness and quietness between the in-breath and the out-breath, then the out-breath, and the second stillness and quietness between the out-breath and the in-breath. This practice allows them to discover the stillness and quietness that exists not only between the breaths, but also underneath the breaths. After they have *experienced* the Still Quiet Place, also known as *pure awareness*, they discover that with practice, they can rest in this place. From the vantage point of stillness, they can watch their thoughts, feelings, and physical sensations (before practice and competition, during a time-out or halftime, after a miss or significant loss). Over time they come to understand that developing the capacity to rest in stillness and observe their experience can enhance their training, competitive performance, and their lives beyond athletics.

Take a moment now and rest your attention on your breath. See if you can *feel* the pure stillness and quietness, between, underneath, and throughout the breaths.

Bringing Awareness to the Body

A common mindfulness practice known as the *body scan* involves *slowly* sweeping attention up from the soles of the feet, *feeling the sensations* in the feet, the legs, and then gently upward through the torso, arms, neck, and head. This practice cultivates the ability to attend to both obvious and subtle sensations in particular areas of the body, as well as to the body as a whole.

The ability to *feel* the body from the inside out is essential for optimal athletic performance. As an athlete, the development of *proprioception*—knowing where the body is in space—is critical. Proprioception allows athletes to discern the subtle adjustments in weight, balance, power, trajectory, and timing that make the difference between a quick powerful start off the blocks and a slower sluggish one, between completing the triple salchow and landing on your backside, between the three pointer that goes swish and the one that bounces off the rim. The practice of bringing awareness to physical sensations with the body scan, with gentle yoga, and ultimately during training enhances proprioception, allowing athletes to naturally receive physical feedback and to fine-tune their execution.

Ultimately, this is the difference between athletes feeling "on," experiencing "flow," and being "in the zone" or feeling "off their game." In fact, a study from France indicated that optimal performance, or "flow," states reveal very similar characteristics to mindfulness and acceptance states. In flow experiences, elite swimmers described being particularly mindful and accepting of their bodily sensations. In another study, mindfulness and acceptance were integrated into a psychological skills training program for seven young elite golfers. Participants improved the efficacy of their training by seeking more relevant internal and external information. The program contributed to performance enhancement in competition (Bernier, Thienat, Codron, & Fournier, 2009). A simple way to incorporate this type of training into your practices is to have athletes warm up or cool down mindfully, in silence, at least once or twice a week. Encourage them to focus their full attention on the physical sensations in their bodies as they move through their usual skills and stretches. You might say something like the following:

"Today we are going to warm up in silence. As you do each activity, see if you can bring your full attention into your body, letting all the thoughts and feelings of the day drift into the background, and really feeling the stretching of your muscles, the stiffness or flexibility of your joints, your energy level, heart rate, breathing.

"However your body is today is fine; there is no need to change anything. Simply bring your full attention to becoming aware of your body as it is in this moment, feeling the stretch in your quad, seeing if you can stretch just a bit more, honoring your limit, not overstretching. Do your best to maintain this quality of body awareness during the rest of today's practice."

A quote from golfer Sam Snead, the winningest golfer in professional history, captures the essence of mindful body awareness: "I figure practice puts your brains in your muscles." In the context of this chapter the quote can be clarified as follows: Mindful athletic practice puts brains in your muscles and awareness in your body. This type of nuanced body awareness not only allows athletes to refine their performance, it is also important in preventing overtraining and overuse injuries. With experience, athletes can distinguish the typical fatigue and the normal aches and pains of training from the deep exhaustion of overtraining and the more insidious stabs and twinges of true injury. Combining mindful body awareness with training logs that document parameters such as workout type, time, intensity, as well as other sport specific measurements (e.g., pitch counts in baseball, power output in cycling) helps athletes find the optimal balance between high-intensity training and equally necessary rest and recovery. Ultimately, mindful body awareness helps an athlete maximize his or her physical abilities, and to simultaneously be aware of, and honor, the body's limits in the present moment.

Getting Your Head in the Game

All too often athletes are distracted by extraneous thoughts—the arguments they just had with their girlfriend, the history final, the last play, the score, a teammate's comment, a parent's scolding, a coach's outburst, or disappointed shake of the head. Once athletes have learned to rest their attention in the Still Quiet Place, they can begin to notice when and where their minds wander. When they become aware that their attention has wandered—whether during mindfulness practice, athletic training, or competition—they can return to the present moment by attending to the breath, the physical sensations in their bodies, or the sights and sounds of the competitive arena.

A wonderful example of mind wandering during competition can be found toward the end of the romantic comedy movie *Wimbledon*, in which the main character is mindlessly lost in thought before a crucial serve. Over time, with mindfulness, athletes can learn to use natural pauses in play to refocus their attention. For example, many tennis players, unlike the character in the movie, use the moments before the serve to breathe, bounce the ball, and bring their attention fully into the physical sensations, rhythms, and sounds of the present moment. In soccer, players can use throw-ins, penalty kicks, and kickoffs to briefly pause, breathe, check in with themselves, and scan the field to note the positions of their teammates and opponents, thus bringing their complete attention into the here and now.

> I try to stay in the moment and remind myself, ice is just ice.
> —POLINA EDMUNDS, 2014 Olympic figure skater (in Almond, 2014b)

> But what the players really needed was a way to quiet the chatter in their minds and focus on the business of winning basketball games. . . . [Mindfulness] is an easily accessible technique for quieting the restless mind and focusing attention on whatever is happening in the present moment. This is extremely useful for basketball players, who often have to make split-second decisions under enormous pressure.
> —PHIL JACKSON, champion NBA basketball player and coach (in Jackson, 2013, pp. 17–18)

> Thinking too much takes me out of my game and I forget what to do with my body.
> —JULIA MANCUSO, 2014 Olympic bronze medalist in women's super-combined downhill skiing (in Almond, 2014a)

You can introduce mindfulness of thoughts in many ways. One of my favorites is having athletes simply rest in the Still Quiet Place and then begin to attend to their thoughts like they are watching a parade. With instruction they can notice that thoughts come and go. They may note that some thoughts are small and shy, whereas others are loud and colorful. Over time they may begin to notice patterns in their thinking, and how their thinking is associated with, and influenced by, their physical sensations and feelings (emotions).

> You have to train your mind like you train your body.
> —BRUCE JENNER, Olympic gold medalist in the decathlon (in Afremow, 2013, p. 29)

Another way to introduce mindfulness of thoughts, or thought watching, after a tough practice, a significant loss, or even a major win (especially when you may be concerned that athletes are getting cocky) is to have your athletes blow bubbles. And yes, this practice can engage even the toughest defensive lineman. Give each athlete a container of bubbles. Invite them to simply blow bubbles in silence of a few moments. Then ask them the following questions:

"What is happening to the bubbles?" —*They are floating, they are resting, they pop.*
"Do they all pop?" —*Eventually.*
"Are they the same size?" —*No, some are smaller, some are bigger.*
"Do they move at the same speed?" —*No, some are faster, some are slower.*
"Does anyone have clumps of bubbles?" —*Yes.*
"Are bubbles like anything that happens in our minds?" —*Yes.* "Here is a hint: What do you call the thing above a cartoon character's head?" —*A thought bubble.*
"How are thoughts and bubbles similar?"—*They come and go. Some are bigger, some are smaller . . . .*
"Do all your thoughts eventually pop and disappear?"—*Yes.*

After this discussion, you might invite them to put down their bubbles, close their eyes, and watch their thoughts. You can, of course, prime their thinking by asking questions such as the following:

"What are your thoughts about the game?"
"How do you think you played?"
"How do you think the team played?"
"What are your thoughts about the upcoming competition?"
"Now can you let these thoughts go? And bring your attention into this moment, the chill in the air, the setting sun, your breath . . . ?"

Then you can either simply let their comments be or guide a discussion about the thoughts they noticed.

Following is an example of a discussion about a thought-watching practice with a group of fifth graders, excerpted from my book *Still Quiet Place: A Mindfulness Program for Children and Adolescents to Ease Stress and Difficult Emotions* (Saltzman, 2014):

One morning, while doing Thought Watching practice in a class where the majority of the boys had been rather skeptical of mindfulness, the boys noticed that many of their thoughts were about the basketball game they'd be playing that afternoon. They had lost the previous game, and now they were up against a team they thought was better than they were. Many of them were worried about losing, playing poorly, and letting their teammates down. . . . They wanted to win.

During our previous sessions, one boy in particular had fairly consistently put effort into being "cool," "funny" (aka "disrespectful"), and less than participatory, in the way that some fifth-grade boys can be. I asked him, "If you're thinking about winning and losing, and the outcome of the game, is your head *really* in the game? Is it really in what's happening right here right now?" His eyes got big. His mouth hung open. He was "in"; mindfulness was now relevant to him. It helped to be able to tell the class that two of the most successful teams ever in the history of professional basketball, the Los Angeles Lakers and the Chicago Bulls, used mindfulness skills to bring their attention to actually playing the game—to the ball, the hoop, their teammates, and their opponents. (p. 79)

Note that by the time you read this, for most kids these references will be ancient history. So you will want to have more contemporary examples such as Kobe Bryant of the LA Lakers; Kerri Walsh and Misty May-Trainor, Olympic gold medalists in beach volleyball; Tim Lincecum World Series Champion pitcher for the San Francisco Giants; and the Seattle Seahawks the 2014 Super Bowl Champions, and 2015 runners up.

> Competitive sports are played mainly on a five-and-a-half inch court, the space between your ears.
>
> —BOBBY JONES, the most successful amateur golfer ever,
> frequently beating the pros (in Justice & Gollnick, 2013, p. 10)

Unkind Mind

Many young competitive athletes are exceedingly hard on themselves. Occasionally this highly critical type of thinking can also be directed at teammates, opponents, coaches, and referees. There are many playful ways of bringing awareness to this negative internal chatter and helping young athletes learn that they don't need to believe or indulge this type of thinking. This gentle, humorous way of relating to overly critical thoughts does not prevent the more constructive habit of objectively evaluating one's performance and considering areas for improvement.

To elicit this type of thinking, which I fondly call *unkind mind*, simply create a novel challenge for your athletes. When choosing an activity, initially it is helpful to select one that is not directly related to the primary sport, and that will be funny, challenging, without risk of injury, and not impossible. This could be a simple dexterity challenge such as dividing your players into two teams, giving each player a small paper clip, instructing the players to put the paper clips in their non-dominant hands, and then having the teams race to connect all their paper clips. Of course, the challenge can be a physical challenge: a yoga pose or series of poses, a rope climb, an obstacle course.

The activity itself is not particularly important; the emphasis in this exercise is encouraging your athletes to notice their thoughts as they engage in the activity. An example of how to do this with the paper clip challenge follows.

"Okay, we are going to do a new and challenging drill. . . . Please notice any thoughts that appeared just as I said that. Were you curious? Excited? Nervous? Did you think 'Ugh, I just want to hit the showers'?

"Please separate and form two lines. Everyone put out your non-dominant hand, the hand you don't write with. [Pass out the paper clips.] Now what thoughts are you having? 'What the heck?' 'Coach, you've lost your mind.' 'What's with the paper clip? This is volleyball!'

"Now please close your eyes and take 10 slow deep breaths [pause]. In a moment you are going to work as a team to connect all your paper clips using only your non-dominant hands. The first player in each line will begin. When that player and the teammate next in line have connected their paper clips, then the second player will begin working with the third player to connect their paper clips, and so on. Any questions on the paper clip part of the challenge?

"There is one additional part to the exercise. While you are connecting your paper clips, do your best to notice your thinking. What do you say to yourself, to your teammates, either out loud or just in your head? Everybody ready?

"1–2–3 Go!"

As teammates attempt to connect their paper clips, note their comments for future reference . . . for example: "F---! I can't get this." "This is too hard." "I got it!" "Hurry up, dude." "You idiot!" "They're winning." When the exercise is complete, invite them to again close their eyes, notice what is happening in their bodies, minds, and hearts, and then to take 10 slow, deep breaths. When they open their eyes, you can discuss the exercise using the following prompts:

"What thoughts did you notice?"
"Were your thoughts kind or unkind? Helpful or unhelpful?"
"Do you have thoughts like these when you are practicing and com-
    peting? When you are doing homework, taking a test, or talking to
    someone you are interested in?"
"I call negative internal chatter unkind mind."
"Perhaps with practice you can learn to watch your unkind mind with-
    out believing it or taking it personally."
"How might this practice of *briefly* noticing your thoughts [and feelings]
    be helpful during training and competition?"
"When you notice you are caught in unkind mind, what can you do?
    Take a deep breath and return your attention to the game, to what is
    happening in the moment."

Your opponent, in the end, is never really the player on the other side of the net, or the swimmer in the next lane, or the team on the other side of the field, or even the bar you must high-jump. Your opponent is yourself, your negative internal voices. . . .

—Grace Lichtenstein, writer and editor
(in Mujtaba & Preziosi, 2006, p. 276)

Being with Emotion

Many athletes and coaches experience intense emotions during competition. Thus it can be helpful to teach athletes to, as I like to say, "have their emotions, without their emotions having them"; this simply means offering them skills for observing their emotions without either suppressing or indulging them. An example of a simple practice to develop mindfulness of emotions/feelings after a difficult competition follows:

> "That was a tough game. After you've cooled down and put on your sweats, please come and lie down on the grass. Allow your eyes to close, settle your attention on your breathing. . . . Rest in the stillness and quietness. When you are ready, gently shift your attention to your feelings. What feeling or feelings are present right now? Anger? Disappointment? Hopelessness? Shame? See if you can simply allow the feeling to be there without minimizing it or pushing it away, or exaggerating it or making it more dramatic.
>
> "Simply breathing and allowing the feeling or feelings. . . . Nothing to change or fix. . . .
>
> "See if you can bring some kindness and curiosity to your feelings. How does the feeling feel in your body? . . . Heavy or light? . . . Cool or warm? . . . Moving or still? . . . Does it stay the same or change with time?
>
> "Continue breathing and allowing the feeling or feelings. . . . Just let the feelings be, allowing them to move through in their own time, noticing their intensity and rhythm. . . .
>
> "When you are ready, shift your attention back to the breath and the stillness and quietness that are always present underneath the breath and underneath feelings. . . . In your own time you may gently open your eyes, roll to your side, and sit up. Intense feelings are a natural part of sports and competition. Over time, with mindfulness practice, you can learn to have your feelings, without your feelings having you; to be aware of and allow your feelings, so that they don't have a huge, negative effect on your performance."

With a few adjustments to the wording, this same practice can also be done at the end of a practice, prior to an event or during halftime. Allowing a specific time and space for simply bringing open compassionate awareness to pre-, during, or post-competition emotions often (though not always) allows them to dissipate. Recorded versions of this practice for young children and teens are available via iTunes and Amazon on my CDs *Still Quiet Place: Mindfulness for Young Children* (available at *www.cdbaby.com/cd/amysaltzmanmd3*), and *Still Quiet Place: Mindfulness for Teens* (available at *www.cdbaby.com/cd/amysaltzmanmd4*).

> You have to be able to center yourself, to let all of your emotions go.
> —KAREEM ABDUL-JABBAR, six-time NBA most valuable player
> (in Mazzoni, 2005, p. 57)

> In my view the key to becoming a successful NBA player is not learning the coolest highlight-reel moves. It's learning to control your emotions and keep your mind focused on the game . . . how to stay cool under pressure and maintain your equanimity after crushing losses or ecstatic wins.
> —PHIL JACKSON, champion NBA basketball player and coach
> (in Jackson, 2013, p. 281)

Breathing Through

Once your athletes have experienced the basics of mindfulness (attending to the breath, the body, thoughts, and feelings), often just one or two breaths will allow them to reset their nervous systems and become fully present. My friend and colleague Todd Corbin, who coaches Little League, encourages his athletes to "breathe through the pitch" and "breathe through the swing." As a coach, you can learn to breathe through a moment of frustration, and then choose if and how you will respond to an athlete, a referee, or a parent.

Beyond the Basics: Using Mindfulness to Teach Life Skills

Thus far we have explored mindfulness for athletes in the moment-to moment context of practice and competition. As a coach, you have a precious opportunity to teach your athletes how to *respond* rather than *react* to challenges in sports, and more importantly, in life. Below are several examples of topics to reflect on with related quotes that you can share with your athletes over the course of a season. Ideally, these offerings will allow them not only to be better athletes, but also better, kinder, more responsive students, friends, employees, bosses, partners, parents, and world citizens.

Mistakes and Rituals

The ability to acknowledge a mistake, note any self-critical thinking, and then reset is essential both during practice and in the heat of competition. This process can often be accomplished with a simple "mistake ritual." In *Elevating Your Game*, Jim Thompson (2011) describes three simple and effective mistake rituals: Flush (making a flushing motion), No Sweat (wiping sweat from the brow), and Brush It Off (lightly brushing the shoulder). Alternatively, athletes can create their own rituals. My daughter used a ritual based on a sweet family moment. When my son was 3, I walked into a closet and found him sitting on the floor, cutting the foam from dry cleaning hangers into little pieces with children's scissors. When I asked him "J, honey, what are you doing?" he responded, "Cutting slack." So when my daughter made a mistake, her ritual was to make a simple scissor like motion with her index and middle finger.

Such rituals support athletes in releasing their attention from the previous play and returning their focus to the immediate here and now of competition. The power of these quick rituals can be enhanced when an athlete shares them with a supportive teammate, parent, or coach via eye contact or a simple smile. Sharing the ritual allows the athlete to feel supported, reminds the athlete that mistakes are part of the game, and encourages the crucial mental reset that facilitates complete return to play.

> What do you do with a mistake?: Recognize it, admit it, learn from it, forget it.
> —DEAN SMITH, U.S. Olympic men's basketball coach
> (in Spainhour, 2007, p. 60)

> Basketball takes place at such a lightning pace that it's easy to make mistakes and get obsessed with what just happened or what might happen next, which distracts you from the only thing that really matters—this very moment.
> —PHIL JACKSON, champion NBA basketball player and coach
> (in Jackson, 2013, p. 53)

Self-Compassion

The power of mistake rituals can be further enhanced by teaching self-compassion.

Kristen Neff, an internationally recognized expert in the field, describes self-compassion as the combination of three capacities:

- Holding one's painful thoughts and feelings in mindful awareness rather than over-identifying with them
- Extending kindness and understanding to oneself rather than harsh self-criticism and judgment
- Seeing one's experiences as part of the larger human experience rather than as separating and isolating (Neff, 2005).

Self-compassion not only enhances well-being, it also increases resilience. Although the research has yet to be done regarding perceived "athletic failure," Neff's (2005) research demonstrates that self-compassion increases undergraduate students' ability to cope with perceived academic failure. As athletes, and as coaches, practicing self-compassion can help us through difficult periods. This attitude is perhaps most succinctly captured in the saying "That's all right; it happens to the best of us."

> I've missed more than 9,000 shots in my career. I've lost almost 300 games. 26 times, I've been trusted to take the game winning shot and missed. I've failed over and over and over again in my life. And that is why I succeed.
> —MICHAEL JORDAN, five-time NBA most valuable player
> (in Westerbeck & Smith, 2005, p. 144)

Positive Scanning and the Magic Ratio

Most of us as human beings, and particularly as athletes committed to enhancing our performance, habitually negatively scan our efforts in practice and competition. We routinely look for and assess what we "did wrong," what we "could do better." And there is value in this type of reflection. However, many highly competitive athletes take this to a potentially self-defeating extreme. Thus, it can be helpful to balance the habit of negative scanning with positive scanning. After each practice or competition, encourage your athletes to acknowledge and appreciate five specific things they did well. Research evaluating effective functioning of marital relationships and business teams indicates that both function optimally when the ratio of positive to negative interactions is at least 5:1 (Gottman, 1994; Losada, 1999; Losada & Heaphy, 2004). Encouraging your athletes to maintain a positive to negative ratio of 5:1 in their self-talk and in their comments to teammates cultivates a culture of excellence and synergy beyond the usual definition of teamwork.

Of course, as a coach, one of the most powerful things you can do for an individual athlete, and for your entire team, is to maintain a 5:1 ratio of positive to negative comments and actions. Perhaps you can commit to making this as part of your own ongoing mindful coaching practice. For a YouTube video that is an excellent demonstration of what the mindfulness practice of maintaining the magic 5:1 ratio looks like in real time, including one small slip in the coach's comments about the receiver, go to *www.youtube.com/watch ?v=9ArAbqy8Lfs&list=PL861401E7490AC619*.

Practice Makes Practice

As athletes, coaches, parents, and human beings it helps if we remember that in reality, despite the popular cliché, "practice makes perfect," the truth is *practice makes practice*. If we strive toward excellence and mastery, there will be periods of progressing, plateauing, and even regressing. Athletes can become complacent or despondent if they believe the latter two are permanent. They are most likely to continue to improve if they cultivate the ability to maintain consistent effort in spite of the external circumstances that suggest "success" and "failure."

> Excellence is not a singular act but a habit. You are what you do repeatedly.
> —SHAQUILLE O'NEAL, four-time NBA champion player
> (in Bergland, 2007, p. 152)

Equanimity and Impermanence

The dictionary defines equanimity as "mental or emotional stability or composure, especially under tension or strain; calmness; equilibrium." A mindfulness teacher noted that we mistakenly tend to think of equanimity as a still pendulum, resting undisturbed at the bottom of its arc. However, this teacher noted that true equanimity is really much more like the anchor point of the pendulum string, the still point that allows the full arc, the highs and lows, yet remains undisturbed. Pleasure and pain, gain and loss, praise and blame, fame and shame—all come and go. Learning to rest in stillness and quietness and allow *all* the physical sensations, thoughts, and feelings that arise and pass away during practice and competition, particularly before and after high-profile events, supports athletes in competing to the best of their ability.

> Keep calm and carry on. A challenging time is just that—a period in time. Taking a few deep breaths and knowing that it won't last forever really allows me to focus on the present moment and task at hand.
> —BETSEY ARMSTRONG, 2008 Olympic silver medalist and 2012 Olympic goalkeeper in water polo (in *Women's Health Magazine*, 2012)

> Sports are more than just games. they're about life, emotion, passion, and some of the greatest highs and lows we can experience.
> —stripedsheep (at *http://boardofwisdom.com/togo/Quotes/ShowQuote?msgid=111807#.U3wL9MerEeI*)

Health and Well-Being

Fatigue, aches, pains, and even injury are an inherent part of an athletic life. There are definitely times to "suck it up and play through the pain." And as athletes, coaches, and a culture as whole, we often take this mindset to an unhealthy extreme. After intense training, a period of rest and recovery is necessary to allow the body to recuperate and assimilate the efforts. If athletes are mindful, they can learn to notice the early physical signs of impending injury, as well as the physical, and often mental and emotional, signs of overtraining, and then back off rather than pushing through and going over the edge. This wisdom, and the willingness to sometimes go against the predominant, glorified "no pain, no gain" culture can often save a season, a career, and occasionally even a life.

> Burned out and exhausted from more than a decade as the standard bearer for U.S. soccer, Landon Donovan needed a break. For four months last winter, soccer was the last concern for the Americans' career scoring leader. He spent time with family and friends, making up for all those holidays and get-togethers he missed over the years. He traveled to far-flung places, reveling in his respite from the harsh glare of the spotlight. And somewhere along the way, he rediscovered his love for the game he'd been so desperate to escape. (Armour, 2013)

> There were physical dimensions to his fatigue, of course, but it was primarily mental exhaustion that forced Donovan away from the game, and he argued that society needs to put greater emphasis on the importance of mental health. (French, 2013)

> [At the end of the 2012 season, after the Galaxy's MLS Cup triumph] I was equally as relieved that the season was over as I was excited that we had won—in retrospect, I realize that is very unhealthy, so that sort of tells you the place I was in. . . . I knew I had to get back to a place where I could enjoy playing again.
> —LANDON DONOVAN, champion professional soccer player
> (in Bennett, 2013)

> A lot gets thrown at athletes these days, and everyone is trying to pull you one way or the other. But as I've gotten older, I've learned that the most important thing is to take care of—and to be true to—yourself.
> — LANDON DONOVAN (in Daniels, 2011)

> If I didn't take this time off, I would have been useless to everybody this year in a professional setting, and probably a personal setting. I absolutely needed [the break] and am very glad that I did it.
> —LANDON DONOVAN (in French, 2013)

"Almost" Moments, Sportsmanship, and Integrity

When I share mindfulness with children and adolescents in the context of an 8-week Still Quiet Place course, we devote a significant portion of our time to exploring how mindfulness can support us in making wise choices. When we discuss the distinction between *responding* (taking some breaths, checking in with yourself, and then choosing your behavior) and *reacting* (acting immediately out of habit and upset), I usually say something like the following:

> "Mindfulness is paying attention here and now, with kindness and curiosity, and then *choosing* your behavior. As you have learned, you can attend to your breath, your body, your thoughts, your feelings, and the world around you. The big benefit of paying attention to your inner and outer experience in this way is that it allows you to choose your actions wisely.
>
> "Let me share an example from my friend Michael. Michael was a fourth grader at a low-income school where I taught mindfulness. One day when we were discussing challenging moments, Michael told us that his new cat had bit him. The bite hurt, and that he wanted to hit the cat. I asked, 'Did you?' He smiled and said simply, 'No. But I almost did.' As a class we dubbed this an 'almost moment.'
>
> "As athletes and coaches, we are presented with many 'almost' moments. Can we be aware of our thoughts, feelings, and urges and then *choose* our behavior, as Michael did? How will *you* respond, in the almost moment, to an opponent's taunt, a ref's bad call, a tough loss, sudden success, one teammate being unkind to another, an offer for performance-enhancing or street drugs, witnessing someone take advantage of a drunk classmate? Ultimately, it is our mindful choices in these moments as much as the final score that determines if we are heroes in our own hearts."

Sports do not build character. They reveal it.
—JOHN WOODEN, 10-time NCAA champion basketball coach
(in Reger, 2012, p. 65)

Coaching with Mindfulness

Thus far we have explored mindfulness for athletes during training and competition, and mindfulness principles in the broader context of sport and life. Now, before concluding, let's turn our attention to coaching mindfully.

Intentionally Creating the Culture

Each season you have the opportunity to establish the team culture. What are your intentions: For yourself? For your athletes? For the team as a whole? Note that intentions are distinct from goals, and they define qualities of *being* rather than specific *outcomes*. When intentions are held in the context of mindfulness, they serve as a behavioral compass. Consider these examples of intentions:

- "We treat ourselves, our teammates, our coaches, our opponents, and the officials with kindness and respect."
- "We commit to coming to practice and games physically, mentally, and emotionally ready to play."

Before the season begins, consider your personal intentions and your intentions for the team. It can be a fun and valuable team-building exercise to create a list of 5–10 intentions on the first day of practice. Many famous coaches acknowledge that their less successful colleagues fail (even though they are technically very skilled and understand the fundamentals and complexities of their sport) because they do not develop an explicit, *intentional* team culture.

Attending to Individual Athletes

Most coaches typically work with several athletes; many coaches work with an entire team of athletes. Each athlete has his or her own personality and physical, mental, and emotional strengths and weaknesses. Early in the season, and several times during the season, set aside time to reflect on each of your athletes. Do your best to see each athlete freshly, with beginner's mind and heart. Initially, it can be helpful to acknowledge your typical attitude about your shortstop, and then to consider other qualities she harbors. What are her strengths and weaknesses physically, mentally, emotionally? What style of coaching is she most responsive to? How does she interact with her teammates? Is she a leader, a follower, a loner, a disruptive force? What do you know about her life outside of softball? How is she doing in school? How are her relationships with her family, friends, and peers? How does she feel about her body? Her playing? What qualities do you want to nurture in her? How can you best support her development as an athlete and a human being? Now that you have held her in your kind and curious attention, how might you coach her differently?

> Look, coaching is about human interaction and trying to know your players. Any coach would tell you that. I'm no different.
> —BILL PARCELLS, two-time Superbowl champion, NFL Football coach
> *http://www.brainyquote.com/quotes/quotes/b/billparcel478066.html*

A common mistake among those who work in sport is spending a disproportional amount of time on "x's and o's" as compared to time spent learning about people.
> —MIKE KREZEWSKI, men's basketball coach, Duke University, Olympic gold medal coach 2008, 2012 (in Howell, 2011, p. 12)

I have learned over the years how to hold a team together. How to lift some men up, how to calm others down, until finally they've got one heartbeat, together, a team.
—BEAR BRYANT, six-time national champion college football coach
(in Williams, 2010, p. 137)

Attending to the Team as a Whole

If you are coaching multiple athletes who play as a team, then once you have reflected upon each athlete individually, expand your attention to consider the team as a whole. How is team morale? How is team energy level? If it is low, would the team benefit from a period of recovery or an increase in intensity? If it is high, is it sustainable through the season or does it need to be tempered slightly? Watch your team as members arrive and depart from practice, partner for drills, recover during water breaks, hang out on the bus, and unwind at meals between events. What is the general tone of the team? Is the banter lighthearted and inclusive? Is there an undertone of tension, resentment, or cliquishness? Do players mix and match, or are there repetitive divisions?

This type of reflection is absolutely critical to getting the most out of your team. In highly competitive environments, if a culture of inclusivity and cooperation is not *actively cultivated* on a moment-to-moment basis, players often engage in an insidious and invisible form of bullying known as *relational aggression* or *emotional bullying*. Ideally, sports provide an environment of true cooperation and compassion (operating together, sharing a passion) and nurturing what is best in each team member. Thus, it is beyond heartbreaking to listen to the mother of an 8-year-old girl describe a textbook case of relational bullying on her local soccer team, or to read about the pervasive culture of bullying on a particular NFL team.

Slowly, athletes, parents, and coaches are becoming aware of and addressing this national epidemic that manifests itself in thousands of almost invisible interactions every day on fields and courts, in pools and locker rooms across the country. Yet, sadly this type of behavior remains incredibly common and frequently unnoticed on sports teams. Following is a brief description of emotional bullying:

> The term "relational aggression" is used to describe a type of bullying . . . a covert use of relationships as weapons to inflict emotional pain. [Relational aggression] can include rumor spreading, secret-divulging, alliance-building, backstabbing, ignoring, excluding from social groups and activities, verbally insulting, and using hostile body language (i.e., eye-rolling and smirking). Other behaviors include making fun of someone's clothes or appearance and bumping into someone on purpose. Many of these behaviors are quite common in [team relationships], but when they occur *repeatedly* to *one* particular victim, they constitute bullying.

The usual motivation behind acts of relational aggression is to socially iso-
late the victim while also increasing the social status of the bully. Perpetrators
might be driven by jealousy, need for attention, anger, and fear of, or need for,
competition. One reason [players] choose this type of bullying rather than more
direct acts of harassment is that the bully typically avoids being caught or held
accountable. Players who appear the most innocent may indeed be the most hostile in their actions. These bullies are often popular, charismatic [players] who
are already receiving positive attention from adults. (*www.teachersandfamilies.
com/open/parent/ra5.cfm*)

The pervasive nature of this issue was reinforced in a conversation with
Bret Simon, the former Stanford men's soccer coach and current Positive
Coaching Alliance (PCA) trainer. Bret shared that a local Northern California school district had engaged PCA to offer workshops to every athlete
within the district. When he asked representatives from the district if there
was anything in particular they would like the PCA leaders to address in the
workshops, the school officials answered unequivocally: bullying.

This behavior has a significant negative impact on each athlete and the
team as whole. Obviously the victims suffer. What is less obvious is that the
bystanders and bullies also suffer. Bystanders live in fear that they will be next
to be bullied, and feel conflicted because they are unsure how to intervene.
Bullies suffer because they know in their hearts that their behavior is unkind
and destructive. It is important to understand that the impulse beneath bullying is most often deep-seated insecurity. As a coach it is your responsibility
to coach constructively, create an inclusive team culture, and set clear expectations about how your athletes treat each other on and off the "court."

> The better the female athletes get along, the better the team will be. If they're
> connected off the field, it really translates on the field and makes a difference in
> those tight games. . . .
> —JON NISHIMOTO, Bishop O'Dowd's girls varsity soccer team coach
> in Oakland, California, and assistant coaching director
> for East Bay United/Bay Oaks (*www.socceramerica.com/article/49845/
> girls-vs-boys-a-difference-in-social-dynamics.html*)

> When you're part of a team, you stand up for your teammates. Your loyalty is
> to them. You protect them through good and bad, because they'd do the same
> for you.
> —YOGI BERRA, appeared in 21 World Series as baseball player, coach,
> and manager (in Brunner & Leventhal, 2011, p. 172)

> The way a team plays as a whole determines its success. You may have the great-
> est bunch of individual stars in the world, but if they don't play together, the
> club won't be worth a dime.
> —BABE RUTH, winner of seven pennants and four World Series
> with the New York Yankees (in Murphy, 2012, p. 309)

It takes a number of critical factors to win an NBA championship, including the right mix of talent, creativity, intelligence, toughness, and of course, luck. But if a team doesn't have the most essential ingredient—love—none of those other factors matter.

> —PHIL JACKSON, champion NBA basketball player and coach
> (in Jackson, 2013, p. 4)

Mindful Communication

As mentioned above, the definition of mindfulness I share with children and adolescents is: "Mindfulness is paying attention, here and now, with kindness and curiosity and then choosing our behavior." It can be helpful to actively bring mindfulness into your communications with your athletes, their parents, and your athletes' communications with you and with each other. In short, mindful communication means taking a moment to breathe, to notice your thoughts, feelings, and physical sensations, and then to *choose* your words wisely: Is this the time to speak? Can you allow the wave of frustration to pass? Can you remember the magic 5:1 ratio? What is it you really want to convey? Is your athlete or team in a place where he or she or they can really *hear* you? Are you really hearing him or her or them? For more detail on mindful communication please turn to (Chapter 8, this volume) where Kramer and Ucok-Sayrak explore mindful communication and "insight dialogue" more deeply.

Then there is player-to-player communication. Do your players know how you want them to communicate with each other during competition? Outside the competitive arena? When things are going well? When they are having difficulties? Are you encouraging them using the 5:1 ratio for feedback? Have you experimented with running a practice in silence so that they can read the game and communicate non-verbally?

Putting It All Together

If you set clear intentions; establish an inclusive and cooperative environment of excellence; foster compassion; maintain the magic 5:1 ratio; teach your athletes to deal with mistakes, loss, and injury; cultivate integrity and a love for the game; and truly train your athletes' minds and hearts as well as their bodies, then your athletes will perform at *their* best, and *be* their best, whether they are third graders or Olympians.

Love of the Game

Sometimes as athletes and coaches we become so focused on performance that we lose sight of our original, natural, pure inspiration for participating.

We lose our love of the game. Although much of the life of an athlete is hard work, blood, sweat, and tears, both athletes and coaches must practice noticing and even cultivating joy. Joy is usually found by being fully in the present moment. It is the feeling of satisfying exhaustion after a grueling, solitary workout, or "nailing it" in the empty gym far away from the adoring crowds.

> Somewhere behind the athlete you've become and the hours of practice and the coaches who have pushed you is a little girl who fell in love with the game and never looked back . . . play for her.
> —MIA HAMM, women's soccer World Cup and Olympic champion (in Downing, 2014, p. 20)

> It's great to win, but it's also great fun just to be in the thick of any truly well and hard fought contest against opponents you respect, whatever the outcome.
> —JACK NICKLAUS, winner of 18 Masters Golf Tournaments (in Taylor, 2001, p. 8)

> I wasn't skating for other people's approval; I had to get back to that pure joy that got me into the sport in the first place. I was determined to enjoy every single practice at the worlds in 1991, to love skating again.
> —KRISTI YAMAGUCHI, world champion figure skater in 1991 and Olympic gold medalist in 1992 (in Brennan, 2014)

> I love winning. I can take losing. But most of all I love to play.
> —BORIS BECKER, former number 1 tennis player in the world and winner of six Grand Slam titles (in Mazzoni, 2005, p. 78)

Although the quotes from famous coaches and athletes are inspiring, I close with a quote from an anonymous softball player whose simple words capture the essence of both the love of the game and mindfulness in sports for devoted athletes at any level:

> You know you love the game when you walk on the field and . . .
> Forget about the drama going on at school.
> Forget the fight you had with your boyfriend earlier.
> Forget the scouts watching in the stands.
> Let everything go, and just focus on the game.
> That's a true athlete.
> (*www.fhslions.com/?PageName=%27SportPage%27&SportID=%2718779%27*)

REFERENCES

Afremow, J. (2013). *The champion's mind: How great athletes think, train, and thrive.* New York: Rodale.

Almond, E. (2014a, February 12). Olympics: Women's downhill tie for gold an alpine first. *San Jose Mercury News.*

Almond, E. (2014b, February 14). Skater Polina Edmunds makes solid Olympic debut. *San Jose Mercury News.*

Armour, N. (2013, July 28). Time off does wonders for Donovan. Retrieved from *www.seattletimes.com/sports/sounders/landon-donovan-leads-us-team-to-sundayrsquos-concacaf-gold-cup-final.*

Bennett, R. (2013, May 16). Landon Donovan's post-sabbatical world. Retrieved from *www.espnfc.com/blog/relegation-zone/71/post/1851563/donovan-happy-to-be-back-at-work.*

Bergland, C. (2007). *The athlete's way: Sweat and the biology of bliss.* New York: St. Martin's Press.

Bernier, M., Thienot, E., Codron, R., & Fournier, J. (2009). Mindfulness and acceptance approaches in sport performance. *Journal of Clinical Sports Psychology, 4,* 320–333.

Brennan, C. (2014, January 31). Kristi Yamaguchi is still winning. Retrieved from *www.usatoday.com/story/life/weekend/2014/01/31/kristi-yamaguchi-is-still-winning/5065529.*

Brunner, A., & Leventhal, J. (Eds.). (2011). *The Yankees baseball reader: A collection of writings on the game's greatest.* Minneapolis, MN: MVP Books.

Daniels, A. (2011, December 30). 10 lessons we learned from athletes in 2011. Available at *www.menshealth.com/fitness/athlete-quotes-2011.*

Downing, E. (2014). *For soccer-crazy girls only.* New York: Feiwel & Friends.

French, S. (2013, March 9). LA Galaxy's Landon Donovan argues mental health should be treated like physical health. Retrieved from *www.mlssoccer.com/news/article/2013/03/29/back-break-la-galaxys-landon-donovan-argues-mental-health-should-be-treated.*

Gottman, J. M. (1994). *What predicts divorce: The relationship between marital processes and marital outcomes.* Hillsdale, NJ: Erlbaum.

Howell, B. (2011). *Inside the sports industry.* Edina MN: ABDO Publishing.

Jackson, P. (2013). *Eleven rings.* New York: Penguin.

Justice, I., & Gollnick, H. (2013). *Triathlete EQ: A guide for emotional endurance.* Bloomington, IN: iUniverse.

Losada, M. (1999). The complex dynamics of high performance teams. *Mathematical and Computer Modelling, 30*(9–10), 179–192.

Losada, M., & Heaphy, E. (2004). The role of positivity and connectivity in the performance of business teams: A nonlinear dynamics model. *American Behavioral Scientist, 47*(6), 740–765.

Mazzoni, W. (2005). *You vs you: Sports psychology for life* (p. 57). Mazz Marketing. *www.amazon.com/You-vs-Sport-Psychology-Life/dp/0966355717.*

Mujtaba, B., & Preziosi, R. C. (2006). *Adult education in academia: Recruiting and retaining extraordinary facilitators of learning* (rev. 2nd ed.). Charlotte, NC: Information Age.

Murphy, S. (Ed.). (2012). *The Oxford handbook of sport and performance psychology.* New York: Oxford University Press.

Neff, K. (2005). Self-compassion, achievement goals, and coping with academic failure. *Self and Identity, 4*(3), 263–287.

Reger, J. (2012). *Quotable wooden: Words of wisdom, preparation, and success by and about John Wooden*. Lanham, MD: Taylor & Francis.

Saltzman, A. (2014). *Still quiet place: A mindfulness program for children and adolescents to ease stress and difficult emotions*. Oakland, CA: New Harbinger.

Spainhour, D. (2007). A season in words: A coach's guide to motivation from the preseason to the postseason. Winston-Salem, NC: Educational Coaching Business Communications.

Taylor, J. (2001). *Prime golf: Triumph of the mental game*. Lincoln, NE: Writers Club Press.

Thompson, J. (2011). *Elevating your game: Becoming a triple impact competitor*. Portola Valley, CA: Balance Sports.

Westerbeek, H., & Smith, A. (2005). *Business leadership and the lessons from sport*. New York: Palgrave Macmillan.

Williams, P. (2010). *Bear Bryant on leadership: Life lessons from a six-time national championship coach*. Charleston, SC: Advantage Media Group.

Women's Health Magazine. (2012, June 29). Olympians share their personal mantras. Available at *www.womenshealthmag.com/fitness/mantra*.

The Young and the Hungry

Marcella Cox
Char Wilkins

Adolescence is a time when young people struggle to eat well and care for their changing bodies. It's also a time of hungering for acceptance, success, and love. Every day, adolescents are assaulted by thousands of media images and their embedded values, while grappling with issues of self-esteem and identity, and inhabiting a body that draws its owner's attention, as well as the attention of others. In addition to self, peer, and media pressure, studies show that both physical and sexual abuse are risk factors for disordered eating among this population.

All of these factors contribute to the misuse of food, which can result in disordered eating, eating disorders, and distorted body image. It's heartbreaking to know that an alarming percentage of girls and boys less than 10 years of age report that they are sometimes or always on a diet, and that many of these diets include such unhealthy practices as skipping meals. In adolescents, disordered eating appears to be even more prevalent, including behaviors such as bingeing; fasting; restricting themselves to only one or two foods; using food substitutes, diet pills, or laxatives; purging (self-induced vomiting); and excessive exercise.

Although body dissatisfaction increases with age, many preteens are dissatisfied with their body size, thinking themselves overweight when they are not, and reporting that they always wish they were thinner. Adolescents, in particular those who are overweight, report being teased about their weight and being bothered by the teasing (Rancourt, Barker, Sato, Lloyd-Richardson, Hart, & Jelalian, 2014). Weight teasing is associated with disordered-eating behaviors that may place overweight youth at increased risk for subsequent weight gain. Knowing all this, we were moved to bring what we've learned personally and professionally about mindful eating to young people. A bit about us:

Marcella Cox, psychotherapist, mindful self-compassion teacher and yoga teacher: Amy Saltzman introduced me to meditation a few years ago when I was in graduate school, and I was immediately drawn to the inner peace it provided me. Now I'm a psychotherapist and yoga teacher, and I work with adolescents and young women with eating disorders, body image issues, and mood and anxiety disorders. I've found that my ability to be present with kindness and curiosity is vital to unlocking the rigidity or chaos that clients are experiencing, and can heal the mind, body, and spirit.

I began to bring mindfulness to my own eating; I have had the good fortune to study mindful eating with Jan Chozen Bays and Char Wilkins, and now teach others to eat mindfully. Mindful eating has not only changed my relationship with food, but it has opened me up to the richness of life. In addition to my meditation practice, my yoga and mindful self-compassion practices have helped me develop compassion toward my body and myself and awaken strength and flexibility that I apply to my life both on and off the mat. I have found that yoga and self-compassion are the most effective tools in helping clients overcome their body image issues.

Char Wilkins, psychotherapist and mindfulness teacher: I must confess I found my way to meditation out of desperation. Twenty years ago I'd often find myself telling people that my mind was driving me crazy, as though I had nothing to do with what was going on up there and someone or thing other than "me" was in the driver's seat.

As I learned to meditate and become more mindful in my everyday life, I realized that I was allowing external circumstances and other people to determine my behaviors in all aspects of my life. I began to see that my reactivity created much of the drama, confusion, and pain in my life. Being mindful allowed me the space and understanding to become more responsive to stressors and take better care of myself.

Now as a therapist, I sit hour after hour, up close and personal with the suffering of others. The women I see individually and in groups often have histories of physical, emotional, verbal, and/or sexual abuse, and frequently struggle with disordered eating: restricting, bingeing, purging, and/or over-eating. It was out of my personal experience that I came to understand that mindfulness could help my clients, because everything, even anorexia and bulimia, is useful on the path to freedom from suffering—or, in teen speak, true "peace of mind." The key for me as a therapist was to see disordered eating not as one more problem, but as a doorway to freedom.

Through the practice of mindfulness meditation, studying and teaching with Jan Chozen Bays, serving on the board of The Center for Mindful

Eating, and working with people of all ages, I came to have a profound appreciation of the healing possibilities of learning to eat mindfully.

Mindful Eating as an Antidote

Mindful eating, in the simplest of terms, is gently bringing a kind, nonjudgmental awareness to what is going on inside—in the body and mind—and outside in the environment, as we prepare to eat, as we eat, and after we eat. When we help adolescents become aware internally and externally, then they can use that information to make better choices about what their bodies need to function at their best. If we can help them better understand why and how certain events and people trigger them, then it may be possible for them to see how they misuse food to sooth, calm, reward, or punish themselves.

What Is Mindful Eating?

To begin, it is helpful to understand some of the basic tenets of mindful eating. We have adapted the guidelines initially developed by The Center for Mindful Eating,[1] a forum for professionals across all disciplines interested in developing, deepening, and understanding the value and importance of mindful eating. We are presenting them here as we would share them with tweens and teens. Mindful eating is:

- Using all your senses—sight, smell, taste, touch, and hearing—in choosing to eat food that is both satisfying to you and nourishing to your body.
- Acknowledging your responses to food (like it, don't like it, neutral) without judgment.
- Becoming aware of the physical sensations in your body that tell you whether your stomach is hungry or full, and using these sensations to guide your decisions to begin or end eating.
- Learning about and respecting your own inner wisdom as you choose and prepare food.

People who eat mindfully do their best to:

- Keep in mind that there is no right or wrong way to eat.
- Choose to pay attention to eating on a moment-by-moment basis.

---

[1] The Center for Mindful Eating (TCME; *www.thecenterformindfuleating.org*) is an international not-for-profit forum for professionals across all disciplines interested in developing, deepening, and understanding the value and importance of mindful eating.

- Learn about how they can make choices that support their health and well-being.
- Become aware of the interconnection of earth, living beings, cultural practices, and the impact of their food choices on those systems.

After presenting these basic tenets of mindful eating, you might give some real-life examples to which kids can relate and dispel some misconceptions about what eating mindfully means, by beginning a conversation something like this:

> "So we can see that mindful eating doesn't have anything to do with dieting; or eating only vegetables; or eating only at certain times; or reading, talking, or thinking about eating mindfully while eating; or chewing every bite 100 times; or counting calories; or eating very, very, very slowly. Although it's true that that most of us eat so fast we don't taste our food, mindful eating doesn't mean that it should take the entire day to eat your morning bowl of oatmeal!
>
> "We live in a fast-paced world where the illusion of multitasking is rewarded, super-sized is the norm, and technology brings everything—including food—to our doorstep. Most of us are disconnected from how the food we eat is grown or raised. It simply appears on a grocery shelf wrapped in smell-proof cellophane, fills a plastic cup at the punch of a button, or can be heated in a microwave. Mindless eating arises in part from this highly stimulating, overwhelming, and disjointed world we inhabit. Learning to eat mindfully can help not only with how, what, when, why, and where we eat, but it can also open the door to a healthier and happier life."

The Consequence of Mindless Eating

It's just as important to talk about what we're doing when we aren't eating mindfully. Engaging youth to think about where, how, and when they eat mindlessly, as well as the consequences of mindless eating, is often a lively and fun discussion that brings new awareness to the many places and times that we multitask while eating. Consider this possible wording:

> "What do you call it when you are not eating mindfully? Mind*less* eating. Every time you eat and are not tuned into your physical or emotional hungers, you're eating mindlessly. What are some examples of when you are distracted from the food because you're doing something else at the same time (texting, surfing the Web, studying, watching TV, walking, driving, talking to friends, etc.)? Often when we eat mindlessly, we are not even hungry. Has this ever happened to you?"

Unfortunately when eating mindlessly we tend to eat quickly, and the faster we eat, the more we eat. It takes 20 minutes for our bodies and brain to signal fullness; however, many people eat a meal in less than 20 minutes, especially kids. In fact, most lunch periods at schools are short, and kids usually eat in under 10 minutes so they can go and play. Researchers found that kids in school cafeterias in New York spent an average of 7.3 minutes actually eating, and in Texas they spent 9.5 minutes (Conklin & Lambert, 2001). Ten minutes is not nearly enough time to know whether you are full.

In addition to eating faster when distracted, we are inclined to eat more and for longer periods of time, because we are not tuned in to how much we are eating. We live in an era of buying large packages of food from wholesale retailers, and studies show that when we consume from bigger packages and larger plates, we consume more food (e.g., Wansink, 2006). The increased size of packages and plates has had the effect of distorting what is an appropriate or normal amount to eat, leading us to serve ourselves more food, which increases the likelihood of overeating when we are not attuned to our hunger and fullness cues.

Brian Wansink (2006) describes an experiment in his book, *Mindless Eating*, in which moviegoers were given as much free popcorn as they could eat in individual medium or large buckets in exchange for answering some questions after the movie. Although the popcorn was popped 5 days prior to the movie, the average person who was given a large bucket ate 53% more popcorn than the participants who had a medium bucket—even though the popcorn was stale and many of them had just had lunch. People eat more when you give them bigger containers, especially when they are distracted.

A fun way to demonstrate this point is to divide your group of kids into pairs and ask them to sit facing each other, close enough so that they can easily hear each other, with some space between the pairs. Pass a bowl of raisins and a spoon and have everyone take a small handful of about 10 raisins. (You can also use potato chips in a bowl, or offer both and let them choose which they want.) Have one person in each pair talk about something upsetting that happened recently with a friend, in school, or with a family member. As the child is telling the upsetting story, he or she is to eat the raisins or chips, just as the child would normally eat while talking. The partner's job is to just listen and watch, without commenting or asking questions, and to simply observe what's happening. After about 3 minutes, switch so that the listener gets to tell his or her upsetting story while eating raisins or chips, and the speaker now listens and watches.

Inquire about this experience by asking, "What did you see when you were the listener?" Then ask, "What did you notice when you were the speaker?" At the end of the sharing, point out that when we are doing other things while eating, we are distracted and don't taste our food, and more often than not, don't feel satisfied after we have eaten. This is the difference between *mindless* eating and *mindful* eating. Explain that we *all* eat mindlessly at times. It really isn't practical to eat with our eyes closed, examining and sniffing each bite of food we eat. We are just trying to be a little more mindful of our eating when we can (Bay, 2009).

Here's a different way to make slowing down and paying attention doable when eating at home or school:

> "Texting, surfing the Web, reading, walking, driving, or talking are things that many of us do while we are eating. 'So is there a problem?' you ask. If you are talking with someone while the two of you are gobbling down a pizza, both of you are probably only half listening to each other. Neither of you feels heard because the pizza is the main attraction. Eye contact is on the pizza, not you, and nobody really wants to look at someone who's talking with pizza in his or her mouth."

Here's a way to eat mindfully and speak respectfully:

- *When eating, just eat.* When the fork, spoon, knife, or glass is in your hand, just eat, just drink. Open your senses and look at the colors, shapes, and textures of the food. Notice the smells and flavors. Listen to the sounds of eating and drinking.
- *When talking, just talk.* Set your utensils down while you speak.
- *When listening, just listen.* Set your utensils down while you listen.
- *Fork up, eat. Fork down, speak.* Up, eat. Down, speak. (Bay, 2011)

Environmental Influences on Eating Habits

Family, culture, advertising, and peer pressure influence the eating habits of adults and youth alike. Bringing mindful attention to eating habits can help us become aware of unhealthy patterns, which we can then choose to change.

In our fast-paced society where everyone is always on the go, families are less likely to sit down and eat together. Children and adolescents eat many snacks and meals in the car on their way to practices or after-school activities, or they eat while distracted in front of a TV, computer, or videogame, even if not physically hungry. This type of eating can set up a pattern of distracted mindless eating that persists throughout a lifetime.

Eating patterns are formed in childhood based on how the family eats. As in all families, there is an emotional atmosphere around the table, be it happy, tense, or something else. Who is present and absent at meals, and who cooks and serves the food, are other factors that affect how children eat later in life. In most families, the person who does the grocery shopping is the person responsible for about three-quarters of what the family eats. Families also have rules around table manners, such as no elbows on the table, no talking with your mouth full, and finish everything on your plate. Youth can't control how their families eat. However, bringing awareness to how family eating patterns affect them enables young people to change how they respond to unhealthy patterns established earlier in their lives.

> Marianne is a 20-year-old college student who has struggled for years with overeating. Growing up, she and her brother would eat together with their father standing over them. Her brother was skinny and didn't like to eat, but Marianne's father wanted him to grow up to be a big football player like himself, so he required the children to eat everything on their plates before leaving the table. Wanting to be a good girl, Marianne would follow the family rule about finishing all the food on her plate, regardless of whether or not she was hungry. Then she would sit with her brother and encourage him to eat, while trying to protect him from their father's intimidation. Years later, Marianne was still finishing everything on her plate, and as a result has struggled with being overweight. Through practicing mindful eating, she was able to understand this eating pattern. She realized that when she is in a relationship with someone who pushes her to eat when she is not hungry, she plays out her childhood behavior at the family table. Through mindful awareness, she has found her voice to tell her current boyfriend that she is not going to eat when she is not hungry.

Fast-food restaurants, larger portion sizes, and convenience foods are part of the cultural food landscape. Fast-food restaurants encourage us to eat fast, and much of the food in these restaurants is full of sugar, salt, and fat (which we are hardwired to crave for our survival). These inexpensive and convenient foods are appealing to many families who are short on time and on a budget. For all of us, bringing mindful attention to what we are consuming and how we feel afterward is essential to figuring out if we want to continue eating these foods.

As adolescents begin to assert their autonomy, peers and the media have a greater influence on their lives, including what they eat. Research shows that when we eat with a group of friends, the average amount others eat suggests the amount that's appropriate for us to eat—which can sway teens to over- or undereat (Wansink, 2006). Furthermore, food companies specifically market their products to children and adolescents, and thereby influence what they eat through advertisements. Studies show that kids who watch more TV are more likely to be overweight than those who don't (e.g., Thomson, Spence, Raine, & Laing, 2008)—likely because they are mindlessly overeating the products being advertised to them.

Almost everyone knows that diets don't work. Ninety-five percent of all people who lose weight on a diet gain it back (Tribole & Resch, 2012). Despite these widely known statistics, we also live in a society where dieting is pervasive. The reason that diets usually don't work is because by continually denying and restricting certain foods, we are likely to crave and binge on these foods later and gain back the weight we lost, plus more. What is even more alarming is that 44% of adolescent girls believe they are overweight, and 60% are actively trying to lose weight—although most of these girls are a normal weight (Ozer, Brindis, Millstein, Knopf, & Irwin, 1998; Field, Camargo, Taylor, Berkey, Roberts, & Colditz, 2001; Field, Camargo, Taylor, Berkey, & Colditz, 1999).

Diets have been shown to be the gateway to eating disorders. Since diets are usually ineffective and have been shown to lead to eating disorders, wouldn't it be far better to teach our children mindful eating, so they can attune to their hunger and feed themselves appropriately throughout their lives?

Some things in our environment we can control, whereas others we cannot. What is important is to bring mindful awareness to how the environment influences the way children and adolescents eat, so that both youth and caregivers can respond in new healthy ways to those influences.

Eight Hungers in One Body

"How do you know you are hungry?" I like to ask adolescents to name ways in which the body tells us we are hungry. This question opens the door for talking about the different ways that we can be hungry. You might begin this exploration of the eight hungers by saying:

> "Did you know that there are actually eight types of hunger? Understanding these eight hungers gives us lots of ways to tune into what's going on in our body and mind, and what we really need in order to take better care of ourselves. Most people say that the eye, stomach, or heart hunger drives their eating, but it may be one of the other hungers for you. All of these hungers are part of being human, and are here to help us learn healthier ways of living. Figuring out which hungers are strongest for you is an important key to when, why, what, and how you eat."

Pause here for a moment and consider the many ways your body tells you that you're hungry. Then, as you read about each type of hunger, consider which hungers are the strongest signals for you.

Eye Hunger

The eyes say, "That sure looks good. I'm full, but . . . I could eat that." This type of hunger is why, even though we are full, we can still make room for dessert. When the waitress hands us the dessert menu and we look at it, our eyes say, "Yes!" even though our stomach says, "Please, no more!" Through the eyes, the body anticipates when food is about to enter the system. That's why our mouths start watering when we see our favorite desserts or look at a slice of lemon. At an all-you-can-eat buffet, our eyes are working overtime, and we often end up eating more than is comfortable for our bodies. Colors, shape, texture, attractiveness: These are the qualities that trigger eye hunger.

Studies have shown that between 35 and 45% of all commercials on children's television are for food, most of it unhealthy. One study showed that on Saturday morning children's television, the proportion of food ads is even higher than at other times, because advertisers know kids are watching then. Seventy-eight percent of ads during this time slot are for food (Byrd-Bredbenner, 2002). These ads are a "feast" for eye hunger.

Ear Hunger

Here is one way you could talk about ear hunger:

> "Have you ever been listening to a friend describe the best burger ever that he or she had last night, and suddenly find yourself salivating and feeling hungry for that very food? That's ear hunger. The sound of some-one munching popcorn in the movies makes us wish we'd bought some. Even the sound inside our head of crunching chips can keep us reaching for another and another—until the bag is empty."

Nose hunger

"I smell pizza! Let's have some pizza!" Scent is one of the ways that our bodies are cued that food is near. Once it's triggered, smell can induce the insulin secretion that makes us think we're hungry. If the fragrance is unpleasant to us, we may not want the food, but if it's pleasant, we may eat even if we're full. Has this every happened to you? Smell is also closely linked to emotion and memory. The smell of bread or cookies baking might remind us of warm and special times spent with our favorite grandmother. Just smell or just sight can turn the appetite on or off, but together they are nearly irresistible.

Mouth Hunger

There's no end to mouth hunger. The mouth just wants more and more tastes, sensations, and intensity of flavors, and it wants different tastes and sensations as well. What taste does your mouth want more and more of? The mouth simply can't be satisfied; it is what we call a "cavern of craving." We may overeat because we are chasing that first fabulous bite that tasted so good. We keep eating and eating, trying to reproduce that first-bite experience so as to feel satisfied, but instead we feel stuffed. That's because taste buds don't have anything to do with the "I'm full, so stop eating" sensors of the stomach.

If you want to enjoy a "party in the mouth," then you have to stay present to the tastes, textures, and experiences; otherwise it's just over the tongue and down the hatch. It's not fun, and there's no party in the mouth if the mind hasn't been invited.

Stomach Hunger

Many of us don't notice signals from our stomachs. Sometimes that's because we have disconnected from that region of the body that is commonly associated with being "fat," and we don't like that. If we don't trust our bodies, then we may allow our minds to override any signals those bodies may be sending.

As you are reading this, you might try tuning into your body for any physical sensations or sounds that alert you to being hungry, full, or satisfied. Sensations that tell us we are hungry or full can be sounds such as growling, gurgling, or burping, or physical sensations such as churning, emptiness, stretching, or constriction. When we feel satisfied, there may be a sense of warmth, contentment, or ease. If we are used to eating at certain times of the day or according to a rigid diet plan, we miss engaging with our internal wisdom, which can tell us when we *really* need to eat to refuel the physical body.

Body or Cellular Hunger

One of the hardest hungers to tune into is cellular hunger. This hunger is a much more subtle hunger than the other seven. A way to get in touch with what cellular hunger feels like is to remember a time when you had the flu or were so sick that you didn't eat for several days. Just the thought of food made the stomach turn over. Then as you began to feel well enough to eat, and thought about what you wanted, certain foods were a "yes" whereas others were an emphatic "no!" Broth was a yes and the favorite chocolate malt was a big no. This is the body's wisdom at a cellular level. Another example is the experience of feeling faint or fatigued and realizing that water or protein is needed. This natural knowing is the body's recognition that it needs fluids, protein, carbs, fat, or minerals.

Mind Hunger

The mind chatters on all day long, and we get lost in endless old stories; or the mind craves more new information that will give it the "right answer." All the "I should eat that" stories, the "I shouldn't eat that" lessons, the media messages, dietary rules, calorie counters, family beliefs, and environmental voices often leave us confused, frightened, and anxious. We may find ourselves so worried about what to eat that we don't eat, or we may overeat because we feel so overwhelmed and worried.

Heart Hunger

When we eat in a particular way that is not in the best interests of our bodies, we are most likely trying to feed a hungry heart. This is what is commonly known as emotional hunger and, because it's a major source of disordered eating, we'll explore it more deeply in this chapter.

Now that you have an idea of what the eight hungers are, you can try this exercise first with yourself, then with youth. Placing just one raisin in your hand, see what you become aware of as you investigate each of these eight hungers. When you lead the kids through this exercise, place one raisin in the palm of each of their hands as you say something like this: "Pretend that you've never seen this small brownish object that is resting in the palm of your hand. Pretend that you have no idea what it is." Or you may need a bit more story to engage their interest, such as they are scientists whose spaceship crashed on a planet and they are running out of food. They have been charged with going out and seeing if there is anything edible on this planet. Unfortunately, all their testing equipment was damaged in the crash, so they must use the only "tools" they have to determine if this object is edible: their own senses.

1. *Eye hunger.* First, investigate this object with your eyes. Look at its color, shape, and surface texture. What does the mind say that it could be? Now rate your eye hunger for this object. On a scale of 0 (not hungry for it) to 10 (must eat it right now!), how much hunger do you have for this object, based upon what your eyes see?

2. *Nose hunger.* Now you investigate it with your nose. Smell it once, then breathe in and out of the nose, and sniff it again. Does it change your idea of whether it might be edible? Now, rate nose hunger: 0–10, how much hunger do you have for this object based upon what your nose smells?

3. *Ear hunger.* Bring the object up to your right ear. Is there a sound? Now hold it next to your left ear, maybe roll it between your fingers. Anything there? Rate your hunger, 0–10, for this object based on hearing.

4. *Mouth hunger.* Now place it in your mouth but *do not bite it*. You can roll it around and explore it with the tongue. What do you notice? Now bite this mysterious object, *but only one bite*. After biting it once, roll it around again in the mouth. Now chew slowly. What do you notice? Now rate mouth hunger. On a scale of 0–10, how much hunger do you have for this object, based upon what the mouth tastes and feels? In other words, how much does the mouth want to experience more of it?

5. *Stomach hunger.* Now you decide if you want to continue eating this unknown object. If you choose to eat it, chew it slowly, noticing the changes in texture and taste. You swallow it. What does the tongue do when you have finished eating it? How long can you detect the flavor? Is the stomach full or

not, satisfied or not? Now rate stomach hunger. How much does the stomach want more of this food?

6. *Cellular hunger.* As best you can, become aware of this object traveling from the mouth to throat down the esophagus to the stomach and passing into the body. Absorption begins as soon as we begin chewing. Are there any sensations that tell you that this food is being absorbed? How are the cells in the body receiving it? Now rate cellular hunger.

7. *Mind hunger.* Can you hear what the mind is saying about this food? (Hint: Often the mind talks in "shoulds" or "should nots.") Now rate mind hunger. On a scale of 0–10, how much would the mind like to have more of this food?

8. *Heart hunger.* Is the heart saying anything about this food? On a scale of 0–10, how soothing or comforting is it? Are there memories connected to this food? Would the heart like you to have more of this food?

Once you've led an individual or group through this exercise, go back through each hunger one at a time, asking what they noticed or observed. Each person's experience is unique, so there will be many different answers. There is no right or wrong answer. Each person's experience is fine, just as it is.

Stomachs Don't Have Taste Buds

Children are born intuitive eaters, knowing when and how much to eat. Research has shown that up until age 5, children eat until they are no longer hungry, and then stop. After 5 years old, children rely on other cues, such as how much is on the plate, being told to finish what is on their plate, or being told how much to eat (Tribole & Resch, 2012). Regrettably, children begin to mistrust their signals for hunger and fullness when parents, often with good intentions, begin to control the type and amount of food they feed their child.

Physical hunger is what most people associate with being hungry, but most people are aware of only two levels of hunger: empty and stuffed (Wansink, 2007). But just as we fill the tank in our car and watch the gallon count rise, there are lots of sensations in our "tank" as we eat that can tell us what our physical level of hunger is. Stomachs don't taste, they just feel volume, and we eat volume. Here's a way to begin to tune into the physical sense of stomach hunger:

> "So what I would like everyone to do is turn their attention inward and 'ask' their stomach how full it is right now. For example, is it empty, a quarter full, half full, three-quarters full, full, or overly full? Write down how full you are. If you can't tell how full you are, it's okay. This is a

skill you can relearn. What's most important is that you are curious, not critical."

It's helpful to draw a "stomach meter," similar to a car's gas gauge, on the board showing the empty to overly full choices.

Now give each person four slices of apple and suggest that everyone first look at a slice, smell it, and then slowly and mindfully eat the slices, reminding them how they paid attention to the raisin with each of their senses in the previous exercise. When everyone is finished, ask them to turn their attention inward and "ask" their stomachs how full they are now; then have them write down how full they feel, using the stomach meter scale (Bay, 2009).

Tuning in

Tuning in to physical sensations of hunger is very important. How do you know you are hungry? Where in your body do you experience hunger? What does it feel like? Here you are looking for words such as *growling, hollow, gurgling, fuzzy minded, tired, irritable,* or *shaky,* which are physical sensations in the body, not conceptual words such as *famished* or *starving.* As words are called out, list them on the left-hand side of the board.

Once you have a list of symptoms of hunger, ask about symptoms of anxiety or nervousness. "When you're anxious or nervous, what physical sensations do you feel?" If they are stuck for answers, you can point to the hunger symptoms and ask: "Does your stomach ever growl or feel hollow when you're anxious?" Write those on the right side of the board. Here's usually what shows up (Bay, 2009):

Symptoms of hunger	*Symptoms of anxiety*
Stomach growling	Same
Hollow feeling in the stomach	Same
Gnawing feeling in the stomach	Same
Headache	Same
Irritable	Same
Lightheaded	Same
Fuzzy mind/can't concentrate	Same
Shaky	Same
Tired/dip in energy	Same

Anxiety and physical hunger cues can often get confused because they are so similar. Eating inappropriate food at inappropriate times can increase anxiety and start a vicious cycle of feeling anxious and eating. For instance, we feel anxious about an upcoming test, and then eat because we confuse the physical sensations of anxiety with hunger. Then we are upset about what we have eaten, and eat to soothe the upset, and then our anxiety increases even more—and we eat more. Ultimately, shame and guilt may arise, and we may continue eating to cope with those feelings. Understanding that anxiety can be mistaken for hunger can help us choose other ways to calm down that don't include eating.

Heart Hunger

It's sad that, here in the United States, a land of plenty, there are people who don't have enough to eat. It seems that every other ad on TV is about food and eating. "Excessive" or "consumed with" might appropriately describe our obsession with food and eating, yet we often hear people say "I'm starving!" The majority of people in this country are not starving.

There's no question that we all want to be loved. During the vulnerable period of adolescence, experiences of connection, approval, love, mastery, and autonomy swirl amid peer and media pressure. Self-esteem, whether high or low, is front and center. The body, with its rapidly changing landscape, is often where all of these mixed feelings and sensations play out.

At one level, we all know that food is not love, and that it provides the energy that sustains our bodies. Yet, at times, we all use food to soothe, pacify, comfort, numb, reward, and punish. We know that whether we are bingeing on chocolate peanut butter cups, canned chickpeas, corn chips, donuts, or baby carrots, it's only a temporary fix, often followed by shame and guilt. Eating is natural and necessary, and using food to fill emotional needs is simply a confused effort to take care of ourselves.

An adolescent's hungry heart is longing for something to ease the pain, but that "something" isn't food. There is no way to fill the hole in a heart through the stomach. When kids can't get the attention or love that they need, they find other ways to comfort themselves. In the practice of mindful eating, we call unmet emotional needs *heart hunger*. If we use food to mask that void, eventually an unhealthy pattern takes root. In order to work with heart hunger, we have to be willing to recognize that thoughts, emotions, and physical sensations result in behaviors that may not get us what we really want.

> Emily is 16 and she tells me, Char Wilkins, that she knows she's an emotional eater, though she has no idea what emotions are driving her to binge on donuts. She is not aware that she's eating her anger, shame, hurt, and sadness because she believes she's not "good enough." These unrelenting critical voices drive her to use food to cope with demands that cannot be met. Additionally, she confides that she thinks about food constantly, but wishes she didn't. The more she tries to control her life by what she does or doesn't eat, the more out of control her life seems. She feels hopelessly trapped in this cycle of shame and blame.

Becoming mindful can help young people become aware of the true origins of their hunger and help them distinguish between physical hunger and heart hunger, so they can take better care of both. Food and eating are doorways into the rest of a person's life; how we use or misuse food to nourish ourselves is usually how we operate in other areas of our lives as well. Anything can be an entryway to understanding ourselves better, and food and eating are keys that open the door of a hungry heart.

Cycle of Emotional Eating

Perhaps it seems too simplistic to get down on the floor with a young person, easel-size paper and a marker in hand, and draw the cycle of emotional eating that feeds upon itself. However, understanding through this visual demonstration of . . .

- how a *thought* leads to an *emotional reaction,*
- how that emotional reaction leads to *using food* to cope with the unwanted *emotion,*
- which, in turn, leads to shaming and fearful *thoughts* that raise more unwanted *emotions,*
- which leads to the *emotional eating* that now consumes this young person's life . . .

can provide a pictorial voice to what has been unmentionable or unknown.

I sat on the floor with Sally, a young woman who, for the past 2 years, routinely restricted her food intake, then binged, and then used excessive exercise to punish herself and regain control. Looking at her life mapped out on the paper, she sat speechless for several minutes as tears ran down her cheeks. She whispered that she had no idea that her behavior was part of an endless circle of thoughts and feelings. She was able to articulate a new feeling for herself: "trapped." In simplest terms the mindless eating cycle looks like this: Feel upset, eat. Feel more upset for eating inappropriately, eat more. Feel upset, etc.

Always keep in mind that people take in information in different ways—whether through auditory, visual, kinesthetic, logical, verbal, solitary, or social channels—so offering not just words but pictures, movement, music, and other age-relevant modalities is essential.

Linking Emotions and the Body

Naming emotions can often be difficult for many in this age group. Carla, a 15-year-old who struggled with binge eating, had only two emotions in her life: sad and happy. Finding a way to invite a gentle knowing of even these two emotions is a place to begin. When working to develop mindful eating, it isn't always necessary to be talking directly about food and eating. In fact, it's helpful to give the topic some space. Food and eating are just the symptoms of what lies below. Bringing a gentle awareness to noticing emotions, as they are experienced in everyday situations, can be a safe way to begin building a connection between emotions, the body, and behaviors. Doing this kind of work in a gender-specific group setting helps to normalize emotions and begins the process of bringing awareness to, and naming, unwanted feelings.

A simple, brief exercise in which the three basic emotions of anger, sadness, and happiness are touched upon in the privacy of each individual's memory provides the opportunity to be with an emotion that may drive restricting and/or bingeing behavior. Bringing kind, nonjudgmental curiosity to the physical sensations that arise in the body with the emotion invites a gentle and kinesthetic understanding of the mind–body connection. For every thought and emotion we have, there is a chemical reaction in the body, and this reaction results in a physical sensation. For many adolescents this is a new and empowering learning. You might say:

> "This exercise will help you begin to connect an emotion and a physical sensation in the body, so that you can take better care of yourself. The body has a wisdom of its own, and can help you know what you are feeling before you are overwhelmed by the emotion."

> Lead a 1-minute breath meditation.

> "Allow a scene or incident to come to mind when you felt *mildly angry*. Perhaps someone cutting line in front of you, or arguing with someone, or a friend lying to you. Don't choose the biggest thing that made you angry, just a small one. Fully imagine this incident, as if you were there. Now, bringing your attention to your body, notice where in your body you experience anger. . . . Let that situation go and bring your attention to your breath.
>
> "Now, allow a situation to come to mind when you felt *sad*, such as losing a game, a tragedy in the world, a friend who was ill, or an animal that was hurt. Recall it fully in your mind. Now, bring your awareness to your body, noticing where in your body you experience sadness, what sensations are there. . . . Let that situation go and bring your attention to your breath.
>
> "For the last part of the exercise, bring to mind a situation when you felt happy, such as watching a pet play, being in a beautiful place in nature, or getting a smile from someone special. Fully experience *happy*. Where in your body do you experience happy? What are the sensations? . . . Let that situation go and bring your attention to your breath."

This exercise provides the experience that thoughts, emotions, sensations, and the resultant behaviors can be identified separately; that we may indeed have some say over what is going on inside; and that there exists the possibility of taking care of ourselves in a way other than via a reactive automatic pilot mode. This exercise also offers the possibility of remaining present with physical sensations rather than the emotions or thoughts about the incident. By not "running" from the physical sensations, but instead bringing a gentle curiosity to where they are felt in the body, adolescents can begin to notice the shape, size, color, texture, and movement of the sensations. By simply allowing them to be present without trying to change them, they will shift, grow smaller, intensify, change, and dissipate. The process of observing may leave students calmer and able to see that there are choices, rather than only one way, to deal with upsetting things in their lives.

Satisfying the Heart

In mindful eating work we plant seeds. We offer possibilities of growth and provide ways of caring for these tender beginnings. Knowing other ways to satisfy heart hunger that don't involve eating gives us alternatives with which to experiment.

Everyone has comfort foods, which can be a doorway to understanding other ways to take care of oneself. A group of young women with eating disorders bonded over this revelation when they heard that they weren't the only ones who craved particular foods. When I asked how their particular comfort food changed how they had been feeling, the underlying emotions driving the craving were made known. One girl said that sometimes, when she gets home from school, she feels driven to eat potato chips. She sits on her bed, eating one after the other, licking the salt off her fingers, and before she knows it, the bag is empty and she is no longer angry. She paused, then said, "Oh, I just realized I said I had been angry. I didn't realize that I want chips when I'm angry." Salt, sugar, and fat do influence our moods and emotions, which is why we are drawn to them. But what might be healthier alternatives?

One direction to go from this place is to ask what is the opposite of the unwanted emotion. For instance, one boy said he eats bags of peanut butter cups when he's feeling lonely, and for him the opposite of lonely is loved. I, Char Wilkins, often hear that the opposite of angry is peaceful, of sad is happy, and of anxious is calm. There's no right answer, just an act of sharing that can broaden into a conversation about which activities (other than eating the comfort foods) they engage in when they feel the "opposite" pleasant emotion. Being in nature, enjoying pets, doing art, talking to a good friend, playing sports, and listening to music are often mentioned. What these have in common is that they are present-moment experiences of connection and intimacy.

How do you know if your hunger is physical or heart hunger? Physical hunger goes away when you feel full and eating leads to satisfaction, whereas with heart hunger, you can still feel hungry after eating and that eating can lead to feelings of guilt or shame.

As an experiment, try one of these activities when an unwanted emotion arises or you are feeling stressed. If you check in with the body and realize that the stomach isn't hungry, then you could see if it's the heart that is hungry and "feed" it in one of these non-food-related ways. And if you aren't in a place where you can take a bubble bath, for example, could you take a few deep breaths and feel your feet on the floor? And even if you figure out that it is the heart and not the body that's hungry, and still choose to eat, you could eat that comforting food slowly and mindfully so you could really enjoy it, consulting with the stomach and body about when to stop.

Healthy Body Image

We can bring mindfulness to any movement, from walking and running to dancing and hiking. The important element is being in the present moment as you are active. There are some physical activities, such a yoga and qigong, where mindfulness is a core feature of the practice. In fact, at the heart of yoga is learning how to accept yourself and your body in this moment, being compassionate with yourself and making peace with who you are. Many schools and yoga studios offer classes for children and teens. Encourage students or clients who are experiencing body image dissatisfaction to try yoga or qigong or a related movement practice. For more information about yoga, movement, and sports, please see related chapters in this book.

As youth enter school, it's natural for them to compare themselves with peers as well as with images in the media—and comparison is the thief of joy. Two recent studies show that social media is having an adverse effect on the self-esteem of young girls. One study reported that 13% of plastic surgeons mentioned that patients wanted a procedure because they did not like their appearance on social media (American Academy of Facial Plastic and Reconstructive Surgery Media Resources, 2014). Many of these patients were teenage girls. A study from Florida State University demonstrated a link between time spent on Facebook and disordered-eating patterns (Mabe, Forney, & Keel, 2014). Choosing wisely the media that one consumes—whether a child, adolescent, or adult—and noticing how it affects us can greatly reduce the dissatisfaction that we feel about our bodies.

Sadly, in our competitive society, people are often valued for their looks and accomplishments rather than for who they are; this superficial type of evaluation can lead to feelings of inadequacy and unworthiness. Our children rarely learn how to be compassionate and kind to themselves, yet self-compassion plays an important role in mindful eating and healthy body image. Research shows that people who have high self-compassion engage in exercise for intrinsic reasons associated with enjoyment, as opposed to extrinsic reasons associated with an outcome (Neff, 2011). Like mindfulness, self-compassion can be learned.

> Amber is a 17-year-old high school student who struggled with body image dissatisfaction, which contributed to her disordered eating. Amber was bullied when she was in middle school and described wanting to shrink so no one could see or hurt her anymore. Through practicing yoga and self-compassion, Amber learned to accept, make peace with, and appreciate her body. When Amber began to practice self-compassion, she declared, "For the first time in my life, I feel it is okay to be kind to myself." She now uses self-compassion to help her with difficult emotions by putting her hand over her heart and silently telling herself: "This is a moment of discomfort. Most people have felt this way at some point in their lives. May I be kind to myself."

Self-compassionate people are also generally more comfortable with their physical appearance and bodies. Learning to accept imperfections and recognizing that beauty comes in different shapes and sizes are part of having a healthy body image.

> To be beautiful means to be yourself. You don't need to be accepted by others. You need to accept yourself.
>
> —THICH NHAT HANH

We are all hard on ourselves, and we all have parts of our bodies that we like and don't like. Addressing body image dissatisfaction among youth isn't easy, especially in a group setting, so here's a short exercise that will let them work individually, with the sense of privacy they are likely to need. Because self-compassion can be such a difficult concept for kids to grasp, this exercise focuses on kindness and acceptance, which are easier ideas for youth to understand. And really, self-compassion is a form of acceptance—accepting ourselves with kindness while we are experiencing discomfort. You'll need to have paper and pencils on hand:

> "I'd like to invite you to make a gentle and kind assessment of your body *for your eyes only*. I'm going to suggest that you start by making a list of the parts of your body that you like. Maybe you like your hair or your eyes. Please remember to consider things like strong arms or legs or that your stomach digests food well. [Give them a few minutes to write.] Now take a couple of minutes and look over your list and let yourself fully appreciate the parts of your body with which you are happy.
> "Naturally, there are parts of your body that you don't like so much. Just about everyone wants some part of his or her body to look or feel different than it does. Maybe you have blemished skin, or you think your legs are too short, or you believe your stomach is too big. Write down

the things about your body that you wish were different. As you do, remind yourself that we all have aspects of our bodies with which we're unhappy.

"Now take a couple of minutes to look over this list and remember, no one is ever 100% happy with his or her body. We all find it hard to feel such strong societal pressure to look a certain way. Just writing these things down can be uncomfortable. So let's be kind, supportive, and understanding toward ourselves as we look at this list.

"Finally, take the list with the parts of your body with which you are dissatisfied, and next to each body part come up with a reason or two you are grateful for what this part of your body does for you; you'll need to focus on the *function* rather than the appearance. Here's a few examples: My skin allows me to touch things and feel sensations of warmth and cold; my legs allow me to walk, skip, and run; my ears allow me to listen to music; my nose allows me to smell food cooking; and my stomach allows me to digest food and fuel my body."

Note: This exercise has been adapted from Kristin Neff's (2001) book *Self-Compassion: Stop Beating Yourself Up and Leave Insecurity Behind* to be more youth-friendly and focused on acceptance rather than change.

Teaching children and adolescents how to eat more mindfully could prevent a lifetime struggle with food, weight, and body image. With patience and practice, the skills learned through eating with awareness can become an intentional way of living and inform all areas of life. Using all of our senses to enjoy not only food, but other things in our lives as well can nourish and satisfy the heart. Slowing down to take in the warming aroma of food cooking can be as pleasurable as stopping to smell a sweet rose or the feel of a warm hug. Reestablishing a healthy and pleasurable relationship with food, eating, body, and mind can open the door to acceptance and compassion in other important areas of a young person's life. We can begin to give our youth the gift of attuning to and nourishing their bodies in loving, fun, and healthy ways so they can lead more balanced lives.

REFERENCES

American Academy of Facial Plastic and Reconstructive Surgery Media Resources. (2014). Statistics on trends in facial plastic surgery. Available at *www.aafprs.org/media/press_release/20140311.html*.

Bay, J. C. (2009). *Mindful eating: A guide to rediscovering a healthy and joyful relationship with food*. Boston: Shambhala.

Brown, J. D., & Witherspoon, E. M. (2002). The mass media and American adolescents' health. *Journal of Adolescent Health, 31*(Suppl. 6), 153–170.

Byrd-Bredbenner, C. (2002). Saturday morning children's television advertising:

A longitudinal content analysis. *Family and Consumer Sciences Research Journal, 30,* 382–403.

Cash, T., & Pruzinsky, T. (2002). *Body image: A handbook of theory, research, and clinical practice.* New York: Guilford Press.

Conklin, M. T., & Lambert, L. G. (2001). Eating at school: A summary of NFSMI research on time required by students to eat lunch. National Food Service Management Institute, University of Mississippi. Available at *www.schoolwellnesspolicies.org/resources/eating_at_school.pdf.*

Field, A. E., Camargo, C. A., Taylor, C. B., Berkey, C. S., & Colditz, G. A. (1999). Relation of peer and media influences to the development of purging behaviors among preadolescent and adolescent girls. *Archives of Pediatrics and Adolescent Medicine, 153,* 1184–1189.

Field, A. E., Camargo, C. A. J., Taylor, C. B., Berkey, C. S., Roberts, S. B., & Colditz, G. A. (2001). Peer, parent, and media influences on the development of weight concerns and frequent dieting among preadolescent and adolescent girls and boys. *Pediatrics, 107,* 54–60.

Hepworth, K. (2010). Eating disorders today —Not just a girl thing. *Journal of Christian Nursing, 27*(3), 236–241.

Mabe, A., Forney, K., & Keel, P. (2014). Do you "like" my photo? Facebook use maintains eating disorder risk. *International Journal of Eating Disorders, 47*(5), 516–523.

Neff, K. (2011). *Self-compassion: Stop beating yourself up and leave insecurity behind.* New York: HarperCollins.

Ozer, E. M., Brindis, C. D., Millstein, S. G., Knopf, D. K., & Irwin, C. E., Jr. (1998). *America's adolescents: Are they healthy?* San Francisco: University of California, School of Medicine.

Rancourt, D., Barker, D., Sato, A., Lloyd-Richardson, E., Hart, C., & Jelalian, E. (2014). Associations among change in overweight status, fear of negative evaluation, and weight-related teasing among obese adolescents. *Journal of Pediatric Psychology, 39*(7), 697–707.

Sanci, L., Coffey, C., Olsson, C., Reid, S., Carlin, J., & Patton, G. (2008). Childhood sexual abuse and adolescent eating disorder : Findings from the Victorian Adolescent Health Cohort study. *Archives of Pediatrics and Adolescent Medicine, 162*(3), 261–267.

Thomson, M., Spence, J. C., Raine, K., & Laing, L. (2008). The association of television viewing with snacking behavior and body weight of young adults. *American Journal of Health Promotion, 22*(5), 329–335.

Tribole, E., & Resch, E. (2012). *Intuitive eating* (3rd ed.). New York: St. Martin's Griffin.

Wansink, B. (2007). *Mindless eating: Why we eat more than we think.* New York: Bantam Books.

CHAPTER 14

Mindfulness in Nature

Iman L. Khan

Nature Is Magic

We are so fond of being out in Nature
because it has no opinions of us.
— FRIEDRICH NIETZSCHE

Nature has a profound effect on the way we experience our lives and each other. One of my earliest memories of the magical essence of nature was as a child, taking nature hikes in the Northern Kettle Moraine State Forest of Wisconsin. This 29,268-acre forest boasts a breathtaking glacial landscape with rolling wooded hills, serene lakes, and over 132 miles of hiking trails. The beauty of a sunny autumn day in Wisconsin is unforgettable; the scenery rich with colors of fiery reds, blazing yellows, burnt and brilliant oranges. Hiking the trails with my family was one of my favorite outdoor activities. I would often find a stick close to the trailhead, perfectly shaped and weighted for my small hands to carry. This stick would be deemed my "magic stick." Leading the way, with family behind me, I would allow my magic stick to choose the direction we would take as we journeyed to nowhere. Each time a fork in the trail would present itself, I would hold my stick out and ask it to point which way we should go. And then, with immense delight that only the purity of innocence can bring, I would burst with excitement as my hand moved either to the left or to the right, indicating which trail we should take. My family graciously indulged my imaginative play, and we carried on consulting the magic stick, walking the paths "it" chose for us. I remember feeling an overwhelming sense of gratitude and peace as I imagined nature to be making the decisions for us. Nature seemed to know just what to do.

As I grew into adulthood, I continued to have experiences in nature that were deeply spiritual and reinforced my connection to all living things. It was nature that led me to learn the formal practices of mindfulness and to later teach them to children and adults as a therapist. My ripened mind, which sought continually to learn and understand, found peaceful respite in the gentle, nonstriving, nonjudgmental quality of mindfulness. The overwhelming effects I experienced from the practice of allowing and accepting, rather than striving and forcing, became life-changing for me.

This change ignited my passion for sharing and teaching mindfulness to children and adults. I was fortunate enough to begin my teaching journey not far from the Kettle Moraine State Forest I had explored as a child. I taught at Nature's Classroom Institute (NCI), an environmental education program in Mukwonago, Wisconsin, where every child, regardless of socioeconomic status, is afforded the opportunity to discover the brilliance of nature. And so it was, my journey began.

Got Nature?

I go to nature to be soothed and healed,
and to have my senses put in order.
    —JOHN S. BURROUGHS

Unfortunately, spending time in nature seems to have become more of a luxury than a necessity. Research shows that children are spending half as much time outside as they did 20 years ago (Juster, 2004). The average American child spends 44 hours per week (more than 6 hours a day) staring at some kind of electronic screen (Rideout, 2005). So, it's no surprise to learn that the prevalence of obesity among children ages 6–11 more than doubled in the past 20 years, to 17% of children in this age group. The rate of clinically obese adolescents (ages 12–19) more than tripled, to 17.6% (Centers for Disease Control and Prevention, 2008).

Since the late 1980s, the percentage of Americans, young and old, taking part in fishing, hunting, camping, and other nature-based activities has declined by slightly more than 1% a year, for a cumulative reduction of 18–25% from peak levels (Pergams & Zaradic, 2008). This lack of direct exposure to nature, or as Richard Louv (2005) refers to it, this "nature-deficit," can negatively impact the physical and emotional health of both children and adults. Some research suggests that the rising rates of allergies and autoimmune disorders might be caused, in part, by less exposure to the healthy bacteria found in nature. And more science has linked reduced exposure to nature to a higher risk for developing obesity, cancer, heart disease, anxiety, and depression in both children and adults (Maas, 2006).

The statistics and consequences paint a grim but very real picture of how disconnected modern society has become from nature. This disconnect has grown and spread, with each new generation inheriting its ill effects (White, 2004). Our children's health and well-being are in jeopardy. The present moment is calling us to awareness—and awareness equals responsibility. And now, there is no turning away; only turning *toward*.

Science Supports Nature

Any fool can know. The point is to understand.
                    —ALBERT EINSTEIN

Scientific studies abound showing the significant results of nature's restorative and healing effects on the body and the mind. In fact, one study suggests that even viewing nature from a window or a picture can improve one's health and mood (Grinde, 2009). Other studies reveal that exposure to natural settings can improve focus and concentration; reduce attention-deficit/hyperactivity disorder (ADHD) symptoms; and lower stress, anxiety, depression, and rates of heart disease (Taylor, 2009; Hull, 1995). Spending time outdoors also raises levels of vitamin D, helping to protect children from future bone problems, heart disease, nearsightedness, multiple sclerosis, and some forms of cancer (American Academy of Pediatrics, 2009; McBrien, 2009). Just being in nature, it seems, can make kids nicer, enhancing their social interactions and increasing their valuing of community and close relationships (Weinstein, 2009). What a tremendous benefit for a generation of children being raised with social media and online gaming as a primary method for learning social and relationships skills.

The findings suggest that nature is important for both our mental and physical health. Being outside in nature generates a sense of feeling more alive. And studies show that this sense of increased vitality exists above and beyond the invigorating effects of physical activity and social interaction within the natural world. Richard Ryan, a professor of psychology at the University of Rochester, said, "Nature is fuel for the soul" (Skye, 2011, p. 148).

Feeding Minds, Feeding Souls

Education is not the filling of a pail, but the lighting of a fire.
                    —W. B. YEATS

NCI focuses on teaching students ecological awareness and fostering community. Mindfulness is taught through developing ecological awareness and nature-based group activities. The program's foundation reflects an educational philosophy of wholeness, which provides integration through individualized learning experiences. Individualized learning enables students of diverse needs to learn at their own pace and level. This approach to education respects both individual learning differences and cultural differences.

The NCI nature-based path to mindfulness begins by helping students discover that despite their differences, they share the responsibilities of taking care of their community and the earth. Thich Nhat Hanh said, "We touch the Earth to let go of the idea that we are separate and to remind us that we are the Earth and part of life" (Hanh, 2008, p. 108). Students at NCI learn how they touch the earth, exploring their individual impact on the planet through their consumption of resources. One way this awareness is taught is by using the online ecological footprint quiz (see *www.myfootprint.org*). A basic sample teaching script follows:

"All living beings have an impact on the Earth and its resources. Human beings particularly impact the environment by how we live on this planet. It is up to us to decide what kind of world we want to live in, and what kind of world we want future generations to live in. [Often teachers will show photo presentations of healthy and unhealthy ecological environments.] The unhealthy ecological environments you see have been caused by humans. But, we do have the power to clean and restore our environment. Has anyone ever participated in any Earth Day events? Here at Nature's Classroom, on Earth Day we walk and pick up garbage along the county roads. We also paint large rain collection barrels that we auction off, and use the money collected for planting in our organic garden. These are just a few ways we work to help save the environment. Does anyone have any suggestions for activities you could do in your community?

"To explore more ways we can protect our environment, we are going to learn about our ecological footprint. An *ecological footprint* is the amount of space that is required to support the resource needs and waste of a single person. Ecological footprints come in all different sizes. A large ecological footprint can be referred to as *overshoot*. Overshoot occurs when a person takes more than the Earth can renew. A small ecological footprint fosters what is called *sustainability*. Sustainability occurs when a person takes less than the Earth can renew. Let's take a look at some examples of overshoot and sustainability.

"Our ecological footprints are calculated by finding out how much energy we use. We use energy for food, water, shelter, and mobility. There are different ways we use energy in our home. [Show pictures of a room in a home.] Look at this picture of the room with the television and lamp. Do you notice anything? The television is on and the light is on, but no one is in the room. The door is also open and the heat is flowing out. The extra electricity we use is a waste and creates air pollution. Now let's look at the next picture, which shows how we can save the Earth. Switching off electronics, appliances, and lights is a great way to save energy; closing doors and insulating windows is another way to reduce consumption by conserving the heat generated from electricity or gas. [Other examples can be provided using automobiles/gas consumption vs. walking, riding a bike, carpooling; Hybrid cars vs. SUV or other high-gas-consumption vehicles; growing food vs. purchasing food; composting vs. garbage.] Now let's take the ecological footprint quiz. If you are not sure how to answer a question, just take a guess; there are no wrong answers. This quiz can also be found online at *www.myfootprint. org*, which you'll see written at the top of your page.

"We had one of our Montessori School students, who is your age, take the quiz online. I am going to use her answers to plug into the online version of the quiz, so you can see what it would be like if you were to take it online. [Plug in answers.] You can see from the result that if you were living like this student, you would need two Earths to live. Now, I would like all of you to complete your quiz. When you are finished, your group leader will help you record everyone's data on the group data sheet. Your table's group data sheet will be collected and we can calculate our total group's ecological footprint."

Upon learning about their individual and group impact on the Earth, students begin to learn positive ways to mindfully reduce their footprint, and they begin to practice some of these during their stay by composting food waste, conserving energy and water, turning lights out and reducing shower time, and so on.

Students feed their minds by acquiring knowledge about the types of ecosystems and their structures and functions. They gain awareness of how human beings contribute to the alteration of ecosystems, for example, through logging, destruction of wetlands, pollution, and so forth. Mindfulness is actively cultivated through students' participation in various sustainability practices on the 300+-acre campus, which includes a biodynamic and organic farm. Composting and controlled prairie burns are two sustainability practices that help students learn about positive human contributions to ecosystems. Students from urban communities, who have never had their bare hands in the dirt or their bare feet on a soft grassy prairie, begin to experience themselves and the environment differently. These experiences are often empowering and cultivate positive change. The opportunity of truly *being* in nature provides many urban students a chance to experience life in ways they have never imagined, from the viewing of stars on a clear dark night, to the sound of sandhill cranes flying overhead. The richness of nature can spark the imagination of students from all walks of life, encouraging them to look at their own communities with a new perspective, and if we are lucky, inspiring them to join the next generation of environmental leaders.

Nature Teaches Tolerance

What is tolerance? It is the consequence of humanity. We
are all formed of frailty and error; let us pardon reciprocally
each other's folly—that is the first law of nature.
—VOLTAIRE

Nature's laws do not discriminate. History has taught us, from the 8.3 earth-
quake near Tokyo in 1923 and the eruption of Mount St. Helen's in Washington in 1980, that the wrath of nature holds no preference for race, religion, or
sexual orientation. Nature does not judge us by the clothes we wear, the color
of our skin, or the balance in our bank account. The lessons we learn from
nature can assist us in the way we live and interact with the world. Yes, we
have come a long way since the civil rights movement of the 1950s and 1960s,
and we still have awareness to cultivate regarding how our own experiences
contribute to how we see the world and each other. Being able to effectively
initiate and facilitate critical reflection on race and gender diversity requires
the ability to critically examine one's own personal beliefs, opinions, and values about racial and gender identity.

Working with and teaching children of diverse populations can be challenging for teachers who lack cultural understanding and self-awareness. The
lens through which a teacher views the student contributes to how the student views him- or herself and the world around him or her. At NCI students
learn about themselves and others through mindfulness-based activities, such
as the ecology footprint, study of ecosystems, and yarn toss (next section);
together these lessons cultivate greater awareness and understanding of interconnection and "interbeing" (Hanh, 2001).

Yarn Toss

To begin, one student holds the end of a ball of yarn and states something
about himself. Then he holds the end of the yarn in one hand and gently
tosses the ball of yarn to another student, who states something different
about herself (e.g., "I have two brothers, I play the piano, I have brown hair,
and I broke my leg when I was 5"). She then holds the segment of yarn,
anchoring it between herself and the first student, and tosses the ball of yarn
to another student. The process continues until the result is an exquisite yarn
web that connects all the students to each other. The following sample script
describes the concept to the students:

"Look around . . . despite our differences, we are all connected. We are
connected in spite of our differences because we are all human beings
who inhabit this Earth, who feel sad, happy, mad, and scared at times.
From systems theory we know that what we do as individuals can greatly

affect and influence one another. We may not be able to predict how or when this influence will occur, but we can predict it will occur. To demonstrate that we are connected and influencing one another, I can simply tug on the yarn. Can you feel the tug? Now I will choose a few of you to gently tug on the yarn. Can you feel their tugs? Now, I would like all of you to gently tug when you feel a tug. Do you notice the ripple of tugs throughout the circle?

"What if I asked one of you now to let go of your string? And now another person can let go. Our connection is disintegrating. Just like this yarn, our actions and our words have a great effect on one another. Negative actions and words do not affect just one person; rather, they affect many. The beauty is in understanding that it works in reverse as well: Positive actions and words affect more than just one person; they affect many."

These mindfulness-based practices help young people reflect on their interconnection in the world even while celebrating the distinct expression of each self.

These practices cannot be taught or modeled authentically unless they are learned, practiced, and lived by the teacher. Mindfulness training and practice for staff are critical in keeping the lenses through which we view our students free of the distortion of judgment and bias. Mindfulness practice cultivates an attitude of letting go, or nonattachment, which is fundamental to positive conflict resolution efforts. We learn to accept students, and situations, as they are, not as we think they should be. We learn to become present to *all that is*, suspending judgment and evaluation. We allow students to be seen and heard for who they are as human beings, not as stereotypes and statistics.

The year I started kindergarten, 1975, was the first year the public school system in Milwaukee implemented the Chapter 220 program. The program's stated purpose was "to facilitate the transfer of students between schools and school districts, to promote cultural and racial integration in education, where students and their parents desire such transfer and where schools serve education interests" (Kava, 2013, p. 1). One of the major goals of this program was to achieve racial balance on a voluntary basis and at no cost to local taxpayers. Although well intentioned, putting students into an environment that is unfamiliar both culturally and geographically comes with many challenges. Though I was just a child, I clearly remember behavioral challenges and frequent fights; the transferred students were struggling to be themselves and to feel like they belonged in an environment that did not know how to support their needs. Perhaps the administrators and teachers were not given the tools they needed to fully understand that these students were more than just numbers, they were human *beings,* raised in a society that told them from the day they were born that they were different and less than, due to the color of their skin. And then they were suddenly outsiders, trying to fit into schools and communities that had little to no diversity. How frightening that must have been.

Practicing awareness also means acknowledging differences. Due to political and economic changes, the diversity in staffing in many places, including NCI, has diminished. The past few years the staff has consisted of mostly European Americans. Rarely do students notice this racial factor. However, during weeks when urban public schools attend, with populations that consist of mostly African and Latino Americans, it is staff members who take notice and begin to consider their ability to relate (Neumann, 2014). The experience of learning in nature is new to many urban students, and the discomfort of unfamiliar situations and experiences can be challenging. Staff members occasionally worry about their ability to cultivate trust and relate to students from different backgrounds; however, they demonstrate respect by sharing their own experiences. Staff members simultaneously acknowledge both the differences and the shared humanity; they speak of their passions and share their stories. They engage not just as teachers, but also as learners, challenging everyone to find opportunities to teach and learn throughout the week.

The adults create an authentic environment of inclusion and respect through their words and actions. Urban students have unique skills in their ability to recognize what is going on around them, and they possess refined interpersonal skills, also known as "street smarts." Urban students are first to recognize authenticity or its lack, and can quickly discern whether an adult really cares about them. Programs where staff members are not traditional classroom teachers have opportunities to develop uniquely powerful relationships with kids in a very short amount of time. Freed from the constraints of standardized learning goals, staff can be authentic and cultivate both intellectual and emotional curiosity.

Of course this advantage comes with its own challenges. Not every student buys into the program's philosophies and approaches from day 1. It is challenging to establish connections with students founded on mutual trust and respect in such a short amount of time. But embodying the values of mindfulness and drawing on the philosophy of individualized education, staff teachers are able to focus on meeting the needs of students regardless of background and abilities. They are committed to having mutually respectful interactions with both students and their chaperoning teachers during field groups, classes, and meals. It is in this gentle interpersonal balance of give-and-take, where students feel a sense of empowerment and inherent value, that an accepting environment is created. One student commented: "The staff [at NCI] are so cool, they really listen to you like what you are saying is the most important thing they've ever heard."

Nature Led Me to It

Choose a job you love, and you will never have to work
a day in your life.
                                        —CONFUCIUS

The work at NCI entails working directly with the staff and the students. Staff is trained in the basic foundations of mindfulness and on techniques for incorporating aspects of mindfulness into the curriculum formally
and informally. Additionally, the staff members are supported in using a nonjudgmental awareness while conducting their classes and activities. Remov-
ing judgment as a teacher, and as a human being, can be an insurmountable
task. We live in a society where we are constantly being judged and judging
ourselves—test scores, GPAs, performance reviews, and more. We are taught
to find value based on the end result, rather than to value the process. The act
of judgment is almost as automatic as the inflow and outflow of our breath.

Practicing nonjudging, present-moment awareness is essential in cultivating an openness to experience moments *as they are*, rather than as we wish
them to be. As NCI teachers, we are encouraged to first bring awareness to
how we judge ourselves, and then to explore how these judgments are often
turned outward, creating a shield to protect ourselves from our inner critic.
Using mindful breathing exercises, we learn to watch our thoughts and stay
present with our emotions. This practice helps us all to understand how fears
and mindlessness alter the way we observe and interact with students. Learning to acknowledge and be responsible for our subjective lenses of experience,
it becomes possible for us as teachers to cultivate a more authentic presence
and create a more open and compassionate space for students to learn how to
be themselves.

Teachers also learned mindful communication and leadership practices,
such as conscious communication (Hanson, 2009). Mindful communication
begins by asking ourselves, "Is what I am about to say *kind, true, necessary*,
and does it *improve the silence?*" Reflecting in this way creates a pause, or as
Victor Frankl (1992) referred to it, a space, between stimulus and response,
during which we can consciously decide how to respond. Staff is also trained
in reflective listening practices, which include skills in positive interpersonal communication (Rogers, 1995). In the mirroring exercise one person
communicates a problem and how he or she is feeling and the other person
reflects back an understanding of what the person has communicated. This
is an excellent mindful communication tool for teaching the practice of nonjudgmental, moment-to-moment awareness, which ensures that both participants stay present and avoid judging or misinterpreting the other's feelings
or emotions. Many students quickly learn that teachers at NCI communicate
in different way than many teachers they have encountered in their schools.
Voices are not raised. Hands are raised only when a teacher wishes to get

the attention of the students. Staff teachers raise a hand indicating a request for silence in order to communicate information. Once the teacher raises a hand, students are cued to stop what they are doing and raise their hands to indicate respect for the speaker and signal their readiness to receive the communication. It is such a beautiful process to partake in, and witness, as silence begets silence. Unfortunately, this way of communicating is often quite distinct from the all-too-frequent shouting, threatening, or provoking used to obtain silence and compliance in other settings. Students report feeling respected and acknowledged when they are addressed in this way. Many teachers have commented that there would be *"no way"* this would work in their classrooms back home. Staff members often respond, "Maria Montessori long professed that if changes in the environment are made then changes in behavior will be observed" (Montessori, 1994). When we take both students and staff out of their usual reinforcing context, it becomes clear how the natural environment, and a new interpersonal environment, impact behavior, and new behavior impacts the environment.

Practicing Mindfulness in Nature

Mindfulness in nature can be cultivated through both informal and formal practices. At NCI, mindfulness is interwoven informally throughout the curriculum. In the following material I offer several practices students find engaging and meaningful. These nature-based practices, both the formal and informal, can be incorporated in any natural environment and adapted to suit the specific needs of the student population.

Walk the Walk

If you seek creative ideas, go walking.
—RAYMOND I. MYERS

Walking meditation or mindful walking is one practice that students seem to particularly enjoy. There are several variations that can be applied, making it a desirable activity to which most youth can relate. One variation, adapted from *Mindful Teaching and Teaching Mindfulness* (Schoeberlein, 2009), is the walking-with-awareness activity. I referred to it as the "Walk As If" activity. This is an excellent introductory activity that seems to appeal to students of all ages and backgrounds, and can be modified for students with physical handicaps. Students are instructed to walk in different ways that communicate and mirror their awareness of specified thoughts, emotions, and sensations. Begin with a short introduction to the activity that includes the guidelines for movement and for processing the session after the activity. A sample script follows:

"Good afternoon, friends. Today we are going to participate in an activity called 'Walk As If.' The intention of the activity is to teach you how your thoughts, feelings, and actions—what you do—are all connected to each other. Now before we begin, I would like to present a few guidelines for our movement. See these boundary markers? [Staff members walk to each one.] These mark the space where we will be moving. Please stay within the space, as it will be important for you to hear instructions during the activity. This activity is conducted in silence, so I will be the only one speaking throughout it. Again, it will be important for you to hear my directions, and practicing silence will also ensure that you are able to hear. We will begin the activity with the sound of a chime, and we will end the activity with the sound of the chime. After the beginning chime, I will give you an instruction that describes a way to walk. As you walk, draw your attention to your experience, how you are walking, what you are thinking, what you are feeling. If at any time you become distracted with other thoughts, or sounds, or observations, just simply bring your attention back to your walking. After about 20 seconds, I will give another instruction that describes a different way to walk. I will do this about nine times. So you will hear a set of instructions about nine times. I will ring the chime again to mark the end of our activity. When we are finished, we will gather quietly here in the center and sit in a circle."

The suggestions for ways to walk are listed next; each one can last about 20–30 seconds. Be flexible and observe what works best for your students. I encourage you to be creative and add your own ideas to this list.

Walk As If . . .
1. You are extremely tired.
2. You are late to meet a friend for a movie.
3. You are very sad.
4. You are feeling very proud and happy.
5. You are in a snowstorm.
6. You have never been outside before and are experiencing nature for the very first time.
7. You are walking barefoot on black concrete in the summer heat.
8. You are walking in the woods on a trail that is overgrown and difficult to follow.
9. You are focusing only on the how your body moves within the natural environment, as it is, in this moment.

Once the activity is over and students are seated in the middle in a circle, the Sharing Circle guidelines can be presented. A sample script follows:

"Now that we are all seated together in our Sharing Circle, I'd love to hear about your experiences during this activity. Has anyone ever been involved in a traditional Sharing Circle? A Sharing Circle is a tradition used in native cultures for the purposes of resolving conflict, sharing stories, and learning. Traditionally a stick, referred to as a 'Talking Stick,' is used to designate the person talking, and also as symbol for courage, respect, and truth. Only the person holding the stick has permission to speak. Because we modify this tradition slightly in order to help guide discussions, I will hold an 'invisible' stick that allows me to moderate the discussion and ask questions from time to time. The general guidelines for sharing in the Sharing Circle are that everyone gets a turn to speak. If you choose not to share, then you may pass the stick on to the next person. We give respect to the person speaking by listening to him or her with our ears and our bodies. In the Sharing Circle, we share our experiences; there are no interruptions, judgments, or putdowns. I also ask that you are mindful of the time, so that all who wish to share have a chance to do so."

The processing portion of the activity can be quite impactful, not only for the students, but also for the teachers. Most of us can confirm that learning the practice of cultivating awareness can be a very vulnerable and emotive experience, so creating an atmosphere that promotes a safe sharing space is essential.

Processing Questions

"What is the purpose of doing this activity?"
"Why is it important to be aware of how we are thinking or feeling?"
"What did it feel like to walk on purpose? What made it easy or difficult?"
"How did changing the way you were thinking change the way you walked?"
"How does paying attention to details influence our experience of the present moment?"
"Can the way we walk, or our actions, have an effect on the way we feel or think about ourselves, each other, the environment? Give examples."

This is where the seeds of mindfulness are planted. Students cultivate awareness and are introduced to the interrelationship among thoughts, feelings, and sensations. They begin to explore how their past experiences can shape their beliefs in the present moment. They also learn how paying attention to things to which they may have never given attention can feel uncomfortable and unfamiliar, and also promote clarity and understanding.

Into the Night

Into the darkness they go, the wise and the lovely.
—EDNA ST. VINCENT MILLAY

Another informal practice of mindfulness that has been particularly popular among our students is the night hike. During a night hike, our senses become more attuned to the present moment—to what is occurring *now*, rather than what was, or what will be.

The students begin with a general introduction to the night hike and learn about local nocturnal animals and their adaptions to living in low-light conditions. They learn about the interactions and interdependences among nocturnal animals and the ecosystems of which they are a part. Students are reminded that everything in the darkness is also there during the daylight hours, just hidden away, like our unconscious thoughts. This is an important concept to process because many students who have not experienced nighttime without the sights, lights, and sounds of the city may have some fears about the dark. With the guidance of staff, students challenge themselves to overcome their fears about the dark and walking outside at night. They learn how to work together to remain safe and to support each other throughout the experience. As the students walk the paths, without bright flashlights, they begin to learn how to rely on all of their senses, rather than relying solely on their vision. Throughout the hike, the students participate in various activities that further their understanding of the basic concepts of science, ecosystems, mindfulness, and community (Khan, 2014).

Before beginning, students are introduced to the rules and safety guidelines. Staff and students do not use flashlights on the night hike. If a light is needed along the way, staff will use a red light first, because it does not degrade night vision as much as a white light. Staff members carry both white and red flashlights in their backpacks with safety gear, just in case.

The hike can begin at dusk or nightfall. With the younger students, we usually start our hikes at dusk to minimize anxiety about hiking in total darkness. If you choose to begin at dusk, this is an excellent time for students to start with a walking meditation. Encourage them to notice the light levels, the color changes in the sky, the scent of the air, the temperature of the air, and the animals they can see and hear before and after the sun completely sets. The more familiar they become with using all of their senses, the more comfortable they will be using all their senses in the transition to darkness.

When it becomes dark, the hike can move into the forest. Walking, students are encouraged to use their senses, first to listen for any nocturnal life. As students continue to walk and stop at various intervals, they listen to stories and learn to practice awareness in the present moment. Below I have listed a few activities in which the students engage in during night walks.

What Color Is It?

Colors are nearly impossible for humans to see at night. To demonstrate this point, at dusk as the night hike begins, students are given a small scrap of paper and a crayon with the wrapper removed. It is best to use basic dark colors such as blue, brown, red, and so forth. Students are instructed to examine the crayon and guess its color. They are asked to write their guess on the piece of paper. The crayons are collected, and the students keep their pieces of paper until the hike is over. Then, in the light, they check to see if they correctly identified the color.

A Pirate's View: Candle Activity

It is said that pirates often fought both in the dark of a ship's hold as well as in the light on deck. Wearing an eye patch would allow them to remove it in the dark and not have to wait for both eyes to adjust to the lack of light—so they would not be easily surprised by an attacker in the dark of the ship's bowels. Our eyes produce a chemical called *rhodopsin* when in low-light situations to improve our night vision. In fact, within 5 minutes of being in the dark, we can see 1,000 times better than when we initially entered the darkness. When our eyes are exposed to light, all of the rhodopsin we have been producing is instantly destroyed, making our night vision poor again. Our eyes are not able to produce rhodopsin again until we are back in the dark.

Students are asked to stand in a circle and to completely cover one eye, so that no light enters. They are then told that a candle is going to be lit and they are to stare at the flame until it is blown out (about 10–15 seconds). As soon as the candle is blown out, students are asked to open and close each eye, one at a time, and to describe the differences between what they are able to see with the eye that was covered and the uncovered eye.

Sitting Solo: Vision Quest

A vision quest is a traditional Native American rite of passage involving several days of solo fasting and prayer done in the secluded wilderness; the purpose of the quest is to obtain spiritual knowledge, clarity and life direction, what is termed the *vision*. Although the core of the vision quest is solitary, traditionally this activity is never done *alone*. There are guides, mentors, or shamans to help prepare and support those who journey (Krown, n.d.). This teaching helps the students understand that although they each have their own unique experiences while on their journey through the woods on the night hike and through life, ultimately, they are not alone. We all walk the path together.

Students are invited to participate in a solo sit. They have the opportunity to challenge themselves by sitting still on the trail by themselves for about 5–7 minutes while staff waits out of sight, but nearby. Sitting times can be extended, but generally 5–7 minutes alone in the dark seems to be an adequate length for students to both reap the benefits of silent sitting and to not be defeated by their fears. Program schedules allow for longer sitting periods with middle school and older students.

Students are instructed to sit in silent reflection, with their eyes open, observing the forest, being mindful of their breath and how their breathing connects them to the ecosystem through the release and exchange of carbon dioxide and oxygen, how their bodies connect to the Earth, and how they connect to the unseen yet supportive community. When the time is up, staff retrieves students, one by one, and their reflections are shared at the next stop.

Shooting Star: Lifesaver Activity

A story or poem is told about the stars and the constellations. Tell your own or choose one you already know; just be sure to make it fun. Before you tell the story, give each student two or three unwrapped, Wint-O-Green Lifesavers. Tell the students not to eat the Lifesavers, and wait for further instructions. At the appropriate point in the story have the students put the Lifesavers into their mouths and bite; this biting down on the minty lozenge creates "shooting stars" in their mouths. Students get a real kick out of this. Our staff often creates original impromptu fiction stories, which specifically lead to a shooting star climax. Have fun with this—be creative!!!

After the story the students are introduced briefly to the concept of triboluminescence, an optical phenomenon in which light is generated through the breaking of chemical bonds in a material when it is pulled apart, ripped, scratched, crushed, or rubbed. When sugar crystals are crushed, tiny electrical fields are created, separating positive and negative charges that then create sparks while trying to reunite. Wint-O-Green Lifesavers work especially well for creating such sparks, because wintergreen oil (methyl salicylate) is fluorescent and converts ultraviolet light into blue light.

This is also a wonderful opportunity to parallel mindfulness, sharing a personal story about breaking apart and coming together. I have used a personal story about my best friend and me. We met when we were 15 years old and have been best friends ever since. Although we only lived in the same city for about 4 years, our friendship continued to grow stronger despite being pulled apart by heading to different colleges and settling down in different states. We even had an argument once that kept us from speaking to each other for almost 2 years! But we learned through a mutual friend that we were both expecting our first baby within a month of each other and we came together, our friendship renewed and our bond strengthened. I love referencing Pema Chödrön's (1997) quote from her book, *When Things Fall*

Apart: Heartfelt Advice for Difficult Times. She says: "We think that the point is to pass the test or overcome the problem, but the truth is that things don't really get solved. They come together and they fall apart. Then they come together again and fall apart again. It's just like that. The healing comes from letting there be room for all of this to happen: room for grief, for relief, for misery, for joy" (p. 10).

The night hike concludes with students and staff walking carefully back to the main campus, listening for an owl's hoot, pointing out the constellations, and invoking all the senses on their journey out of the forest. The energy of the returning students is markedly different from their energy when they departed. Students report feeling empowered, proud, and grateful, with a new appreciation for the Earth and its inhabitants. Having experienced a few moments in time where they were not separated by gender, skin color, age, or the clothes they wore, students display a deepened respect for themselves and each other. They appreciate the opportunity to experience the world without bias or judgment, to rely on all their senses to keep them present in the here and now. They have learned to trust themselves and each other. A principal from a visiting school shared this report: "Our school teachers get to watch the students' metamorphosis from a nervous, unsure student to a confident, courageous person. We are city slickers learning botany and zoology out of a textbook or internet. At NCI, they [students] are IN it, living it and taking the students out of their comfort zone; walking in a dry riverbed that was once a river and looking for fossils and creatures. Challenges were not about winning, it's about the process of learning . . . how you collaborate" (Lubel, 2012). Mindfulness, the practice of cultivating a concentrated awareness in the present moment, is both a daily habit and a lifelong process.

The last mindfulness practice is adapted from Thich Nhat Hanh's (2013) *Planting Seeds: Practicing Mindfulness with Children*. It is called the Pebble Meditation. I have adapted it quite a bit, and the original version can also be found online or in the book.

Ripple Effect: Pebble in the Pond Meditation

Breath is the bridge which connects life to consciousness, which unites your body to your thoughts. Whenever your mind becomes scattered, use your breath as the means to take hold of your mind again.
—THICH NHAT HANH

This practice is one of my favorites because it gets to the heart of mindfulness and to the benefits of practicing it. It also explains the neuroscience of how we process emotions, visually and metaphorically, which is important knowledge not only for students, but for all of us! When we begin to understand how the brain works, we can learn to work with, rather than against, nature. We can learn that acceptance is not defeat, but rather an act of freedom that releases us from the struggle of trying to resist what is here, now.

The practice begins by instructing students to find three small pebbles or rocks, small enough to fit all three in one hand. This designation of size is important, as there is usually one or two students who will find rocks the size of small boulders. Once the pebbles are found, students find a safe spot next to a still body of water—anything from a puddle to a pond can work. Students are instructed to look into the water, focusing first on their in-breath and their out-breath, while noticing their reflection in the water. Students are then asked to bring to mind something that is unpleasant, perhaps a recent argument or a situation that is making them sad or frustrated. With the next in-breath students are instructed to express something they are feeling, such as, "Breathing in, I'm feeling anger." They are instructed to carefully drop the pebble into the water as they say their feeling, and with their out-breath they are instructed to say, "Breathing out, I let it go." Students are invited to repeat this process two more times, using their remaining pebbles.

Then we discuss how our thoughts and emotions are like the stones, and our minds and our bodies are like the water. When the stones enter our minds and hearts, they have a ripple effect. Both "positive" and "negative" thoughts have a ripple effect. When we learn to breathe and simply allow our thoughts and emotions to come and go, like ripples in the water or waves on a shore, the mind becomes still. And it is in the stillness that we can see most clearly. If we do not learn how to pause and allow the ripples to subside, we may react mindlessly and make choices we regret. When we learn to breathe and simply watch our thoughts, allowing our emotions to come and go like waves on a shore, like ripples in the water, the mind will become still. And we will begin to see things as they are, not as they appear to be. It is only our thoughts and emotions that take us away from the present moment, and from the appreciation that we are already whole, just as we are. We are already perfect, just as we are; everything we need is already with us. We just need to be still long enough to be able to see it clearly.

Working with Resistance

It is easier to resist at the beginning than at the end.
        —LEONARDO DA VINCI

Not every student will arrive with an open heart and an open mind. As a professional who works with youth and adults, I do not believe it is my job to tell individuals to open their hearts or their minds. But I *do* believe my job is to open my heart and mind first. My job is to *be*, and in *being*, invite others to become comfortable and learn how to be themselves.

The well-known idiom "Do as I say, not as I do" references behavior that is hypocritical. This saying has its origins in social learning theory; implicit in it is the understanding that youth are powerfully influenced by observing and modeling adult behaviors, attitudes, and emotional reactions. Fortunately, when working with children from all backgrounds, adult hypocrisy will not go unchecked. For students, any incongruity between what we say and what we do is confusing and frustrating. Students who come from social learning environments that are harshly authoritarian and powered by disrespect, mistrust, and fear are particularly sensitive to just being "told" to act respectfully. Telling them to do what I say is just another reason for them not to do so. These students are conditioned to believe that in order to gain respect, it must be taken away first. We must not only speak of respect, but we also must *be* respect.

Yes, boundaries and guidelines need to be provided from the start and then upheld consistently. And *how* that is done has more of an impact on resistance then what is said. Students who are resistant usually are more so in the beginning of our work together, when there is no relationship established or trust built. When I open my heart, share a story, reveal myself, I become me, a woman with a name, Ms. Iman. Being authentic is the number one antidote to resistance; kids see right through pretenses. When we become real with ourselves, we become real with each other. It is no longer them against us, or you against me; it is now *we*: we, the collective; we, the individuals. Just like snowflakes, each one diverse in splendor and design, we all have unique characteristics and gifts that are ours alone. And just like snowflakes, when we are working together, blanketing the earth with our individual purposes, those differences are much harder to see. All that can be seen is light and beauty.

Conclusion

I only went out for a walk and finally concluded to stay out till sundown,
for going out, I found, was really going in.
—JOHN MUIR

Teaching mindfulness in nature begins first by practicing it ourselves. Reconnecting with the Earth and rediscovering our childlike nature as it emerges when we walk barefoot on the yielding green grass, or when we attempt cartwheels in the cool sand on the beach at sunset. When we meditate beneath a tree, with the weight of our bodies cushioned by the soft soil below, we find our place in and on this Earth, literally and figuratively. We ground ourselves in what is real and alive within us and strengthen our connection to all that is alive around us. We begin to understand that nature has its own mindfulness practices: The practice of letting go naturally occurs each autumn as the leaves change their colors and let go of their hold of the branches; the practice of opening up, as the buds burst forth and the flowers begin to bloom each spring. Mindfulness in nature restores our senses, brings us back, again and again, to what is now, to what is present. May we all be inspired to cherish this gift by giving back through conservation and sustainability practices, through educating our youth and enjoying nature's gift together. May we all be blessed with the patience, the courage, and the compassion to continue to inspire our young learners to love themselves, to love their Earth, and to love each other.

REFERENCES

American Academy of Pediatrics. (2009, October 26). Many children have suboptimal vitamin D levels. Available at *www.aap.org/en-us/about-the-aap/aap-press-room/Pages/Many-Children-Have-Suboptimal-Vitamin-D-Levels.aspx*.

Centers for Disease Control and Prevention. (2008). *Childhood obesity*. Washington, DC: National Center for Chronic Disease Prevention and Health Promotion, Division of Adolescent and School Health.

Chödrön, P. (1997). *When things fall apart: Heartfelt advice for difficult times*. Boston: Shambhala.

Frankl, V. E. (1992). *Man's search for meaning*. Boston: Beacon Press.

Grinde, B. P. (2009). Biophilia: Does visual contact with nature impact on health and well-being? *International Journal of Environmental Research and Public Health, 6*(9), 2332–2343.

Hanh, T. N. (2001). *Thich Nhat Hanh: Essential writings*. Mary Knoll, NY: Orbis Books.

Hanh, T. N. (2008). *The world we have: A Buddist approach to peace and ecology*. Berkeley, CA: Parallax Press.

Hanh, T. N. (2013). *Planting seeds: Practicing mindfulness with children*. Berkeley, CA: Parallax Press.

Hanson, R. M. (2009). *Buddha's brain: The practical neuroscience of happiness, love and wisdom*. Oakland, CA: New Harbinger.

Hull, R. M. (1995). Nature-based recreation, mood changes, and stress reduction. *Leisure Sciences, 17*, 1–14.

Juster, F. T. (2004). *Changing times of American youth: 1981–2003*. Ann Arbor, MI: Institute for Social Research, Child Development Supplement.

Kava, R. (2013). School Integration (Chapter 220) Aid. *Wisconsin Legislative Fiscal Bureau, 25*, 1–16.

Khan, N. I. (2014, April 4). Night hike experiences (I. L. Khan, Interviewer). (Personal Interview with Noor Khan, participant at NCI program)

Krown, M. K. (n.d.). Vision fasts and training. Retrieved from *www.schooloflostborders.org/content/huffington-post-what-vision-quest-and-why-do-one*.

Louv, R. (2005). *Last child in the woods: Saving our children from nature deficit disorder*. Chapel Hill, NC: Algonquin Books.

Lubel, H. (2012). Personal interview with principal from Beren Academy in October 2012.

Maas, J. V. (2006). Green space, urbanity, and health: How strong is the relation? *Journal of Epidemiology and Community Health, 60,* 587–592.

McBrien, N. M. (2009). What's hot in myopia research: The 12th International Myopia Conference, Australia, July 2008. *Optometry and Vision Science 86*(1), 2–3.

Montessori, M. (1994). *Discovery of the child.* New York: Random House.

Nature's Classroom Institute. (1995–2013). *Curriculum manual.* Mukwonago, WI: Author.

Nature's Classroom Institute. (2014). Available at *www.discovernci.org.*

Neumann, L. (2014). *Overcoming personal and group challenges.* Unpublished essay. Mukowengo, WI.

Pergams, O. Z., & Zaradic, P. A. (2008). Evidence for a fundamental and pervasive shift away from nature-based recreation. *Proceedings of the National Academy of Sciences of the United States of America, 105*(7), 2295–2300.

Rideout, V. E. (2005). *General M: Media in the lives of 8–18 year olds.* Washington, DC: Henry J. Kaiser Family Foundation.

Rogers, C. (1995). *Client centered therapy.* London: Constable.

Ryan, R. W. (2010). Vitalizing effects of being outdoors and in nature. *Journal of Environmental Psychology, 30,* 159–168.

Schoeberlein, D. S. (2009). *Mindful teaching and teaching mindfulness: A guide for anyone who teaches anything.* Somerville, MA: Wisdom.

Skye, A., Meera, L. & Dean. C. (2011). *Self-care for life: Find joy, peace, serenity, vitality, sensuality, abundance, and enlightment—each and every day.* Avon, MA: Adams Media.

Taylor, A. K. (2009). Children with attention deficits concentrate better after walk in park. *Journal of Attention Disorders, 12,* 402–409.

Weinstein, N. P. (2009). Can nature make us more caring?: Effects on immersion in nature and intrinsic aspirations and generosity. *Personality and Social Psychology Bulletin, 35*(10), 1315–1329.

White, R. (2004). *Young children's relationship with nature: Its importance to children's development and the Earth's future.* Kansas City, MO: White Hutchinson.

Wisconsin State Park System, Kettle Moraine State Park Southern Unit. (n.d.). Available at *http://dnr.wi.gov/topic/parks/name/kms.*

CHAPTER 15

Mindfulness with a Beat

Embodied Practice in the Key of Song

Betsy Rose

"If you're happy and you know it—clap your hands!" How many of us can sing (and clap) this all-too-familiar childhood song, decades after we first heard it in preschool? It is truly remarkable that long after memories from our earliest years have faded beyond recall, a simple tune can be on our lips—and in our hands—at a moment's notice. From annoying advertising jingles, to camp songs, spiritual music, or a hit on the radio when you were a teen, music has emotional staying power, sticking power, making it a wonderful tool for helping mindfulness practice "stick" in the minds and hearts of people of any age.

I often use these "sticky" familiar tunes to create mindfulness songs for young people; one example is my rewrite of "The Happy Song":

If you're happy and you know it—
Take a breath! [All breathe slowly in and out.] [Repeat.]
If you're happy and you're breathing
Oh your joy will be increasing
Breathing in and out is sweet—
So take a breath!

What is it about music that sticks to our brain? Why is music such a universal source of happiness, emotional uplift, community connection, and spiritual nourishment across cultures and time? What does any of this have to do with mindfulness practice for youth? And does one have to be a musician to incorporate music into mindfulness practice?

In this chapter I explore all of these questions and offer a variety of ways that music can enhance your time with young people, whether as a classroom teacher, musician, therapist, camp counselor, or parent. I draw primarily on my own musical repertoire of original songs, with reference to a wider range of resources from other musicians and mindfulness practitioners. Exploring how the expression of sound, song, and rhythm are activities of body, mind, and heart that both parallel and enhance mindfulness. I focus primarily on singing, but also touch on other musical forms such as the use of percussion, bells, wordless vocal toning, and sound. I provide specific songs, as well as styles and subjects that work well with youth of different ages and backgrounds. Along the way, you will find some neurological information about the unique way the brain processes music and song. Most important, I hope to leave you with a sense of enthusiasm, adventure, and confidence about your ability to integrate music into your life and the lives of young people. Even those who are protesting "But I cannot carry a tune!" can teach, lead, and even enjoy making mindful music with the young people in your life.

If you aren't an experienced musician/song leader, you may be wondering how you can put the teachings and practices in this chapter to use in your own work with youth. For your ease, all the musical/song references in this chapter can be heard, downloaded, or linked to through my mindful music website *mindfulsongs.org*. And for those versed in musical language and leadership, these audio resources may be useful as well, providing melodies and further lyrics to songs I reference that may not be familiar to you.

Some of us (myself included) are seasoned musicians, choral directors, or music teachers. The learning edge for me in integrating mindfulness into music making has been to add to the familiar performance criteria (e.g., pitch, enunciation, accuracy, tempo) the vital dimension of the internal experience of the musician—body awareness, emotional presence, relaxation, awareness of self-judging or critical thoughts, and more. As Melanie DeMore, a youth choral leader and professional singer/song leader, puts it: "Music opens up a space inside people—both the listener and the musician. With music, we create a space where people can feel their larger self. It's important for the singer to get off the printed page, and tune into the three-dimensional, embodied experience" (Melanie DeMore, personal communication, January 21, 2013). Your own experience with mindfulness will guide you best in how to integrate the practice into your musical leadership. And what a gift it will be to the youth, the listeners, and yourself!

Music and Mindfulness: Natural Partners

Music is a natural vehicle for mindfulness practice. Like mindfulness, singing involves breath, body, brain, and heart. It is an embodied practice. Our heartbeats, breath, and other body processes are naturally rhythmic; rhythm is felt deeply and naturally in our bodies. The body vibrates internally in response to musical sound, most especially when singing or sounding a musical tone. Music involves silence and sound, listening and expressing, inward and outward. Master vocal teacher Kristin Linklater, (1976) among others has pointed out that in singing, our breathing naturally deepens and lengthens; the very act of singing, even a lively song, can have a naturally occurring calming effect on the entire energy system. And singing together is a connecting force, unifying and harmonizing a group, which you probably have already experienced. Of course, you hardly need an expert to tell you this. Anyone who has joined in the joy of a community chorus, drummed in a circle, engaged in freestyle rhymes and beats with friends, cranked up the radio in the car, crooned a lullaby to a child, or sung in the shower knows that body and spirit are nourished by music. If you haven't experienced this particular form of nourishment lately, here's a little introductory practice to try.

Experience Music with Beginner's Mind

Take a moment to sit or lie down, take a few easy breaths, and become aware of your body and sensations. Relax. Slowly sing or hum a simple song you know, perhaps from childhood. Any song that comes easily with little effort or recall works well—something as basic as "Twinkle, Twinkle Little Star," "Swing Low, Sweet Chariot," or "Kumbaya." Slow the song way down, taking easy breaths when your body asks for them. Do not dwell on the sound you are making; rather, focus on the inner experiences of vibration, breath, warmth, and any other sensations that arise. Become curious and nonjudgmental. You may encounter some resistance or even critical thoughts about your voice (often painful residue from childhood shaming), or questions about whether this is a waste of time, or whether you are doing it "right." With mindfulness now in the musical mix, you can make room for these thoughts without giving them free rein to undermine your singing. Bring your focus back again and again to the simple sensations of breathing, the body's experience of singing, and noticing where you feel vibration or sensation (chest? head? throat?). Perhaps you can experiment with changing the volume or intensity of your sound, and noticing the accompanying physical changes of vibration, warmth, relaxation, or tension. Notice how your mind, body, and heart feel.

The Musical Brain

I have been writing and singing songs with children and adults for over three decades, and am convinced that music—both listening to, and creating it—is fundamental to our humanity. My message to people of all ages who are shy about singing is, "Singing is not a skill, it's a birthright!" Singing is as natural to humans as breathing and feeling. And science is now discovering and clarifying the unique ways that music benefits the brain.

- Music is a "whole-brain" activity" represented in mechanisms widely distributed throughout the brain, rather than localized in a single region, as are (some) other kinds of information, such as visual or movement information (*www.childrensmusicworkshop.com/advocacy/brain.html*).
- Music engages the areas of the brain involved with *paying attention, making predictions,* and *updating (an) event in memory* (*http://med. stanford.edu/news_releases/2007/july/music.html*).
- Researchers suggest that music stimulates areas deep within the amygdala and hippocampus, where *emotion and long-term memory are processed* (Shulman, 2008).
- Recent study found that singing increases *oxytocin, a "feel-good" hormone* associated with breastfeeding, connection, and nurturing in both men and women (*www.ncbi.nlm.nih.gov/pubmed/12814197*).

Music: The Universal Language

From preschools to at-risk youth programs, from inner-city classrooms to affluent private schools, and in the poverty-ridden *jugghi* (slum) neighborhoods of Delhi, teachers, musicians, and mindful leaders are finding innovative ways of using music to create pathways into mindfulness practice, self-awareness, and emotional balance for youth of all ages. Here's a lovely example, from a memorable classroom visit to a low-income, very diverse school in San Francisco, of how music can gather and stabilize a restless group:

> Darine, a mindfulness teacher with the Mindful Schools program, had warned me that this particular first-grade class would be a challenge. She was near the finish of a 6-week mindfulness program at the school. She confided to me that she had barely been able to move beyond the first day's lesson, listening to bell and breath practice. Week after week the lesson had focused solely on bell listening and breathing; each session felt like starting all over again.
>
> As we entered the classroom, I took a long breath and listened for some inner guidance on how to gather, settle, and connect with this band of squirmy bodies and stimulated, active minds. Darine had chimed the bell several times, and a small portion of the class had begun to sit and "put on their mindful body," while others jumped up to touch my guitar, roll on the carpet, and call out questions. "It" just wasn't happening.
>
> So I put down my guitar and drew a different tool from the kit of possibilities for moments like this: the human voice in song. With a brief preface—"If you can hear my voice, repeat after me"—I launched a call-and-response chant with a simple tune:
>
> "Mindfulness is in my heart"—I wave my hand to invite them to echo. A few voices echo "Mindfulness is in my heart." Mostly the chaos persists.
>
> "Mindfulness is in my bones"—A few more voices echo. The restless ones, hearing their classmates joining in, listen up. (Am I missing something? What's going on?)

"Mindfulness is in my mind"—The tide is turning! The sound of many voices draws in the last stragglers and for several precious moments, we are attuned and together. Handclaps and thigh slaps accompany the rhythmic back and forth.

"Mindfulness is in my hands"—Smiles on faces, small bodies sway with the rhythm. The kids make up more lines: ". . . in my feet . . . in my breath," and so on. When the song ends, Darine is ready with the bell and her warm smile, inviting them into a moment of breath and silence. The focus and presence may be tentative, but they have arrived, and another song is quick to follow.

"If you're happy and you know it—take a breath! . . ."

The 15 minutes have flown by, and we close with a quick goodbye song (to the tune of Stevie Wonder's "Isn't She Lovely?"): "May you be happy / May you be peaceful / May you be filled with love."

Darine and I exit the classroom with big smiles and sighs of relief. Like the children, we have been energized, calmed, and rebalanced by the magic of harmony, mindfulness, and a positive shared experience. Where the breath and bell had failed to gain a foothold, music had found a way in.

Music: The Ultimate Mindful Multitasker!

Here is a list of what I've discovered about the profound and practical ways that music brings an individual or group into harmony:

Harmonizing the individual mind–body

- Singing is a present-moment, embodied experience involving breath, mental focus, listening, body awareness, relaxation and pleasure. Sound familiar?
- Music engages multiple areas of the brain that are exquisitely coordinated to integrate rhythm, language, auditory sensation, emotional centers, pleasure and reward centers, and more.
- Music "sticks" in memory; a lesson, practice, or concept that is sung is more likely to be retained and recalled, and more likely to be fun. Consider how teachers use songs to announce cleanup time, snack time, or other challenging transition times of day for young children.

Harmonizing the community

- Singing together creates group cohesion and supports inclusion. Everyone is breathing, sounding, and listening together. Groups create a sound that is richer and somehow bigger than the sum of their parts. Many "me's" become a "we," creating a satisfying sense of belonging and intimacy across differences.
- A song sung together helps pull a group into focus, and can provide a transition from a state in which energy and distraction are spilling in all

directions, toward cohesion, unity, and a common purpose. For many reluctant participants, hearing the voice of a friend invites participation, as self-consciousness and judgment are transcended by the song.

• Songs offer an anchor in a classroom or group—for example, a "touchstone" song that is sung everyday at a certain time or to begin a mindfulness period, end a session, or mark a transition. For those children who live unstable lives with little predictability, this consistency can be deeply reassuring.

• Youth with different learning styles can participate fully, regardless of reading, writing, language, math skills, or even the ability to focus on academic tasks.

• Singing "mindfulness practice" offers the highly active youth an alternative to the more traditional sitting practice. Music is physical and kinesthetic, and can easily include movement. Let's face it, who doesn't want to dance and move their body to the rhythm of a great tune?

Embodied Vibration: The Inner Experience of Sound

Are you eager to get started, but uncertain how your group (or you!) will respond to actually singing songs? Not everyone is immediately comfortable launching into a song with a group. So here's a playful and nonthreatening practice I've developed that can ease a group into the singing process. For shy or reluctant singers, this activity can circumvent resistance and serve as a bridge to actually singing. It's fun and evokes curiosity, not judgment. It reliably draws the entire group into enthusiastic participation. For those of you who are professional music teachers, this practice is one way to introduce mindfulness to your instrumental or vocal students. Playing or singing with attention and awareness and noticing process more than outcome can enhance their sensitivity and skill as musicians—and it's fun!

Where Is Your Voice?

The fourth graders look at me quizzically. "The voice is located in your body, of course, but where? Touch some part of your body that you think has to do with your voice."

Tentatively, fingers land on the throat, or the chest, or the mouth. A few touch their heads.

"You're *all* correct! It takes many different parts of your body to create your voice. Who wants to say what part they thought of?"

"Lungs!"

"Throat!"

"Mouth!"

"Brain!"

"Heart!"

"Feet??"

"All of the above! Now, try this! Put two fingers lightly on your throat, and we will all make a soft sound together on the vowel 'eh.'"

The class follows my lead on a long tone that gently sets the vocal cords vibrating. Smiles spread across a few faces as they feel the vibrations under their fingertips.

"Those vibrations travel up into your mouth, then bounce off your teeth and hard palette [I have them touch the roof of their mouth with a finger to feel the hard palette]. You are an amplifier! Those vibrations echo around your mouth and skull just like when you shout into a cave."

We play with creating a tingle in the lips by softly closing the lips over the sound. "Now you can *really* feel the vibrations; they are making your lips tickle, aren't they!" And by creating a rising and falling "siren" on a hum, we send the vibrations up into the skull, setting the sinuses, forehead, and temples humming as well.

This playful activity incorporates mindfulness (paying attention to bodily sensations, feelings, sound), inviting curiosity and discovery rather than performance and evaluation. It helps to circumvent "judging mind" and thoughts of "How do I sound?" This can be particularly helpful with fourth-grade and older boys whose voices may be changing and whose peer consciousness is high. And it is easy for non-English speakers to participate without having to deal with singing words. It's a little scientific, a little playful, and it's about *all* of us, and our universal capacity to create sound. And it has deep roots in our shared human history. Toning, chanting, drumming, and instrumental melodies have been used for millennia in the service of fostering individual healing, shifting inner experience, and creating community cohesion.

"Now that we've warmed up our instrument, let's use it to sing this song." And we're off!

A final note: When there are group members who are really resistant to singing, I encourage them to mouth the words silently (the brain seems to learn both the words and music when mouthing without sound, along with others singing). Also, inviting reluctant singers to join in as a scientific experiment, noticing their physical experience of making sound (as in the opening exercise on p. 278), can help defuse the embarrassment.

Keep It Simple, Keep 'Em Involved: Simple Song Forms for Inclusion, Mindfulness, Transitions, and More

If your musical skills feel shaky, it can be helpful to remind yourself and your students that people without formal musical training created much of the music we love and sing and remember. Children's playground rhymes, field hollers from the days of slavery, sea shanties, and myriad types of spiritual community singing are all forms of music that spring from the human impulse to bring the community together, lighten the workday, express ourselves, and work and play in rhythm. Anyone can lead, and anyone can follow.

You don't need to play an instrument to lead a song. Most songs will work fine with just voices. Songs have an internal beat that drives the music along. Lightly tapping your thighs or a simple drum for extra rhythm support can help keep everyone together. Additionally, you may find parents of your students who have musical skills and can be a resource. And you can use recorded songs from my mindful music CD *Calm Down Boogie* and other resources, but be sure that *you* sing along. For specific tips and tools for leading songs and using recordings, see pages 290–292.

Three song forms I have found to be faithful allies in my work with youth and adults have been zippers, call and response, and parodies.

Zipper Songs

In this form, participants contribute to an existing song structure by "zipping in" a new word or phrase. If you have ever sung "Old MacDonald Had a Farm" or "She'll Be Coming 'Round the Mountain," you have sung a zipper song. This flexible, open-ended song form invites creativity, collaboration, and inclusion. And the act of co-creating a new song or musical entity provides an empowering sense of ownership and pride—an experience the heart and mind will long remember.

Much of the American song library and many songs about social justice and human liberation are indebted to the African American singing tradition and are themselves zippers. Songs such as "We Shall Overcome," "We Shall Not Be Moved," and "Oh Freedom" are all songs that have been sung, updated, revised, and made new again with social justice movements such as labor, civil rights, and the empowerment of women, people with disabilities, those from LGBTQ communities, and more.

Call-and-Response Songs

These songs are a traditional way for a community to sing, drum, and sound together, making music instantly accessible to everyone. The "leader" sings a short line, and the group echoes the phrase or sings a second response, which is then repeated after each new "call." There is nothing to read or learn, just careful listening, repetition, and maybe some embellishment. This style reaches far back into the histories of work, play, worship, protest, and celebration.

Many spiritual songs follow this structure, and many children are familiar with it through their own worship tradition. "Oh When the Saints Go Marching In" is an example of both a zipper and a call-and-response song.

> Oh when the saints (oh when the saints)
> Go marching in (go marching in)
> Oh when the saints go marching in (marching in)
> Oh how I want to be in that number
> When the saints go marching in.

Traditional zipper lines include "Oh when the sun refused to shine" and "When the trumpet sounds the call." Your zipper lines could include group guidance ("Oh when we all clean up the room") or mindfulness practice ("Oh when I sit and feel my breath").

Parodies

Parodies take a familiar tune and add new words to it (see "If You're Happy and You Know It, Take a Breath"). Who can forget, or wishes they *could* forget, "Jingle Bells, Batman Smells," or "Weird Al" Yankovich's marvelously irreverent pop parodies. In current popular music, layering a new lyric or song over a familiar older hit is part of the remix/mashup trend. Parody is a truly democratic, open-source art form: imitation combined with wit and creativity. Parodies seldom fail to delight, and the catchier and more contemporary the tune, the easier it is to impart a lesson through parody lyrics.

Songs as Touchstones and Anchors

Group leaders can use a touchstone song to open and/or close a session, and with repetition over time, the song sinks "into the bones," as the first few bars cue the group to what is coming and what's expected (e.g., put away schoolwork, gather together, sit in a circle, "put on mindful body"). Familiarity with and repetition of a song creates a sense of rhythm to the day, thereby responding to the human need for the underlying, reliable order that signals safety. A few songs I've found useful as touchstones follow.

"This Little Light of Mine"

This is a great touchstone and zipper song, one that is familiar to many adults and youth. It can easily be adapted to mindfulness.

> This little light of mine, I'm gonna let it shine. (Repeat twice.)
> Let it shine, let it shine, let it shine.

It can be used to express well wishing for others (loving-kindness):

All around my family I'm gonna let it shine.
All around my classroom . . . my neighborhood (etc.) I'm gonna let it shine.

And it can remind us of the inner feelings of compassion, well-being, and kindness that can help us in hard moments:

When I'm feeling lonely, I'm gonna let it shine.
When I'm feeling sad . . . When my friend is feeling bad, I'm gonna let it shine.
Deep within my heart.

"Bring Your Voice into the Circle"

In this touchstone/gathering song, a favorite of mine, the group can "zip in" elements needed to create a circle of song and mindfulness:

Bring your body into the circle (repeat twice)
It's time for mindfulness (or, it's time for circle time)

The group can zip in "bring your heart," "bring your mind," "bring your breath . . . your love . . . your sadness . . . your energy . . . your focus. . . . "

"May You Be Happy"

I close every school mindful music assembly or classroom visit with "May You Be Happy" (to the tune of "Isn't She Lovely?"). Adults often report that this song—a simple and singable way to send good wishes to each other—becomes a touchstone part of their family or community routines. After I visited a school in Vancouver, British Columbia, Canada, the teacher was delighted by the idea of having students lead the whole school in singing this every morning as part of the broadcast morning announcements!

You can probably think of examples of zippers or short, accessible, or familiar tunes that can be adapted for transitions; for gathering, settling, or closing a session; or to make chores like cleaning up a little more fun. A list of familiar tunes to get you going can be found on my website (*www. mindfulsongs.org*).

Mindful Music for Older Youth

So far, many of the songs we've considered are most appropriate for younger children. How can music be part of mindfulness practice for older elementary and teenage youth? We know that preteen and teenage youth are actively absorbing music from outside of the classroom and family. They are often wary of music generated by adults rather than their youth culture. The sight of me, gray-haired and playing a visibly nonelectric guitar, can be a real initial barrier. Here are some approaches that I have found lead to positive experiences of mindful music with older elementary and middle school children and teens.

What Is the Sound of 600 Hands Clapping?

In the hollow echo chamber of a suburban Massachusetts school cafeteria, it could be deafening, but today we are actually attuned and in sync! Three hundred fifth and sixth graders, sitting cross-legged, join me in rhythmic thigh slaps—*short short*—and a chest slap—*loooong, one two threeeee, one two threeee*. I have an adolescent urge to break into "We will, we will rock you, rock you!" Instead, I start the "Loving-Kindness Rap," chanting the verse in rhythm to their body percussions:

> Out on the playground things can get rough
> Kids act mean, kids act tough
> You're glaring at me, I thought we were friends
> Do not know what I did, but this could be the end
> What am I gonna do . . . ?"

Middle-school-age youth can be at a challenging age to capture and captivate. Rocking a bit of rhythm and spoken word can bridge the gap between generations and cultures. Sure enough, the smirks transform into smiles as they thump away, listening. We reach the chorus, I swing into the guitar, and they sing along:

> What about loving-kindness,
> Talkin' 'bout loving-kindness.
> That's right
> Send it direct from my heart to you
> It can break down walls it can cut right through
> And it makes me feel strong down deep inside
> I got—(*clap*)—loving-kindness—that's right!

Amber Field, a vocal artist and teacher who includes the didgeridoo (a wind instrument developed by aboriginal Australians) and a variety of percussion instruments in her work, has this to say about working with preteen and teenage youth:

> "Rhythm and participation work really well. We start a clap–stomp circle where I start a beat, the next person adds in something a little different but connected, with hands and/or feet, and so on around the circle. We

do this with vocal sounds too. Body percussion, using the whole body as instrument, is great too. I see them become focused, alert, and engaged as they follow and participate in rhythm making." (Amber Field, personal communication, January 24, 2013)

I often open my sessions with upper elementary or middle school youth with "Woke Up This Morning with My Mind (Stayed on Freedom)." This song is a wonderful example of a zipper song, and it's effective as a touchstone or transition song. The lyrics offer a springboard for discussions on focus, attitude, and goals. *Staying one's mind* means choosing what to focus on and staying with it despite distractions and setbacks. Historically, the song was used in the civil rights movement, and we can ask the youth what *they* "stay their mind on" when faced with one of life's myriad challenges. We then zip their ideas into the song ("stayed on friendship . . . my mom . . . my dog . . . hope . . . love . . . confidence . . .").

A song from *Calm Down Boogie* that reliably engages youth of all ages is "Equanimity." The song has catchy sing-along chorus, and the verses describe various situations young people face in which slowing down and taking a breath can make all the difference (e.g., a moment of fear, taking a test, being teased by a sibling). Early on in the song I take a pause, once they've heard the chorus, and make sure the participants have some kind of working definition of *equanimity* (building vocabulary here!). We discuss emotional balance, the importance of responding rather than reacting, the impermanence of emotions, and the ways our minds can make situations better or worse. This exploration leads to conclusions about the importance of noticing our thoughts and "not believing everything we think."

Equanimity! Everything gonna be all right
Equanimity! I've got balance deep inside
Equanimity! I don't have to fight or flight
I can breathe and be still, trust all is well
Offer some calm to whatever's going on
With equanimity.

A fourth grader from Oakland, California, demonstrates his understanding of equanimity when he says, "I like when it says you don't have to fight or flight. I don't have to use my fist or my legs, and I don't have to run away with my legs."

Another fourth grader, from Tacoma, Washington, wrote, "It was fun singing with you. I feel so peaceful now. When my mom gets mad (even though she doesn't show it), I will sing her your song!"

And a ninth grader from Menlo Park, California, said, "Equanimity helps me whenever I encounter a challenge. I have actually written multiple verses of the song when I have gotten into sticky situations."

This older age group is often interested in how the brain works. The phrase "don't have to fight or flight" can open up a short, informative talk (which I often embed in the middle of the song—a spoken interlude between verses) about what happens when the brain is flooded by fear, anger, shock, sorrow, and how the fight–flight–freeze response can be eased by slowing down, taking a mindful breath, noticing thoughts, and responding skillfully to the situation.

Mindfulness and the Wider World

I have learned over the years that the older elementary and middle school youth are eager to make connections between mindfulness and the wider world, and to see its practical uses in the "real world" where certain realities are more and more a part of their lives. They learn that mindfulness is more than a "feel-good" avenue to better concentration or personal peace. Mindfulness is an empowering, inner resource that allows them to become peacemakers and agents for social change in the world they inhabit. And I give them examples.

"We Still Have a Dream"

In 1983, tens of thousands of people gathered on the Lincoln Mall to celebrate the 20th anniversary of Martin Luther King, Jr.'s historic 1963 march on Washington. I wrote a song for the occasion, "We Still Have a Dream," and performed it at the march. For many years now I have been singing this song with upper elementary and older groups, linking Dr. King with Gandhi, who may be less familiar to this age group. The two leaders shared a practice of nonviolent social change. Their power as changemakers was rooted in the practice of slowing down, turning inward, accessing an inner voice of wisdom, waiting before acting, and always having compassion for those oppressing and opposing them. In the movie *Selma*, we see the character of Dr. King pausing in a moment of great intensity, facing armed state troopers, and then kneeling on the bridge, seeking guidance. It is a riveting moment of mindful awareness in the midst of danger and fear. This practice of pausing, listening, feeling and finding wisdom is of enormous benefit to young people living in our modern culture. The chorus of "We Still Have a Dream" is call and response:

> We still have a dream (we still have a dream)
> We still have a dream (we still have a dream)
> Every step of the way . . . brings on a better day . . .
> And the spirit is willing . . . and the journey is long
> And we've got to be strong . . . 'cause we still have a dream. . . .

In the classroom or small group, this structure becomes a template for the group writing their own lines. The children can create verses articulating their own dreams for our world. In a larger group, I ask for examples of a vision they have of a better world, and sing their vision back to them, or share verses created by other students that express that vision. (The responses are inspiring and often include a world without pollution, war, animal cruelty, poverty, and, of course, without homework!) A fourth-grade class wrote:

Well, I have a dream (well I have a dream). . . . People won't be mean (echo)
We'll work together. . . . Respect one another. . . .
No matter your age. . . . No matter your size. . . .
Don't judge the outside. . . . Just count the inside. . . .

The Role of Music in the Retention of Mindfulness Practice

Many children take naturally to mindfulness practice. Being present and embodied, seeing the world with fresh eyes is, after all, their specialty! The unique "staying power" of music, activating both kinesthetic and mental memory, makes it a valuable resource for offering children lasting practices in awareness, emotional balance, insight, self-soothing, and resilience.

A second-grade teacher in a classroom of primarily Asian students in the Sunset District of San Francisco introduced mindfulness in her classroom through music. Using the *Calm Down Boogie* CD, she and the students began learning and singing the songs together. The students created a complex circle dance to one song ("We Are a Circle within a Circle") and energetic hand and body motions for another ("Equanimity"). The group had taken the raw material of the song and made it a community work of art and a central and enduring part of their classroom culture. When I visited the classroom, I found that these students knew every word of the songs; as we discussed some of the teachings within the songs, the children's grasp of mindfulness would inspire many a grown-up!

Another inspiring school experience occurred at an Afro-centric K–6 public school in Northern California, where I shared a mindful music assembly with the school just before their winter break. Later in January, I met a mindfulness teacher at the school and she told me this:
She met with the children after a 2-week vacation, expecting a few days of review to get back up to speed with material. She asked the children what they remembered about mindfulness from the fall. Several first graders spontaneously burst into song, singing word for word a rather long song I had performed in the assembly. Though they had heard it just once, it was all there, along with hand motions and a little new choreography they had created.
Another classroom teacher at the school added, "With the singing, and with them owning those words, it makes a big difference. They say things

like 'in that song we say we used our heart,' 'in that song we say may you be peaceful.' It sticks with them."

One last example of music and retention is the fact that many children go home and sing/teach the songs to their parents and siblings, thus subtly introducing the practices to a wider community. Songs not only stick, they travel well!

Using Recorded Music for Mindful Listening and Singing

Listening mindfully to sound and song is yet another modality for engaging youth of all ages. Here are a few practices I have learned from other mindfulness teachers:

- A teacher in Mexico volunteers with teenage girls in a local orphanage. These stressed and restless teens loved lying on the floor and breathing while listening to recordings of "Somewhere over the Rainbow," a Spanish version of "Imagine," and other calming songs.
- In one New York City public school, sixth-grade teacher Jeffery Pflaum (see Chapter 18, this volume) had the children record their own mix of favorite songs. They listened on headphones while relaxing at their desks, then wrote about what they felt, saw, and thought while listening to the music. The writings were read aloud anonymously and discussed.
- At the King Street Center in Burlington, Vermont (serving at-risk youth and young refugees from African nations), mindful leaders introduced the "Mind the Music" program, using recorded music chosen by the teens as a vehicle for helping them focus on relaxation, presence, breath and body awareness, and their own emotions.
- In one second-grade classroom, the mindfulness teacher has the children listen to the recording of "I Am Breathing" as they breathe and listen mindfully, then respond to his follow-up questions: "What did you hear about where you can practice mindful breathing? Did she leave anything out? Where else can you practice mindfulness? Let's listen again, and this time sing along."

Now It's Your Turn!: Practical Tips for Teaching and Integrating Mindfulness and Music

By this point, my hope is that you feel inspired about the possibilities of weaving together the joyful practices of music and mindfulness. Before concluding, I would like to offer a few tips for organizing and leading a session of music and mindfulness.

Some Basics on Song Leading and Group Participation

If you are working in a classroom or group, know that most children *love* when the teacher/leader sings. Singing reassures them and invites them in on many levels. Your singing creates safety! One obvious truth is that a *singing* teacher is not an angry, about-to-blow-up teacher. If you feel a bit unsure or awkward, be transparent (e.g., "I haven't done this much before, and I know you'll help me"). Once you get going, the children will sing along and drown you out. Sharing in this way, you demonstrate leadership and courage, and convey the important message of inclusiveness: Making music *is* for *everybody,* not just the select few.

Many children in so-called "developed" nations are growing up in a time where cultural *consumption* is the norm. Yet in many "undeveloped" nations, children are creating culture and art out of necessity. For example, children in Paraguay are playing in an orchestra with instruments made entirely of materials scavenged from trash heaps (*www.youtube.com/watch?v=yiYFcuIkBjU*). I have found that in the United States, many young people have rarely, if ever, participated in live group singing. The notion that they themselves could create their own music and message (e.g., through zipper songs) is an experience of engagement and empowerment that teaches children that their voices and ideas are needed and valued; they are creators and contributors, not just observers or consumers. Teaching self-expression through music, or any creative activity, is a vital part of helping nurture world citizens who feel connected and empowered as they come of age.

Although most children tend to pick up words and music very quickly, and listening to a song once may be enough, for some populations or age groups, you might need to adapt your teaching. Should you want or need to teach the songs more carefully, here are some tips:

Learning a Melody

- Sing the song a little more slowly, and teach one line at a time: You sing it, and the community sings it back (echoing).
- Repeat any difficult lines two or three times.
- If the melody seems tricky, have everyone hum it, without words.
- If the song is a little long, teach it line by line and put the lines together, two at a time or four at a time, rather than trying to sing the song straight through after singing each individual line.

Learning Rhythm and Words

- If a song has many words said quickly, or a tricky rhythm, or it just seems hard for singers to form all the words, practice chanting the song without melody, in the rhythm of the song several times, then go back to singing.

- Encourage kids to visualize what is happening in the song, as if they were watching a movie in their minds, or to make movements acting out the song.
- Remember that songs with a simple rhyming structure will be easier to remember.

Creating a Mindful Music Session[1]

Some of you may be in a situation where you are able to spend 20–30 minutes or more on mindfulness practices with your group, whereas others may only have 5–10 minutes. Either way, there are components that can make a mindful song session rich and engaging. Here is a sample flow for a 20- to 30-minute session:

- Gathering song
- Settling/unifying song
- Song or songs to introduce or support a specific teaching or practice (mindful breathing mindful eating, sending kind thoughts, awareness of body sensations, etc.)
- Discussion or further practice of the "lesson"
- Closing/farewell song
- And of course, simple bell and breathing practices can be part of the flow at any point.

For examples of songs that fit nicely into these functions, see the Teachers Guide on my website (*www.mindfulsongs.org*).

Music and Special Audiences

Non-English Speakers

Many of you may be teaching youth who are English language learners, or you are teaching in a multicultural setting. Many of the song examples in this chapter might not be relevant to your groups. But every language and culture has iconic songs—tunes virtually everyone knows from childhood, and those are the melodies that can become your mindfulness "parody" songs. Two examples are "Arirang" (popular Korean folk tune) and "Feliz Navidad" (a favorite Mexican holiday song). I make every effort to bring mindfulness songs to my groups that in some way reflect their cultures both because doing so creates a sense of inclusion and also a sense that mindfulness is not some foreign, imported activity, but is universal, human, belonging to all of us.

---

[1] I am indebted to Sarah Pirtle for this lesson plan concept, from her excellent social skills curriculum, *Linking Up* (1998).

Individual or Group Trauma

Many of our youth have experienced painful individual losses and frightening experiences, the death of a relative or beloved pet, incarceration of a parent, violence in the neighborhood, and/or various forms of abuse. An entire group and community can be impacted by an event such as the Boston Marathon bombing, the Newtown school shootings, or extreme weather disasters.

Songs and singing together have always been a vital resource for individual and community healing and comfort. Music positively modulates the nervous system and brain chemistry; it is calming and relaxing by its very nature. Songs provide a safe entryway into a difficult topic, and can be a springboard for talking about a specific situation. They offer an indirect way of addressing underlying feelings and hard realities of life, without necessarily dwelling on the particulars, which are often not appropriate for younger children. Here are a few suggestions, should you be faced with a situation that impacts your group:

• Stay with soothing, reassuring melodies and simple words. Be alert to the ways that songs already familiar to the group, and perhaps part of their mindful music repertoire, can address this new issue or situation. "My Mind Is a Clear Blue Sky," "This Little Light," and "Kumbaya" provide the space to "zipper in" current situations and feelings.

• The late Tom Hunter, a renowned and gifted songwriter and educator, reminds us that the classic folk song "Go Tell Aunt Rhody (the old gray goose is dead)" allows us to sing about grief, loss, and the importance of "going and telling"—talking about it when we are sad or scared. And "Kumbaya" reminds us that joys and sorrows come to *everyone*, are part of life.

• In the case of a not-too-intense loss or scare, "Equanimity" has an upbeat positive message, with stories of kids facing hard situations and the reassuring chorus reminding us of how mindfulness can help. Singing together the phrase "Everything gonna be all right" imprints that reassurance—a good takeaway for a challenging time.

Special Needs

I'm grateful for the mindfulness leaders who have shared their stories with me of how special groups of young people have been touched and helped by mindfulness and music. I'll share two of them here.

In a Vancouver inner-city elementary school, where 70% of the children are from First Nation (indigenous) or immigrant families, therapists Joan McNeil, Heather Scott, and Ly Hoang co-lead a special mindfulness group for young girls who come from families traumatized by the impact of governmental policies that tore apart First Nation families through involuntary displacement, removal to schools, adoption, etc. These girls are largely unable to learn and function well in a typical classroom setting, due to their neurological and emotional stress. Joan and her co-leader, Ly Hoang, sang "Breathing In, Breathing Out" with the girls, and over several weeks, they were able to sing along to some degree:

> Breathing in, breathing out . . .
> I am blooming as a flower.
> I am fresh as the dew.
> I am solid as a mountain.
> I am firm as the earth.
> I am free.

Understanding and retaining words was very hard for them. One day as they lay on big cushions with their "stuffies" singing, they spontaneously began creating hand motions for the song with the arms of the animals, singing to them and clearly absorbing more of the song through the addition of touch and movement with safe objects. The girls then initiated a puppet show, with the stuffies leading the singing and movement! This activity engaged them for the full 50-minute session—an unusual amount of focus and calm for them. In subsequent weeks, the retention of the song and the anchor it provided were evident in how they asked for it and participated.

Ly Huong added a few words about her own experience: "I needed those songs as much as the girls did. Sometimes I felt so overwhelmed with their needs and behaviors that singing those songs helped me to calm down."

In an inner-city Oakland school, the mindfulness teacher introduced "Breathing In, Breathing Out" to a class for children with various learning and emotional challenges. She found that the music was essential in helping the children absorb core mindfulness practices such as focusing on the breath and sitting with calm and ease. With one child who often became agitated, flailing and unable to control her movements, the teacher joined with the child as the music played, interlacing their hands and mirroring body movements as they breathed and swayed to the rhythm of the song. The child was able to find her breath and calm herself. She also sat and rocked to the music as she made sounds that followed the voice singing; the teacher noted that when the girl sang, "her whole self exhaled, and the whole room responded." Seeing the effect on the child and the group, the classroom teacher began to play the song at the start of each class to invoke that inner peace and help cultivate some calm and focus. The song became a touchstone for the class.

Beyond Singing and Songs: Using Instruments for Embodied Practice

My own history as a singer and songwriter makes me partial to the uses of language and voice to practice mindful music. But there are many other ways to engage body, mind, and heart in awareness through sound. Here, in a rather shorthand form, are several ways to expand your use of music and mindfulness.

Bells and Bell Practices

• Sound a bell—could be a "singing bowl," a chime, or even a metal triangle—and ask participants to listen closely (with eyes closed or lowered) until they cannot hear any further sound, and then to raise their hands.

• Ask group members to close or lower their eyes and take a few moments to notice exactly when the breath is going in and exactly when it is going out. At a random moment, chime the bell and then ask them whether they were on an in-breath, out-breath, or in-between when they heard the bell. Answering this question requires concentration and staying with the breath—valuable practices.

• In a mindful bell-ringing practice, each participant who wishes to do so rings the bell while the others practice mindful breathing. I take the time to illustrate the gentle way of "inviting" the bell rather than "striking" it. We pay attention to how we experience the impact of the sound from a hard strike, then from a mindful one. *Discussion points:* The concept of eliciting rather than demanding sound can expand into discussions of empathy, mindful listening to others, patience, and how it feels to be invited rather than pressured (e.g., to join a game, have a playdate, or, for older youth, peer-related situations).

• Using bowls or bells of various sizes, I arrange them in a group on the floor and invite the students to sit in a rough circle around them, getting as close as they can. If confined to desks or chairs, I invite students to close or lower their eyes while I walk among them, toning the bell near their backs, chests, or heads. I ask the students to notice where they feel the vibration in their bodies. Larger bells resonate differently than smaller, of course, and each individual body is different; thus many different experiences of the sound are reported. *Discussion points*: Differences in perception, people hearing and feeling differently in response to the "same" sound and vibration.

Percussion

Practice mindful listening by shaking or striking various instruments and have the students, without looking, experience the sound as if for the first time. Consider asking these questions:

• "What feeling does it elicit?"
• "What is the instrument 'saying'?"
• "Is it big, small, gentle, bold, shy?"

- "Is your experience of the sound pleasant, unpleasant, neither?"
- "Do any pictures come into your mind with particular sounds?"

Rain sticks create a dreamy and mysterious sound and can accompany a group period of breathing and settling. When participants take a turn with the rain stick, the group can explore the ways different movements create different kinds of sounds (e.g., quick, sharp shakes; slow, steady tipping). They can play with how slowly they can upend the stick and how the sound changes the slower they go. Both practices—bell ringing and the rain stick—provide a concrete embodied experience of slowing down, noticing minute changes and experiences, and impulse control.

No instruments available? The human body is an excellent percussion instrument that we always carry with us. Thigh slaps, handclaps, chest thumps, and foot stomps not only create rhythm, but also engage the whole body and increase bodily awareness. The impact of feet on the floor or hands on the body can be grounding and even soothing, especially for youth with sensory or attention differences.

A simple rhythmic handclapping call and response (i.e., leader claps or drums out short rhythm pattern, group echoes) helps focus and unify the group in a fun way, encouraging concentration, attention, and self-control.

Adding in Movement

- The group can move or dance to music or drumming, paying close attention to the tempo and mood of the music as it speeds up, slows down, and changes character.
- Young children often spontaneously use their hands and arms to express the words of a song; keep your eyes out for this and invite the other children to watch, imitate, or make up their own movements in a way that will not lead to distraction or disruption.
- Feel free to make up your own choreography to songs, encourage the participants to "listen to" movements their body asks them to make, or explore movements suggested on *Calm Down Boogie* (DVD files of some movement options are embedded in the CD).

In Closing

This chapter has been chock-full of stories, tools, songs, and hopefully inspiration for you. Although not all of it will be useful to everyone, I hope that some part of what is offered here will launch you more fully into sharing the gifts of leadership, mindfulness, music making, and connecting deeply with others. Music is like the breath—natural, innate, always available, and a source of grounding and returning to our inner home. So I encourage you to sing, move, and make music—with your mind, body, and heart. Writing and sharing music with others has been unquestionably the most meaningful, healing, empowering, and spiritual activity of my life. I deeply hope that you will experience some of these gifts on your own path of mindfulness and music with youth.

REFERENCES

Linklater, K. (1976). *Freeing the natural voice*. New York: Drama Book Specialists.
Pirtle, S. (1998). *Linking up*. Cambridge, MA: Educators for Social Responsibility.
Shulman, M. (2008, July 17). Music as medicine for the brain. *U.S. News and World Report*. Available at *http://health.usnews.com/health-news/family-health/brain-and-behavior/articles/2008/07/17/music-as-medicine-for-the-brain*.

CHAPTER 16

Mindfulness and Art

Vanessa CL Weiner

"Art" can take many forms. We may think of it in a traditional way to include photography, painting, cooking, or dance choreography. Or, we may think of it in a less traditional way to include the presentation of a school report, how we convince the judge in a mock trial, or accessorize an outfit. When we approach the creative process inherent in all these activities with an intentional contemplative perspective, the benefits can be far-reaching.

Scientists studying creativity find that neurological patterns shift in a beneficial way in people who regularly engage in creative activities. They also report that the benefits of strong creative skills include better relationships and greater confidence in one's ability to succeed (Bronson & Merryman, 2010). The workplace values creative skills. A poll of 1,500 CEOs identified creativity as the most important leadership competency of the future. Over "rigor, management discipline, integrity, or even vision—successfully navigating an increasingly complex world will require creativity" (IBM, 2010). Thinking "outside the box" has been cited as a way to "distinguish your child from others. . . . If children practice thinking creatively, it will come naturally to them now, and in their future career" (Strauss, 2013).

Schools also see benefits of incorporating art as a creative process, because it is shown to produce positive change in the school environment, enhance cognitive and social skills, and increase literacy, standardized test scores, and motivation to learn (Ruppert, 2006). One school in New York considers art the "communication side of the Common Core" (Robelen, 2012) and values its students' abilities to convey messages through the creative process. There is a movement underway to change the acronym STEM (science, technology, engineering, and math) as core competencies in our educational system to STEAM, where the *A* is for *art*, because creative practice develops such critical skills.

A colleague shared a story in which her daughter called from boarding school and asked that her mother send markers and paper to her. At first unable to figure out why her teenager was asking for coloring supplies, this colleague quickly realized that in the high-pressure environment, her daughter was seeking an "escape" or "coping mechanism." In the field of mindfulness, we might call this an opportunity to be fully present, such that the external pressures may release their grip for just a moment.

There is a term used frequently in mindfulness teachings: "dropping in." Similarly, people often talk about "being in the zone" when referring to athletes, artists, or authors. These terms imply a single-pointed focus and steady concentration without distraction. When in this state, we are better able to trust our instincts to make wise decisions for ourselves. As one artist friend said, "When you're present with yourself, the possibilities open up. The ideas just flow, as opposed to being a to-do list [or an assignment]." Just like my colleague's daughter, when we connect to this creative flow, we can find a moment of pause in the repeated stimulus–reaction pattern that can drive our day, possibly allowing us to connect with ourselves and others from a deep, compassionate inner space.

Ultimately, setting up an environment for children to experience success has an impact far beyond the art that is created there and then. My colleague's daughter may not become a famous artist, but she did know that art making would support her during times of stress and would increase her resilience to handling the demands of the work in front of her. The following material offers a framework for fostering the creative process in children, and it can be used in conjunction with activities in the next section.

The Creative Wheel Process

Creativity lies not in the done, but in the doing.
—JULIA CAMERON (2002)

Where art and mindfulness intersect is in the process. By focusing on the process, as opposed to the product, we sustain our attention through engagement of the senses. Kids who connect to art making find that this medium allows increased awareness, self-knowledge, and confidence as they mature.

Figure 16.1 notes five stages of a path of self-discovery through creativity:

1. Looking to structure attention.
2. Seeing to increase creativity.

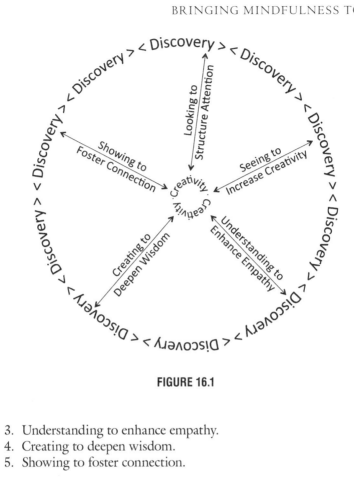

FIGURE 16.1

3. Understanding to enhance empathy.
4. Creating to deepen wisdom.
5. Showing to foster connection.

One young artist might flow through these steps in a linear fashion, whereas another might find him- or herself engaged in a wheel–spoke pattern, flowing in and out of the center, along the various stages of the process, in no particular order. There is no right or wrong way to approach the creative process. More important is the art-maker's *connection* to the creative flow.

Looking to Structure Attention

The capacity for delight is the gift of paying attention.
                                        —JULIA CAMERON (2002)

We use our eyes to see all day long. Sometimes something really captures our attention, and we focus on it for a while. Perhaps we are on a walk in the spring and we smell a flower, or we photograph a beautiful tree in bloom. Other times, we take in the visual stimuli around us, our focus shifting and flitting about, like a butterfly flying, landing, and moving on again. At times the visual stimuli can feel like overload—there are too many colors, shapes, and lights. The busy-ness we see through our eyes is reflected in our minds. When we become present to look at everything in our environment, we can learn a lot about the world around us, and how we interact with it.

To begin structuring attention, it is helpful to build awareness of when and how we look. Equally beneficial is to become aware of moments of distraction. Perhaps this "distraction" is the moment of inspiration for the next photograph or color family to use in a painting. Or maybe it is something that piques our curiosity and could eventually lead to a doodle, or germinate into something bigger. Either way, we are waking up to the visual language of the world around us, which has the power to inspire our innate creativity. The more we look, the more we will see. . . .

Seeing to Increase Curiosity

I shut my eyes in order to see.
—PAUL GAUGUIN

As Gauguin notes, we don't see only with our eyes. We can hear and smell and even taste our surroundings. Esref Armagan, a Turkish artist who was born blind, uses his hands, instead of a brush, to put onto paper what he feels in his environment. The realism of his work illustrates this beautifully (*www.esrefarmagan.com*).

Learning to "see" with all our senses requires a keen awareness and clarity. When we focus on something with a curious nature, we can generate an internal need for further investigation. A colleague talks about playing with salt that she sprinkled on the table as the inspiration for a painting; or walking on a beach and getting really curious about barnacles, which inspired a series of photographs.

Think of a time when something caught your attention and inspired curiosity—you wanted to reach out and touch that soft puppy, cock your head to see the sculpture from a different perspective, or smell a newly flowering tree. I remember seeing a construction site where workers had excavated around a huge, old tree, exposing its root structure. I was so fascinated by the gnarly pattern and how deep it went into the earth that I took a photograph to share with students during applicable lessons.

A recent study showed enhanced observational skills in nursing students who were trained to study art. The nurses in the experimental group were able to offer more objective clinical findings and more alternative diagnoses than their peers in the control group (Pellico et al., 2009). The nurses trained to study art are putting their "seeing" practice to practical use. With deepening curiosity, we can all be more inspired by and engaged in the world around us.

Understanding to Enhance Empathy

Savor the blankness. Marvel at nothing. Be swept away
by the glorious, wonderful, empty page.
              —PETER REYNOLDS, author and illustrator

This stage of the process can be profound. One colleague described a walking meditation in the woods behind her house as the inspiration for her latest
sculpture, representing the Native American tribe that had lived on that land
long before she was there. By engaging with the world around her, this artist
felt inspired to create a sculpture installation, which increased her curiosity
for greater discovery and ultimately led to a deeper connection to the history
and cultures around her.

I remember the first time I learned to use a traditional Japanese callig-
raphy brush. I first learned the history of the art form, how the brush was
made, what materials were used, how to hold it, and then to recognize the
beginning, middle, and end of each stroke. This new knowledge deepened
my connection to the work and helped me to honor those who have been
practicing for years. Using that connection, I was able to remain present
with the feel of the brush as it created each individual stroke, and occasionally connect it to a particular story in my memory. Art is a communication vehicle. As our external environments communicate, so do our internal
environments—bodies, minds, and hearts. When we let go of preconceived
notions and remain clear, we allow a deeper understanding to come through,
fostering empathy.

Creating to Deepen Wisdom

Life shrinks or expands in proportion to one's courage.
                            —ANAÏS NIN

Deepening wisdom comes from drawing upon our own well of courage and
creativity, and trusting ourselves enough to let this inner-knowing flow.
Frida Kahlo, a famous artist from Mexico, was known for her self-portraits.
She would review her work after finishing the painting as though the image
were mirroring who she was at that time in her life. This introspective nature
came through in her portraits, which were often described as honest. Her
process culminated in contemplation, where for others contemplation may
precede creation.

For some, creating can be the most exciting and rewarding part of the
process, and for others, the most daunting. We all have that voice inside that
tells us that our work isn't very good. I've heard this voice referred to as the
censor or the gremlin. This inner critic is often very unkind and impedes
our ability to access our creative flow. Author Julia Cameron says, "Who

wouldn't be blocked if every time you walked out into the open, somebody (your Censor) made fun of you?" (2002).

The courage to trust ourselves is at the core of unlocking our creativity—courage to express ourselves, courage to respond to a voice, a message, an image, a random inspiration that has provided this energy to create. We must trust that seed of creativity inside with the courage to experiment, to find joy in the process, to let go of expectations, to stretch beyond comfort zones, follow our inner wisdom, and repeat the process over and over again.

"Wonder is the beginning of all wisdom," says Socrates. Wrapped up in wonder are wisdom, passion, and creativity, which lead many people to use their art for social justice. AG Saño, artist and environmental activist in the Philippines, was so overcome with emotion after watching a documentary about injustices against dolphins, that he began painting murals to raise awareness for this cause. One study showed that through "creating activist art, students developed skills for critical thinking, leadership, community engagement, and communication" (Dewhurst, 2009). By understanding and connecting with communal injustice, students are inspired to create an artistic message. This experience builds lifelong skills of inquiry and self-knowledge.

Showing to Foster Connection

There's a crack in everything. That's how the light gets in.
—LEONARD COHEN

We live in a society of judgment. Remember a time when you made up your mind about something before you even . . . met the person, experienced the situation, tried the food, or really looked at the art? It is human nature to connect or disconnect with everything around us—liking or not liking our surroundings, food, people, styles, books, and the list goes on. The showing stage of the creative process encourages an openness to both observing and being observed as a way to foster connection. The National Endowment for the Arts reports that "individuals who attend arts events at least once a year are more likely to participate in various civic associations, exhibit greater tolerance towards racial minorities and homosexuals, and behave in a manner which regards the interest of others above those of oneself" (Jacobs, 2012, p. 17).

Consider the installation that Marina Abramovic did at the Museum of Modern Art in New York in 2010 where she *was* the show, sitting, physically present, for almost 3 months. This work, called "The Artist Is Present," shows her courage to be physically present in this unique art show, as well as the self-trust to bring this idea to fruition (film trailer of this installation and other videos are available on YouTube). Her physical presence allowed the audience to connect with the person behind the art, and she with her audience. She created a space for this installation in which everyone simply had an experience just by showing up. In viewers' looking, seeing, and understanding, there is a powerful connection evident on all the stories and videos.

For the purposes of this chapter, *showing* doesn't necessarily refer to a formal gallery display; allowing another trusted person to witness the work—a family member, a friend, a teacher, or a therapist—is just as valid. When skillfully facilitated, showing our work encourages self-confidence, courage, self-compassion, and a deeper connection to self. Similarly, in observing others' work, we learn to build external connections and reduce judgment.

Exercises

Drawing is a small but powerful act. One that everyone can do.
It's a pencil, ballpoint pen, or charcoal on paper. It's a mark in
the sand or chalk on the sidewalk. Drawing is a visual language.
—DEBORAH PUTNOI, Author

We may not think so, but as Putnoi declares in the quote above, all of us can draw. "Drawing is not about making straight lines. The world of drawing is infinite. Drawings, like the people who create them, are individual" (Berkowitz, 2012). The exercises in this chapter are all intended to facilitate experiential learning through sensory awareness, wherein mindfulness and creativity intersect to bring deep presence and connection, increased awareness, and a moment of stillness.

Often when I introduce art activities in classes, there will be a few groans in the room from kids who say, "I'm not good at art." I often explain that these activities aren't intended to produce museum-ready pieces, but rather to offer children a road to learning a little more about themselves. Despite the groans, I continue to be struck by the silence that takes over a classroom or my own home when the kids are participating in an art activity. With a single-pointed focus, kids are resting in the stillness of creativity and *not* ruminating about, for example, that locker-room incident, worrying about the next test, wondering if there will be food for dinner, replaying the conversation on any number of social media outlets, or thinking about what to do when this activity is over. Such anxiety-provoking thoughts can make it difficult for kids to pay attention, be present, and access their natural creativity.

There are so many wonderful art activities to do with children. I find that children are most able to experience success, connecting with the mindfulness and art-making intersection, in the activities described in the following sections. The first set of activities encompasses all stages of the creative wheel process, and the additional exercises focus more on a specific step of the process. The recommended age groups are listed at each activity and focus on children 5 years and older.

Art Activities Encompassing All Aspects of the Creative Wheel

Art Journal

Creating their own journal to house their creations and reflections can be inspiring to children both in the moment and when they look back on their experiences. The journal can also serve as a safe space, preventing work from getting lost, protecting it from unintended or premature viewing, and allowing the student to choose when and where the work is viewed. Additionally, because it is recommended that kids keep the creative process going after class concludes, the journal can serve as a central container for all that to happen.

Helpful Tips for the Facilitator

These general suggestions include practices that will facilitate a successful experience for both you and your students/clients.

- Allow time for reflection, slowing down, and stillness. Kids today are feeling the fast pace of our society.
- Be sure to be present for your students/clients. They intuitively sense your authenticity, as well as your availability and ability to really see them in that moment.
- Establish guidelines of no judgment from you or the students; this encourages them to be uninhibited.
- The goal of each of these exercises is simply the experience—no grade, no judgment, no art show. Let students develop their own sense of necessity. This allowance empowers students to make discoveries for themselves about things that are meaningful to them, and how to represent those in a visual form.
- Interconnectedness can be fostered by the sharing of experiences. Get a sense of whether your student might like you to create your own work at the same time.
- For many children, being creative is an act of courage that needs support and recognition.
- Creation also takes concentration. Let your students/clients know that they can get up and walk away, look from another perspective, change their seat or lighting. There are distractions at every turn. The goal is to discover these distractions and return to the project—and eventually, to the test, the conversation, the book, or simply the breath.
- Surroundings have an effect on everyone. When possible, create a comfortable atmosphere; maybe a pillow on the chair or a favorite stuffed animal, a plant, or even different lighting to increase comfort and creativity for the art-makers.

• If art is foreign to students/clients, then these exercises can be like learning a new language. If art is something they already love, then this resonance may be present from the first exercise. Encourage a regular practice over the course of a few weeks so that the children have the opportunity to try multiple activities.

A Moment of Stillness

Before beginning any creative work, it can be helpful to take a few deep, centering breaths as a way to connect to the flowing creativity in each one of us. Below is a sample relaxation exercise you could do with your students or clients:

> "Take a moment to find a comfortable seated position, noticing your feet on the floor, feeling yourself supported by the chair, and your spine growing tall out of that seat. Allow your eyes to close or look down at the table or floor in front of you. Taking one hand to your belly, and one hand to your heart, begin to feel your breath. [Pause.] Breathing is something we do all day, but often we don't notice it. Maybe you can feel the breath in your nose, feeling cool air coming in and warm air going out. . . . [Pause two breaths.] Maybe you can feel the breath in your chest as the hand that is resting there rises and falls when the lungs fill with air and then let it all out. . . . [Pause two breaths.] Or maybe you feel the breath in your belly like a balloon, with your hand there rising as you fill your abdomen with air, and then returning gently downward as you let the breath out. [Pause.] Maybe you can't feel the breath at all, and that's okay too. Keep breathing . . . and when thoughts come in to your mind, which they do for all of us, see if you can gently come back to the breath. . . . Sometimes saying to yourself 'breathing in' and 'breathing out' can help you stay focused. [Pause three breaths.] Coming back to the breath over and over again is okay. . . . Thinking is what the mind is supposed to do . . . we just don't have to follow that train of thought right now. We are staying with the breath, noticing if the thoughts get a little judgmental, like 'I can't do this' or 'I'm not creative.' It's okay if these thoughts show up. You can notice they are there and return to your breathing. [Pause three breaths.] And then together we will share three deep breaths in, and out, and then return our attention to the room." [Breathe together. Then make eye contact when ready.]

Glitter Jar (All Ages)

This activity is a tangible way for kids to see the storm that may often be their minds, as well as a visual anchor in which to rest, facilitating that ever-important pause.

DIRECTIONS FOR THE ART-MAKER

"You're going to make your own glitter jar to use whenever you need it. Some kids use it when they can't fall asleep at night, some when they're having trouble focusing on their homework, and others when they need to take a few breaths to cool down. Start by selecting a jar. With all the colors of glitter in front of you, pick up the first one you're drawn to and start shaking it into the jar. While you're shaking, answer this question out loud or to yourself, 'What are some things you worry about?' Pick your next color and shake it in, answering a different question. Keep going as you make your way through a set of questions, shaking enough glitter in to generously coat the bottom of the jar. Some sample questions might include:

'What makes you feel shaken up/stormy like the glitter jar?'
'What makes you feel strong?'
'What are you ready to let go of?'
'What do you want to learn from these experiences?'

"Once you've covered the bottom of the jar, add water all the way to the top. Seal the jar and tape it closed. Now you're ready to give it a good shake. Once all the colors are swirling around, put the jar down and just watch the glitter settle. Notice your breathing and your state of mind when the water becomes still. Know that this settled stillness exists inside you all the time! So shake away, using your jar, or your imagination, anytime you need to return to this stillness."

HELPFUL TIPS FOR THE FACILITATOR

- Know your audience; plastic bottles are often a safe choice.
- Have your own glitter jar that you use to introduce the idea.
- Up to age 6 or 7, kids may not be able to articulate answers to many of the questions, in which case just shaking in the glitter is great. Or you can try to simplify the questions, knowing your audience.
- Small spice jars or even small plastic water bottles work well. You may find that you start keeping all the old salsa, spice, and jelly jars, as they all make good jars, in size and shape, with the labels soaked or peeled off.
- If working in a group, walk around with a few colors so that there is choice. In a one-on-one setting, putting out a few colors will offer the same artistic license.
- Metallic or plastic-shaped confetti-like hearts or stars offer a fun and effective focusing tool for kids to watch during the settling process.

• A few drops of dish soap will reduce the surface tension of the water in the jar and help the glitter to sink.

• A teaspoon to a tablespoon of glycerin will thicken the water so that the glitter settles more slowly. This is helpful in small jars where it doesn't take long for the swirl to quiet.

• Using a funnel over a small jar opening will contain the mess.

• Add enough glitter to cover the bottom of the jar or bottle generously. Then add the water all the way to the top of the jar.

• Seal the jar with Duck Tape®, which now comes in many colors and patterns. If using spice jars with the holes in the lid, it is helpful to seal the inside of the lid before sealing the outside so that the water doesn't leak through the holes.

Draw a Story (Ages 8+)

In this experience, kids are responding to auditory stimuli and connecting to the responses in their bodies and minds through their drawings.

DIRECTIONS FOR THE ART-MAKER

"Observing can be done without using your eyes. [Have the grown-up in the room tell the students a story.] Open your ears really wide to listen with all your concentration effort, and then you're going to draw what you hear. You can draw pictures or shapes and swirls that represent the feeling of the story. What do you hear and feel, and how is that reflected in your art? Trust your instinct to allow some visual representation of the story to come through, and then, if you feel comfortable, please share your story about the art you created.

"Remember, experimenting, making marks, making 'mistakes,' and even being completely unsure of the work you are doing is all okay! This is a practice of staying present and being here, now, with the story and your art."

Consider Figure 16.2 as an example. I didn't actually tell this student a story in the traditional sense, but was sharing the creative wheel with her, and this is the drawing she created while I was talking. Her characterization of the wheel goes like this: She was listening (structure attention) to me talking about the creative wheel, when something piqued her interest (build curiosity). Upon deeper listening to my words and to her own inspiration (facilitate connection), she created this work (deepen wisdom). I watched her stop and look at her drawing, show me, and then go back to sketching (showing, understanding, creating, showing, repeat). When she was done, I asked her

FIGURE 16.2

to share it with me; she described the detail of the lines around the eye as all the things to look at (developing focus), the eye representing the structured attention. The trail of stars represents the understanding, the paintbrush as the creation, and the whimsical swirl as the showing.

HELPFUL TIPS FOR THE FACILITATOR

• Young artists can do this exercise too. You're likely to get very literal drawings.

• Children ages 10 and up will show greater introspection about what they heard.

• Remember to tell secular stories.

Five Photographs (Ages 12+)

My good friend Tina Tryforos, a photographer and teacher, does a similar version of this exercise with her high school students, and it demonstrates a wonderful cycling through all the stages of the creative wheel.

DIRECTIONS FOR THE ART-MAKER

"For this experience, you're going to head outside with a digital camera and take pictures. While outside, notice what captures your attention and where you're spending extra moments with increased curiosity. Print the pictures and then spend some time really looking at and seeing them. Select five photographs and see if you can put them together into a sequence where the order (narrative, associative, decorative, or otherwise) helps to create a connection within the group of images. Finally, share your work and explain the process in ordering them the way you did."

HELPFUL TIPS FOR THE FACILITATOR

• To streamline the exercise, if necessary, this can be a homework assignment, wherein you send the children home with instructions for taking pictures in nature and they come back with the printed photographs.

• Offering a time limit for the picture taking can be helpful.

Nature Walk: A Group or Solo Activity (All Ages)

Being out in nature often facilitates connection and inspiration. This exercise allows as much freedom or structure as you, the facilitator, are comfortable giving.

DIRECTIONS FOR THE ART-MAKER

"As you step outside, take a moment to inhale and notice what you smell. Practice mindful walking while you connect with the nature around you. Spend some time stopping and seeing, not only with your eyes, but also your sense of touch, smell, and sound. See if something really captures your attention. Perhaps you're interested in drawing or painting something you see, or carrying an item(s) back with you to build a collage, take a photograph, or just to journal about what each one means to you and why you picked it up. When you're done, consider sharing your creation with your facilitator, or someone in your group."

HELPFUL TIPS FOR THE FACILITATOR

• Know your audience, and be sure that if you take kids outside in your environment, it is a safe choice.

• Encourage kindness in nature (e.g., "Please do not pick the neighbors' flowers or disturb new grass growth").

Thirty-Second Scribble (Ages 8+)

This is a fun and accessible introductory drawing exercise for reluctant artists. Enthusiasts also love it, and even when repeated, most students find something different each time.

"This exercise is just about scribbling! Put your pencil in the middle of the paper and see what happens if you don't lift it for the next 30 seconds while moving all around your paper. One extra thing . . . no peeking! Try either looking away or closing your eyes. Ready, set, go!

"Once you're done, take a close look at your paper and find an image/shape/object . . . something that comes through in your art. You can stand back from the paper and even rotate it through all perspectives. When you find that one thing, color it in or mark over it with a darker color—something to make it stand out. Now give your picture a title and keep it in your scrapbook, journal, or folder of special artwork."

After reviewing my 30-second scribble (Figure 16.3), I quickly noticed a bow in the upper left corner holding together all the busy-ness and craziness of life right now, but with an accessible, still center ready and waiting.

HELPFUL TIPS FOR THE FACILITATOR

• Younger kids often are more successful if their paper is taped to the table or desk.

• Depending on your participants, they may or may not be able to find an object in the picture. That's okay! They can still name it and keep it.

• Older kids will be able to share deeper reflections, whereas younger kids will generally point out more literally what they see and title the picture.

• Encourage rotation of the scribble to see it from all angles.

Squiggle (All Ages)

Making something from nothing is rewarding and can build confidence and trust when complete. For this activity, students will need a partner or group with which to create.

DIRECTIONS FOR THE ART-MAKER

"Start with a blank piece of paper and something with which to draw. Take a breath and then make a mark on the paper—a line, a swirl, a shape, a dot, anything you feel called to do. Then, pass this 'squiggle' to the next person in the group [or to your partner]. Spend a few quiet moments just looking at that squiggle you received, and then when you're ready, turn it into a drawing! Remember to trust your instinct—there is no wrong picture!"

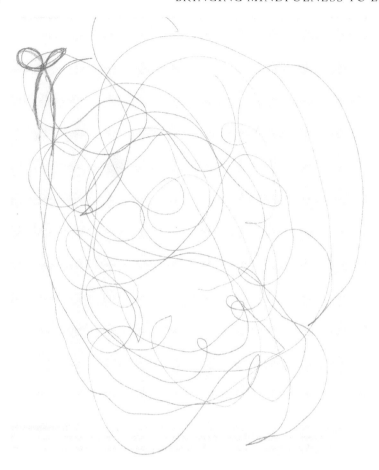

FIGURE 16.3

In the example in Figure 16.4, a second grader was given the squiggle you can see in the darker outline along the top of the hat and the brim. He immediately saw in it the hat he loves to wear, complete with the button detail on top.

HELPFUL TIPS FOR THE FACILITATOR

- This activity can be done in pairs or groups.
- Invite rotation of the paper if a child seems stuck.
- When everyone uses pencil, it is difficult to tell what was the original line and what is the new artwork. When each person uses a different color, you get a different effect. Both are helpful in the final results.

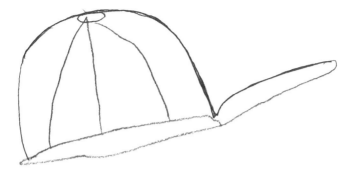

FIGURE 16.4

Name Art (All Ages)

Names are unique and personal, and can be a starting point for articulation about who we are as well as inspiration for deeper reflection.

DIRECTIONS FOR THE ART-MAKER

"This self-confidence-building exercise starts with your name. Simply draw your name in the middle of a piece of paper in large block or bubble letters. Next, spend a few moments thinking about these questions one at a time:

'What are your hobbies?'
'What things are you good at?'
'What are things you're known for?'
'What are things that you'd like to be known for?'
'What are things you're grateful for?'
'What makes you smile?'

"You can write the answers to your questions in your journal or draw them right into your name. For each question spend a few moments reflecting with your eyes closed to find your true answers. With each answer, see if you can notice what color, shape, and size it is. Use these cues to represent the answers in the bubble/block letters of your name."

HELPFUL TIPS FOR THE FACILITATOR

• Kindergarteners and some first graders may need you to help them with their name, or even give them block letters that they can fill in.

• There will be a very different level of introspection between a 5-year-old and an 18-year-old. Setting everyone up for success may include simplifying the exercise for the younger kids, and adding additional layers of introspection for high school students. You can even make a form on a separate piece of paper where younger kids can answer the questions first, then use the answers to fill in their name.

• It is helpful to have a wide variety of media on hand, such as crayons, colored pencils, Cray-Pas, and colored paper and scissors to really encourage self-expression.

• Depending on how much time you spend with your group, this exercise can often be spread out over a few sessions. Children will be more apt to slowly and thoughtfully answer each question when they know they have multiple sessions to complete the work.

• If in a group setting, this exercise offers a wonderful community-building exercise with both sharing and learning about the group members.

Peaceful Place Discovery (All Ages)

We all have a peaceful place inside us. This exercise offers a guided visualization for accessing it, and the opportunity to draw it afterward. Visual learners may have an easier time accessing this place when they've been able to make a picture of it as a way of remembering—another opportuniy to incorporate the art journal.

SAMPLE GUIDED VISUALIZATION

"Take a moment to find a comfortable, seated position. Feel your feet on the floor and then wiggle your toes and spread them out so wide that you can feel the edges of your shoes. Lift your shoulders up to your ears and slide them back down, keeping your spine really tall. See if you can relax your whole face, and even take your tongue away from the roof of your mouth. [Pause.] Now begin to imagine a place that makes you feel calm, peaceful, and completely safe. [Pause.] It can be under your bed, in a forest, or at the beach—there is no right or wrong place. . . .

"As you arrive in this peaceful place, take a look around . . . what do you notice? [Pause.] Is it daytime or nighttime? Is it inside or outside? Is it dark or light? Is it large or small? What colors do you see? [Pause.] Shifting your attention to your ears, listen for the sounds in your peaceful place. Do you hear birds? Ocean waves? Leaves rustling in the wind? Voices off in the distance? Just notice. [Pause.] Now notice smells in your peaceful place . . . take a deep breath in. Maybe you can smell the ocean air, or the spring rain, or fresh cookies coming out of the oven. If your peaceful place is a somewhere where you can take a walk, see if you can watch yourself slowly moving, step by step, and when you get to something that is interesting, reach out and touch it. If your peaceful place isn't somewhere that you want to move, then just stay right where you are and reach out and touch something nearby. . . . Maybe it's the fibers of your carpet, or the bark on a tree. . . . Notice what that object feels like, almost like you're touching it for the first time. Is it bumpy, rough, wet, soft, smooth, or warm? What do you notice? [Pause.]

"As we finish up here, take one last look around your peaceful place. [Pause.] This place exists *inside* you and is with you every day. Bringing your awareness back to your breath, remember that with just a few breaths, you can come to this place any time you need to—when you're falling asleep, before a test, after a fight with your BFF, or when you just need a moment to yourself. [Pause.] Whenever you're ready, bring your attention back to this room."

HELPFUL TIPS FOR THE FACILITATOR

• Go slowly through this exercise, and really let the child(ren) experience this inner peaceful place.

• When the guided visualization is over, provide blank pieces of paper and various colored pencils, Cray-Pas, crayons, or markers to allow the children's drawing to come through while the details are still vibrant.

"Looking"-Focused Activities

The following three exercises offer an entry to the creative wheel to develop focus and structure attention.

Daily Looking (All Ages)

DIRECTIONS FOR THE ART-MAKER

"We can go through our day without really noticing our surroundings. This exercise offers an opportunity for you to find something new every day. It might be something new on your way to school, or to the lunchroom, or in the car on a drive you take regularly. It may be that you've never noticed that blooming tree or front porch light, or sign in the hallway. See if you can notice it without judgment—without saying if you like it or don't like it, or that it would be better if it were taller, colored differently, or cleaner. Keep track of at least one new thing in your journal each day as you expand your awareness of the world around you."

• Sometimes kids will need reminders to do their daily looking.

• You can facilitate this process by adding a sentence starter in their journal; for example, "Today I noticed _____ when I was _____."

• It is often a shock to kids when they discover something new that has always been there. Encourage this curiosity by taking it to the next step of the creative wheel. Maybe they want to study it, read a book about it, draw it, paint it, or make a clay sculpture of it.

Blind Contour Drawing (Ages 8+)

Drawing without looking at the paper and without lifting the pencil is a challenge! See if your students/clients can use this exercise to connect what they're seeing to how their drawing hand is moving.

DIRECTIONS FOR THE ART-MAKER

"Place your pencil in your dominant hand, the hand you usually use for writing. Place the elbow of your other hand, which is called your *nondominant* hand, on the paper in front of you so that it doesn't move [if this movement is complicated for anyone, you can tape down the paper as a simple alternative]. Take a good look at your nondominant hand. Without rushing (or tracing!), draw what you see in one continuous line without lifting your pencil and without looking down at the paper.

"Once you're done, take a look and notice the shape, size, and detail of the drawn hand.

"Now switch hands and do it again. Notice what the experience is like when drawing with your nondominant hand.

"You can try this exercise any time, with anything that catches your eye, particularly things in nature, or if you're feeling really adventurous. For example, try drawing your own face when looking in a mirror!"

HELPFUL TIPS FOR THE FACILITATOR

• This exercise often requires a little cheering from us to encourage and remind our students not to look down at their paper, which is a natural instinct.

• After your students/clients try this exercise with both hands, offer the opportunity to try it with something outside in nature or with a printed picture of something in nature—single palm tree, a fence on a mountain, or a close-up of a blooming flower all work well.

Colored Feelings (All Ages)

Often youth don't have the vocabulary to describe a feeling or emotion. Color can facilitate that self-expression, and it is used in this activity to build awareness, word choice, and the mind–body connection.

DIRECTIONS FOR THE ART-MAKER

"In this experience, you will be guided through a colorful visualization. Try to follow along, even if some of the instructions feel unusual. Have your journal handy so you can write a few things down on a page titled 'Colored Feelings.'"

HELPFUL TIPS FOR THE FACILITATOR

• Guide your students/clients to experience a color and then share a word that goes along with that color. After starting with breathing exercises, offer a guided visualization of breathing in a rainbow and breathing out all the colors except the one you're planning to work with at the moment—for example, green. Allow your students/clients to experience breathing in green all the way down to their fingertips and toes, and have it get brighter and brighter with each inhale. When their whole bodies are filled up with green, ask them what green feels like, and where that feeling resides in their bodies.

• Invite students/clients to write or color their responses in their journal. Some teachers and parents find this exercise to be a helpful check-in for learning how their students or children are feeling in a given moment.

• If working in a group, you can collect all the words and write them collectively on a colored piece of paper (use the color you're working with). Collecting all the words on the colored paper and keeping all the papers together can be a helpful tool for kids to refer to when they are learning to express how they are feeling. Laminating helps with longevity.

• A ring of single-colored paint chips also serves as a helpful reference tool.

• As an alternative, you can spread out a stack of colored paint chips and invite the children to pick the one that most feels like them today—the one to which they are most drawn. Then offer the color practice as a way to link words with that color. Glue these paint chips into their journals and have them write the corresponding words for future reference.

• With younger kids, it can be helpful to start this exercise by reading a book called *My Many Colored Days* (Seuss, 1998) to offer an example of how colors can be linked to feelings.

"Seeing"-Focused Exercises

Mindful seeing is a practice that can begin to develop curiosity. There are a number of art-related ways this type of seeing can be facilitated.

"What's Going On in This Picture?" (Ages 8+)

The *New York Times'* Learning Network posts a photo without a caption every Monday to encourage students to access their curious nature in determining what is going on in the picture.

DIRECTIONS FOR THE ART-MAKER

"Spend a little time looking at the picture. Look carefully for clues that would help you write a caption if you had to do so. Think about the following:

'Where was the picture taken?'
'What is happening in the picture, and how do you know?'
'What time of day is it?'
'Are there any clues that help you determine the year or decade?'
'Notice what this picture evokes in you.'"

HELPFUL TIPS FOR THE FACILITATOR

• Depending on the age of your students/clients and their access to and permissions for online time, they can participate directly on the website. Discussions are facilitated by Visual Thinking Strategies on Mondays from 9:00 A.M. to 3:00 P.M. EST. The next day, the *New York Times* posts additional information about the picture and asks how viewers see the image differently with the caption and additional information.

• It can be equally successful to explore the picture with your students/clients offline by printing it, or even exploring it on the screen together, with and without the additional information and caption.

Mindful Seeing Art Chart (Ages 10+)

This exercise offers a structured way for students/clients to notice both how their perceptions may change over time, and also to experience the mind–body link.

DIRECTIONS FOR THE ART-MAKER

"You're looking at a famous painting. Many, many people have commented on this piece of art. Some like it and some don't. Some have even changed their mind over time. This experience isn't designed to determine whether you like it or not, but to encourage you to get really curious about what you see in the painting. Sometimes your initial reaction can shift with repeat reflection.

"As you continue to look and see and understand, notice if that curiosity follows you into your surroundings. Ask yourself, what do you need to do to really notice what's around you? It takes courage to stay focused and continue seeing. Notice when you are called to look away, and see if you can return to the looking, or to your breathing.

"A student once shared with me that he wasn't really sure why he continued to look and relook, but something called him back to this painting. At the end of the week's exercise, he noticed he had stronger feelings toward the artwork, almost like he had developed more of a relationship with it than when he started.

"Staying open will help strengthen your natural curiosity as opposed to shutting down to something you don't like—whether this piece of art, an assignment, a book, or even another person. After the time period of observation is complete, share your findings."

HELPFUL TIPS FOR THE FACILITATOR

• Print a copy of a famous painting and secure it to a page in the art journal. Include a chart or list of questions for your students/clients to fill out over the course of a week.

• Questions can include:

"What is the first thing you noticed today?"
"What works well in the painting?"
"What doesn't work well in the painting?"
"How do you feel when looking at the painting?"
"Where do you notice that feeling in your body?"
"What is your relationship to the painting today?"

Understanding Exercises

Everyday Items, Mystery Draw (Ages 8+)

Kids love this activity, not only for the challenge of not looking at the item, but also for the opportunity to access other senses for this exploration. By placing simple, everyday objects in a bag for kids to pick from, *but not look at*, they have the opportunity to engage their senses of smell, touch, and hearing in order to visualize what it is they are asked to draw. Items can include paper clips, marker caps, shaped erasers, small plastic or rubber animals, tea light candle, wrapped peppermint candy, or a shell.

DIRECTIONS FOR THE ART-MAKER

"When we draw, we are very accustomed to using our eyes to see the subject. In this exercise, you are going to draw an everyday item that you pull from a bag without looking at it. Using your senses of touch, smell, and sound, discover how much you can learn about your mystery item before putting the pencil to the paper. You may know right away what it is, and it may take you a little while to figure it out. Either is fine. Just stay focused on not looking at the object in your hand, and on trying to draw it from memory."

HELPFUL TIPS FOR THE FACILITATOR

• Offer to take the object back from any child who may find it too tempting to peek while he or she is drawing.

• Kids generally love this exercise, and you can even have them divide their paper into four quadrants so they can repeat the exercise multiple times.

• Invite an age-appropriate conversation about using other senses and about the temptation to peek. This is a great place to introduce Esref Armagan's work (*www.esrefarmagan.com*).

Sensory Drawing (Ages 9+)

Connecting mind and body through this exercise give kids the opportunity to trust their responses, knowing there is no right or wrong way. Use the chart of words and phrases below as a guide (see Figure 16.5).

DIRECTIONS FOR THE ART-MAKER

"Your objective is simply to make lines/shapes/marks that represent the words and/or phrases I'll say out loud. Take your time and really see if you can feel the line almost drawing itself. You might be thinking, 'How do I draw a line that represents *sour*?' The idea is to let go of any preconceived notions and trust your first instinct of what *sour* might look like. The good news is that there's no right or wrong. Whatever line/shape/mark you make on your paper is absolutely fine, and interestingly, if you do this exercise on a different day, your line for the same word might be different. What does that tell you?"

FIGURE 16.5

HELPFUL TIPS FOR THE FACILITATOR

• You're working toward mind–body connections in this exercise to encourage a state of flow. The more lines the kids draw, the more they'll connect to the exercise.

• Encourage the drawing of a line without lifting the pencil, noticing the beginning, middle, and end of each line.

• Watch for completion of each mark before calling out the next word or phrase for the next line, but with a balance so that there's not too much time for kids to start the thinking process where judgment and looking at others' papers starts to interfere.

• Kids will ask, "Like this?" Remind them that there is no right or wrong way. This is an exercise that is intended to build knowledge of that inner voice to work toward trusting their intuition and to practice being less judgmental.

• Older kids may be able to try variations, including not looking at their paper, reflecting on their drawing to see if there are any patterns that jump out, seeing if they can recognize the word each line represents, what about the line communicates the word, and do the various marks evoke any feelings or emotions?

- Feel free to use this list as a jumping off point, and add your own as you are inspired to do so!

Straight	Short	Bold
Jagged	Long	Sour
Fast	Tired	Direct
Curly	Sleepy	Fall leaf pile
Zigzag	Lazy	Fresh fallen snow
Angry	Pokey	Introduce two lines to each
Slow	Awkward	other
Curvy	Timid	Prickly cactus
Bent	Spiral	Fluffy clouds
Thick	Love	Peeling bark
Gentle	Bird	Soft Play-Doh
Sad	Mountain	Jiggly water balloons
Jazz music	Sky	Cuddly stuffed animals
Scared	Tree	Fresh-baked cookies
Bossy	Sick	Rock in your shoe
Round	Rain	Cold ice water
Tall	Generous	New flowers of spring
Small	Thankful	Crisp apple
Crooked	Hungry	Hip-hop dance

"Create"-Focused Exercises

This stage of the process gets mixed reactions. Some kids love making things come to life, whereas others put a pencil to the paper and get stuck. We've all experienced creative blocks—writers, math test takers, composers, and artists. Even the most talented and successful artists are using practices such as mindfulness to connect and reconnect with their center and their creativity. Giving voice to that part of each of us who has ever felt stuck in creative endeavors or otherwise can often be the key to moving past it.

Clay Pinch Pot (Ages 6+)

A pinch pot is an easy-to-make small bowl that children of any age enjoy creating from a block of clay.

DIRECTIONS FOR THE ART MAKER

"Your job is simply to mold this block of clay into a bowl. Remember, there is no right or wrong shape of the final product. More important is to notice the clay in your hands, and how it feels as you squish it, stretch it, and form it. Notice how you respond when it begins to take shape. See if you can respond to how the clay wants to be shaped, as opposed to forcing a shape onto it. Notice if you're rushing to create a vision you have in your mind. If you are, try putting the clay down and taking a few breaths before going back to your pinch pot. This is an opportunity for you to connect with the creation—no matter how it turns out—nail marks, uneven edges, odd shapes, different heights and sizes."

HELPFUL TIPS FOR THE FACILITATOR

- In a one-on-one setting it may be helpful for you to create with your student/client. It can often be distracting if a student feels watched, and it creates a sense of connection if you work side by side.
- Molding/air-dry clay works well for this activity, but offers less of a sensory experience than water-based art clay.
- You can also make your own clay. Many recipes can be found online using standard household ingredients.
- If using store-bought clay with young children, check for safety and how washable it is.

Artful "Book of Awesome" (Ages 6+)

Gratitude inspires us to see the bright side and increases happiness and well-being. When author Neil Parischa found himself quite sad and depressed at a point in his life, he began blogging about the positive things in his life as a way to feel more optimistic. He ultimately published *The Book of Awesome* (2011), which became an international bestseller. The book offers a great model to inspire kids to create their own.

DIRECTIONS FOR THE ART-MAKER

"Start a page of your journal that is titled 'Awesome,' and at any moment add items to your list of awesome things. Try to be really specific, like 'the way the sun streams into the fifth-grade classroom,' as opposed to saying 'Fifth grade is awesome.' This list will become a central source of inspiration for your 'awesome' pages. When you're ready to make a page, select one item from the list and draw what this looks and feels like to you. You can even narrate the illustration. Once you or your group decide that you have enough pages for an *Awesome* book, staple or bind it together to keep as a reminder for those times when you might need a little extra smile."

• If working in a group, have everyone participate in creating the book's front and back covers to deepen the connection to the work and among group members.

• Have a variety of media ready for the illustrations!

"Showing"-Focused Exercises

Activities for this stage of the process center around observation and reflection—both on one's own work and the work of others.

The creative process helps art-makers to focus more on the experience rather than the end result. When sharing work with others or receiving feedback, however, it is not uncommon to see youth shifting the focus back to the product and the feelings that can bring. However, with guided questions as part of the observing process, and the constant reminder of breath as an anchor, we can help students stay mindful of the experience, and not slip into judgment of themselves or others. The *Washington Post* reports that in receiving constructive feedback, children come to understand "that this is part of learning and not something to be offended by or to be taken personally. It is something helpful" (Strauss, 2013).

Self-compassion is important to address here as youth are developing their own identities. It isn't uncommon to hear kids say they're terrible at something, or for them to join in the laughter when sharing something that isn't their best work. This self-talk is a metaphor for life. I often share with students that when my daughter was learning to throw a Frisbee®, she would constantly say "I can't do this" just before trying to sail it across the lawn to where I was standing. Imagine her surprise when she tried telling herself "I *can* do this" before she threw the next one, and it came right to me! Our negative self-talk has far-reaching effects, yet we all continue this self-deprecating language. Use these exercises as a launching point for discussion around the connection to self and its effect on everything we do.

Self-Reflection (Ages 12+)

DIRECTIONS FOR THE ART-MAKER

"It is natural to want to evaluate your own work, and sometimes we might not say such nice things about it, particularly if comparing it to someone else's. In this exercise, see if you can answer the following questions (either out loud or writing in your journal) using language that isn't critical of yourself or your effort."

REFLECTION QUESTIONS

"How do you feel when you look at your work?"
"Where do you notice that feeling in your body?"
"What works well in the art piece?"
"What area isn't as successful and why?" [Be specific here—color, area, lighting, shape, etc.]
"What changes would you make to improve that area?"

HELPFUL TIPS FOR THE FACILITATOR

• Younger kids can look at their work and identify areas that are strong or that they're proud of. With students as young as fifth grade, you may be able to invite them to share what was difficult for them, or what didn't come out as planned. They may be able to identify "mistakes" that turned into something positive, or even an area that they worked on but aren't feeling that it integrates with the rest of the work.

• Help kids to avoid blanket statements of what they see as needing improvement, and guide them to specific areas and detailed use of words.

• As students are being observed, encourage them to refer back to trusting themselves in the process of visual creation, to practice listening to the feedback in a nonjudgmental way, and to take a deep belly breath to pause before responding.

Reflecting on Others' Work (Ages 12+)

DIRECTIONS FOR THE OBSERVER

"As the one looking at another art-maker's work, practice your looking and seeing with discernment rather than judgment. For example, you might say 'I notice the light comes from the left at the top of the picture but then shifts to the right toward the bottom' as opposed to 'the representation of light is not correct.' Remember that you, too, have had your work on display!"

QUESTIONS TO CONSIDER

"How is the balance of space and form?"
"What movement do you see? What stillness?"
"How does the work communicate with you?"
"What is the message in the work?"
"What is something that speaks to you in the art? What does it say?"

"How do you feel when looking at the art? Where do you notice that feeling?"
"What's happening in the picture?"

HELPFUL TIPS FOR THE FACILITATOR

• Help kids increase their vocabulary for descriptive words to grow beyond *good* and *bad* or generic statements such as "I like it" or "I don't like it."

• Encourage conditional language "this *could* be" as opposed to "this *is*" as a way to maintain openness.

Keep Creating . . .

Painting is just another way of keeping a diary.
                                        —PABLO PICASSO

Encourage your students/clients to keep creating! If they've connected to the experiences in this chapter, suggest that they continue to use the journal that you've been working with together, or to start a new journal to capture creative moments, encourage doodling/scribbling, collecting images or colors ripped from magazines, photographs, things they're grateful for, pleasant images, or even writing down words that evoked a beautiful image. With the digital age upon us, older kids may appreciate (and utilize more) a digital journal. With various apps they can use a smartphone to capture images that they want to preserve and store them in a digital notebook that can become their art journal.

REFERENCES

Berkowitz, D. (2012). The drawing mind: Silence your inner critic and release your inner creative spirit. Retrieved May 11, 2013, from *http://psychcentral. com/lib/2012/the-drawing-mind-silence-your-inner-critic-and-release-your-inner-creative-spirit*.

Bronson, P., & Merryman, A. (2010, July 10). The creativity crisis. *Newsweek*. Retrieved from *www.newsweek.com/creativity=crisis=74665*.

Cameron, J. (2002). *The artist's way* (10th ed.). New York: Tarcher/Putnam.

Dewhurst, M. (2009). *A pedagogy of activist art: Exploring the educational significance of creating art for social justice*. Unpublished doctoral dissertation.

IBM. (2010). IBM 2010 global CEO study: Creativity selected as most crucial factor for future success [Press release]. Retrieved from *www-03.ibm.com/press/us/en/pressrelease/31670.wss*.

Jacobs, T. (2012, November 5). Do the arts open hearts? *Pacific Standard*. Retrieved from *www.psmag.com/books-and-culture/need-help-try-a-lover-of-the-arts-49123*.

Parischa, N. (2011). *The book of awesome*. New York: Putnam.

Pellico, L. H., Friedlaender, L., & Fennie, K. (2009). Looking is not seeing: Using art to improve observational skills. *Journal of Nursing Education, 48*(11), 648–653.

Robelen, E. W. (2012, December 11). Arts seen as a Common Core partner. Available at *www.edweek.org/ew/contributors/erik.robelen.html*.

Ruppert, S. S. (2006). *Critical evidence: How the arts benefit student achievement*. Washington, DC: National Assembly of State Arts Agencies.

Seuss, T. (1998). *My many colored days*. New York: Knopf Books for Younger Readers.

Strauss, V. (2013, January 23). Top 10 skills children learn from the arts. *The Washington Post*. Retrieved April 7, 2015, from *www.highbeam.com/doc/1P2-34156068. html*.

CHAPTER 17

Mindful Games

Deborah M. Plummer

Ten-year-old Maisy is joining in with a game of musical chairs—a game chosen by group facilitator Jenny to highlight simple listening skills and have fun at the same time. Maisy is one of eight children in the group, all of whom stutter. They have just finished practicing some speech control techniques. Maisy has done well with these but is generally very self-critical with regard to her speech. She is disappointed with the level of control that she achieved. She is also not a particularly agile child. Nevertheless, during the game she manages to get to a chair every time the music stops until there are only three children playing and two chairs left on which to sit. She suddenly screeches loudly and bursts into tears. The game comes to an abrupt halt. "What happened?" asks Jenny, rushing forward. "I hurt my arm!" says Maisy, through her sobs. No one saw this happen but all attention is now diverted to Maisy and away from the game.

Have you ever played musical chairs? What have your experiences of this game been? Do you have fond memories, or do you remember trauma and tears? During a recent workshop with a group of university students, I asked for recollections of party games. Whereas a few students reported happy memories, many recalled feelings of tension and anxiety ("I hated party games—I was too slow to move, so by the time I joined in, they'd already chosen someone else"; "I'd get so worked up, I'd end up crying and then feel embarrassed"). Perhaps you too recall the buildup of tension or the mindless pushing and shoving to reach a chair before the music started again. Perhaps you have also experienced what I call "game apprehension." By this I mean a generalized dislike or even *fear* of games. Some of the fears that children may face in even the simplest of games include worries about personal outcome ("Will I fail?"); evaluation apprehension ("Will I embarrass myself?" "Will I be left out?"); feelings of low general efficacy ("Will this help me to learn?" "I don't know why we are playing this"); and low self-efficacy ("Will I feel useless?" "Will I understand the rules?"). Although games played as ways to get kids moving or as rewards can be exciting and fun, the experience of playing games "mindlessly" can undoubtedly be a less than pleasant experience for some children. Mindful games, on the other hand, are an enriching experience for all participants, including the facilitators.

What, then, makes for a *mindful* game? In this context the term *mindful* refers to a way in which we can engage in games in order to promote mindfulness and maximize personal and social well-being in young people from age 4 and older. Mindful games are specifically and overtly based on the enhancement of awareness and the ability to direct and sustain attention for increasing periods of time. The games help children pay attention to the inner world of images, ideas, and feelings in the present moment in a nonjudgmental, accepting way, and to focus mindfully on the outer world of people, objects, and events.

The "mindfulness" of mindful games also includes enhanced awareness of how we, as adult facilitators, influence the children in our care—a sort of "extended" mindfulness, if you like. This means that, not only are we engaged mindfully (in the moment) in the games ourselves, but we are also mindful of how we have set up the game process, how we can maximize feelings of safety and comfort among the participants during play, and how we can maximize the opportunities for building well-being and for integrating these skills into each child's daily life. Three mindful adaptations of musical chairs are offered later in the chapter.

Why Use Games?

The universality of play and traditional games highlights the developmental importance of this aspect of children's learning. We know that play activities can help to promote thinking and language skills as well as the self-regulation of cognitive, emotional, and social behaviors. These benefits can, in turn, have a profound impact on a child's learning and future success in school, relationships, work, and life.

Games hold a unique place in the world of play. The rule-governed nature of games means that children can build competency and a strong sense of self-efficacy in a variety of skills within the safety of a structured activity. Games can help children develop social awareness and conscience, and they create opportunities to explore concepts of fairness and equality. Through the medium of games, children can (1) experience the process of making rules and develop the ability to select and modify rules appropriately, (2) see how games reinforce previous learning, and (3) learn the *social* value of individual achievements. In games, children who may have difficulty in understanding and expressing their feelings verbally can begin to explore difficult emotions in safety, with a spirit of "play," thereby strengthening their emotional resilience.

Reflections on Experience

The development of mindful games in my own work as a speech and language therapist and then as a senior lecturer in health studies in the United Kingdom began 20 years ago when a good friend of mine gave me a book called *Healing and the Mind* (Moyers, 1993). In this treasure trove of interviews with people working at the forefront of their professions, I found a chapter entitled "Meditation" (Kabat-Zinn, 1993). The interview was with Jon Kabat-Zinn, founder of the Stress Reduction Clinic at the University of Massachusetts Medical Center. Kabat-Zinn's description of the now iconic "eating a raisin" exercise particularly struck me. In this exercise participants are asked to eat three raisins, one at a time, "paying attention to what we are actually doing and experiencing from moment to moment" (Kabat-Zinn, 1990, p. 27). There is a detailed explanation of this exercise in Kabat-Zinn's book *Full Catastrophe Living* (1990, pp. 27–29). In brief, participants first bring their attention to "seeing the raisin," then feeling the texture and noticing colors, being aware of any thoughts that they might have about raisins and food in general, noticing the smell of the raisin, the movement of hand to mouth, the touch of the raisin on the lips, the impulse to swallow, and so on. Kabat-Zinn describes the experience to an interviewer:

> In this exercise, people realize, "My goodness, I never taste raisins. I'm so busy eating them that I don't actually taste them." From there, it's a very short jump to realize that you may actually not be in touch with many of the moments of your life, because you're so busy rushing someplace else that you aren't in the present moment. Your life is the sum of your present moments so . . . you may be tuning out of all sorts of inner and outer experiences simply because you're too preoccupied with where you want to get, what you want to have happen, and what you don't want to happen. . . . Once we do the raisin exercise, people begin to realize that there's nothing magical about mindfulness. (1993, pp. 117–118)

The idea that there is "nothing magical about mindfulness" appealed to me. My work with children and young people was already heavily based around the use of play, structured games, and the encouragement of children's natural imaginative abilities in the enhancement of personal and social well-being. The increased element of mindfulness seemed a natural extension of the therapeutic (and teaching) process. Gradually, the concepts grew into a framework for "mindfulness play" based on eight foundational elements for well-being (Plummer, 2007, 2012, 2014). In the context of this chapter, it is useful to be aware that playing structured games with children, particularly where there is a focus on mindfulness, can help children build and strengthen these foundational elements. Very briefly, the elements consist of:

1. *Self-knowledge.* Building a strong sense of self and a sense of belonging.
2. *Self and others.* Understanding the joys and challenges of relationships and the importance of mutuality.
3. *Self-acceptance.* Recognizing the areas that we can change or are already working on and accepting those that would be much more difficult or impossible to change.
4. *Self-reliance.* Promoting feelings of being in control and able to anticipate what might happen next as a consequence of our own behaviors.
5. *Self-expression.* Understanding how our interactions reflect beliefs about ourselves and others.
6. *Self-confidence.* Developing a strong sense of self-efficacy and the ability to set goals and solve problems.
7. *Self-awareness.* Being perceptually and emotionally intelligent.
8. *Beyond self.* Deepening our engagement with the awe and wonder of life.

(For further explanation of these elements and ideas for activities based on each one see, e.g., Plummer, 2007.)

Noncompetitive Games

There are, of course, many different types of games: board games, puzzle games, sports games, computer games, and so on. Some can be played by just one player; others require a partner or a larger team effort. Some are competitive, whereas others are definitely not. In some, perhaps the only element of competition comes in trying to beat one's own score. There are games that require a high degree of specific knowledge; others demand a greater degree of imagination and the freedom to invent. Whereas some childhood games are culturally specific, others can be found in various forms across different cultures or regions (e.g., see Let's Play Asian Children's Games [Dunn, 1978]).

Every game will engender different responses and feelings among the players. Each person's enjoyment and participation in certain games will alter over time as he or she matures, learns new skills, discovers new talents, or rejects activities as not being "right" for him or her. Every game can be played mindfully or mindlessly.

It is helpful to remember that a mindful element can be introduced into *any* type of game. However, noncompetitive games make for a good starting point. Younger children and those who are particularly vulnerable to low self-esteem will often find it extremely difficult to cope with competitive games. They will first need to develop a degree of emotional resilience, competence, and self-efficacy in order to be able to enjoy and benefit from the competitive element. These qualities can be fostered effectively through their engagement in noncompetitive activities.

Iona and Peter Opie, renowned in the United Kingdom for their study of children's folklore, conducted extensive observations of children's street games in the 1960s. They noted that

> children like games in which there is a sizeable element of luck, *so that individual abilities cannot be directly compared*. They like games which restart almost automatically, *so that everybody is given a new chance*. They like games which move in stages, in which each stage, the choosing of leaders, the picking-up of sides, the determining of which child shall start, is almost a game in itself. . . . Many of the games, particularly those of young children, are *more akin to ceremonies than competitions*. In these games children gain *the reassurance that comes with repetition*, and the feeling of fellowship that comes from doing the same as everyone else. (1976, pp. 394–395, emphasis added)

These observations are useful points to bear in mind when choosing, adapting, or creating mindful games. For example, three noncompetitive games that involve repetition and "doing the same as everyone else" are Pass a Smile, in which players sit in a circle and "unzip" a smile to pass to another player; the Old Family Coach, which involves players listening for their name in a story told by the facilitator and responding with an appropriate action; and Splodge Tag, which involves children tagging each other to form larger and larger groups until everyone is part of one group, all holding hands. These three games utilize observation or listening skills and mindfulness of other group members, but what else are the players learning and developing? Self-knowledge? Self-awareness? Self-reliance? Self-expression? Self-confidence? If you spend a few moments thinking about the different foundational elements involved in these games, it will quickly become apparent that there is a lot more going on than at first glance! This is where our own mindful awareness is important. We need to be aware that any game can touch on life experiences and skills other than those we might be specifically teaching. So how can we structure such games in order to maximize feelings of safety and fun for children?

As you read through the following sections, I suggest that you try to keep a particular child or group of children in mind and consider how the ideas might be used or adapted to suit their unique situation and needs.

The Structure of Mindful Games

Mindful games have an element of predictability and safety; they should be relevant to everyday outcomes so that children can see the benefits of playing them; and they should have an immediacy for the children—that is, the learning will be applicable immediately in daily life. Let's consider each of these elements in turn.

Predictability and Safety

Psychologist Catherine Garvey describes games as play activities that are structured with "explicit rules that can be precisely communicated" (1977, p. 101). Games follow sequences that are accepted by the players and that can therefore be replicated at other times and in different situations. These "process rules" provide a sense of predictability and security, which helps children make informed choices within games and may even reduce feelings of game apprehension. Two of the most important rules for facilitators to make clear are:

1. Children are *always* given the choice of staying in or out of the game. For some anxious children, observing others engaging in a game without feeling included could allow the buildup of negative emotions, whereas for others it gives them the opportunity to prepare themselves to join in by watching what happens and familiarizing themselves with the rules. For children who opt out frequently, you may want to suggest an alternative role, such as timekeeper, to encourage some initial involvement.
2. Children who are reluctant to take part straight away may choose to join in at any time by giving an agreed-upon signal. (Note: If the group appears generally restless, do not insist on continuing for a certain number of set rounds of a game; take it as an indication that it is not the right time to play this game or that it is not the right game for this group.)

Further rules should be established for any discussion time related to the games. For example, in order for children to feel comfortable in contributing to these sessions, they need to know that their ideas and opinions are valued and that they will be listened to without interruption or judgment from others.

Games typically have clear start and finishing points and a clearly defined play area. These characteristics are also important with regard to mindful games. If possible in your setting, try to use the same designated space in which to play mindful games. Remind the children that this space is a place where they learn about being mindful. Once they enter the space, encourage them to remain focused. It is the facilitator's task to "hold" the intention of mindfulness during this time so that it continues while the children are in the mindful space.

Playing mindful games involves making certain guidelines explicit. However, constant insistence on adherence to adult-imposed rules in games may begin to have a negative effect on the process, resulting in children's disengaging from the games, rebelling, or becoming passive. Rules should therefore remain flexible enough to accommodate different types or levels of response.

Relevancy

It is not necessary for children to analyze games in the ways in which adults might do so. It is, however, important that we help them to see the relevance of playing games as part of developing a mindful approach to life. This can be achieved through reflecting aloud and linking games to daily experiences. For example, you could remind children of particular games when relevant. For example: "Do you remember when we played the listening game? That is how mindful we are going to be during this next activity."

The reflective aspect may range from a brief discussion or drawing activity about the general experiences of a game to more in-depth discussions about what was felt, learned, and intuited during and after the process of playing a game. For example, you may want to ask for a show of hands after a game in response to a few key questions, such as "Who feels that they are listening more mindfully?" or "Who feels that they have learned something new about being mindful?" Or you may want to encourage more depth to the exploration by asking questions such as the following:

> "How do you feel after playing this game?"
> "How could this game help us to . . . ?"
> "Was it easy or difficult to keep concentrating on the game? Why was this?"
> "What sort of things made it easier/harder for you to listen/observe/concentrate?"
> "Did you see/hear anything that you haven't noticed before?"
> "Was this an easy or difficult game? Why was that? What might make this game easier? What might make it harder?"

Although I have found it helpful to have a few questions prepared to ease the discussion with younger children, I would always recommend encouraging their initial personal reflections, however basic or brief or elaborate they might be.

You may find that a few children have misperceptions about being focused and aware (concentration can be seen as hard work!), but the fun element of games will soon dispel this notion. Children may also misunderstand how an active game might help them to focus better and to be mindful. It is therefore important to be *explicit about the skills being taught and reinforced*, and to openly invite questions and personal insights from the children. Valuing children's views about a game session is likely to foster motivation to engage more fully in the learning process, and their comments about a particular game or activity can guide you in choosing another one to address that specific issue or skill. As they learn more games, children should also be encouraged to choose familiar games and activities (perhaps from a small selection of possible options) that they think might be relevant for a particular learning outcome. This process of choosing can engender useful discussions about how skills are learned and developed.

Immediacy

Mindful games carry the greatest impact if they have immediate relevance for an activity just undertaken or for your next intended activity. For example, if you are intending to tell a story, you might play a listening game. Or, if you have just shared a story with a particular theme, such as friendship, you might want to play a game involving an aspect of sharing, cooperating, or negotiating, such as team machine, wherein teams pantomime machines for others to guess, with each member of each team acting out a different component of the machine.

Self-Motivation

Mindful games are structured so that fear of negative evaluation or ridicule by others does not inhibit motivation. Where such feelings linger, despite our best efforts at facilitation, then we need to be aware of them and help the children to understand their fears and worries. We must be mindful to be ready and able to support children, and should we observe these fears arising, help them to observe, understand, and respond to their thoughts and feelings in a nonjudgmental way.

We can also encourage self-motivation in children by ensuring that mindful games are *intrinsically* rewarding; the games should be fun for each child and also lead to a tangible change in self-belief (e.g., through the experience of mastering a skill). Additionally, games should be *extrinsically* rewarding. For example, children might notice a positive difference in how other people respond to their growing ability to be mindful in daily life. For this reason a skill emphasized during a mindful game should be appropriate for the child's age and level of understanding. Aim to build upon the child's current knowledge and memory abilities and minimize possible stress about remembering the rules and procedures.

Try not to mix too many skills or modalities (e.g., listening and observation) in a single game. Aim to build skills gradually. Start with a short observation, listening, or taste game. For example, observation games such as Kim's Game (in which players try to remember a number of different objects that have been placed on a tray or table and then covered with a cloth) and I Spy can both be played in a way that initially minimizes the memory load and gradually increases the element of focus and concentration. This might be achieved by limiting the objects to be remembered or spied upon, or perhaps by making the objective of the game to detect something unusual about a familiar item—something that the child has not noted before. These simple games (1) help children become aware of their own ability to focus on single elements in their environment and (2) will facilitate the introduction of body and movement awareness at a later stage. Work gradually toward games that require more complex thinking skills and monitoring of thoughts. Be prepared to increase or decrease the complexity of the game elements according to the abilities and motivation of the children involved. The next section provides an example of how this might be done with a listening game.

Sound Tracking[1]

THE BASIC GAME

Group members sit silently in the center of a darkened room with their eyes closed. The game facilitator hides a ticking clock in the room. Each player tries to locate the clock through listening only, without moving from his or her seat. The player who is the most accurate in his or her description of the clock's location (e.g., next to the door, on top of the bookcase) takes the next turn to hide the clock.

ADAPTATIONS

- The clock is hidden before players enter the room.
- Players can be blindfolded, and all point in the direction of the clock at the same time. Two clocks are placed in different locations and players have to find both of them.
- Use hidden speakers to play soft music.
- Players sit with their eyes closed and try to identify as many different sounds as possible (e.g., a ticking clock, the sound of breathing, traffic noises outside, someone walking past the door).

---

[1] See also Plummer (2012, pp. 93–94).

EXPANSION QUESTIONS

"How easy or difficult is it to sit very still and listen? What makes it easier? What makes it harder?"

"Did you hear noises that you hadn't been aware of before?"

"When is it useful to be able to choose what we listen to and what we ignore in the sounds around us?"

"What might make this choosing to listen versus ignoring a difficult task?"

"What sounds do you like to listen to? What sounds in the environment don't you like?"

Giving genuine, descriptive praise throughout the games will also help children become more confident and self-motivated in their use of mindfulness. For example: "I really noticed the way that you relaxed your shoulders and calmed your breathing as soon as you sat on the carpet," or "When you were working with Alex, I could see that you were using mindful listening, and that helped Alex to stay focused too." And, of course, there are plenty of other ways to convey to children that their efforts are noted and admired. I suspect that anyone who is reading this book will have a wealth of wonderful ideas with regard to praise! My suggestion to you would be to revisit these and ask yourself how you might specifically bring your tried-and-trusted methods into the realm of mindful games (see also Plummer, 2010, pp. 17–20; Plummer, 2012, pp. 44–46). Don't be afraid to use the same basic format over and over again with only small changes over time. Remember, predictability adds security to the process, and you will soon start to hear the children using the same language to praise each other: "I noticed that you were really concentrating well," or "I noticed that you looked after Jo when she didn't know what to do." Our unconditional acceptance and genuine constructive feedback will help children to learn and grow in confidence and motivation. The way in which we give feedback will also help them internalize our acceptance and thus promote the important foundational element of *self*-acceptance.

Adapting Familiar Games

Let's go back to Maisy and her game of musical chairs. The game has structure and predictability but no overtly discussed relevancy or immediacy for children. Maisy's prime motivation appears to be to win the game and to demonstrate that she is the best in the group. She may or may not be aware of her emotions, but Jenny does not have the chance to explore this aspect with her.

What if Jenny had introduced the game in a different way? Or structured it so that there was no competitive element? There are plenty of ways in which familiar games can be adapted to integrate and emphasize mindfulness.

Considering the key elements of mindfulness described in this chapter and elsewhere in this book, ask yourself how you would adapt the musical chairs game to make it a more meaningful experience for the participants. Spend a few minutes writing down as many ideas as you can and then have a look at the three versions outlined in the following material. Each of these adaptations can be extended by asking children to notice their thoughts and/or feelings at any stage (see the earlier section on relevance and skills). Once children begin to form a good understanding of mindfulness, this can be a great exercise for them to do as well. They can work in pairs or small groups to devise mindful adaptations of favorite games, and to discuss the various aspects of mindfulness within the adaptations.

Three Possible Adaptations for Musical Chairs

1. Set up chairs in a circle, but only enough for half the group. Children tiptoe around the chairs while music is played very quietly. When the music stops each child who is left standing sits on another child's lap. When the music starts again, each pair of children walk around the chairs and attempt to breathe mindfully and in unison with each other.

2. Walk around the chairs in different ways according to the "mood" of the music—confidently, calmly, quickly, playfully, sadly, etc.

3. Children walk around the chairs in silence, focusing on their breathing or on the movements of their feet and the feel of their feet touching the ground. After a few moments the facilitator rings a bell or quietly says "Change over," and everyone moves in the opposite direction. Again after a few moments the facilitator quietly says "Sit down," and each child sits on the chair that is nearest to him or her or on someone's lap. As you take away more chairs, children will end up in pairs. The last two players left (or one, if you have an odd number) become the "callers." Add a variety of instructions to increase or decrease the complexity of the game.

Maisy's Dilemma

As already indicated, games provide facilitators with an opportunity to observe children's interactions and to gain valuable insights into their temperaments, learning styles, developmental progress, thinking skills, and levels of empathy. After reflecting on the game process, Jenny realized that Maisy's fragile confidence had led to her cry from frustration. Maisy was sure that she was about to be "out" and was embarrassed by her reaction. What should she do? She made up a story about hurting her arm. This is a typical reaction for Maisy. Because of her speech difficulty, she is in a state of heightened anxiety in most group situations. Easily reduced to tears, she covers her embarrassment by inventing physical reasons for her distress.

The way a child acts and reacts in games is likely to reflect his or her life experience in some way and therefore also reflect how he or she behaves in other situations. Without being overly analytical or too literal in our interpretations of children's behavior during games, it is nevertheless important for us to be aware of general patterns. Are there children who take a long time to warm up to each activity? Are there some who consistently "take over"? What happens when children become frustrated or cannot tolerate waiting their turn? Are they able to recognize personal achievements and those of others? Do they behave independently or always look to others to take the lead? Are they able to take on different roles at different times or for different types of activity?

Realistically, it is not possible to be mindful of all that is happening with every child, and every group. However, if we approach the playing of mindful games with focused attention; a high degree of respect for each child and for the process itself; a sense of valuing each child for who he or she is, not what the child can achieve; and an understanding of the world from the child's perspective, we will quite naturally tend to think and behave in ways that will encourage each child's enjoyment and learning during games. Our interactions will be further enhanced if we are also willing to reflect on our own thoughts, feelings, and actions objectively and to make adjustments as needed. With these points in mind, you might want to ask yourself the following questions when you start to use mindful games:

"What are my personal feelings about the games I have chosen? If I was this child/part of this group, would I enjoy playing these games?"
"Are the games appropriate for the age/cultural background of the child/children in the group?"
"Are the games appropriate for the cognitive and developmental profile of this child/group?"
"Are the games appropriate given the mental health profile [history of trauma, anxiety, etc.] of the children in the group?"
"Who, if anyone, in the group will find the games difficult/challenging/easy?"
"Do I need to adapt the games in any way to encourage full participation of all group members?"

Jenny might review the game of musical chairs and decide that, rather than abandon this as a useful and fun way to highlight important listening skills, she can adapt the game to make it much more mindfully based, taking account of individual abilities. She can also change the way that she introduces and facilitates the session. This would help the children to be more mindful of each other and of their own thoughts and feelings and to have a better understanding of the different aspects of the game. Jenny could also ensure that there will be time for a discussion after the game, allowing her the opportunity to support the children and demonstrate acceptance of their emotions in a nonjudgmental way.

Putting It All Together

With all the above guidelines informing the process, a suggested format for starting and ending mindful games is as follows:

• Ask the children to sit quietly, being as still as possible, in the space designated for mindful games. Give them specific instructions about how to achieve this stillness. For example, show them how to be aware of and feel the flow of their breath in and out, or have them visualize breathing in and out each color of the rainbow in turn. Offer positive feedback on how well the group members are achieving this, noting the benefits to the group as a whole. Don't worry if there are some who find this aspect of the process difficult. Some children will naturally become still and attentive within the space, whereas others may take many weeks to get to this stage.

• Set the scene for the game with an introduction such as the following: "Today we are going to play a mindful game called the *old family coach*. This game is all about listening." Or "We are going to play a mindful story game today. We start by sitting in a circle. I will tell you/show you how to play. This story game will help you with mindful listening."

• Explain the game briefly and clearly, making the rules, roles, and time frame explicit. Keep instructions concrete, short, and simple, and demonstrate if necessary.

• If the game involves the need to be quiet, make this clear up front and explain the reason. For example: "When we swap places with our partners, we are going to do it without talking so that we can make/keep a lovely, quiet space."

• Play the game.

• Sit quietly for a few moments after the game so that the children can "wind down." If the game has been lengthy, you may find it useful to also incorporate a specific wind-down activity. For example, after a brief silence, you could finish with each person having the chance to say one sentence beginning with "I feel . . .," "I have noticed that . . .," or "Today I learned that. . . ."

• If you have scheduled enough time for reflection, you could invite the children to draw a picture. Younger children might simply draw something that happened or an aspect of the game that particularly stood out for them; older or more able children can be encouraged to draw something that somehow shows what they felt or experienced during the game. Feel free to encourage both literal and abstract expressions of experience through drawing.

● Invite the children to talk about their pictures if they want to.

● Thank the children for their participation and offer brief positive feedback.

● Finish with an affirming comment to the whole group about your own experience of sharing the mindful game(s) with them. It is important to acknowledge when the children have a positive effect on you, simply by being themselves (e.g., "I really enjoy your company").

● Make a link with the next or previous activity, but do not belabor this point. Children will soon get used to the format and will be able to suggest their own links before long.

● "Tiptoe" out of the space, or move quietly to the next activity.

Reinforcing, Extending, and Generalizing the Skills and Insight of Mindful Games

Undoubtedly, many of the ideas given in this chapter will already be familiar to you, although perhaps in different contexts. This familiarity is an important point, because once we know about mindfulness and have some knowledge of child development and well-being, then we might instinctively create appropriate frameworks for mindful games. However, making this tacit knowledge explicit helps us to evaluate what we do in a creative and mindful way, and this holds true for children as well. One of the most effective ways of extending and generalizing the skills learned during mindful games is to have children explain and facilitate these games with younger children, or indeed, to explain and even play them with parents, siblings, and friends.

Part of my perspective is informed by "Imagework," a model that involves "developing the receptive ability to tune into the images that guide us, and the active ability to create new images that enhance our health, happiness, and creativity" (Glouberman, 2003, p. 6). My aim is always to encourage children to use their *own* eminently creative imaginations to deepen their experience of mindfulness. The ability to imagine is an important aspect of learning, creativity, and problem solving. It is also vital for empathy—the ability to see things from another person's point of view and to be aware of other's needs. Imagination allows us to be more effective in directing our attention both internally (to images, feelings, and thoughts) and externally to our environment and to other people. For example, we can aid self-awareness and concentration through the use of guided visualizations (Plummer, 1999). We can imagine objects, sounds, and smells and focus our attention on these internally without the actual object, sound, or smell being present. We can recall images, colors, and so on to focus our attention away from the ceaseless chatter of our minds. We can heighten the focus of our attention on someone else (and move our attention away from our own concerns and troubles) by imagining what it might be like to *be* that other person.

I often give children the opportunity to create their own images to represent their experience of playing a game. Once children have drawn or described an image associated with a game, the facilitator can encourage deeper exploration of aspects of the image to enrich the experience. For example, Zoë, age 5, drew a pink blanket with a silk border (she apparently has one at home that she likes to wrap up in) to represent how she felt after playing a calming and focusing game that involved children giving and receiving a gentle shoulder massage in pairs. I suggested to Zoë that she could pretend to *be* the pink blanket for a while and get a sense of what that felt like ("warm and calm"). We then used this image as a helpful link for Zoë to regain the same feeling in other, more stressful situations (e.g., "Do you remember the feeling that you had when you were imagining your pink blanket? Imagine yourself being that blanket now and feel what that is like").

Children of all ages are usually capable of constructing their own stories to illustrate different aspects of mindfulness. "Before" and "after" pictures can spur storytelling. For example, Zoë's *before* picture might have shown her without a blanket, feeling 'unmindful.'" I might then prompt Zoë to tell me a story about how she "found" the blanket, or even to tell a story from the blanket's point of view—how it helped Zoë to become more mindful. Encouraging children in the creative use of their imaginations empowers them to build a unified sense of their inner and outer worlds. Imagination also serves as a window into the often profoundly intuitive and sensitive insights experienced by children during mindful games.

Another important way of helping children to internalize their experience of mindfulness is to integrate the terminology from mindful games at other points during the day, such as referring back to a "quiet space," to calmness, focus, awareness, and mindfulness when relevant and appropriate. Point out connections and praise children when you see them naturally generalizing their experiences into daily life.

Possible Challenges

The benefits of playing mindful games far outweigh the challenges, but here are a few thoughts and common questions that may help in your preparations.

Who Facilitates?

The facilitator's role will naturally change according to the nature of the group and the type of game being played (e.g., teacher/arbitrator/timekeeper/

observer). In the same way, the role played by each child can change and evolve over time so that group members all have the opportunity to be the game coordinator, the "ideas" person, the referee, or the "teacher." Children who understand the rules of games and can explain them to others may naturally take on the role of arbitrator or game coordinator, leading others in making choices and in ensuring that the rules are understood and followed by all participants. Children who initially find this role difficult can be gradually encouraged and supported in leading and monitoring fairly. The children who have plenty of experience in arbitrating and leading games can also be encouraged to allow others to have a go.

How Long Should a Game Last?

Games in which children are engaged in focusing and concentrating should be fun and not feel like hard work. With that in mind, we need to start small and begin gently. When you are just starting out, playing a focus game, such as identifying sounds in the environment, for just 3–4 minutes is better than a half-hour session of several games, or one long game. To help with time boundaries, I sometimes give out games pieces (e.g., marbles, a puzzle piece, or cards) each time a round of the game is finished, explaining, "When you have all the pieces, then the game will end and you can make the puzzle or play the card game."

Spreading the Good Practice

As I described earlier, the very word *games* can elicit all sorts of preconceptions in adults as well as children. When working with colleagues in a teaching or therapeutic environment, or when putting forward the idea of mindful games to a senior management team, it is important to be aware that many adults will have already built up a high degree of *game apprehension*. Here, making a short presentation to clarify the nature and purpose of these particular games may be useful. It is often helpful to emphasize that many play activities already in place can be adapted to give them a mindful focus.

Be kind to yourself when reviewing your current efforts to share mindful games with the children you serve. Pinpoint where there are already elements of mindfulness in a particular game, and work to capitalize on these.

Jon Kabat-Zinn (2003) suggests that mindfulness "cannot be taught to others in an authentic way without the instructor's practicing it in his or her own life" (p. 149). This is also true in the context of mindful games. As adults, we can engage fruitfully in a mindful, playful approach to life, and we can all benefit from understanding and using the simple precepts of mindful games in our day-to-day living. If *we* engage fully and playfully with the concepts, then this personal integration of mindfulness will undoubtedly add authenticity to our game playing with children (Plummer, 2012).

It took a while for my own ideas to crystallize into the present format of mindfulness play, perhaps because I, too, was busy "rushing someplace else" in my career. However, I can look back on the last 20 years and say with conviction that on those occasions when I have been mindful in my interactions with children, and when I have been able to support a child in being mindful too, then between us we truly have achieved something worthwhile—and we've had fun doing it!

REFERENCES

Dunn, O. (1978). *Let's play Asian children's games*. Tokyo: Asian Cultural Centre for UNESCO.

Garvey, C. (1977). *Play*. London: Fontana/Open Books.

Glouberman, D. (2003). *Life choices, life changes: Develop your personal vision with Imagework* (rev. ed.). London: Hodder & Stoughton.

Kabat-Zinn, J. (1990). *Full catastrophe living: How to cope with stress, pain and illness using mindfulness meditation*. London: Piatkus Books.

Kabat-Zinn, J. (1993). Meditation. In B. Moyers (Ed.), *Healing and the mind*. London: Aquarian/Thorsons.

Kabat-Zinn, J. (2003). Mindfulness-based interventions in context: Past, present, and future. *Clinical Psychology: Science and Practice, 10*(2), 144–156.

Moyers, B. (Ed.). (1993). *Healing and the mind*. London: Aquarian/Thorsons.

Opie, I., & Opie, P. (1976). Street games: Counting-out and chasing. In J. S. Bruner, A. Jolly, & K. Sylva (Eds.), *Play: Its role in development and evolution*. Harmondsworth, UK: Penguin.

Plummer, D. M. (1999). *Using interactive Imagework with children: Walking on the magic mountain*. London & Philadelphia: Jessica Kingsley.

Plummer, D. M. (2007). *Helping children to build self-esteem* (2nd ed.). London: Jessica Kingsley.

Plummer, D. M. (2010). *Helping children to cope with change, stress and anxiety: A photocopiable activities book*. London & Philadelphia: Jessica Kingsley.

Plummer, D. M. (2012). *Focusing and calming games for children: Mindfulness strategies and activities to help children to relax, concentrate and take control*. London & Philadelphia: Jessica Kingsley.

Plummer, D. M. (2014). *Helping adolescents and adults to build self-esteem*. London: Jessica Kingsley.

CHAPTER 18

The Contemplation Music Writing Project

"Get into It, and Get It Out"

Jeffrey Pflaum

Introducing Inner Experience to Children

Inner space is the real frontier.
—GLORIA STEINEM

It may seem strange to have to think about how to introduce children to their own inner experience, but I realized one morning that was exactly what needed to happen to help them feel relaxed, focused, and themselves in my classroom. "It shouldn't be this way," I thought, so on a whim, as the unsettled students returned to their unsettled teacher after lunch, I found myself playing one of my favorite albums on the boom box. I suggested they place their heads softly down on their desks and close their eyes—something perhaps I too was craving. The kids paused, slowed down, and truly listened to the music in the moment, and were able to settle before starting the afternoon lessons.

The resulting calm was a pleasant outcome, but as an inner-city elementary school teacher, an academic component felt important, especially after seeing the music prepare them to work. Eventually, these regular music experiences showed them a new educational "TV" channel: viewing their own inside worlds—the images, feelings, and thoughts that flowed through their minds and were theirs to discover. Over time, through trial and error, a writing curriculum developed, "The Contemplation Music Writing Project," elements of which are described in this chapter, which I invite you to use in its entirety, or select aspects of it, whichever you prefer. Each exercise follows a similar routine: (1) activity; (2) recall, reflect, and/or contemplate the experience; (3) writing; and (4) discussion.

Practice 1: The Counting Technique, an Introduction to Inner Experience

(Total time, 25 minutes: counting, 5 minutes; recalling/writing, 10 minutes; discussion, 10 minutes.)

The counting technique is one way to show kids their inner lives and to provide a strong introduction to contemplative practice. A student introduced this exercise to me; another teacher had used it to refocus students' wandering attention after lunch. Her simple practice involved counting backward from 50 to 1. The counting technique offers children immediate access to their inner worlds. Here are the instructions I give:

> "Close your eyes and count backward by ones, silently and slowly, from 50 to 1. Rest your head on the desk, if you like, and don't rush to finish counting. When you do finish, open your eyes and take a minute to recall what happened inside yourself while you were counting. The second part of the lesson is to write about *whatever* you experienced inside, and anything is allowed. Ask yourself: 'What happened as I counted backward? Where did my mind take me?' At the end, I will read some of your answers out loud and we will discuss your responses."

Note: As an introduction, it can help to list experiences that might occur while counting: fantasies, memories, present-moment events, body sensations, daydreams, mind pictures, feelings, thoughts, and ideas to normalize such mental events. Describing the experience with words also provides students with a *framework* for comprehending the richness of their own inner landscapes.

Sample Student Counting Experiences with Discussion Questions

Next are some examples from my fifth-grade class. The suggested questions were prompts used to clarify the student writings and also to help kids understand and appreciate their inner experiences. This inquiry technique is the same throughout all of the contemplation writing practices:

- "While I was counting, I thought I was in a place like the moon. It was so dark, I thought I got lost." —Yvette Nieves

- *Experience*: fantasy, present-moment event.

- *Discussion questions for the class*: Describe the student's counting experience. Did anyone else feel "lost in the dark"? What feelings do you think the writer experienced? Why does she feel like she is on the moon? What happened to the numbers?

- "While I was counting back, I thought about the time me and my cousins and brother were playing in the hall. My grandmother came out with a broom, and we all got away except Diana. She started hitting her and we laughed. All this happened a long time ago, but I just remembered it now. It was like doing it all over again." —Carlos Rivera

- *Experience*: memory.

- *Discussion questions for the class*: What would you call this experience? What feelings are expressed? Did anyone see silly or funny pictures in their mind? What is meant by "It was like doing it all over again"? Did *you* experience a memory while counting?

- "I saw myself as if there was a mirror, and I saw myself in the mirror counting the numbers in my mind." —Belinda Garcia

- *Experience*: present-moment events/mind pictures.

- *Discussion questions for the class*: What happens in this experience? What is this "mirror" described by the writer? What does she see? Did you visualize yourself in a "mirror" counting? How could an imaginary mirror inside your mind be important? Could it help you in your life? Why or why not?

Discussing, Questioning, and Expanding Insight into Inner Experiences

The counting technique introduces kids to their interior worlds. Many wonderful, absurd, and surprising events emerge during the simple act of trying to focus on counting backward. The main objective was to initiate the students into inner journeys: to discover the creativity of their own minds and help them wake up and become mindful and peaceful human beings, beginning by making peace within their own minds. When children establish a regular practice of looking inward, this seemingly idealistic goal can be accomplished.

As practice leaders, the questions we ask to expand students' understanding of their own and their peers' experiences are critical. Leading a discussion on writing and learning to ask reflective questions and follow-ups in the moment are not easy skills to develop. Practicing an inquiry or question-and-answer technique enables teachers to create questions spontaneously and probe the writings to offer kids greater awareness and insight. Student responses tend to be best when fresh, but their writings can be taken home and reflected on, with questions developed and asked the next day in class. For you, reviewing the kids' responses overnight can also shape your future questions for follow-up exercises, such as The Contemplation Music Writing Project lessons.

One way to discuss the students' responses is to treat them as if they were *reading comprehension passages* in academic, social, and emotional learning. Suggested basic questions include the following:

"Describe what happened in the writer's counting experience. What mind pictures are triggered by the writing?"
"What feelings and thoughts are sparked by the mind pictures?"
"What did the writer mean by this word, line, or phrase?"
"What name would you give the experience?"
"How would you define a *fantasy, memory,* or *present-moment event*?"
"Give an example of a fantasy, memory, or present-moment event *you* had while counting."
"Did *you* learn anything from the experience about yourself or the world?"

The underlying lessons of this practice are many, but few key themes include:

- Awareness of all the things happening inside the mind by just counting backward, an activity that takes less than 2 minutes.
- A consideration of everyday life and what goes around in the mind and imagination—the thoughts, feelings, and images.

As a classroom teacher, a therapist, or other professional, you may think of other thematic questions used to steer children toward particular insights or ideas. Examples: Why do we have memories? Why do they come up while counting? Did it happen to you? What did you remember and how did it feel? How "real" did the memory feel? Did anyone visualize a fantasy while counting? Why do you think fantasies are imagined? How do fantasies affect our lives, for better or worse? Did anyone notice negative thoughts? How do they affect us? How can we change these thoughts and feelings?

Such basic and in-depth questions expand insight and encourage self-reflection. Questioning increases awareness of both self and other, while encouraging identification of the differences and similarities among individual experiences. The individual counting experiences are important, but they become more relevant and insightful when kids listen to their classmates' responses. They enjoy what others have to say—one key to having accompanying, lively discussions. Through directed inquiry, students become active participants, listeners, and observers of their own lives; ultimately internalizing this process prepares them for other contemplative writing experiences, such as The Contemplation Music Writing Project lesson.

Four practice counting technique lessons serve as a good introduction to a wide variety of inner experiences, before getting too repetitive or boring. To create a more challenging exercise for older or more experienced young people, start the counting at 100; they will certainly be ready to express themselves after that longer inner journey.

Through the practice of the counting technique, students begin to appreciate mindfulness: an awareness of what happens *inside*. This appreciation is key before introducing music or other stimuli to lead them through landscapes of mind, imagination, and spirit. As the kids develop and strengthen their *inner sight*, they can be encouraged to use the ability to improve and expand their imaginations in other realms and creative endeavors. With these initial positive and affirming creative experiences, the motivation to journey into greater self-discoveries and self-awareness increases.

Practice 2: Contemplation Music Writing

(Total time for the contemplation lesson, 30 minutes: music listening/contemplating, 10 minutes; writing, 10 minutes; discussion, 10 minutes.)

The next practice is the contemplation music writing sessions, in which children listen to music for 10 minutes with their heads down on their desks and eyes closed. When the music stops, they write about *whatever* happened inside their minds and imaginations while listening. The instructions are simple:

"Please remember that there is no talking or eye contact with classmates during the music. Focus on yourself, on whatever is happening inside, and be ready to write about your experiences in a paragraph. *Contemplate your experiences*. Look closely and carefully at the events in your mind. You will have a minute to recall what went on inside before you start writing. Do your best to be open and honest about what you experienced. Do your best to *get into it, and get it out on paper*. Consider what you just experienced and contemplated, and express it in your writing. I'll read aloud some of your contemplations anonymously, and then we will discuss them. If you don't want your work read out loud, please write 'Do not read,' and I will honor that."

A range of music genres—including top 40 songs the children enjoy as well as classical, meditation, and other styles of music—can stimulate a variety of inner journeys. Over time, let the children make their own playlists to share with each other, with the instruction to *find music that will motivate your classmates to contemplate their experiences*: "If your playlist puts them in the mood for contemplation, you have done your job as DJ for the day."

Defining and Illustrating the Activity of "Contemplating Your Experience"

It can help to be deliberately vague or at least open-ended about directing the writing experiences. There are no other prompts beyond writing about whatever happened internally and the process of "contemplating your experience."

What does it mean to *contemplate your experience*? And how can we explain it to a group of 10-year-olds? What were the kids experiencing while the music played? Some simple definitions: "To *contemplate your experiences* means to look at them carefully and closely. It is to view whatever is happening in your mind thoughtfully, or to focus on what is going on inside. Be aware or mindful of what is going through your head in the present moment." Deeper understanding of the phrase *contemplating your experience* comes with regular practice, ideally a few times a week. To illustrate the concept visually, the facilitator can draw a human head with space to draw examples of the mind pictures, thoughts, and feelings that emerge during the exercise.

Class Discussions and Illustrations of the Contemplation Writings

After writing, the contemplations can be read aloud and questions posed to cross-fertilize students' experiences with those of their classmates'. Longer-range goals include inspiring greater awareness, mindfulness, and inner sight by keeping the doors of the mind and imagination open toward accepting and becoming curious about all internal experiences as they occur.

To enrich students' understanding of the contemplation experience and to play to varying strengths of different students, experiences and reflections can be illustrated on the board or on paper, either literally or symbolically.

Developing a Vocabulary of Experience Words and Phrases

One of the benefits of writing and discussion is that it gives kids a language with which to understand and share their emotional experiences. In my own classrooms from grades 4 to 6, a vocabulary began to emerge, creating common language and understanding that defined and described inner experiences from the writing and the contemplation experiences. Examples included terms such as *inner eye* or *mind's eye*, *imaginary TV*, or *movie screen*. Self-awareness, self-discovery, self-understanding, self-knowledge, and self-discipline became important themes, along with countless words describing emotions and terms such as *mindfulness*, *reflection*, *meditation*, and *visualization*. If a student expressed a particular feeling such as fear in a contemplation writing piece, the class collaborated on a definition by looking up the word in a dictionary and/or a thesaurus. Words for *experience* were also defined in an impromptu manner; for example, *self-discovery* means to find out things about ourselves and *present-moment events* describe things happening at this moment or now.

Sample Student Contemplations with Suggested Follow-Up Discussion Questions

As a teacher, expect anything and everything and remain open to the joys of surprise. Students will write about *whatever* they experience while listening to music. Using music to access mindfulness unlocks and opens kids' inner worlds, many for the first time, so expect and welcome diversity in their contemplation experiences. After reading through a year, or even a month's worth of contemplation writings, you will come to know a child from the *inside out*—a stark contrast to how we usually approach kids, especially when hurried or stressed. In my early work with struggling elementary school children, I did not push them to write a lot. Yet even in a few words or sentences, their contemplations left them with a deeper awareness of, and a greater appreciation for, *what makes them who they are.*

The following contemplations come from a high-achieving, inner-city, sixth-grade class, with the type of experience defined, followed by suggested discussion questions for the class.

Contemplation 5

- "I thought about me, not just me, but my family, like my father. He works from 9 A.M. till 1 A.M. at night. I hardly ever see him—just on the weekends. If I want to visit someone with him, he gives me money and tells me to go buy something for myself. My mother comes out of work at 3 P.M. and goes straight to college. If I want to go out with her, she tells me to leave her alone, she's too busy, or to go ask my father. After school I have nobody to talk to unless it's on the phone. I feel that I don't care about anything."
—Glennie Llano

- *Experience*: present-moment event, feelings.

- *Discussion questions for the class*: Can you describe the writer's situation? What is she thinking? What is she feeling? What could she do about it? What do you think of her parents' behavior? How does the writer end her contemplation? Does anyone else feel neglected at times by his or her parents?

Contemplation 27

- "While the music played, I thought about the letter Mr. Pflaum wrote home to me this weekend. His last line on the letter said a lot about what I'm doing in school—which isn't much. He wrote: 'I'm an old song which can become a sad one if I keep doing what I'm doing in school.' Now I think I understand about putting more effort into all my work instead of just saying, 'Well, this is easy so I'll do it another time when I can do it quickly.' I also found out that my father went through the exact same thing I'm going through now. I said to him the next day, 'If you know what happened to you, tell me before I go through that same phase of life.' I realized that I have to get my butt back on course before I end up working as the guy in the zoo who picks up after the elephants." —Hiram Quesada

• *Experience*: present-moment event.

The contemplation demonstrates important social–emotional and emotional intelligence skills the contemplation music writing can generate in older children, such as self-awareness and self-motivation. Other skills were revealed in his writing, such as visualizing a behavior and reflecting on its consequences to make changes. Through the process, Hiram was able to be honest in his self-evaluation in that moment. The student's writing prompted a larger class discussion on contemplation and personal values, which then led us to the importance of being honest with ourselves and how contemplation music writing was about self-awareness and knowing yourself, as opposed to self-deception.

• *Discussion questions for the class*: What main idea is the writer communicating? What thoughts came to your mind after hearing the piece read aloud? How might the writer feel? Describe his attitude toward doing his schoolwork. What does he realize about himself? What does he see as he looks into the "mirror" inside himself? What mind picture stands out most? Was he being honest about himself and his behavior? According to the writer, how can he avoid making the same mistake twice? Is this a good solution to bring into the future? Will the writer end up being "an old song that becomes a sad one"? Do you get positive and/or negative vibes from the contemplation? Can you explain Hiram's self-realization in this particular situation? What self-realizations have *you* made in *your* contemplations? What does this contemplation stimulate you to think about and change in your own life?

Over time, what had begun as a way to relax a stressed out and boisterous classroom evolved into a curriculum that incorporated vital academic and emotional skills. When the contemplation, writing, and discussion components were added, fundamental skills for learning and *learning how to learn*, as well as life skills resulted. Contemplation music writing introduced and inspired social, emotional, and academic skills in a fun and self-directed way, and changed and clarified the way young people saw themselves, others, and their inner and outer realities.

Assessing The Contemplation Music Writing Project Experience

A major component of The Contemplation Music Writing Project, and certainly any program in public school settings, are student assessments. These too can be contemplative, such as is demonstrated in the following exercises of "Contemplation Comprehension," "Sight-Ins," and "The Student Contemplation Questionnaire." The questions invited my students to reflect on what happened inside their hearts, minds, bodies, and imaginations. As a teacher, I wanted to know—would they take their awareness and knowledge with them to the next class and next level? How effective and affective was the project? What were my students actually learning?

Assessment 1: Contemplation Comprehension

(Total time for the evaluation, 30 minutes: writing, 20 minutes; discussion, 10 minutes.)

The class reads a past student contemplation and answers several questions to informally assess their EIQs, or *emotional intelligence quotients*, defined as the ability to understand how to identify emotions and their influence on thought, decisions, behavior, and interpersonal interactions. The purpose was to see if students were developing insight into their own and their classmates' experiences. The instructions are simple and nonthreatening as far as assessments go:

"This contemplation comprehension exercise will show how much effort you put into contemplating, writing, and listening during discussions. You will read a student's contemplation and answer questions about it in writing. Respond using the same energy given to your own contemplation writings. Your answers will show how much inner sight and awareness you developed about emotions and behavior after writing and discussing the contemplations. We will discuss your answers later."

As discussion leader, first take a few moments to see how *you* would respond to the questions for the following contemplation:

- "I imagined being a soccer pro. I was a goalie. Nobody scored on me. I was the best and then they left me on the bench for most of the game. The score was 6 to 6 and they put me back in the game as goalie. The other team scored on me and I wasn't so professional anymore." —Cesar Torres
- *Contemplation comprehension questions for the class*: What thoughts arise as you read the contemplation? If *you* were the goalie, what might you be thinking while sitting on the bench? What might you be thinking 2 hours

after the game? Describe one mind picture you can see clearly. How do the goalie's feelings change from the beginning to the end of the game? Why isn't the goalie "so professional anymore"? What do you think the writer is trying to express?

   • *Discussion leaders*: How good is your sports EIQ? Answer the questions in writing and see for yourself.

The contemplation comprehension evaluation can be done as often as you want to assess students. The most useful results tend to come from midway through the end of the unit, or year, if you are integrating contemplative writing into the full academic calendar. The students' responses reveal their progress in mindfulness of thought and emotion: Have they learned to identify and manage thoughts, feelings, and behavior *in the light of awareness*? Could they apply this new ability to other facets of life, from school to sports and to daily living? What do they realize now that they did not know before starting the project? Overall, what is the progress on individual and collective EIQs?

Assessment 2: Sight-Ins

A second evaluation, which I term *sight-ins*, presents students with a quotation alongside related questions. These assessments also come toward the end of my yearlong program, but can be used toward the end of an abbreviated version, integrating themes that emerged in writing and discussion. Examples of quotations used that reflected each classroom's experience:

   • "Know thyself." (Thales)
   • "To thine own self be true." (Shakespeare)
   • "My eyes make pictures, when they are shut." (Coleridge)
   • "The only thing we have to fear is fear itself." (Franklin D. Roosevelt)
   • "Nothing can bring you peace but yourself." (Ralph Waldo Emerson)
   • "I think, therefore I am." (Descartes)
   • "Knowledge is power." (Hobbes)

Insights from the discussions were reflected in the quotes: self-knowledge, visualization, thoughts, feelings, and empowerment. The different quotations helped the children organize and make sense out of their experiences, clarify values, and see that they were not alone in their internal experiences, but rather that they were in the company of humanity's greatest thinkers.

Notes: There is a plethora of quotes to choose from online (many grouped by theme or subject) that can be selected based on the common experiences of the class.

To introduce sight-ins, define *quotation* first. Here is an example: "A quotation can be a saying or a line(s) taken from a novel, play, poem, song, or speech. It usually shows a great deal of wisdom, knowledge, and understanding of our human experiences. The quote tells us something about ourselves as human beings, the way we act, think, and feel. Quotations can give us inner sight."

Sample Sight-In Lesson

The sight-in lessons include an opening activity, discussion questions, introduction and clarification of the quote, written responses, and a discussion of responses. The five-part lesson can be presented over multiple days, depending on facilitator's time. Here I describe the details of my class experience with this lesson.

DAY 1/STEPS 1, 2, AND 3

(Total time for Day 1/Steps 1, 2, and 3, about 50 minutes: Contemplation plus writing, 20 minutes; discuss answers to questions, 15 minutes; and oral reading/discussion of peace contemplations, 15 minutes.)

Step 1: Emerson's quote, "Nothing can bring you peace but yourself," opened the assessment with a 2-minute contemplation on *peace*, followed by free writing about the experience: "Contemplate the word *peace* and then write about *whatever* thoughts, ideas, feelings, pictures, memories, dreams, and/or fantasies you experienced inside."

In *Step 2*, students were asked follow-up questions:

"What is *your* definition of peace?"
"What is the dictionary definition?"
"What are synonyms for peace?"
"What does the quotation mean?"
"Do you agree or disagree with it?"
"Why?"
"What are three ways *you* find peace?"

In *Step 3*, the student contemplations on peace were read aloud and discussed. These three steps can easily be done in one day.

DAY 2/STEP 4

(Total time for Day 2/Step 4 was 40 minutes for writing.)

Step 4 followed with questions related to the quotation and the kids' experiences. The class wrote responses to *all* of the reflection questions below:

"Does freedom give you peace?"
"Would being in nature bring you peace?"
"Can you develop peace by fantasizing or daydreaming?"
"Does peace come from being kind to others?"
"Do you get peace from listening to music?"
"Does reading a book bring you peace?"
"What about TV?"
"Can you feel peace after or during exercise?"
"Do you receive peace from contemplating or meditating?"
"Can you get peace from your friends?"
"Is it easy or hard to find peace in your life?"

The above list of questions is comprehensive, and I have found that students will answer many questions if they connect with their lives and make them think, feel, and experience things, especially at the completion of the project.

STEP 5

(Total time for Step 5 was 30 minutes for discussion.)

For *Step 5*, facilitators review the answers to the reflection questions to prepare for discussion. For each question, have several students read their responses out loud and then discuss them as a group. The lesson allows children to focus on a long-range intention of the project, and a theme that emerges over the year—which, in my classroom experience, was inner peace. After spending a school year listening to music, contemplating, writing about and discussing inner experience, expanding awareness, and building a contemplative outlook on their adolescent lives, the end result for my students appeared to help both stabilize and calm at-risk students. Awareness, with the help of music and contemplation, led to a more peaceful, yet more awake, classroom atmosphere.

Assessment 3: The Student Contemplation Questionnaire

(Total time for questionnaire, 2½ hours: rereading contemplations, 90 minutes; answering survey questions, 30 minutes; discussing student responses to questions, 30 minutes.)

Sample questions from a self-evaluation survey are shared below. The survey was administered at the end of the full program; it provided a format to receive direct feedback from the children. Students reread *all* their contemplations and reflected on them before responding to the questions. The kids' impressions from reviewing the writings created a *stream of experiences* needed in order to answer the questionnaire.

Students were instructed to slow down and give each question thought before responding so as to get a good feel for what they said and tried to express at the time. Comments can be added by the facilitator before opening the discussion, which ideally comes soon enough after reviewing writing, when everything is still fresh in the their minds.

Survey Questions with Sample Student Responses from Fifth-Grade Inner-City Students

- *Question*: "Did you learn anything about yourself after reading the contemplations?"
- *Responses*: "I learned that I have to get out my feelings." "I learned that you have to have knowledge and power to understand yourself."

- *Question*: "Do you think contemplation has been helpful to you?"
- *Responses*: "It helped me learn how to write and read." "It helps you think about your problems."

- *Question*: "Do you enjoy the contemplation periods? Why or why not?"
- *Responses*: "I enjoy [contemplation periods] because I get a chance to express my feelings and thoughts." "It makes me feel strong and happy and I like it." "I enjoy the meditation period because it helps you to get to know yourself better."

- *Question*: "Can contemplation help you face a problem? How? Give an example."
- *Responses*: "If you're mad and you do contemplation, it makes you happy." "I can tell what my problem is and I feel good." "If you can't relax, contemplation helps by making you not worry."

- *Question*: "What do you think would happen to the school if everyone, all the students and teachers, contemplated during the day?"
- *Responses*: "The school would cool down a little and the kids would have fun and learn a lot." "They would realize that life is easy, resting, relaxing, and contemplative."

- *Question*: "What don't you like about the contemplation periods? Why?"
- *Responses*: "I like everything, the music and putting my thoughts down on paper." "I don't like to write after I hear the music."

• *Question*: "Do you have ideas or suggestions to improve the contemplation periods?"

• *Responses*: "Change the writing part, and instead, tell it to a friend." "I want to write while the music is playing and not after the music stops because I forget things."

• *Question*: "What two things would you like to change in yourself?"

• *Responses*: "I would like to stop fighting and lying." "I want to change my reality and my way of acting." "I want to change my bad temper and have patience."

• *Question*: "What are your last thoughts and feelings about contemplation?"

• *Responses*: "I wish the whole school did contemplation." "I like to meditate every day."

Summary of the Student Contemplation Questionnaire's Results and Findings

The answers after a year showed greater thoughtfulness. After rereading approximately 100 contemplations that they had done, the children became very emotional as they reentered their private inner worlds, which had been hitherto unknown to them. Students appeared to realize, as a result of contemplating three times a week, that they had many thoughts and feelings, that it helped them to focus on their internal experience, to be mindful, rather than distracted or on autopilot. students learned to live the motto of contemplation music writing—*to get into it, and get it out*—which allowed them to go inside and identify, express, and release feelings in a healthy way. Contemplation taught them to deal with distractions in the mind, face painful past events, learn to solve problems more effectively, and feel peaceful, all while improving reading and writing skills. The students' answers showed they could more frequently face their feelings and not become overwhelmed by their intensity, and could take this newfound knowledge and inner sight with them *wherever* they go in life.

Music Writing Leads to Original Mindful Writing Formats and Greater Self-Awareness

Contemplation music writing opens kids up to themselves and others, to creativity and mindfulness, and taps into intrinsic motivation. After the initial introduction, they may venture into their inner landscapes with other mindful or contemplative writing activities. Once my students grasped the idea of contemplation, it was not difficult to present new exercises and prompts to expand their access to insight.

Sample Here-and-Now Meditative Writing Exercises

Word Contemplation

(Total time for Exercise 1, 45 minutes: list/word selection/contemplation, 10 minutes; recalling/focusing on experience, 5 minutes; writing, 20 minutes; discussion, 10 minutes.)

Children are asked to compose a list of words that make them feel good or happy, although a range of emotion-laden words can be brainstormed, depending on your goals for the activity. Examples of words from my students' lists included *eating, playing, friend, gym, money, toys, family, peace, present, holiday, mom, dad, music, sharing, smiling,* and *summer,* among others. Suggested instructions to your class:

> "When you hear, see, imagine, or read this word, something happens inside that makes you feel good. Take a few minutes to complete the list and pick a word for your contemplation. Contemplate the word by saying it silently, over and over again, for 1 minute. Be aware of what is going on inside as you repeat and focus on the word. Take another few minutes to recall and focus on *any* mind pictures, thoughts, ideas, and feelings you experienced. When you finish, write about your contemplating-a-word experience."

The following sample writing and follow-up discussion questions were a response to contemplating the word *smiling*:

- *Smiling*: "I pictured this morning, we're outside in the yard, and everybody was smiling and glad to be in school. I was smiling because I saw my friends again, and they are my best friends. I have to be with them all the time. And now I am smiling because I know that I am going to eat and run around the yard. I have been smiling since the morning, but let me tell you something: I better stop smiling before I get 'smilitus,' like the man in the television commercial that won the lottery and didn't stop smiling for the rest of his life. That's the way I am going to be if I don't stop smiling. Ha, ha! I made you smile. Keep on smiling. Don't stop now!" —Yesenia Vargas, grade 6

- *Discussion questions for the class*: Do you think the writer got into the word *smiling*? Why or why not? Why do friends bring a smile to her face? Describe the feelings communicated in the writing. What mind pictures do you visualize? What thoughts are triggered by the contemplation? What feelings in your body? What do you think about the ending? Why? What comes to mind if you think about the word *smiling*? What did you experience while contemplating your word?

Staring Game and Contemplation

(Total time for Exercise 3, 45 minutes: staring, 5 minutes; recall/contemplation, 5 minutes; writing, 20 minutes; discussion, 15 minutes.)

Children are paired for this activity. Suggested instructions to your class:

> "Sit and face each other, staring eye to eye, with no faces or gestures of any kind, for 5 minutes. If you start laughing or cannot focus, just relax and bring your attention back to staring at each other. Keep track of what happens inside and outside you. When you are finished, take 5 minutes to recall and contemplate the whole experience before you write about it. Here are some *reflection questions* to help you with the writing: What are you experiencing? What do you see on the outside? What thoughts, feelings, and images come to mind?"

The following writing, by Venus Diaz (grade 4), showed self-awareness, mindfulness, and liveliness to the point where the class experienced the activity along with her:

- "I felt as if I was going to burst out laughing. I tried to hold it in, but I couldn't stop laughing. I also felt like sleeping because I looked deeply into his eyes and became hypnotized. His eyes would turn different colors, and every time I looked, I would get dizzy. It got funnier and funnier. His eyes would go up and down, and also sideways, just so he wouldn't start laughing. After that I got a stomachache. I held my breath in order not to laugh. I let go because I couldn't hold it anymore. Mr. Pflaum still did not say, 'Stop looking at your partner.' Then, finally, he said, 'Stop.' I took a deep breath and let go. Boy, was I relieved. Soon as he said to start writing, I wrote a lot. Every time I wrote, I would think of another idea. I noticed that I had many things to say."

Her contemplation modeled a core skill of contemplation music writing and its practical application in here-and-now writing: a state of awareness, combined with social awareness, playing an absurd game without losing concentration in what went on, in front of, and inside her. Venus's present-moment contemplation detailed what she observed about her partner's contortions (outside world) and the emotions, thoughts, and body sensations she experienced (inside world). In all the project's writing formats, whether it was contemplation music writing or another method, detailed descriptions and a connectedness to the words expressed were keys. These were achieved by integrating mindfulness into writing, and writing *into* mindfulness activities.

• *Discussion questions for the class*: Describe the writer's awareness and concentration during the activity. What does she experience inside herself? What is the writer thinking? What does she see on the outside? What did she imagine was happening on the inside for her partner? What do *you* imagine her partner was feeling? Why is she constantly taking a deep breath? Why do you think the student had many things to say? Did anyone notice physical sensations during the activity? Did *you* feel hypnotized at any time? What holds your attention in this contemplation? Could the writer concentrate during the contemplation? Could *you*? What did it feel like to keep staring at someone? Did you feel close to or far from your partner? Did it feel strange, weird, and/or awkward? Why?

Home Practices: Experimental Present-Moment Contemplation Writing

Early Morning Contemplation Exercise

(Total time for Exercise 4, 45 minutes: contemplation, 5 minutes; recall/writing, 20 minutes; discussion, 20 minutes.)

The contemplation exercises can also be expanded at home; of course, motivation is difficult, but ideally such practices help kids get in the habit of becoming aware of their emotional state at the start of the day. Suggested instructions to your class: "Contemplate your feelings and thoughts for 5 minutes as you get up in the morning. Recall and then write about it for 20 minutes. We will discuss your contemplations after I review them." The aim is to continue to build awareness practice into all aspects of life. The following writing is a student's response to the homework assignment:

• "When I woke up this morning, I was very angry because I got up at 7:30. I asked my mother why she woke me up late today, and she said because I did not set the alarm. I got so mad and said that next time she should set the alarm on the clock. And she said, 'Don't answer me back, okay?' and I began to cry. I got dressed and was ready to leave. I did not have my keys and could not find them. I was so mad. It took me 5 minutes to find the keys. Then my mother asked if I wanted to eat something and I said, 'No, I am already late for school.' She asked me if I had my bus pass and I said, 'I think so.' She told me to look inside my book bag. When I checked inside it was not there, but my mother found it. When I looked at the time it was 7:59. I left very fast and took the bus to school." —Laureen Rivera, grade 6

• *Discussion questions for the class*: What feelings does the student experience in the morning? Why did her feelings get worse? Is she thinking clearly? Why or why not? Why do you think she cried? What mind picture from the contemplation stands out? Why? Why is the writer frustrated? How do you think she felt getting on the bus? How do you think she would feel in school?

Does the writer control her feelings, or are the feelings controlling her? Why? Have you ever gotten up in the morning feeling like this student and then your feelings changed? How do you respond to angry feelings? How do you calm down when you experience anger?

Sitting Alone

(Total time for Exercise 5, 75 minutes: sitting alone, 30 minutes; contemplation, 5 minutes; recalling/writing, 20 minutes; discussion, 20 minutes.)

This more advanced practice asks students to reflect on what happens if they do *nothing* but observe their experience, sitting alone in a room without television, music, videogames, computer, Internet, or cell phones. This was the aim of this experimental present-moment contemplation. Suggested instructions to your class:

> "Sit or lay down in a room for 10 minutes [or more, depending on the age] with no TVs, cell phones, music, videogames—just yourself. Contemplate your experience for 5 minutes afterward and recall *whatever* happened while sitting alone. Examine your inside and outside worlds and then write about them for 20 minutes: Ask yourself: 'What am I thinking, feeling, and imagining inside? What am I experiencing on the outside?' Please contemplate before describing your experience."

Following is one student's response to the homework activity in contemplation:

• "While I was in my room, I thought about when I was on a baseball team. It was the bottom of the ninth inning, no outs, man on first, second, and third, and me batting. The pitcher throws the ball, I swing and hit the ball—it's a home run! Now it is seven-up, still no out. My cousin is batting, the pitcher throws the ball, and he hits it for a single. My friend Billie comes up, he hits the ball, it is a single. Now, man on first and second and Jessie comes up and hits another single. Now up with the bases loaded is Freddy and he hits a pop fly to second—he's out. Next up is Alex, who hits another pop-up to right field—two outs. David is next: swings, strike one. He swings again: strike two. He takes one more swing—strike three. But the catcher misses the third strike as the ball rolls to the backstop and the runner on third scores. We win in the bottom of the ninth!!" —Claude Sharpe, grade 6

Some students, like Claude, avoided the present-moment experience of sitting alone and instead wrote about memories or ventured into fantasies. This might be interesting to follow up on in discussion. Others expressed frustration and boredom, feeling trapped in a room unable to hang out with friends or do anything—another rich topic for discussion. Sitting alone was difficult because kids, and we adults, now live in a world of constant distractions and are no longer used to being alone "without diversions" for any span of time—there's *always* something happening on our phones or online.

The larger goal is for young people to expand their ability to focus on the *here and now and observe their experience* through contemplation or mindful writing exercises. Studying, thinking, learning, writing, and reading are academic skills that require sustained periods of concentration, and students need to give a lot of energy and effort to get a lot back in return. Reflection, self-knowledge, clarity, and calm are some of the emotional skills built through these exercises. Many young people "check out" if there's too much interference when working or reflecting, opt for the distractions of the digital world or other forms of escape from the present moment.

● *Discussion questions for the class*: What happened in the writer's experience of sitting alone? Why do you think he recalled a memory? Is he aware of the present moment of sitting alone for 10 minutes? What mind picture from the memory stands out? What feelings and thoughts does the memory trigger in you? What feelings does the writer experience? Was sitting alone with nothing to do hard for you? Did you stay in the present while sitting alone? Rate your ability to stay in present time while sitting alone on a scale from 0 to 10, where 0 = totally unable, and 10 = totally able to stay focused on the now. What rating would you give to this writer's ability to sit alone and remain in the present moment for 10 minutes? Why?

Conclusions

Once the children have experience with contemplation music writings, other mindful writing methods could be applied because of the combined academic and life-oriented skills learned in the foundational process. From this 1-year project, students took away these *fundamental prerequisite skills* necessary for learning *anything*.

Along with the skills development came insightful writing exemplified by the student-created themes found in their contemplation music writings. Moving from the introductory exercises for contemplating and writing to its practical applications was made easier because students experienced a self-motivating form of experiential writing. The here-and-now meditative writing exercises and experimental present-moment contemplation writings showed that kids, from fourth- through sixth-grade classes, made powerful self-discoveries and self-realizations, and accessed mindfulness to keep them focused in the present moment.

The assessments along the way—in the form of contemplation comprehension, sight-ins, and a questionnaire—supported the fact that they had learned their lessons via music, contemplating, writing, and discussing their lives with classmates. Class discussions and the inquiry technique enabled kids to connect with each others' experiences, building common language and understanding, and to engage in a cross-fertilization of ideas and inner sight they could take with them for the rest of their lives.

The mindful writing methods improved communication skills and shifted the overall classroom environment to a peaceful, sensitive, caring community within a larger tough and chaotic inner-city school. The students made peace with themselves, made sense out of their experiences, and created their own awareness and inner wisdom, the way adolescents usually like it— that is, to do it freely and autonomously, with a little help from their friends.

I still hear from former students, many well into their 30s and 40s, describing how they continue use music and contemplation to soothe and focus themselves when life becomes difficult—perhaps the best evaluation of the enduring qualities of the project. The experiences written years ago became lifelong lessons, which are still practiced today.

RESOURCES

Go to my website, *www.JeffreyPflaum.com*, for published articles, blog posts, sample student contemplations, themes from the writings, Internet radio interviews, and newspaper articles connected to the project. I am a regular blogger on the BAM! Radio Network's blog, EDwords (*www.bamradionetwork.com/edwords-blog/blogger/ listings/jeffpaul*) with many posts about contemplation and emotional intelligence. As a guest blogger on Edutopia (*www.Edutopia.org*), I wrote posts under the title "Music Writing." I can be contacted about my work at *jeffreyppflaum@gmail.com.*

PART III

THE SCIENCE
OF MINDFULNESS

CHAPTER 19

Mindfulness Training for Children and Adolescents

Updates on a Growing Science with Novel Applications

David S. Black
Marvin G. Belzer
Randye J. Semple
Brian M. Galla

In today's world, youth are challenged by an array of social challenges psychological stressors, including time pressures, high attentional demands, early-age resource competition, and an intense media barrage. Given this contemporary social world, we are all challenged to provide our nation's youth with mental and social–emotional skill sets that can boost resilience against psychological stressors and engender healthy development and prosocial behavior across the human lifespan. Addressing this challenge is a wise investment in the future of our species.

New and promising intervention modalities used to foster such skill sets are emerging. Mindfulness training is one approach that can boost prosocial and social–emotional development and promote resilience in youth. The objective of mindfulness training is to provide youth with a set of tangible and self-sustaining skills that can be implemented, when needed, during early years of life and across the course of life. Skill sets are founded on an ethical lifestyle framework and center around a mental foundation of paying attention "on purpose, in the present moment, and nonjudgmentally to the unfolding of experience moment by moment" (Kabat-Zinn, 2003, p. 145). Inherent in mindfulness training is also a focus on acquainting children and adolescents with skills in self-regulation (e.g., behavioral inhibition, emotional regulation, and attentional control); awareness of thoughts, feelings, and associated bodily sensations without needless reifying of these experiences, and kindness and compassion for self and others. Given that mindfulness-based interventions can help cultivate this broad set of skills, they may serve as one possible antidote for the psychological and existential struggles faced by today's younger generation.

In this chapter, we present recent scientific findings in the relatively young albeit growing field of mindfulness training with children and adolescents. A review of the effects of mindfulness interventions on health outcomes among youth has been published previously (Black, Milam, & Sussman, 2009). At the time, that review reported on only 10 mindfulness intervention trials, and many of those studies contained several limiting factors, such as small sample size, uncontrolled study designs, inactive controls, and lack of generalizability due to clinical or homogeneous samples. Now, at the time of this writing, just 6 years later, at least 40 mindfulness intervention studies with youth have been published (Black, 2013). To refrain from redundancy, the following section reviews some of the newer findings among nonclinical samples (i.e., 2010 and later) and, for the first time, includes recent etiological findings linking dispositional mindfulness and health. The chapter concludes with an illustration of a novel retreat environment that is currently being used to deliver mindfulness training to youth in a more intensive manner than previously administered.

New Evidence for Mindfulness Training among Nonclinical Youth

Neurocognitive and Social–Emotional Domains

Mindfulness training targets skill development in present-focused awareness, sustained and concentrated attention, compassion toward self and others, and affective self-regulation. These skills appear to be associated with certain cognitive capacities related to executive function and social–emotional function. *Executive function* (EF) refers to a set of interrelated cognitive skills and associated brain processes involved in planning and carrying out goal-oriented activity, behavioral self-regulation, and response inhibition (Pokhrel et al., 2013). These skill sets are essential to learning and prosocial behavior. Poor EF is often found to be associated with cognitive deficits, impulsivity, emotional problems, and poorer academic performance (Biederman et al., 2004).

Although EF normally increases with age, young people demonstrate variability in the developmental trajectory of EF. Many youth with poor EF may be vulnerable to delayed social–emotional development or unsatisfactory academic progress (Biederman et al., 2004). Consequently, mindfulness training may offer opportunities to improve EF during early development, especially among otherwise healthy youth who have relatively poor EF capacity. A randomized controlled study (i.e., randomization stratified by classroom, gender, and age) conducted at the University of California,

Los Angeles, examined the effect of a mindfulness training program, called Mindful Awareness Practices (MAPs), on the EF capacity of 64 children in second- and third-grade classrooms (Flook et al., 2010). Findings from this trial shed light on the effects of mindfulness training on EF development during early childhood.

The objective of the MAPs program is to promote states of heightened and receptive attention to the present moment by using sustained attention to the inhalation and exhalation of the breath and bodily sensations (e.g., up and down movements of the belly and sensations of the body walking or moving through space). When attention wanders from this focus, students are gently invited to refocus their attention back to the present awareness of the body. The practice of cultivating kindness and compassion toward others is also implemented by having students practice a loving-kindness meditation, which focuses attention on sending well-wishes for other beings and oneself to be safe, happy, and free from suffering.

Based on teacher and parent reports of students, Flook and her colleagues (2010) found that children in the MAPs group, who began the program with low EF, showed statistically significant improvements in behavioral regulation, metacognition, and EF after the training, relative to controls. More specifically, mindfulness practices improved children's ability to shift, initiate, and monitor their attention. Indeed, improvements in these three domains may reflect the skills practiced, which include bringing focused attention to physical sensations (initiating), continuing to observe these sensations and attentional direction (monitoring), and redirecting attention back to the sensations (shifting). These findings are very promising, particularly since teachers and parents both reported similar improvements in the children.

These findings provide initial evidence that mindfulness training in schools may be particularly beneficial for otherwise healthy youth who have relatively low EF capacity. Moreover, changes in EF and other factors may offer an explanation for the medium to large effect sizes found in a separate study, which reported improved social and emotional competencies following a mindfulness intervention with children (Schonert-Reichl & Lawlor, 2010). This study does not address whether those with relatively high EF could benefit from advanced training in mindfulness, yet it is possible that all youth might show benefits in the social–emotional domain. Advanced training in mindfulness may include longer and/or more frequent sessions of practice throughout the day and week. Currently, it is unknown how long the effects of MAPs last on EF and social–emotional functioning, beyond completion of the program. Studies with longer-term follow-up assessments are needed to answer this question.

Separate studies have explored the influence of mindfulness practices in healthy urban youth living in an economically disadvantaged area. In Baltimore, Maryland, four classrooms of fourth- and fifth-grade children were randomized to a 12-week mindfulness intervention that included yoga or a wait-list control condition (Mendelson et al., 2010). Students met with the mindfulness group trainer for 45 minutes, 4 days per week, to learn and practice mindful awareness activities. Relative to the control conditions, mindfulness training was associated with significant improvements in involuntary responses to stress, rumination, intrusive thoughts, and emotional arousal. Statistical trends indicated some improvements in impulsive actions and physiologic arousal. These findings suggest that a combination of movement-based and seated or lying-down mindfulness practices might be an effective means to improve stress resilience and to reduce unhelpful automatic responses to social stressors. This finding has important implications for the development of stress reduction methods and stress management skills during childhood, especially for low-income, at-risk youth.

The United States is not the only country evaluating the effects of mindfulness practices on social–emotional and health outcomes among youth. A recent study conducted in Hong Kong, China, evaluated the effects of a 6-week mindfulness program (12 hours), including a single-day retreat (7 hours) among 48 healthy 14- to 16-year-old adolescents who were attending lower-performing public schools (Lau & Hue, 2011). Mindfulness practices included mindful awareness during gentle stretching exercises and body postures, daily mindfulness activities (mindful sitting, walking, lyvving down, and eating), body scans, and loving-kindness practice. Results showed that participation in this program was associated with greater mindful presence per the Freiburg Mindfulness Inventory (FMI; Walach, Buchheld, Buttenmuller, Kleinknecht, & Schmidt, 2006), a dimension of well-being, and reduced depressive symptoms relative to controls. Qualitative evaluations of the program from participants in the mindfulness condition showed high rates of program acceptance.

Positive Psychology

A growing area of interest has focused on reframing the disease model toward a model of well-being. This area, broadly known as *positive psychology*, studies the positive attributes of mental health and well-being, such as hope, wisdom, compassion, mindfulness, optimism, and creativity (for an introduction to positive psychology, see Seligman & Csikszentmihalyi, 2000). Positive psychology is especially relevant to children because personality and behavioral characteristics, at least to some extent, are defined during early stages of development (Caspi et al., 2003). Therefore, interventions that attempt to bolster positive psychological attributes and prosocial behavior in children and adolescents may advance the well-being potential of children throughout the lifespan.

Although research linking mindfulness practices and positive psychology is in its infancy, some initial evidence suggests that this may be a promising area for future investigation. For example, 246 students in Canadian elementary schools (i.e., grades 4–7) were enrolled in a nonrandomized controlled trial to compare mindfulness practices to wait-list controls (Schonert-Reichl

& Lawlor, 2010). The 10-week mindfulness program consisted of sustained attentional focus on the breath and sounds, mindfulness of sensations and emotions, managing negative emotions, and acknowledgment of self and others. Guided mindfulness was practiced three times daily for up to 3 continuous minutes each session. Results from the study showed that those in the mindfulness group reported significant increases in optimism over time, as compared to the control group. A nonsignificant trend was also found for an increased positive emotional state in the mindfulness group, relative to the control group.

Other studies also suggest the utility of mindfulness practices to the field of positive psychology. For example, mindfulness training has been shown to increase self-awareness among urban youth who face significant social stressors (Kerrigan et al., 2011). However, the relationship between mindfulness training and positive psychology remains mostly unstudied. Given that mindfulness practices offer training in self-awareness, self-regulation, gratitude, nonjudgment, and compassion for self and others, we suggest that they are likely to promote many of the personal attributes studied in the field of positive psychology as well as enhancing social–emotional learning (for more on social–emotional learning, see Zelazo & Lyons, 2012).

Behavioral Domain

Mindfulness training can, in some cases, positively influence child and adolescent behaviors. One study enrolled children in grades 4–7 in a 10-week mindfulness training intervention, and teachers with students in the mindfulness condition reported that these children showed improvement in their oppositional behaviors (Schonert-Reichl & Lawlor, 2010). Black and Fernando (2013) reported findings from an uncontrolled field intervention trial of the Mindful Schools curriculum, delivered to 409 lower-income, ethnically diverse, elementary school children. Results showed that teachers reported improved classroom behavior of their students (i.e., paying attention, self-control, participation in activities, and caring/respect for others) that lasted up to 7 weeks postintervention. Thus, initial evidence suggests that training in mindfulness may promote prosocial behavior in the primary learning environment. However, an important limitation in both of these studies was that teachers who rated behaviors were not blind to the treatment condition. Much remains to be discovered about the link between mindfulness and prosocial behavior, which is relevant to healthy interpersonal relationships, social–emotional functioning, and learning.

Dispositional Mindfulness

The inherent disposition of mindfulness (i.e., mindfulness measured as a naturally occurring trait rather than in response to mindfulness practice) has also been explored in relation to health behaviors among youth. Beyond training programs in mindfulness, recent studies suggest that even a naturally occurring dispositional trait of mindfulness plays a role in mental health and health habits.

Youth relatively higher in trait mindfulness on average report lower levels of depressive affect, perceived stress, anger, anxiety, and other mental illness indicators (Black, Sussman, Johnson, & Milam, 2012c; Brown, West, Loverich, & Biegel, 2011). Trait mindfulness is also shown to moderate the relationship between negative life events and mental health status: Higher trait mindfulness, as measured by the Mindful Attention Awareness Scale (MAAS; Brown & Ryan, 2003), appears to weaken the link between negative life events and some mental health outcomes, including depression, anxiety, and stress (Marks, Sobanski, & Hine, 2010). Additionally, a series of studies from a large and representative sample of high school youth in China found that higher levels of trait mindfulness, as measured with the MAAS, were inversely associated with smoking behaviors (Black, Sussman, Johnson, & Milam, 2012a).

These findings also suggested that the mechanism for the protective effect of mindfulness on smoking behaviors may function through a reduction in perceived stress, aggression, and depressive affect (Black, Sussman, Johnson & Milam, 2012b), while bringing greater awareness to the decision-making cognitions underlying smoking behaviors (Black et al., 2012c). Such findings may have important implications for future intervention modalities among youth in developing regions such as China, where smoking is a main contributor to the leading causes of mortality (Ezzati & Lopez, 2004). Interestingly, recent research with adult smokers suggests that mindfulness training can be more effective than current standard treatments for the cessation of smoking (Brewer et al., 2011).

Physiological Domain

Promoting healthy physiology in youth has public health implications for health promotion and disease prevention across the life course. For example, cardiovascular, metabolic, and inflammatory-related diseases (e.g., heart disease, diabetes, obesity, stroke, cancer) are among the leading causes of morbidity and mortality in the United States (Minino & Murphy, 2012; Mokdad et al., 2011; Zimmet, Alberti, & Shaw, 2001). Biobehavioral factors associated with chronic stress, such as overeating, sedentary lifestyle, and neuroendocrine dysregulation, contribute to the onset and progression of these disease states. Training youth in self-administered and self-sustaining stress reduction techniques that have the potential to create immediate and lasting physiological changes, reflected in healthier cardiovascular profiles, is essential. Mindfulness training therefore has implications for preventing stress-related disease outcomes by reducing the cumulative effects of psychological stress and its physiological effects across the lifespan—that is, if the mindfulness practices are persistently maintained.

Previous literature reviews suggest that mindfulness and other forms of meditation training offer benefits related to perceptions of psychological stress, and modify measures of cardiovascular functioning (e.g., blood pressure, heart rate, and sodium excretion rate) among youth and adults (Barnes & Orme-Johnson, 2006; Black et al., 2009; Grossman, Niemann, Schmidt, & Walach, 2004). The biological changes that have been identified suggest a shift toward better cardiovascular health. However, physiological findings come primarily from studies of homogeneous samples of African American youth, which limits the generalizability of these findings to other demographic groups. More recently, a randomized controlled trial compared a core mindfulness practice (i.e., breathing awareness meditation) to two other recognized school-based programs, including Botvin LifeSkills® Training and basic health education (Gregoski, Barnes, Tingen, Harshfield, & Treiber, 2010). African American youth in the mindfulness condition outperformed youth in the two other interventions on hemodynamic (blood flow) function, which represents a healthier cardiovascular profile. At present, however, implications that may be drawn from this finding are limited to African American youth.

Novel Opportunities for Intensive Mindfulness Training for Adolescents

To date, the delivery of mindfulness training to children and adolescents has occurred mainly in school, clinic, or home settings. Given that mindfulness training is a small portion of the total educational experience in these settings, competing commitments and other responsibilities may limit the effectiveness of mindfulness training. Training may also become fragmented due to the time limitations associated with school testing and absenteeism. Identifying new ways of delivering mindfulness training in more intensive settings is warranted to determine if intensity of practice bolsters previously observed positive effects on health. The following section provides a description of intensive teen "retreats" as a novel delivery method of mindfulness training that may be a promising avenue for future investigation.

Teen mindfulness meditation retreats have been offered for over two decades in the United States. Those taking place currently are mostly organized by the program Inward Bound Mindfulness Education (IBME; *http://ibme.info*), based on retreats that began at the Insight Meditation Society in Barre, Massachusetts in the 1980s. We describe and discuss the benefits of this format as an example of intensive mindfulness training for adolescents.

The IBME-style teen meditation retreat protocol includes a 5-night residential stay for groups of 30–55 teens (15–19 years old). An experienced mindfulness teacher oversees activities and staff. Adequate staffing is the first essential need; the ideal teen-to-adult staff ratio is 3 to 1. The various staff roles are described in the retreat protocol (Henry & Smith, 2005). In addition to offering support and guidance to teens throughout the retreat, adult staff participates fully in all retreat activities.

These retreats include organized periods of silent mindfulness meditation, small-group relational mindfulness exercises, guided activity periods, and free time. As with adult retreats, there are five basic behavioral guidelines for the duration of the retreat: (1) Do not kill, (2) do not to steal, (3) be respectful in speech, (4) remain celibate during the retreat, and (5) refrain from using intoxicants. Teens are expected to maintain silence during certain periods throughout each day; this differs from adult mindfulness retreats, in which participants are encouraged to maintain complete silence. The teens on retreat transition in and out of silence several times each day.

Program Format

Mindfulness meditation instructions include techniques for cultivating concentration (e.g., focusing attention on the breath, body, or sounds) as well as ones designed to promote acceptance of moment-by-moment physical and mental experiences. These methods are taught in separate sessions devoted to sitting, standing, and walking meditation. The meditation sessions each last 25–30 minutes. Mindfulness practices are also used to help teens cultivate positive emotions such as gratitude, kindness, joy, and forgiveness, and to better manage difficult emotions.

Groups of 7–10 teens are assigned to two adult staff. Each group meets twice each day for 1 hour. The groups function to build intimacy in a safe context by using mindfulness activities that cultivate attention to self and others. Group activities focus on ways to be more at ease with oneself when interacting with others. For many, these activities function as doorways into greater awareness of their own emotions and thoughts.

Participants are also taught how to develop and maintain mindfulness while engaging in routine daily activities (e.g., eating, speaking, listening, athletic activities, and creative expressions). The daily schedule varies based on practical needs, but in general takes the following format. Each day begins at 6:30 A.M., with the first morning meditation at 7:00 A.M. The day ends around 10:30 P.M. The teens observe silence for about half the day, during which they engage primarily in periods of sitting and walking meditation. On the final evening of the retreat, there is a party that provides a "community sharing" opportunity. A closing ceremony takes place on the last morning.

Initial Evidence for Intensive Teen Retreats

The meditation retreat is a novel environment for the empirical examination of the effects of mindfulness training for youth. In general, intensive retreats permit investigation into how intensive periods of mindfulness practice might alter psychosocial and biobehavioral health. In addition to providing opportunities to study intensive periods of practice, pre–post data collection can be completed relatively quickly and easily, since all participants are in one place. In contrast, clinic and school-based settings are limited by unanticipated clinical discharges and/or absenteeism. The retreat environment also allows for in-depth qualitative data collection from both individuals and the small groups.

Whereas a number of studies have documented beneficial effects associated with intensive retreat practice in adults (e.g., Chambers, Lo, & Allen, 2008; Jacobs et al., 2011; Lutz et al., 2009), only two studies have examined the influence of intensive retreats among youth. Emavardhana and Tori (1997) explored the effects of a 7-day vipassana retreat on indices of self-representation among Thai youth. One of the main findings showed that those who completed the retreat reported improvements in overall self-esteem (e.g., satisfaction with oneself) as compared to an inactive control group. Findings were mixed for ego defensiveness (e.g., increases in denial, but decreases in repression). Tori (1999) found that participation in a 3-day meditation retreat promoted positive changes in emotional maturity and sympathetic warmth in Thai teenage girls compared to an inactive control group. Positive changes were also noted in a third group, which participated in a 3-day Roman Catholic retreat. However, teens who participated in the meditation retreat showed the greatest relative improvement. These preliminary studies suggest some initial efficacy for the use of mindfulness training with youth in an intensive retreat format.

In an effort to extend this knowledge base among samples of youth from non-Buddhist countries, in the summer of 2013 one of us (Brian M. Galla) gathered data from ongoing teen meditation retreats (Galla, 2015). Retreats were open to all youth interested in meditation practice. No previous meditation experience was required. A total of 132 youth (61% female) between the ages of 14 and 20 participated in the study. Immediately before and immediately after the retreat, and then three months post-retreat, participants completed a battery of self-report surveys designed to measure multiple aspects of social-emotional functioning (e.g., mindfulness, self-compassion, perceived stress, life satisfaction).

Significant improvements were found across nearly every measure immediately following the retreat and three months later. Interestingly, improvements in mindful attention and self-compassion during the five-day retreat were correlated with indices of social-emotional functioning three months later. These findings suggest that improvements in mindfulness and self-compassion might be one mechanisms of action for improved mental health outcomes observed in youth after retreats. This single evaluation is not intended to be definitive, and the study is limited because it was an open-trial pilot with no control group and no follow-up assessments. However, this study does present promising pilot data to support the delivery of mindfulness training to youth in intensive retreat settings.

Conclusions and Future Directions

The pool of scientific evidence on mindfulness training for children and adolescents remains relatively small compared to the literature on adults, an age group wherein the research base has been more robust for stress-related ailments and health behaviors (Goyal et al., 2015; O'Reilly, Cook, Sprujit-Metz, & Black, 2015; Black, 2014; Black, O'Reilly, Olmstead, Breen, & Irwin, 2015). However, the research has grown steadily over the last decade, and will likely continue to grow. It seems evident from the published literature that mindfulness training is feasible and can be successfully delivered to and accepted by children and adolescents across different settings and in different formats. Of the studies reviewed in this chapter, there is growing evidence that mindfulness practices delivered to youth can improve various outcome measures representing multiple domains of child and adolescent health (i.e., neurocognitive and social–emotional functioning, behavioral health, and physiological functioning).

The lack of replication of studies to date limits our ability to make any definitive statements about the efficacy or effectiveness of any particular mindfulness training program for youth. This inability is not surprising, given that the field is in its infancy—and ripe for further exploration and discovery. To continue the empirical journey to discover the potential impact of mindfulness training on child and adolescent health, we suggest that researchers consider the following suggestions for future research exploration:

- Determine the effect of mindfulness training using validated measures of multiple health outcomes; if possible, simultaneously assess neurocognitive, social–emotional, behavioral, and physiological outcomes. For understanding mechanisms, measure levels of mindfulness with validated scales adapted for youth (e.g., Mindful Attention Awareness Scale—Children; Lawlor, Schonert-Reichl, Gadermann, & Zumbo, 2013; Black et al., 2012a), and adapt newly validated scales for youth comprehension (e.g., Li, Black, & Garland, 2015; Hanley, Garland, & Black, 2013).
- Include long-term follow-ups beyond immediate postintervention to determine the sustained effects of mindfulness on the trajectory of youth health and development.
- Evaluate factors that facilitate or limit the implementation and dissemination of mindfulness practices. Some of these may include class size, teacher and/or student resistance, and school culture that promotes or opposes mindfulness practice.
- Use active control groups that match the time, group, attentional, and expectancy effects of mindfulness programs. These might include sports camps, team-building groups, or creative or performing arts groups.
- Recruit larger numbers of participants from diverse demographic and ethnic backgrounds so as to increase the generalizability of previous findings to broader categories of youth.
- Report research trials using the Consolidated Standards of Reporting

Trials (CONSORT) guidelines (Altman et al., 2001) to make study methodology and results transparent and easily reproducible.

These recommendations are only a handful of strategies that we encourage be used to further advance our understanding of the effects of mindfulness practices on the health and development of youth. The significant and new environmental and psychosocial stressors encountered by youth today require equally significant and innovative psychological interventions to cultivate mental and emotional health and resilience. Mindfulness practices may offer practical insights into how these interventions can be designed, and may themselves be well worth further integrating into treatments and investigations.

REFERENCES

Altman, D. G., Schulz, K. F., Moher, D., Egger, M., Davidoff, F., Elbourne, D., et al. (2001). The revised CONSORT statement for reporting randomized trials: Explanation and elaboration. *Annals of Internal Medicine, 134,* 663–694.

Barnes, V. A., & Orme-Johnson, D. M. (2006). Clinical and pre-clinical applications of the transcendental meditation program in the prevention and treatment of essential hypertension and cardiovascular disease in youth and adults. *Current Hypertension Reviews, 2,* 207–218.

Biederman, J., Monuteaux, M. C., Doyle, A. E., Seidman, L. J., Wilens, T. E., Ferrero, F., et al. (2004). Impact of executive function deficits and attention-deficit/hyperactivity disorder (ADHD) on academic outcomes in children. *Journal of Consulting and Clinical Psychology, 72,* 757–766.

Black, D. S. (2013). *Publication database.* Los Angeles: American Mindfulness Research Association. Retrieved January 29, 2013, from *www.goAMRA.org.*

Black, D. S. (2014). Mindfulness-based interventions: An antidote to suffering in the context of substance use, misuse, and addiction. *Substance Use and Misuse, 49*(5), 487–491.

Black, D. S., & Fernando, R. (2014). Mindfulness training and classroom behavior among lower-income and ethnic minority elementary school children. *Journal of Child and Family Studies, 23*(7), 1242–1246.

Black, D. S., Milam, J., & Sussman, S. (2009). Sitting-meditation interventions among youth: A review of treatment efficacy. *Pediatrics, 124*(3), 532–541.

Black, D. S., O'Reilly, G. A., Olmstead, R., Breen, E. C., & Irwin, M. R. (2015). Mindfulness meditation and improvement in sleep quality and daytime impairment among older adults with sleep disturbances: A randomized clinical trial. *JAMA Internal Medicine, 17*(4), 494–501.

Black, D. S., Sussman, S., Johnson, C. A., & Milam, J. (2012a). Psychometric assessment of the Mindful Attention Awareness Scale (MAAS) among Chinese adolescents. *Assessment, 19*(1), 42–52.

Black, D. S., Sussman, S., Johnson, C. A., & Milam, J. (2012b). Testing the indirect effect of trait mindfulness on adolescent cigarette smoking through negative affect and perceived stress mediators. *Journal of Substance Use, 17*(5–6), 417–429.

Black, D. S., Sussman, S., Johnson, C. A., & Milam, J. (2012c). Trait mindfulness helps shield decision-making from translating into health-risk behavior. *Journal of Adolescent Health, 51*(6), 588–592.

Brewer, J. A., Mallik, S., Babuscio, T. A., Nich, C., Johnson, H. E., Deleone, C. M., et al. (2011). Mindfulness training for smoking cessation: Results from a randomized controlled trial. *Drug and Alcohol Dependence, 119*, 72–80.

Brown, K. W., & Ryan, R. M. (2003). The benefits of being present: Mindfulness and its role in psychological well-being. *Journal of Personality and Social Psychology, 84*, 822–848.

Brown, K. W., West, A. M., Loverich, T. M., & Biegel, G. M. (2011). Assessing adolescent mindfulness: Validation of an adapted mindful attention awareness scale in adolescent normative and psychiatric populations. *Psychological Assessment, 23*(4), 1023–1033.

Caspi, A., Harrington, H. L., Milne, B., Amell, J. W., Theodore, R. F., & Moffitt, T. E. (2003). Children's behavioral styles at age 3 are linked to their adult personality traits at age 26. *Journal of Personality, 71*(4), 495–514.

Chambers, R., Lo, B. C. Y., & Allen, N. B. (2008). The impact of intensive mindfulness training on attentional control, cognitive style, and affect. *Cognitive Therapy and Research, 32*, 303–322.

Emavardhana, T., & Tori, C. D. (1997). Changes in self-concept, ego defense mechanisms, and religiosity following seven-day Vipassana meditation retreats. *Journal for the Scientific Study of Religion, 36*, 194–206.

Ezzati, M., & Lopez, A. D. (2004). Regional, disease-specific patterns of smoking: Attributable mortality in 2000. *Tobacco Control, 13*(4), 388–395.

Flook, L., Smalley, S. L., Kitil, M. J., Galla, B. M., Kaiser-Greenland, S., Locke, J., et al. (2010). Effects of mindful awareness practices on executive functions in elementary school children. *Journal of Applied School Psychology, 26*, 70–95.

Galla, B. M. (2015). *Intensive meditation retreates and psychological well-being in adolescents: A three-month longitudinal study.* Manuscripts in preparation.

Goyal, M., Singh, S., Sibinga, E. M. S., Gould, N. F., Rowland-Seymour, A., Sharma, R., et al. (2014). Meditation programs for psychological stress and well-being. *JAMA Internal Medicine, 174*(3), 357–368.

Gregoski, M. J., Barnes, V. A., Tingen, M. S., Harshfield, G. A., & Treiber, F. A. (2010). Breathing awareness meditation and LifeSkills training programs influence upon ambulatory blood pressure and sodium excretion among African American adolescents. *Journal of Adolescent Health, 48*, 59–64.

Grossman, P., Niemann, L., Schmidt, S., & Walach, H. (2004). Mindfulness-based stress reduction and health benefits: A meta-analysis. *Journal of Psychosomatic Research, 57*, 35–43.

Hanley, A., Garland, E. L., & Black, D. S. (2013). Use of mindful reappraisal coping among meditation practitioners. *Journal of Clinical Psychology, 70*(3), 294–301.

Henry, W., & Smith, T. (2005). *Teen retreat staff manual.* Unpublished manuscript.

Jacobs, T. L., Epel, E. S., Lin, J., Blackburn, E. H., Wolkowitz, O. M., Bridwell, D. A., et al. (2011). Intensive meditation training, immune cell telomerase activity, and psychological mediators. *Psychoneuroendocrinology, 36*(5), 664–681.

Kabat-Zinn, J. (2003). Mindfulness-based interventions in context: Past, present, and future. *Clinical Psychology: Science and Practice, 10*(2), 144–156.

Kerrigan, D., Johnson, K., Stewart, M., Magyari, T., Hutton, N., Ellen, J. M., et al. (2011). Perceptions, experiences, and shifts in perspective occurring among urban youth participating in a mindfulness-based stress reduction program. *Complementary Therapies in Clinical Practice, 17,* 96–101.

Lau, N., & Hue, M. (2011). Preliminary outcomes of a mindfulness-based programme for Hong Kong adolescents in schools: Well-being, stress and depressive symptoms. *International Journal of Children's Spirituality, 16,* 315–330.

Lawlor, M. S., Schonert-Reichl, K. A., Gadermann, A. M., & Zumbo, B. D. (2013). A validation study of the mindful attention awareness scale adapted for children. *Mindfulness, 5*(6), 730–741.

Li, M., Black, D. S., & Garland, E. (2015). *The Applied Mindfulness Process Scale (AMPS): A process measure for evaluating mindfulness-based interventions.* Manuscripts submitted for publication.

Lutz, A., Slagter, H. A., Rawlings, N. B., Francis, A. D., Greischar, L. L., & Davidson, R. J. (2009). Mental training enhances attentional stability: Neural and behavioral evidence. *Journal of Neuroscience, 29,* 13418–13427.

Marks, A. D. G., Sobanski, D. J., & Hine, D. W. (2010). Do dispositional rumination and/or mindfulness moderate the relationship between life hassles and psychological dysfunction in adolescents? *Australian and New Zealand Journal of Psychiatry, 44,* 831–838.

Mendelson, T., Greenberg, M. T., Dariotis, J. K., Gould, L. F., Rhoades, B. L., & Leaf, P. J. (2010). Feasibility and preliminary outcomes of a school-based mindfulness intervention for urban youth. *Journal of Abnormal Child Psychology, 38,* 985–994.

Minino, A. M., & Murphy, S. L. (2012). *Death in the United States, 2012.* U.S. Department of Health and Human Services, Data Brief, No. 99.

Mokdad, A. H., Bowman, B. A., Ford, E. S., Vinicor, F., Marks, J. S., & Koplan, J. P. (2001). The continuing epidemics of obesity and diabetes in the United States. *Journal of the American Medical Association, 286*(10), 1195–1200.

O'Reilly, G. A., Cook, L., Spruijt-Metz, D., & Black, D. S. (2014). Mindfulness-based interventions for obesity-related eating behaviours: A literature review. *Obesity Reviews, 15*(6), 453–461.

Pokhrel, P., Herzog, T. A., Black, D. S., Zaman, A., Riggs, N. R., & Sussman, S. (2013). Adolescent neurocognitive development, self-regulation, and school-based drug use prevention. *Prevention Science, 14*(3), 218–228.

Schonert-Reichl, K. A., & Lawlor, M. S. (2010). The effects of a mindfulness-based education program on pre- and early adolescents' well-being and social and emotional competence. *Mindfulness, 1,* 137–151.

Seligman, M. E., & Csikszentmihalyi, M. (2000). Positive psychology: An introduction. *American Psychologist, 55,* 5–14.

Tori, C. D. (1999). Change on psychological scales following Buddhist and Roman Catholic retreats. *Psychological Reports, 84,* 125–126.

Walach, H., Buchheld, N., Buttenmuller, V., Kleinknecht, N., & Schmidt, S. (2006). Measuring mindfulness: The Freiburg Mindfulness Inventory (FMI). *Personality and Individual Differences, 40,* 1543–1555.

Zelazo, P. D., & Lyons, K. E. (2012). The potential benefits of mindfulness training in early childhood: A developmental social cognitive neuroscience perspective. *Child Development Perspectives, 6*(2), 154–160.

Zimmet, P., Alberti, K. G., & Shaw, J. (2001). Global and societal implications of the diabetes epidemic. *Nature, 414*(6865), 782–787.

CHAPTER 20

Mindfulness, Executive Function, and Attention-Deficit/ Hyperactivity Disorder

Bringing It All Together

Mark Bertin

Most people immediately recognize the benefits of practicing mindfulness once they encounter the definition: *Paying full attention to our moment-to-moment experience with openness and compassion.* Without mindfulness, we remain lost in distraction, skipping over the details while acting habitually and frequently reactively through much of our lives.

Mindfulness, although not an inherently spiritual practice, in many ways reflects values of the traditional serenity prayer: "God grant me the serenity to accept the things I cannot change, the courage to change the things I can, and the wisdom to know the difference." Deliberately cultivating an attitude of open-minded responsiveness to whatever life throws our way has extraordinary value. Expanding our ability to proactively address ingrained mental habits, which may seem fixed and permanent, represents a significant step forward for most of us.

So how do the benefits of mindfulness relate to attention-deficit/hyperactivity disorder (ADHD)? ADHD causes a range of impairments in a mental skill set known as *executive function*, which includes all of the cognitive abilities that manage and coordinate day-to-day life. ADHD potentially impacts anything we attempt that requires focus, forethought, impulse control, or long-term planning. Without skillful intervention, ADHD impacts entire families, classrooms, relationships, after-school activities, and countless other endeavors from childhood onward.

Recognizing ADHD as a brain-based developmental delay in executive function, the rationale behind various interventions becomes clear. Integrating *mindfulness* into traditional ADHD care starts with an understanding of the full scope of this complex medical disorder. For parents, teachers, and providers, this chapter offers an overview of how mindfulness uniquely supports both individuals and families living with ADHD.

Executive Function: What It Is

If you were to depend on the average 4-year-old child to make dinner one night next week, you would not end up with much. With some grown-up supervision, perhaps you'll eat peanut butter and jelly—as long as you've done the shopping and have peanut butter and jelly at home. Planning ahead in that way isn't too likely for a tot. If the child does muster a sandwich, he or she probably will not get it on the table by any particular time. Actually, the child might not bother with the table at all. And cleaning up afterward is not likely without reminders and prompting.

By 14 years of age, most kids could pull off a meal, making at least a sandwich if they felt like it, if not something more balanced. Of course, they might prefer a bag of chips and a pint of ice cream. And some teens would struggle to coordinate finding recipes, shopping, or juggling the timing of cooking instructions. Something has changed since preschool, but not yet fully matured.

By 24 years of age, most young adults live independently. They make meals, attend school, or hold jobs—maybe even work as a chef. They navigate relationships, negotiate and compromise with others, and are capable of reflecting on their pasts and futures. Many young adults make long-sighted choices about eating, exercise, and lifestyle habits. By 34 years of age, their perspective often shifts to consider retirement plans, health insurance, their children's education, and other life necessities as they start to contemplate their future selves . . . all while getting some kind of dinner planned, eaten, and cleaned up night after night.

So what happens between the ages of 4 and 34? Unlike what we thought only a few years ago, the brain continues to develop well into early adulthood. It grows up. More specifically, the parts that act as our "brain manager" reach peak performance some time near 30 years of age.

This cognitive skill set that comprises the brain manager is referred to as *executive function* and includes abilities ranging from monitoring our immediate behavior to regulating our emotions and from organizing our lives to managing our time. Executive function does not represent *what* we know but instead *how* skillfully we access and apply our underlying intelligence and morality. Before these skills develop, we lack full capacity for actions such as following through on a long-term project (e.g., menu planning) or the wherewithal to stick with a new overall plan for healthy eating.

If there is one shared goal for providers and parents working and living with children, it is to positively influence their long-term well-being. Many predictors of lifelong achievement, such as cognitive skills or social disparities, are near impossible to address individually. On the other hand, abilities related to executive function and self-regulation may be influenced by direct instruction. As much as any skill set we can teach children, executive function allows them to handle the bumps (or sometimes mountains) they inevitably encounter along the road of life.

Executive Function in Childhood: Why It Matters

One illustration of executive function in action is the oft-cited "marshmallow study" conducted by Walter Mischel and colleagues in 1972 and updated since (Mischel, Ebbesen, & Zeiss, 1972; Casey, Somerville, Gotlib, et al., 2011). The setup was simple. Preschool children sitting with a researcher were told that they could have a less-preferred treat now (e.g., one marshmallow) or a more-preferred treat later (e.g., two marshmallows) if they could wait until after the grown-up left the room and returned. The intent was that the children would find it difficult to choose while the treats remained on the table.

Unsurprisingly, waiting was not straightforward for preschool children. Many grabbed a treat right away ("low delayers" in the study). Others struggled a while before giving in. One third of these children managed to wait for the adult to return and give them their preferred treat ("high delayers").

Years later, the researchers tracked down many of the children from this original study (Casey et al., 2011). Based on this single measure of preschool self-regulation, as teenagers the high delayers were described as more socially competent than low delayers. They demonstrated higher standardized test scores. Later as adults, they were found to have a decreased risk of being overweight. A related study published in 2013 examined the association between preschoolers' ability to attend to a task and their long-term academic success (McClelland, Acock, Piccinin, et al., 2013). Those with a higher ability to focus attention were nearly 49% more likely to graduate college by the age of 25.

An early childhood ability to self-regulate, such as controlling impulses and monitoring long-term consequences, apparently influences a lifelong path. A 2011 study out of New Zealand found that "differences between individuals in self-control are present in early childhood and can predict multiple indicators of health, wealth, and crime across three decades of life in both genders" (Moffitt, Arseneault, Belsky, et al., 2011). For example, children identified as having lower skills before 5 years of age were more likely to be single parents or struggling with substance abuse as adults.

It's important to recognize that these studies only monitor trends. Not every child who fails to resist a pile of marshmallows is fated to a life of crime and underachievement. Yet on a foundational level, executive function at only a few years of age appears to correlate with adult well-being. Among all the complex variables that influence the development of a human child, executive function skills appear remarkably predictive of long-term success through a range of measurements. Since a growing body of research describes improved executive function as a potential outcome of mindfulness, this practice may represent a direct choice parents and teachers could make to positively influence a child throughout life.

ADHD and Executive Function

For children and teens with ADHD, executive function explains the vast array of difficulties they may encounter at home, school, and elsewhere. ADHD (a term that also encompasses the nonhyperactive, inattentive subtype: attention deficit disorder, or ADD) is a condition that has long outgrown its own name. It is neither a disorder of inattention nor hyperactivity alone, but includes a much larger umbrella of cognitive challenges related to deficits in executive function.

For most individuals, devastating troubles lurk below the ADHD surface regarding organization, time management, emotional self-control, or any of countless related skills. Because executive function skills coordinate all of our daily-life functioning, ADHD can undermine everything from sleeping and eating habits to social and communication abilities. An ever-expanding list of studies documents ADHD-related risks, including low self-esteem, school failure, social problems, marital strife, accidents, eating disorders, early drinking, and many other behaviors related to difficulties with self-regulation.

Conceptualizing ADHD as a developmental delay in executive function is a shift in perspective that can change lives. Through this lens we more accurately recognize a child's level of development and define a proactive plan for long-term success. Children with ADHD do not elect to act out behaviorally, fall behind academically, or perform below their potential, but instead lack specific skills that would otherwise allow them to thrive.

Executive Function, ADHD, and Everyday Living

One common framework for evaluating everyday executive function comes from Thomas Brown (2008), who has categorized these abilities as *focus, action management, activation, working memory, emotional regulation*, and *sustained effort*. Each of these labels refers to a coordinating and supervising cognitive skill set. By understanding the implications for daily life, we more easily meet the evolving developmental needs of individual children.

Focus (which can also be described as *attention management*) is the ability to direct our attention where we want without becoming distracted. Strong attention management skills permit us to keep on task even when things are not utterly exciting. It also represents the ability to shift between activities with ease. When children or adults lack attention management abilities, as is the case with ADHD, they often have difficulty switching attention away from what they are doing (e.g., playing a videogame, checking their smartphone) when someone talks to them or asks them to switch tasks. Children with ADHD can focus very well if something completely engages them, but struggle otherwise to wholly or partly disengage.

Action management refers to the ability to monitor our physical behavior both internally and in relation to others. It represents the ability to sit still when required and to control our impulses. Without this skill set, people often experience excessive fidgeting or seem "driven by a motor." Or, they may have a hard time resisting the various cravings and desires that arise for all of us throughout the day.

Activation (similar to *task management*) describes the ability to organize, plan, learn from mistakes, and look toward the future. Delays in activation explain why a young child with ADHD cannot typically manage a long-term, multistep project without the help of an adult, or why even an adolescent may require significant supports with something like a research paper. Although hyperactivity and impulsiveness typically decrease with age, difficulty with task management often persists into adulthood, making everyday logistics related to school, jobs, and households an ongoing challenge.

Working memory (analogous to *information management*) is where all the moment-to-moment triage and organization of thoughts occur. Working memory holds information in the human brain temporarily while it is being used, organized, or sorted. Until strong working memory develops, tracking mental to-do lists and multistep directions (e.g., "Go up to your room, get dressed, and brush your teeth") without external prompts and accommodations remain difficult.

Working memory also allows us to pull together information from our own minds and integrate it with whatever is going on around us. It then allows us to maintain a linear discussion while holding those ideas in mind. Deficits in working memory therefore may impact skills such as narrative writing or communication, especially when combined with other difficulties related to executive function.

Effort is the capacity to sustain alertness, perform hard work, and complete mental tasks efficiently. This executive function component is neurologically based, yet when someone struggles in this area, it is often perceived as *choosing* not to try hard. On a neurological level, the brain must be able to keep itself on target for a specific period of time even when the task is less than thrilling—a skill often lacking in ADHD. Just as some people have more innate physical strength or natural endurance, some people find it easier to sustain mental effort.

Emotional regulation (managing emotions) refers to the capacity to experience emotion without immediately acting on it. Although we all experience unsettling emotional experiences, individuals developmentally behind in this aspect of executive function become frustrated easily and are often quick to lash out or shut down. They do not yet have the filter or skill set to become internally rattled and then settle down before responding.

Studies of mindfulness (Flook et al., 2010) have shown improvements in various measures of executive function. Potential benefits start with an ability to sustain attention, shift attention, and to return more quickly from distractions. For action management, building responsiveness to replace reactivity is an integral part of training, as is developing moment-to-moment awareness, instead of remaining on "autopilot" through much of the day. Working memory has also been a measure in mindfulness research. Studies have tracked outcomes related to emotion, including growth in areas of the brain related to emotional regulation after as little as 8 weeks of mindfulness training (Lazar, et al. 2005).

Mindfulness and Evidence-Based ADHD Care

ADHD treatment is not a concrete entity that can be prescribed identically for everyone. Although traditional ADHD care breaks down into *behavioral interventions* (targeted at children, parents, or teachers), *educational interventions*, and *medical options*, no single choice "fixes" everything. In addition, when an individual has ADHD, it strongly influences relationships with family, friends, and teachers. As outlined in the following material, mindfulness encourages a broader approach by supporting stress management, flexibility in behavioral planning, communication skills, and many other oft-overlooked aspects of ADHD, while potentially strengthening executive functioning.

Mindfulness, ADHD, and Stress on Caregivers and Children

Stress is inevitable. Certainly, some stress motivates or keeps us safe, but our bodies and brains are not wired to handle chronic, excessive levels. When unchecked, chronic stress negatively impacts physical and mental health. Stress also affects our ability to monitor the "big picture" (instead of only immediate crises) while flexibly and skillfully addressing challenges as they arise.

Parents and caregivers of children with ADHD consistently report higher levels of stress and lower opinions of their own self-efficacy (Primack,

Hendricks, Longacre, et al., 2012). They report higher levels of anxiety, depression, marital strife, and even divorce (Barkley, 2006). Behavioral and educational interventions for ADHD require consistency, compassion, and ongoing creativity in problem solving, all of which are compromised by chronic stress.

Both children with ADHD and the adults supporting them are impacted by its effects on everyday life. Whereas the average 9-year-old child may need little adult assistance to get ready in the morning, those with ADHD may require constant parental involvement just to make the bus on time. That same degree of effort and stress spills over into classrooms, homework, social situations, and anywhere imaginable. And when adults become overwhelmed or burned out, interactions with children drastically alter; few of us are at our best when overly stressed. One recent survey even suggested that children of stressed-out parents are far more likely to report feeling stressed themselves (American Psychological Association, 2010).

A vital addition of mindfulness to ADHD is its emphasis on self-care and stress management. Giving parents, teachers, and health providers the tools to manage stress has implications that ripple beyond their own immediate well-being. Mindfulness practice often impacts how they relate to others, most likely through changes in affect, responsiveness, and communication skills. Studies show increased empathy and improved patient satisfaction when therapists and doctors practice mindfulness (Krasner, Epstein, Beckman, et al., 2009; Escuriex & Labbe, 2011; Irving, Park-Saltzman, Fitzpatrick, et al., 2014). Other studies suggest that mindfulness decreases the stress and burnout that frequently plague overworked parents, caregivers, teachers, and health providers (Epstein-Lubow, McBee, Darling, et al., 2011; Benn, Akiva, Arel, et al., 2012; Beer, Ward, & Moar, 2013). A 2013 study that included adolescents with ADHD and their parents reported both improved stress levels for parents and decreased reports of ADHD symptoms as seen on behavioral rating scales (Haydicky, Shecter, Wiener, et al., 2013).

ADHD and its associated problems not only create stress, but also compound the issue by deeply affecting how stress itself is managed. No other disorder so directly influences the ability to handle the routines of everyday life, impacting individuals, parents, and teachers. Tasks mastered by peers far earlier remain daily battles. Moment-to-moment reactivity escalates for everyone involved. In fact, the ability to manage emotions and frustration is directly impacted by ADHD, further amplifying stress.

Mindfulness strengthens the ability to respond instead of simply reacting reflexively when challenged. Pausing and paying attention allow the individual to make more intentional choices by stepping out of autopilot and entrenched communication patterns. An increased ability to remain settled and clear of thought benefits not only adults but also the children in their lives.

As a starting point of bringing mindfulness to individuals with ADHD, parents, teachers, and providers can augment ADHD care by diminishing the negative impact of stress on themselves. ADHD can be exhausting to live or work with, but mindfulness allows adults to sustain the long-term effort required to care for someone with ADHD. Energy spent on one's own well-being and resilience enables adults to consistently evaluate and address the unexpected situations with all the skill, compassion, and clarity with which they are capable.

Nonjudgmental Awareness of ADHD

Children with language delays or traditionally defined medical disorders (e.g., asthma, cerebral palsy) are never expected to catch up to their peers through effort alone. Yet children with ADHD are often not afforded the same compassion or accommodation, with their difficulties attributed to poor effort or intentional misbehavior. To thrive, these children instead require an approach that objectively evaluates their delays and emphasizes incremental progress and long-term planning.

Many common misperceptions continue to impact ADHD treatment: "ADHD is not real." "ADHD is caused by parents." Or perhaps "ADHD medications are too dangerous to ever use safely." In trying to gain an understanding of ADHD, some people believe similar myths, which amplifies their stress and distorts their decisions. Others are overwhelmed by the perceived judgment of family or friends when it comes to treatment decisions. Many believe not only external storylines but internal narratives as well, such as "These symptoms are my fault, and I need to do better."

The results of years of genetic research, biological studies, and neurological imaging convincingly demonstrate that ADHD is a medical disorder (Barkley, 2006). The genetic heritability (i.e., the odds of transmission from parent to child) for ADHD is similar to that of adult height. Studies show that immediate relatives of those with ADHD have a two- to threefold higher likelihood of having it. These statistics hold regardless of whether or not family members have lived together. Environment may influence the expression of these genes, but at its core ADHD is a genetic disorder.

ADHD diagnosis remains one of clinical judgment (there is no test for ADHD yet), so the potential for misdiagnosis is there. But for any individual who truly has ADHD, the effects are, *by definition*, significant. Demonstrated impairment in some aspect of life is required to make the diagnosis.

With ADHD, a mindful perspective of nonjudgmental awareness transforms care. There is a difference between something that is upsetting but manageable ("My child has ADHD and I need to do something about it") and everything we add to that situation ("If only I had been stricter, he wouldn't have ADHD at all; if he doesn't get his act together now, he is going to have no friends and never graduate from college"). More skillful decisions follow when ADHD is recognized as a result of a particular neurological condition without adding assumptions about traits such as low motivation or willfulness.

Throughout life our thoughts and emotions are influenced by inferences, emotional states, or even unconscious biases. Many seem concrete and factual (e.g., "The answer is that he has to try harder; we've tried everything else"), even when they are not. But as the old bumper sticker suggests, "DON'T BELIEVE EVERYTHING YOU THINK" is an important reminder for all of us. In reality, some thoughts we have are valid, some less so, yet we tend to give them all equal weight.

So much of ADHD can appear within a child's direct control even when nothing more exists than another frustrating manifestation of delayed executive function. Without open-minded awareness it is easy to assume a child engaged in an art project is ignoring our request to stop and get their homework done . . . even though individuals with ADHD simply cannot transition their attention the way their peers can. The behavior appears deliberately oppositional, when the underlying issue is one of attention management.

Through the practice of mindfulness we become more discerning in observing our immediate experience. We honor the basic reality for a child with ADHD: *He is supremely bright, creative, and friendly, yet 3 years behind in the ability to monitor his own behavior. She is quick to lash out and often angry because she doesn't have strong enough skills to manage her emotions.* From a mindful stance we also address the frustrations and expectations of daily life for parents, teachers, and classmates.

We aim to see executive function delays for what they are: nothing more and nothing less. Mindfulness practice allows us to maintain this perspective. It is impossible (and not a goal) to force any particular mindset, and there's no need to celebrate the fact that anyone has ADHD. Nonjudgmental awareness means seeing the impact of ADHD as clearly as possible, where it begins and also where it ends, noticing the impact on both children and adults, and taking skillful action from there.

Mindfulness as a Facilitator for Behavioral Change

Mindfulness does not replace any aspect of ADHD care; rather, it augments most approaches. Changing entrenched behaviors is not easy yet is often demanded. In fact, behavioral habits reinforce themselves neurologically over time (a concept called *neuroplasticity*), making them challenging to alter. With sustained effort we can "rewire" more productive habits, but we must start with awareness that they exist in the first place. Mindfulness helps us discover and then address these often overlooked cognitive and behavioral patterns, whether we are living or working with those who have ADHD.

Behavioral programs for ADHD depend on parents and teachers for implementation. Youth with ADHD are delayed in the exact executive function abilities needed to address their difficulties in the first place. Most adults have the capacity to establish a plan and stick to it over time, but most young children do not, particularly with ADHD in the mix. An emphasis on parent training and classroom management is vital not only for redirecting inappropriate behaviors, but also for providing children with a framework that will help them catch up wherever they have fallen behind.

We can use an understanding of executive function as a tool for everyday life. If children have a deficit in attention management, they may be *unable* (as opposed to unwilling) to shift attention away from a game. If they cannot manage their homework independently at 10 years old because their organizational skills are those of a 5- or 6-year-old child, what type of plan would best meet both their short- and long-term needs?

At home or school, adults can examine a child's day-to-day pitfalls through this lens. How might we set up a household or classroom to minimize demands on working memory? *Stick to consistent routines, and don't ask children with ADHD to keep track of things in their head.* How might we make even simple requests easier? *Be sure to have their full attention before asking, and keep requests concise.*

Classroom management represents another foundation of ADHD care. Behavioral programs that emphasize success should proactively anticipate difficulties, rather than waiting for troubles and negative feedback to begin. Reward-based systems (which counterbalance the frequent redirection and behavioral limits children with ADHD require), well-structured classrooms, direct supports around organizational skills, and countless other details are vital for children with ADHD. They not only further academic progress but increase the likelihood of appropriate behavior by creating a positive classroom experience for those who otherwise may chronically feel harried and at a loss trying to keep up.

As a side note, individual behavioral therapy in early childhood typically has a different role when used to treat ADHD, addressing related concerns such as low self-esteem or anxiety without as much impact on "core" ADHD symptoms (e.g., impulsiveness or distractibility). Behavioral therapy may also improve parent satisfaction and family dynamics. Theoretically, children involved in therapy may require lower doses of ADHD medication. As a growing number of therapists incorporate mindfulness into their interventions, this is another opportunity to introduce the practice to children.

Observing life with more compassion and less reactivity facilitates behavioral interventions, since so much is missed when perception is distorted by anxiety, anger, or other emotional states. Planning requires an objective review of triggers and consequences on either end of problematic behaviors, as well as emphasizing on-task, prosocial behaviors even under stress. Pausing, we may notice that something actually related to poor executive function (e.g., the inability to keep track of a mental to-do list) only *appears* to be intentionally avoidant, or maybe we find something to adjust in our own response. There is little point in hassling someone for not handing in schoolwork if the underlying problem is not yet having the skills to manage it.

We all develop ways of managing situations, communicating with others, and relating to ourselves and to the world. Viewing these traits more clearly as habits (and therefore not fixed or permanent), we can engage in more intentional actions or even affect patterns of thinking. Maybe having traditionally avoided confrontation, we pause, notice an instinct to withdraw, and remember to stand firm this time. Much of what we take for granted about ourselves ("I'm a shouter," "I always procrastinate," "I'll never be any good at this") is not actually written in stone, and the same is true of the children we encounter every day. Encouraging not only responsiveness but also an increased awareness of habit encourages a flexible, open-minded approach to ADHD care.

Mindfulness and Educational Planning

Mindfulness can be incorporated directly in the educational setting to augment self-regulation and executive function in children, as outlined elsewhere in this book. Classroom interventions can supportz focus, impulse control, and other aspects of executive function. A wide range of programs have been developed from preschool to high school settings, from urban centers to leafy suburbs.

From tailored interventions to curriculum planning, educational decisions profoundly impact the odds of success. Regardless of a child's age or apparent motivation, we establish short-term safety nets (e.g., a 504 or individualized educational plan) to support his or her lagging executive function skills and prevent the child's falling further behind, with adults fully supporting organization and planning as needed. At least half of children with ADHD also have specific learning disabilities that require remediation in reading, writing, math, or language. Alongside any immediate supports, we create long-term plans that build individual skills and foster greater independence and self-sufficiency. It is not through effort alone that a child several years behind in executive function development will catch up.

The same interventions that support children with ADHD benefit everyone in the classroom. As noted above, well-structured classrooms that minimize distraction and emphasize routine help to reduce extraneous cognitive demands for students. Evidence-based curricula establish fluency in individual skills, further easing demands on executive function *before* emphasizing experiential learning and increasing the odds for *any* student to thrive.

Although mindfulness is often discussed as a method of building specific skills for individuals, it is meant to impact how we interact with the world. Educational planning is often a stressful and at times contentious experience. Remaining calm and empathic not only to the impact of ADHD on a child in the classroom but to the stresses carried to the table by parents and teachers supports the process.

Complementary and Lifestyle Approaches for Treating ADHD

For any complementary or alternative approach to medicine, we can follow several basic guidelines to sort out potential risks and benefits. First and foremost, is this potentially untested intervention safe? Second, does the underlying rationale make sense? Third, is the intervention affordable in terms of both time and money? And last, what does the relevant research suggest? Many complementary interventions are supported by preliminary studies, whereas others have already been largely disproven.

Unlike many areas of medicine, research supports potential benefits of complementary care for ADHD. Unsurprisingly, researchers have suggested that regular exercise and quality sleep may improve symptoms (Pontifex, Saliba, Raine, et al., 2013; Paavonen, Raikkonen, Lahti, et al., 2009; Touchette, Cote, Petit, et al., 2009). Nutritional interventions, such as addressing deficiencies in iron intake or perhaps avoiding certain food dyes, may benefit some individuals as well (Pelsser, Frankena, Toorman, et al., 2011; Cortese, Angriman, Lecendreux, et al., 2012; Millichap & Yee, 2012). Computer-based trainings and even neurofeedback have had some success with improving attention and executive function, although results have been mixed and remain inconclusive regarding generalizing these skills outside of the research setting.

And then there is mindfulness, which has been so well studied that the National Institutes of Health no longer consider it "complementary care" at all. Mindfulness is a practical and accessible supplement to almost every medical or mental health condition studied to date. Research, much of it described in greater depth elsewhere in this volume, suggests benefits to physical and emotional well-being when we build our capacity to cultivate attention and responsiveness, create new and more productive mental habits, manage stress, and develop increased compassion for ourselves and others.

Mindful Decision Making for Caregivers

An entire phenomenon in the field of ADHD has been labeled "decision-making angst" for parents. A 2009 study in the journal *Pediatrics* defined this phenomenon as the chronic toll that ADHD takes on parents debating the best course of action at any moment in time (Brinkman, Sherman,

Zmitrovich, et al., 2009). Beyond whatever else ADHD causes, parents suffer deeply in deciding what to do about it. These choices, and the stress around making them, in turn impact the teachers and providers who interact with these families and their children.

When mindfulness supports decision making, we pause and observe the nuances of any particular situation while striving to separate fact (e.g., "My child has ADHD") from opinion (e.g., "His grandmother says he'd be fine if he only worked harder"). Gathering our thoughts, we make a choice, acknowledging all the fear and uncertainty around it. Afterward, we aim to remain open to adjustments, accepting that we did the best we could, even if it may not have worked out as expected.

None of us would intentionally make a challenging situation worse. When a child misbehaves, we try to find a way to guide him or her toward something more appropriate, and the child may or may not react as we hoped. Recognizing that we've been trying our best but that we always have more to learn, we remain open to the possibility of altering our path forward.

Perhaps the most emotionally fraught decision in ADHD for families involves medication. Understandably, parents fear fundamentally changing their child in some way, or making a choice that will cause long-term harm. But another way of perceiving medication use is this: Children are inherently good; they are trying to succeed and be happy, but ADHD is getting in the way. Appropriately prescribed, medication should allow children to be their own best self more consistently, nothing more.

Research suggests that 75–80% of patients respond positively to well-managed medication, with a marked improvement in ADHD symptoms (Barkley, 2006). Far lower response rates have been shown for children receiving intensive behavioral interventions alone. Integrating medication into an overall plan may allow a child to thrive who otherwise struggles against his or her own neurology.

That said, ADHD medications are not a miracle cure. They do not always work, they do not address all executive function deficits, and side effects may be unavoidable for a small percentage of individuals. And yet, nothing else has yet been shown to as effectively improve common issues such as an inability to focus, sustain effort, sit still, or to control impulses.

Pausing and allowing the mind to settle, we may notice emotional reactions to the concept of medication ("Never for my child") or preconceived notions ("It's dangerous"), or we may simply stop wrestling as much with the choices we've made ("We're not trying them now, and we'll see how it goes"). Any medication has potential side effects. Of course, so does untreated ADHD, which has been shown to increase the risk of everything from car accidents to divorce, school failure to obesity (Barkley, 2006; Dempsey, Dyehouse, & Schafer, 2011; Larson, Russ, Kahn, et al., 2011; Klein, Mannuzza, Olazagasti, et al., 2012; Narad, Garner, & Brassell, 2013). Thankfully, decisions around ADHD treatment are not set in stone. Whatever choices we make today, exploring the nuances with less reactivity and more flexibility encourages a more balanced approach to long-term planning.

Mindfulness, Relationships, and Communication

Choosing to pay attention, with intention, has benefits for children and relationships in general. Children thrive when they can count on consistent time and positive feedback from adults. When we pay attention, we may also become more familiar with how everything from our body language to tone of voice, emotional states, and cognitive habits all influence how any situation unfolds.

The nuances of communication unconsciously influence the outcome of any interaction, whether we are talking with our spouses, students, children, clients, or anyone else. Imagine a battle over schoolwork, whether at home or in the classroom. In one situation, having been down the same path of homework resistance dozens of times before, an adult enters, already frowning, and says, "Why isn't your homework done yet? You need stop screwing around and get it done. When are you going to get your act together?" Who would not respond with defensiveness, retaliation, or escalation, especially someone with the impulse control deficits frequently related to ADHD.

Regardless of what is going on around us, we can control only our own actions. This remains true even when circumstances seem out of our control (e.g., someone else has ADHD). Without letting go of our own needs, we can acknowledge that our choices steer the path of any conversation we have. How we comport ourselves affects not only outcomes but also models for children on how to deal with conflict in their own lives.

As an alternative to the scenario above, we could choose a measured response that does not give up on the importance of homework. Pausing, we might settle for a moment. Perhaps we could picture how we would advise a close friend to communicate in the face of a similar challenge: "I realize you are frustrated. Your homework needs to get done before you play, and I know you'd like to earn your reward for getting it done. Let's take a few breaths, and then figure out what you need to do first."

Attention Training, Executive Function, and ADHD

Similar to working out our bodies to improve fitness, if we train our attention, our ability to attend improves even if we cannot alter our entire physiology. Although there is no evidence yet to suggest that we can erase ADHD through cognitive training, we may make a significant difference through an intentional practice of focused attention. The brain *is* capable of rewiring itself in response to any action that we practice repeatedly, mentally or behaviorally, just as our body grows muscles and becomes fitter through physical exercise. An additional benefit of mindfulness practice may be a direct impact on ADHD itself.

Many of the best-studied clinical applications of neuroplasticity examine the effects of mindfulness. Numerous adult studies have shown that an ability to sustain attention, shift attention, and regain focus can be strengthened. One of the first pilot studies specific to ADHD was conducted at UCLA by Lidia Zylowska and colleagues (Zylowska, Ackerman, Yang, et al., 2008). These researchers adapted the traditional 8-week mindfulness-based stress reduction (MBSR) program by shortening meditations and adding in-depth information about ADHD and its effects. Zylowska et al. demonstrated that people with ADHD benefited from, and were capable of finishing, an 8-week MBSR program. Participants also experienced decreased stress and increased well-being as measured by self-report. Compellingly, posttest neuropsychological testing showed improved executive functioning!

Lisa Flook, also of UCLA, and her colleagues conducted a classroom-based study of mindfulness that tracked executive functioning of second- and third-grade children (Flook, Smalley, Kitil, et al., 2010). Similar gains were observed. Perhaps the most exciting finding showed greater improvements for children whose executive function abilities started among the lowest; those children who needed it most seemed to gain the most, and began to catch up to peers. Several other studies of mindfulness in ADHD have shown improvements in attention, executive function, stress levels and other related benefits (e.g., van de Weijer-Bergsma, Formsma, de Bruin, et al., 2012; Carboni, Roach, & Fredrick, 2013).

Classroom studies of mindfulness curricula have shown improved behavior, emotional regulation, and executive function skills in students practicing mindfulness (see the chapters in Part I, this volume). Mindfulness training may improve communication skills and increase compassion for others and self. As noted earlier, a meta-analysis of social–emotional programs suggested that children who complete programs emphasizing self-regulation and emotional skills in early childhood appear to *academically* outperform those who complete preschool programs that are purportedly "academic" (Durlak, Weissberg, & Pachan, 2010).

Another aspect of mindfulness addresses self-doubt, a cognitive habit often propagated by ADHD. Although we all live with some degree of self-judgment (e.g., "I should be doing better," "Everything is my fault," "I let everyone down again"), concerns regarding self-esteem and anxiety are amplified by ADHD. A lifetime of trying to thrive, putting in effort but being let down by poor executive function skills, undermines self-confidence and increases the amount of daily effort required just to get by. Practicing mindfulness balances an ability to observe the reality of our immediate experience with compassion not only for everyone else in the world, but also for ourselves. So beyond only attention training, introducing mindfulness may help address the insidious impact of self-judgment on children living with ADHD.

Invariably, parents or professionals who discover the benefits of mindfulness ask about how to share it directly with children. They read the research about stress or inattention, or perhaps experience the benefits in their own lives. They may already be noticing changes in the midst of the typical chaos of home life. But children are hardwired to learn from adults, both through direct instruction and what they observe. Mindfulness benefits children with ADHD through many avenues, but before explicitly teaching it to kids (as reviewed elsewhere in this book), the foundation begins when parents, teachers, and caretakers truly live it themselves.

Making Mindfulness Work with ADHD

Jon Kabat-Zinn and his colleagues created MBSR in the late 1970s to expand access to mindfulness in the West. They translated traditional Eastern spiritual practices into secular Western terms for a predominantly blue-collar population in Massachusetts. Programs have proliferated ever since, with adaptations for all walks of life and a range of mental and physical conditions. Although the core teaching points remain the same, the language and style have been adapted for each audience. Common modifications to mindfulness practices for parents, adults with ADHD, and children often overlap for reasons in the following sections.

Organizational Supports

Finding or making the time to meditate is difficult for most of us. For a family, it can be a challenge to juggle school, homework, after-school activities, meals, family time, jobs, and all the rest. Parents are exhausted and often feel pressured to put their children and other life demands first, leaving little time for true self-care.

ADHD compounds this challenge, impairing the ability to manage time and stick with a schedule. Although someone can believe and know that setting aside a few moments a day will help, actually making that happen is rarely so simple. Though already an emphasis in the traditional MBSR curriculum, an even greater need exists to discuss exactly how to fit these new practices into busy lives when working with either parents or individuals with ADHD.

There also may be a perceived need for "permission" to meditate at work, on the train, or wherever the time can be found. Although a pristine, serene setting for meditation is certainly not required, people often imagine that it is. Figuring out *when* to schedule (first thing in the morning, at lunch, before bed, or linked to other regular daily routines), *where* to meditate (anywhere is okay, even someplace noisy), and *how* to stick to a schedule are challenges to practice, which can be offset by supportive mindfulness teachers or a community.

Shortened Meditation Practices

Research remains unclear regarding which components of the MBSR curriculum and how much time practicing make a difference. The original program recommended an immediate, radical change for most people and asked students to schedule 45 minutes of daily meditation. On the other hand, studies have shown benefits when people meditate as little as 20–30 minutes a day, 5–7 days a week (Tang, Ma, Wang, et al., 2007; Chen, Yang, Wang, et al., 2013). Dialectical behavior therapy (DBT), commonly used in patients with borderline personality disorder, often incorporates informal mindful awareness practices without a detailed discussion of formal meditation.

When adapting the practices for families and for anyone with ADHD, meditation periods are frequently shortened. A 10- or 15-minute session may be perfect on a day when a child's homework takes an hour longer than planned. Discovering a short gap of time during the daily grind to take a few mindful breaths is a valid and powerful mindfulness practice.

Multiple programs exist that introduce mindfulness to children, as described elsewhere in this book. For children, mindfulness is often practiced only a few minutes at a time, sometimes through meditation but often through related, play-based activities. Tools to engage children, such as brief games, playfulness, and humor, are essential (and of course can be equally effective with adults). For children or adults with ADHD, an allowance both for attention deficits and ADHD-related behaviors also can be addressed while the basic techniques remain the same.

Emphasizing Informal Practices

Research has not yet determined the ideal "dosing" for mindfulness benefits. Benefits from mindfulness are often shown despite self-reports of little time meditating. Mindful awareness is still possible in everyday life even without traditional meditation practice. Many common mindfulness exercises require no additional time. There are numerous ways of approaching life with awareness, pausing and redirecting our attention throughout the day. One example is described by unpacking the meaning of the acronym STOP:

- Stop what you are doing.
- Take a few breaths.
- Observe what's going on right now, and then, with intention . . .
- Proceed (or pick a next step).

These simple steps summarize the basic practice of mindfulness. In any moment, we can pause and check in, seek a clear view of our experience, and move forward with intention instead on autopilot. STOP represents a habit that can be reinforced through repetition, until it becomes more automatic, and is straightforward enough for a child or adult to understand and use.

Engaging the steps of STOP impacts the course of ADHD in everyday life. Redirecting distracted attention in this way cultivates responsiveness and decreases reactivity and impulsivity. Practicing STOP throughout the day creates a space to consciously respond, one that could be otherwise limited by the distracted, impulsive symptoms of ADHD. A quote (usually attributed to Viktor Frankl) states, "Between stimulus and response there is a space. In that space is our power to choose our response. In our response lies our growth and our freedom."

As another example, people with ADHD often describe an experience full of partially completed tasks. Meals are cooked but not cleaned up, schoolwork started but not handed in, or clothing removed before bedtime but left on the floor. By using the STOP acronym, we reinforce a new habit of pausing at transitions or the start of tasks, addressing this stress-inducing and self-perpetuating habit. Rising from the table . . . *STOP* . . . then observe . . . and then perhaps remember to clear the table or put homework in the backpack.

Other informal mindfulness practices can fit naturally into a daily routine. Mindful eating and walking both introduce mindfulness into everyday activities and serve as a bridge between formal and informal practice. At any moment when we are interacting with children, we can aim to bring our full attention to all the experience of eating dinner or playing a game. When the mind wanders, we return it back to a chosen activity with a new clarity, offering ourselves and our child a moment of undivided attention.

Although the original MBSR program includes meditating daily for up to 45 minutes, as mentioned, finding that kind of time can present a huge hurdle for any individual reaching for mindfulness, particularly a stressed-out parent or burned-out teacher. Busy and overwhelmed, how can we fit in one more activity? A more manageable approach for some of us may be to emphasize bringing mindfulness to whatever our situation or task may be. Though there may be different benefits found with formal mindfulness practice when time allows, we can still start right now, wherever we find ourselves.

Loving-Kindness Practice

Developing compassion for ourselves and others is a significant part of any meditation practice. The ability to notice when we are distracted, and then return to our intention without self-criticism (e.g., thinking, "I'm bad at this"), frustration ("I just want to relax"), or any other mental self-judgment is, fundamentally, a practice of compassion. We strengthen the ability to discover that we are off-target in some way and readjust without adding self-recrimination to the mix.

One addition to mindfulness training for both parents and children living with ADHD is an explicit loving-kindness meditation. Without forcing ourselves to feel anything we don't feel, we offer our best wishes to ourselves and to others, as we might for a close friend in need. We practice giving ourselves a break when rattled, and in turn become more patient with the world around us. We may notice that although we feel we have erred in a particular situation, we still deserve peace and well-being, along with our children, friends, the grocery clerk, or anyone else with whom we come into contact in daily life.

Difficulty maintaining motivation and following through on plans impact self-esteem and shape the internal narrative we often create about their lives. By using mindfulness to reframe ADHD, we change our relationship to voices of internal self-judgment (e.g., "It's my fault," "I need to try harder," "I always screw things up"). In similar fashion, the judgment of adults toward children with ADHD can be swayed away from misperceptions of poor effort or willfulness through mindful, compassionate awareness training.

With practice, we come to recognize that everyone is driven by the same basic motivations in life as they seek their own version of health and well-being. Some actions may appear unskillful, frustrating, or inappropriate, but we can remind ourselves that behind any action is a simple human goal of happiness. We also come to find that we can simultaneously be compassionate and yet still have likes and dislikes, be angered by injustice in life, and take decisive action toward change.

Research into compassion practice has shown promising results. Studies reveal changes in how we relate to others, such as an increased likelihood of donating to charity (Weng, Fox, Shackman, et al., 2013). One study that evaluated a "kindness curriculum" in preschoolers found increased sharing in those who completed the curriculum (Flook, & Pinger, 2013). Self-compassion—the ability to treat ourselves with the same kindness we would treat a loved one—has been shown to enhance well-being and resilience.

Fully accepting ADHD while still pushing for change is a balance that mindfulness helps us to maintain. We can love our children, our students, and our patients; feel near-boundless empathy for their suffering; yet still struggle to see that many difficulties are rooted in ADHD. What does it mean for a child when we can balance a clear vision of frustration and sadness about his or her ADHD with full acceptance and compassion for his or her struggles as a fellow human? Through a wide-ranging, compassionate, and open-minded perspective, we set individuals and families living with ADHD on a long-term path toward well-being and success.

Although mindfulness training is not the homeopathic "cure-all" for ADHD that some people await, it offers a lifelong promise of improving cognitive skills for those with ADHD and their caregivers. Mindfulness supports children with ADHD in educational settings through the new ability to notice thoughts as thoughts, impulses as impulses, distractions as distractions; to pause when caught up in overwhelming emotions; and to move forward with a willingness to change. Cultivating responsiveness, resilience, and compassion helps every child, with or without ADHD, as well as those of us who care for and about the next generation.

REFERENCES

American Psychological Association. (2010). Stress in America: Findings. Retrieved September 18, 2013, from *www.apa.org/news/press/releases/stress/index.aspx*.

Barkley, R. A. (2006). *Attention-deficit/hyperactivity disorder: A handbook for diagnosis and treatment* (3rd ed.). New York: Guilford Press.

Beer, M., Ward, L., & Moar, K. (2013). The relationship between mindful parenting and distress in parents of children with an autism spectrum disorder. *Mindfulness, 4*, 102–112.

Benn, R., Akiva, T., Arel, S., et al. (2012). Mindfulness training effects for parents and educators of children with special needs. *Development Psychology, 48*, 1476–1487.

Brinkman, W. B., Sherman, S. N., Zmitrovich, A. R., et al. (2009). Parental angst making and revisiting decisions about treatment of attention-deficit/hyperactivity disorder. *Pediatrics, 124*, 580–589.

Brown, T. E. (2008, February). Executive functions: Describing six aspects of a complex syndrome. *Attention*, 12–17.

Carboni, J. A., Roach, A. T., & Fredrick, L. D. (2013). Impact of mindfulness training on the behavior of elementary students with attention-deficit/hyperactive disorder. *Research in Human Development, 10*, 234–251.

Casey, B. J., Somerville, L. H., Gotlib, I. H., et al. (2011). Behavioral and neural correlates of delay of gratification 40 years later. *Proceedings of the National Academy of Sciences of the United States of America, 108*, 14998–15003.

Chen, Y., Yang, X., Wang, L., et al. (2013). A randomized controlled trial of the effects of brief mindfulness meditation on anxiety symptoms and systolic blood pressure in Chinese nursing students. *Nurse Education Today, 33*, 1166–1172.

Cortese, S., Angriman, M., Lecendreux, M., et al. (2012). Iron and attention deficit/hyperactivity disorder: What is the empirical evidence so far? A systematic review of the literature. *Expert Review of Neurotherapies, 12*, 1227–1240.

Dempsey, A., Dyehouse, J., & Schafer, J. (2011). The relationship between executive function, AD/HD, overeating, and obesity. *Western Journal of Nursing Research, 33*, 609–629.

Durlak, J. A., Weissberg, R. P., & Pachan, M. (2010). A meta-analysis of after-school programs that seek to promote personal and social skills in children and adolescents. *American Journal of Community Psychology, 45*, 294–309.

Epstein-Lubow, G., McBee, L., Darling, E., et al. (2011). A pilot investigation of mindfulness-based stress reduction for caregivers of frail elderly. *Mindfulness, 2*, 95–102.

Escuriex, B. F., & Labbe, E. E. (2011). Health care providers' mindfulness and treatment outcomes: A critical review of the research literature. *Mindfulness, 2*, 242–253.

Flook, L., & Pinger, L. (2013). Kindness curriculum study with pre-kindergarten students. Retrieved September 18, 2013, from *www.investigatinghealthyminds.org/cihmProjEducation.html*.

Flook, L., Smalley, S. L., Kitil, M. J., Galla, B. M., Kaiser-Greenland, S., Locke, J., et al. (2010). Effects of mindful awareness practices on executive functions in elementary school children. *Journal of Applied School Psychology, 26*, 70–95.

Haydicky, J., Shecter, C., Wiener, J., et al. (2013). Evaluation of MBCT for adolescents with ADHD and their parents: Impact on individual and family functioning. *Journal of Child and Family Studies, 24*(1), 1–19.

Irving, J., Park-Saltzman, J., Fitzpatrick, M., Dobkin, P. L., Chen, A., & Hutchinson, T. (2014). Experiences of health care professionals enrolled in mindfulness-based medical practice: A grounded theory model. *Mindfulness, 5*, 60–71.

Klein, R. G., Mannuzza, S., Olazagasti, M. A., et al. (2012). Clinical and functional outcome of childhood attention-deficit/hyperactivity disorder 33 years later. *Archives of General Psychiatry, 69*, 1295–1303.

Krasner, M. S., Epstein, R. M., & Beckman, H., et al. (2009). Association of an educational program in mindful communication with burnout, empathy, and attitudes among primary care physicians. *Journal of the American Medical Association, 302*, 1284–1293.

Larson, K., Russ, S. A., Kahn, R. S., et al. (2011). Patterns of comorbidity, functioning, and service use for U.S. children with ADHD, 2007. *Pediatrics, 127*, 462–470.

Lazar, S. W., Kerr, C. E., Wasserman, R. H., Gray, J. R., Greve, D. N., Treadway, M. T., et al. (2005). Meditation experience is associated with increased cortical thickness. *NeuroReport, 16*(17), 1893–1897.

McClelland, M. M., Acock, A. C., & Piccinin, A., et al. (2013). Relations between preschool attention span-persistence and age 25 educational outcomes. *Early Childhood Research Quarterly, 28*, 314–324.

Millichap, J. G., & Yee, M. M. (2012). The diet factor in attention deficit/hyperactivity disorder. *Pediatrics, 129*, 330–337.

Mischel, W., Ebbesen, E. B., & Zeiss, A. R. (1972). Cognitive and attentional mechanisms in delay of gratification. *Journal of Personality and Social Psychology, 21*, 204–218.

Moffitt, T. E., Arseneault, L., Belsky, D., et al. (2011). A gradient of childhood self-control predicts health, wealth, and public safety. *Proceedings of the National Academy of Sciences of the United States of America, 108*, 2693–2698.

Narad, M., Garner, A. A., & Brassell, A. A. (2013). Impact of distraction on the driving performance of adolescents with and without attention-deficit/hyperactivity disorder. *Journal of the American Medical Association Pediatrics, 167*(10), 933–938.

Paavonen, E. J., Raikkonen, K., Lahti, J., et al. (2009). Short sleep duration and behavioral symptoms of attention-deficit/hyperactivity disorder in healthy 7- to 8-year-old children. *Pediatrics, 123*, e857–e864.

Pelsser, L. M., Frankena, K., Toorman, J., et al. (2011). Effects of a restricted elimination diet on the behaviour of children with attention-deficit hyperactivity disorder (INCA study): A randomised controlled trial. *Lancet, 377,* 494–503.

Pontifex, M. B., Saliba, B. J., Raine, L. B., et al. (2013). Exercise improves behavioral, neurocognitive, and scholastic performance in children with attention-deficit/ hyperactivity disorder. *Journal of Pediatrics, 162,* 543–551.

Primack, B. A., Hendricks, K. M., & Longacre, M. R., et al. (2012). Parental efficacy and child behavior in a community sample of children with and without attention-deficit hyperactivity disorder (ADHD). *Attention Deficit Hyperactivity Disorders, 4*(4), 189–197.

Tang, Y. Y., Ma, Y., Wang, J., et al. (2007). Short-term meditation training improves attention and self-regulation. *Proceedings of the National Academy of Sciences of the United States of America, 104,* 17152–17156.

Touchette, E., Cote, S. M., Petit, D., et al. (2009). Short nighttime sleep-duration and hyperactivity trajectories in early childhood. *Pediatrics, 124,* e985–e993.

van de Weijer-Bergsma, E., Formsma, A. R., de Bruin, E. I., et al. (2012). The effectiveness of mindfulness training on behavioral problems and attentional functioning in adolescents with ADHD. *Journal of Child and Family Studies, 21,* 775–787.

Weng, H. Y., Fox, A. S., Shackman, A. J., et al. (2013). Compassion training alters altruism and neural responses to suffering. *Psychological Science, 24,* 1171–1180.

Zylowska, L., Ackerman, D. L., Yang, M. H., et al. (2008). Mindfulness meditation training in adults and adolescents with ADHD: A feasibility study. *Journal of Attention Disorders, 11,* 737–746.

CHAPTER 21

Neurobiological Models of Meditation Practices

Implications for Applications with Youth

Willoughby Britton
Arielle Sydnor

Many meditation and awareness practices derived from contemplative religious traditions are increasingly studied in clinical and scientific circles. In traditional[1] contexts, meditation practices are used to attain "insight" or a perceptual shift in the experience of self and world called "awakening." In modern secular contexts, similar practices are being used to address a wide range of psychological disorders, including anxiety (Evans et al., 2008; Kim et al., 2009), depression (Bondolfi et al., 2010; Kuyken et al., 2008; Ma & Teasdale, 2004; Teasdale et al., 2000), bipolar disorder (Williams et al., 2008), suicidal behavior (Williams, Duggan, Crane, & Fennell, 2006), psychosis (Chadwick, Hughes, Russell, Russell, & Dagnan, 2009; Johnson, Penn, et al., 2011), personality disorders (Soler et al., 2012), pain (Kabat-Zinn, Lipworth, & Burney, 1985), eating disorders (Wanden-Berghe, Sanz-Valero, & Wanden-Berghe, 2011), addiction (Hsu, Grow, & Marlatt, 2008), autism (Spek, van Ham, & Nyklicek, 2013), and traumatic brain injury (Bedard et al., 2003). Beyond the individual patient in the clinic, meditation practices are also being used and studied in both K–12 classrooms (Greenberg & Harris, 2012; Kaiser-Greenland, 2010; Meiklejohn et al., 2012; Mind and Life

---

[1]While the term "traditional" could refer to any religion, including Christianity, Hinduism, Islam, and Buddhism, in this chapter the term "traditional" refers specifically to Buddhism. Similarly, the term "Eastern" also refers to Buddhism and not other Eastern cultures or religions.

Education Research Network et al., 2012) and in higher education settings (Shapiro, Brown, & Astin, 2011).

The growing interest in meditation in the culture has been matched by an interest in the scientific study of meditation, especially in relation to clinical applications and brain sciences. However, neuroscientific models are faced with the daunting task of sorting out and integrating the effects of different practices into a unified theory that might explain, beyond placebo effects, why these practices could be beneficial for so many different kinds of conditions and problems. Despite the challenges, a few models are gaining traction. This chapter reviews the neurobiological research supporting the idea that certain functions of the prefrontal cortex associated with mental health and well-being can be strengthened through contemplative practices such as meditation and mindfulness.

Regions Associated with Distress That Respond to Meditation Interventions

The prefrontal cortex is perhaps the most important area of study in understanding how meditation operates in the brain. It is located just behind the forehead and underlies functions that include thinking, planning, and keeping behavior in line with goals (Miller & Cohen, 2001). The "cognitive control" element of the prefrontal cortex is also called "executive function" and is described in more detail by Mark Bertin (Chapter 20, this volume). Executive function includes controlling and shifting attention, cognitive flexibility, self-monitoring, planning, impulse control, and working memory capacity (Roth et al., 2006; Wood & Smith, 2008). The prefrontal cortex also controls aspects of the limbic system and the default mode network, another important process in understanding meditation that is described below.

The limbic system is a set of interconnected brain areas that includes the hippocampus, amygdala, and nucleus accumbens, among others. These regions are involved in memory, emotion, motivation, and reward (Morgane, Galler, & Mokler, 2005). The amygdala, which is involved in detecting emotional salience, works closely with the endocrine and sympathetic nervous systems. It triggers the "fight–flight–freeze" response, and so is often associated with the expression of emotional reactions (Davidson, Jackson, & Kalin, 2000). The prefrontal cortex exerts inhibitory control on limbic structures such as the amygdala (Davidson et al., 2000; Mayberg et al., 1999; Ochsner, Bunge, Gross, & Gabrieli, 2002; Ochsner & Gross, 2005; Ochsner et al., 2004; Urry et al., 2006). Lack of such inhibitory control results in a hyperactive amygdala (Siegle, Steinhauer, Thase, Stenger, & Carter, 2002; Siegle, Thompson, Carter, Steinhauer, & Thase, 2007) and an associated increase in emotional disturbance, reactivity, and sympathetic hyperarousal (Baxter et al., 1989; Bench, Friston, Brown, Frackowiak, & Dolan, 1993; Blumberg et al., 2004; Clark, Iversen, & Goodwin, 2002; Davidson, 2000; Mayberg et al., 1999; Meyer et al., 2004; Siegle & Hasselmo, 2002; Siegle et al., 2002).

Some areas of the prefrontal cortex, along with other brain areas that are involved in attention (the dorsal attention system, or DAS) also inhibit a group of brain areas that are often called the "default mode network," or DMN. This network of midline brain structures is active during "rest," or when the brain is not otherwise engaged. The system is also thought to be involved in mind wandering and self-referential thought (Qin & Northoff, 2011). The DAS and the DMN are typically "anticorrelated" (Fox et al., 2005), which means that when one is highly active, the other is less active. The real-life experience of this makes sense: If you are raptly engaged in reading this chapter, the DAS is engaged—and you haven't been planning your grocery list or worrying about the future because the DMN is suppressed. Conversely, if you notice that your mind is producing a lot of thoughts that have nothing to do with this chapter, the DMN is geared up, and therefore your ability to sustain attention on something specific has suffered, because the DAS is less active.

It is the DMN that is partly responsible for creating a sense of an enduring or continuous "self." It is dependent on the construction of a self-narrative—"the story of me"—that connects disparate experiences over time into a whole of "self" (Gallagher, 2000). Because this sense of continuity must be continually constructed, such self-related processing represents the DMN of our brains and is always active except when our attention is otherwise engaged. Essentially, when we are not busy, our minds just get back to work creating and sustaining self-narrative. However, even though thinking about ourselves appears to be a favorite human pastime, such self-referential processing is highly associated with distress, anxiety, rumination, and depression (Buckner & Vincent, 2007; Farb et al., 2007; Gentili et al., 2009; Hamilton et al., 2011; Lemogne, Delaveau, Freton, Guionnet, & Fossati, 2010; Segal, 1988; Sheline et al., 2009; Whitfield-Gabrieli et al., 2009; Zhao et al., 2007).

Low activation in the prefrontal cortex ("hypofrontrality") is associated with a wide range of psychological disturbances with negative affect (Clark, Chamberlain, & Sahakian, 2009; Couyoumdjian et al., 2009), such as unipolar depression (Baxter et al., 1989; Bench et al., 1993) and a number of disorders characterized by poor affect regulation, including bipolar disorder (Blumberg et al., 2004; Clark et al., 2002; Meyer et al., 2004), obsessive–compulsive disorder (van den Heuvel et al., 2005), schizophrenia (Carter et al., 1998; MacDonald & Carter, 2003; MacDonald et al., 2005), and addiction (Goldstein et al., 2009; Hester & Garavan, 2004). Because poor prefrontal control appears in a range of psychiatric conditions, we think of hypofrontality as a risk factor for many disorders and as the very condition we want to change. If hypofrontality is associated with numerous problems, it stands to reason that treating it has the potential to alleviate or prevent such problems. Later in the chapter we examine the positive impact of meditation on hypofrontality more specifically.

Neuroplasticity and "Cognitive Rehabilitation"

The growing understanding of neuroplasticity—the idea that the brain structure can actually change in response to experience or practice—is one of the most important paradigm shifts in modern science and medicine. Rather than being fixed, our brains, along with our personalities and behaviors, are in fact quite malleable. Just as exercise and training strengthen physical muscles within parameters, the brain can be strengthened and even grow in gray matter in corresponding neural networks. For example, networks related to spatial processing increase in taxi drivers as they develop interior maps of city streets (Maguire, Woollett, & Spiers, 2006), and other parts of the brain change in response to practicing music (Rodrigues, Loureiro, & Paulo Caramelli, 2010) or juggling (Draganski et al., 2004). Whether or not we realize it, we are *always* practicing something and therefore always changing our brains. *Choosing* which qualities or abilities to cultivate and which ones to let wither is the fundamental principle of contemplative practice. Choosing to cultivate certain types of mindful attention appears to reverse hypofrontality and its related problems described earlier (Lazar, et al. 2005). Other regions of the brain (described below), many associated with psychopathology, also appear to change for the better after meditation.

In adults, restoration of the prefrontal cortex can be achieved by engaging the region through cognitive training over time. Because impairment in the area plays a central role in so many psychiatric disorders, many studies have attempted to use cognitive "remediation" exercises to restore and boost prefrontal functioning. The rationale behind what is generally termed "neurocognitive rehabilitation" is that training on prefrontal cortex-dependent tasks—or "working out" the area with sustained attention task—will improve functioning and subsequently improve emotion regulation and dysfunctions that are associated with its impairment.

In patients with schizophrenia, Penades et al. (2006) found that 12 weeks of multicomponent attention training improved performance on prefrontal cortex-dependent tasks and appeared to decrease hypofrontality and psychological distress. In another study of "cognitive control training" in unipolar depression, Siegle, Ghinassi, and Thase (2007) used two types of focused attention tasks to increase prefrontal functioning and decrease mood disturbance. Wells's attention training (Papageorgiou & Wells, 2000) is a 15-minute task in which participants focus on a single sound and an arithmetic task that engages working memory and executive control. Results of the six-session attention training protocol indicated improved depressive symptoms and emotion regulation, with reduced hypoactivation in parts of the prefrontal region and reduced hyperactivation in the amygdala.

Meditation and associated practices can be considered as neurocognitive rehabilitation approaches aimed at increasing prefrontal cognitive control and thus addressing hypofrontality and its associated problems. In this way, such intensive attention training can lead to better affective regulation and emotional well-being. Many studies of adults have found that meditation practices increase activation of the prefrontal cortex; decrease limbic and DMN activity; and improve attention, emotional reactivity, rumination, addictions, and mood disorders, and are associated with increased activity in parts of the prefrontal cortex (Allen et al., 2012; Baerentsen, 2001; Baron Short et al., 2010; Brefczynski-Lewis, Lutz, Schaefer, Levinson, & Davidson, 2007; Farb et al., 2007, 2010; Hasenkamp, Wilson-Mendenhall, Duncan, & Barsalou, 2012; Ritskes, Ritskes-Hoitinga, Stodkilde-Jorgensen, Baerntsen, & Hartman, 2003) and even with a larger volume of gray matter with practice (Hölzel et al., 2008; Lazar et al., 2005; Luders, Toga, Lepore, & Gaser, 2009). These studies demonstrate most clearly that meditation raises prefrontal activity.

Meditation practices have been found to improve a range of attention and executive function tasks associated with the prefrontal cortex (Brefczynski-Lewis et al., 2007; Bushell, 2009; Chambers, Lo, & Allen, 2008; Chan & Woollacott, 2007; Davidson, Goleman, & Schwartz, 1976; Jha, Krompinger, & Baime, 2007; Lazar et al., 2000; Lutz et al., 2009; Pagnoni & Cekic, 2007; Slagter et al., 2007; Srinivasan & Baijal, 2007; Tang et al., 2007; Valentine & Sweet, 1999; Wenk-Sormaz, 2005), including sustained attention (Jha et al., 2007; Kaul, Passafiume, Sargent, & O'Hara, 2010; MacLean et al., 2010; Valentine & Sweet, 1999) and self-regulation (Chambers et al., 2008; Heeren, Van Broeck, & Philippot, 2009; Ortner, Kilner, & Zelazo, 2007; Tang, Yang, Leve, & Harold, 2012; Tang et al., 2007; Zeidan, Johnson, Diamond, David, & Goolkasian, 2010; Zylowska et al., 2008). Bertin (Chapter 20, this volume) describes the importance of executive function as the foundation for lifelong mental health and functioning. Still, not all studies have found positive effects on attention from meditation practice (e.g., Anderson, Lau, Segal, & Bishop, 2007).

Another explanation for how meditation practices work comes from studies of the amygdala, site of emotional reactivity. A number of studies with adults have found decreased activity in the amygdala following different forms of meditation (Brefczynski-Lewis et al., 2007; Creswell, Way, Eisenberger, & Lieberman, 2007; Desbordes et al., 2012; Farb et al., 2007; Taylor et al., 2011; Way, Creswell, Eisenberger, & Lieberman, 2010).

Multiple studies have found that various forms of meditation training are associated with decreased DMN activity, the region that is associated with the creation of a sense of self and the associated problems (Baerentsen, 2001; Baerentsen et al., 2009; Berkovich-Ohana, Glicksohn, & Goldstein, 2011; Brewer et al., 2011; Farb et al., 2007, 2010; Goldin, Ramel, & Gross, 2009; Hasenkamp et al., 2012; Taylor et al., 2011; Travis et al., 2010). However, others have found increased DMN activity (Goldin et al., 2009; Goldin, Ziv, Jazaieri, & Gross, 2012; Goldin & Gross, 2010; Hölzel et al., 2011).

A number of studies of various meditation practice found decreased sympathetic hyperarousal in meditators (Barnes, Treiber, & Davis, 2001; Carlson, Speca, Faris, & Patel, 2007; Maclean et al., 1994; Ortner et al., 2007; Sudsuang, Chentanez, & Veluvan, 1991; Tang et al., 2007), but increases in arousal have also been reported (Britton, Haynes, Fridel, & Bootzin, 2010; Holmes, 1984). The sympathetic nervous system is associated with stress and the fight–flight–freeze response, and a range of research points to the multiplying effect of stress on a variety of physical and psychological disorders. Thus by decreasing sympathetic arousal and lowering stress, we create the conditions that better facilitate the healing process.

Other studies have also suggested a relationship between mindfulness and reduced reactivity to stress and emotion, including dampened emotional responses to threat and faster recovery from transient negative emotions (Arch & Craske, 2006, 2010; Brewer et al., 2009; Britton, Shahar, Szepsenwol, & Jacobs, 2012; Broderick, 2005; Campbell-Sills, Barlow, Brown, & Hofmann, 2006; Erisman & Roemer, 2010; Goldin & Gross, 2010; Kuehner, Huffziger, & Liebsch, 2009; McKee, Zvolensky, Solomon, Bernstein, & Leen-Feldner, 2007; Ortner et al., 2007; Pace et al., 2009; Proulx, 2008; Raes, Dewulf, Van Heeringen, & Williams, 2009; Tang et al., 2007; Weinstein, Brown, & Ryan, 2009).

Meditation and Mindfulness: A Closer Look

The research described above, although offering some promising evidence that various forms of meditation practice change the brain in regions associated with the problems we see in learning, behavior, and mental health, should be regarded as preliminary. The state of the research suffers from a wide range of limitations, including nonstandardized meditation practices, methodologies, control conditions, and a mix of different populations, including both secular clinical novice meditators as well as advanced meditators. Making research more difficult, scientists who study meditation are confronted with a wide range of different practices that are collectively *meditation* or *mindfulness*.[2] A

---

[2]The terms "meditation" and "mindfulness" are common but ambiguous terms that refer to a wide range of contemplative practices. Jon Kabat-Zinn used the word "mindfulness" as an "umbrella term" and "a place-holder for the entire dharma" or all of the teachings of the Buddha. While the program that he developed, Mindfulness-Based Stress Reduction (MBSR), draws heavily from both Theravada and Mahayana (Zen) Buddhist meditation practices, it also includes approaches derived from Hindu Vedanta and other non-Buddhist spiritual teachers (Kabat-Zinn, 2011). Thus, what is commonly called "mindfulness meditation" may refer to any number of practices from different religious traditions, and has led to much ambiguity in science and much criticism from Buddhist scholars (Lopez Jr., 2009).

recent U.S. government report cited "confusion over what constitutes meditation" (p. 209) as the central obstacle in meditation research (Ospina et al., 2007), preventing any strong conclusions about meditation's benefits.

Because of this confusion, researchers are attempting standardize terms and practices in a way that both honor traditional theory and reflect the practicalities of clinical applications and research. Antoine Lutz et al. created the terms "focused attention" and "open monitoring" as two broad categories of practices that are thought to have different neural underpinnings and different cognitive, affective, and behavioral consequences (Lutz, Slagter, Dunne, & Davidson, 2008; Rapgay & Bystrisky, 2009). Close study of the mindfulness-based stress reduction (MBSR) and mindfulness-based cognitive therapy (MBCT) manuals indicate that these 8-week programs spend about half of the time on focused attention and the other half on open monitoring (Santorelli & Kabat-Zinn, 2003; Segal, Williams, & Teasdale, 2002), so the widespread but ambiguous term *mindfulness meditation*[3] could also be described in terms of a mixture of the two practices.

Focused Attention Meditation

Focused attention (FA) practice involves intentionally directing and sustaining attention on a chosen object or anchor of attention (e.g., the breath, a visual object, a sound) while "deselecting" other stimuli. Thoughts, emotions, and body sensations that are not the meditation anchor are viewed as distractions. The meditator's goal is to remain anchored, monitor the mind's wandering, and return attention to the object when the mind has wandered. Beginning this practice involves effort and frustration, and can produce fatigue and sleepiness, not to be confused with meditative calm. Such sleepiness is counteracted with renewed vigilance and energy (Britton, Lindahl, Cahn, Davis, & Goldman, 2013). Progress in FA is measured by the ability to hold attention on the object without distraction, which becomes easier with practice. Sustaining and redirecting attention back to an object (e.g., the breath) over and over again builds the attentional "muscle" of the DAS (Hasenkamp et al., 2012). When this system is strong and engaged, the limbic (amygdala) and DMN systems become less active, with the possible result being a calm and tranquil mind. Tranquility and mental calm are nice side effects, but are actually not the goal of many traditional or secular meditation practices.

Because the tranquility is transient and easy to get attached to, many teachings downplay the advanced cultivation of focused attention in favor

---

[3] In many Buddhist systems the term *shamatha* or *samatha* is used to describe initial focused awareness or "tranquility" practices. However, this term becomes confusing, because in some systems (Theravada), *shamatha* refers to focusing on an object, but in other systems (Tibetan), later stages of *shamatha* are objectless and therefore no longer fit the criteria for focused awareness.

of the more enduring transformations that come through "insight." Nevertheless, some mastery of concentration is important as a foundation, just as physical exercise and stretching cannot be done without a foundation of some muscle strength. From the inside, strengthening the DAS network is like sharpening the focus of a microscope or telescope, or "keeping the tripod steady." When our telescope is steady and in focus, we now see that what appear to be stars are, in fact, planets. Or, through a microscope, we can see that an onion skin is not "solid," as we perceive it by the naked eye, but made of individual cells. When our minds are calm, we can see everything more clearly, including the subtleties. Thus, the ultimate purpose of FA is to stabilize the mind for deeper inquiry and insight.

Open-Monitoring Meditation

In contrast to FA practice, open-monitoring (OM) practice involves a continuous monitoring of any and all stimuli (thought, emotions, body sensations, sounds, etc.) that arise in experience, without privileging any particular object. In such practice, all stimuli—including disturbing thoughts, judgments, and emotions—are possible *objects* of meditation, and are not viewed as distractions or any other type of problem or obstacle. In Theravada Buddhism as well as MBSR (Kabat-Zinn, 1990, 2011), the goals of practice include insight into the "three characteristics"—the impermanence, unsatisfactoriness, and non-self—of all phenomena. In other forms of Buddhism (Mahayana), insight is described in terms of the "emptiness" of persons and phenomena. In either case, the development of insight involves a "reperceiving" (Shapiro, Carlson, Astin, & Freedman, 2006) of the self and the world, so that they come to be understood as less solid and fixed.

At an experiential level, we can now see that the emotions that we have identified with as intrinsic to ourselves are nothing more than passing thoughts (mental images, words) and body sensations (pressure, tightness, heat). Because they are fleeting and insubstantial, thought and emotions are neither reliable nor able to give lasting satisfaction or threat. Seeing thoughts and emotions as transient events rather than as accurate views of reality has been called "metacognitive awareness" (Teasdale et al., 2002), "decentering" (Watkins, Teasdale, & Williams, 2000), and "cognitive defusion" (Masuda, Feinstein, Wendell, & Sheehan, 2010). Whatever the term, this state is characterized as a spacious, nonreactive way of observing the mind's process, like a bird's-eye view.

On a neural level, this ability to see thoughts as thoughts is apparent when the dorsal anterior cingulate cortex (dACC) is coactivated with the DMN (Brewer et al., 2011; Hasenkamp & Barsalou, 2012) without a decrease in amygdala activity (Taylor et al., 2011). Usually these two brain areas are anticorrelated: For example, it's hard to daydream or worry *and* pay attention at the same time. But if we are monitoring, we can make the worry or daydream itself become the object of our meditation. *Unpleasant thought, body sensation, or memory?* Not a distraction and not a problem!

Selflessness

As we get better at watching our minds, we eventually see that all of these fleeting thoughts and body sensations are not who we really are, nor do they necessarily reflect how the world really is: *I am not my thoughts, and my thoughts and perceptions do not necessarily reflect objective reality, if there even is an objective reality.* These "mental events" no longer feed into to DMN to construct a solid or permanent "thing" called a self that we have to defend, protect, or worry about being good enough.

This change in how we think about ourselves and the world may represent an unusual neural shift whereby the awareness/monitoring area (dACC), which is usually mutually exclusive with self-referential thinking/mind wandering DMN, turn on at the same time (Brewer et al., 2011; Hasenkamp & Barsalou, 2012; Josipovic, Dinstein, Weber, & Heeger, 2012). This coactivation creates the opportunity to remain aware *while* the process of self-construction is happening, instead of losing the metacognitive awareness as emotional patterns take over. When both are active, then we can truly step back and observe the way we construct ourselves, seeing how the sense of self is built from a complex set of images, narratives, and associated body sensations. So rather than suppressing the DMN, as in focused attention (which is still a good skill to have), the narrative self arises—but it can be observed, even if not believed, as a solid, permanent entity.

Like looking under the hood of a truck to see the running motor, we can get a closer look at the process of consciousness as it unfolds, and by doing so, we are less captivated or in thrall. The experience is akin to knowing the illusion behind the magic show; the illusion loses its ability to trick us. Such insight into selflessness can be sudden or gradual, and may be liberating or distressing, depending on the context and theoretical preparation provided (Castillo, 1990). These factors of context and preparation underscore the need for knowledgeable and experienced teachers.

As scientists begin to collaborate with practitioners and scholars of contemplative traditions, a more complex picture of meditation is emerging that challenges the often simplified notions that appear in research and clinical applications. In particular, the confusion about the differences in the goals of concentration/FA and insight/OM practices has led to a conflation of the term *mindfulness* with the practice of insight/OM. However, many of the outcomes from "mindfulness" programs such as MBSR and MBCT are more in line with the goals of cognitive control and mental calm, which are more associated with FA. Furthermore, although "mindfulness meditation" is often considered an "insight" practice, there has been very little actual research on the process and experience of insight. These distinctions have profound implications for the applications of meditation-based practices in both adults and youth, as certain practices may be more suitable for certain goals and populations than others.

Contemplative Practices for Youth

Because of the widespread popularity, application, and scientific study of meditation in adults, there has been much interest and enthusiasm in applying these practices earlier in life, during childhood and adolescence. There is a strong empirical rationale for this idea, as hypofrontality appears to start early in life with similar consequences. The idea that we could, at an early age, build resilience to so many forms of distress is appealing for a number of reasons.

In children and adolescents, poor prefrontal control and impaired executive functioning, including self-regulation problems and attentional control difficulties, are associated with a host of negative outcomes across the lifespan, including behavior problems, aggression, antisocial behavior, attention-deficit/hyperactivity disorder (ADHD), problems with peers, school failure, depression, substance abuse, and criminal offenses, as described elsewhere in this volume (also see Eigsti et al., 2006; Ivanov, Schulz, London, & Newcorn, 2008; Mahone & Hoffman, 2007; Moffitt et al., 2011; Perner, Kain, & Barchfeld, 2002; Riggs, Blair, & Greenberg, 2003). Conversely, better executive functioning is associated with greater professional and academic achievement; relationship success; and positive social, emotional, behavioral, economic, and health outcomes (Blair & Peters, 2003; Blair & Razza, 2007; Carlson, Mandell, & Williams, 2004; Carlson & Moses, 2001; Lefevre et al., 2013; Moffitt et al., 2011).

Given that prefrontal control and executive function predict such a wide range of outcomes in both adults and children, there has been considerable interest in offering attention training techniques, such as meditation and mindfulness, to the developing minds of young people. The prefrontal cortex does not fully develop until young adulthood, and so is highly susceptible to influences on development throughout childhood and adolescence (Davidson & McEwen, 2012; Huttenlocher & Dabholkar, 1997; Mind and Life Education Research Network et al., 2012). Because neural plasticity and behavior change are more possible in children than adults, training executive function at a young age may be, from a prevention and public health perspective, the best time to intervene (Dahlin, Nyberg, Backman, & Neely, 2008; Diamond & Lee, 2011). Diamond (2013; Diamond & Lee, 2011) reviewed programs designed to foster self-regulation and executive function in youth, and concluded that executive function can be improved through training, with the strongest evidence from well-designed trials for computerized training, interactive games, martial arts, and specific school curricula, with positive results but weaker-quality research for aerobics, yoga, mindfulness, and other school curricula (Blair & Diamond, 2008; Dahlin et al., 2008; Diamond, 2013; Diamond & Lee, 2011). Many such programs are described in greater detail earlier in this volume.

Mindfulness and meditation-based interventions have been applied to both clinical and nonclinical populations of children and adolescents. On the clinical side, mindfulness-based programs have been applied to a range of psychological problems, including anxiety, (Beauchemin, Hutchins, & Patterson, 2008; Biegel, Brown, & Shapiro, 2009), rumination and depression (Napoli, Krech, & Holley, 2005), and attention problems (Semple, Lee, Rosa, & Miller, 2010; Zylowska et al., 2008). In addition to clinical populations, numerous schools have adopted mindfulness and meditation-based programs, either as electives or institutionwide curricula (Meiklejohn et al., 2012; Schoeberlein, Koeffler, & Jha, 2005).

Notes of Caution

Both the scientific research and the subjective accounts of meditation training have occurred almost exclusively with adults. Even in countries where monastic training has been commonplace for centuries or millennia, historical accounts suggest that meditation played a very minimal role in the lives or training of monks, and almost no role in the lives of laypeople, until the 20th century. Most young monastics spend their preteen and teenage years engaged in the memorization of liturgical and philosophical texts and are rarely required to meditate as part of their training. Very few people within large-scale monastic institutions engage in extensive practice before completing their scholastic study, a process that can take upward of 20 years of training in some cultures (Dreyfus, 2003; Sasson, 2013; Sharf, 1995). Thus, like the modern Western idea of using meditation practices to treat psychopathology, the idea of using meditation with children is a novel and mostly untried concept, both East and West. Nor do Eastern models of psychology have a clear theory of child development or age-appropriate practices from which to draw; rather, existing practices are being adapted now.

Training the developing brain through meditative practices offers a promising opportunity to correct or even prevent certain types of developmental trajectories, especially those associated with poor prefrontal control and its associated difficulties. However, since the only existing neuroscientific studies are of adults, and we have little idea how meditation may affect the developing brain, a note of caution is warranted. It may be worth asking whether certain capacities need to be established before engaging in certain forms of training. For example, the idea of a self emerges between ages 2 and 3, solidifying through childhood and adolescence into early adulthood. The emerging sense of self is highly malleable and strongly influenced by developmental changes in brain structure and the resulting cognitive abilities (Harter, 2006; Lewis & Carmody, 2008). As described, brain areas associated with self-concept (the DMN) are often deactivated during different meditation practices, and self-concept is deliberately deconstructed during insight practice. Psychologist Jack Engler (1984) warns that a fully "cohesive and integrated self" is a prerequisite for insight meditation and suggests that this practice may be contraindicated for individuals who have not yet established a fully mature and coherent sense of self.

The research in adults is starting to ask whether mindfulness or meditation training is equally beneficial for everyone, or whether some individuals may be better off with other forms of treatment. Indeed, studies in adults have found that preexisting characteristics predict treatment outcome (Cordon, Brown, & Gibson, 2009), and that mindfulness or meditation-based interventions may be maximally effective (Arch & Ayers, 2013; Ma & Teasdale, 2004; Teasdale et al., 2000), ineffective (Jazaieri, Goldin, Werner, Ziv, & Gross, 2012; Mularski et al., 2009), or even "contraindicated" for certain types of people (Arch & Ayers, 2013; Ma & Teasdale, 2004).

Many school-based programs are implemented at the institutional level so that all students receive meditation as part of the school day—not by individual choice—making the question of individual differences in response to meditation even more urgent. So far, the effects of mindfulness-based training programs with children and adolescents have been found to be affected by preexisting characteristics, including baseline levels of executive function (Flook et al., 2010), developmental age (Schonert-Reichl & Lawlor, 2010), family environment (Barnes, Gregoski, Tingen, & Treiber, 2010), and gene-by-environment interactions (Gregoski et al., 2012), indicating that some children benefit more than others, and some do not benefit at all.

Since possible side effects of meditation (Epstein & Lieff, 1981; Lazarus, 1976; Shapiro, 1992)—including depersonalization (Castillo, 1990; Kennedy, 1976), psychosis (Chan-Ob & Boonyanaruthee, 1999; Kuijpers, van der Heijden, Tuinier, & Verhoeven, 2007; Sethi, 2003), epilepsy (Lansky, 2006), and mania (Yorston, 2001)—have been reported in some adults (Lustyk, Chawla, Nolan, & Marlatt, 2009), it has been recommended that "researchers need to be cognizant of the possibility of iatrogenic effects that certain practices could have with children of different ages and characteristics" (Greenberg & Harris, 2012, p. 164). Indeed, studies of children have also reported unwanted effects. An 8-week randomized controlled trial of a yoga-based mindfulness intervention with fourth- and fifth-grade girls found that girls in the yoga intervention reported larger increases of perceived stress than wait-list controls, and that this increase in distress was associated with amount of home practice (White, 2012). Mark Greenberg cautions, "Consumer interest and marketing have expanded such practices without sufficient knowledge of their outcomes, which might be positive, minimal, or even iatrogenic. . . . Because there is currently little quality research on outcomes, widespread use is premature" (Greenberg & Harris, 2012, p. 121). Christine Burke (2009) offered sound advice for the future of the field:

> Advancing the empirical research is vital, as it is clear that the popularity of mindfulness-based approaches is on the rise in all age groups, including children and adolescents, despite the absence of empirical evidence of the efficacy of these interventions with younger populations. Now, with a reasonable base of support for the feasibility and acceptability of mindfulness-based interventions with children and adolescents, it is time that the field embarks upon a more rigorous course of gathering empirically sound evidence of the efficacy of these interventions. (p. 11)

REFERENCES

Allen, M., Dietz, M., Blair, K. S., van Beek, M., Rees, G., Vestergaard-Poulsen, P., et al. (2012). Cognitive–affective neural plasticity following active-controlled mindfulness intervention. *Journal of Neuroscience, 32*(44), 15601–15610.

Anderson, N., Lau, M., Segal, Z., & Bishop, S. (2007). Mindfulness-based stress reduction and attentional control. *Clinical Psychology and Psychotherapy, 14,* 449–463.

Arch, J. J., & Ayers, C. R. (2013). Which treatment worked better for whom?: Moderators of group cognitive behavioral therapy versus adapted mindfulness based stress reduction for anxiety disorders. *Behaviour Research and Therapy, 51*(8), 434–442.

Arch, J. J., & Craske, M. G. (2006). Mechanisms of mindfulness: Emotion regulation following a focused breathing induction. *Behaviour Research and Therapy, 44*(12), 1849–1858.

Arch, J. J., & Craske, M. G. (2010). Laboratory stressors in clinically anxious and non-anxious individuals: The moderating role of mindfulness. *Behaviour Research and Therapy, 48*(6), 495–505.

Baerentsen, K. B. (2001). Onset of meditation explored with fMRI. *NeuroImage, 13,* S297.

Baerentsen, K. B., Stodkilde-Jorgensen, H., Sommerlund, B., Hartmann, T., Damsgaard-Madsen, J., Fosnaes, M., et al. (2009). An investigation of brain processes supporting meditation. *Cognitive Processing, 11,* 57–84

Barnes, V. A., Gregoski, M. J., Tingen, M. S., & Treiber, F. A. (2010). Influences of family environment and meditation efficacy on hemodynamic function among African American adolescents. *Journal of Complementary and Integrative Medicine, 7*(1), 1326–1328.

Barnes, V. A., Treiber, F. A., & Davis, H. (2001). Impact of transcendental meditation on cardiovascular function at rest and during acute stress in adolescents with high normal blood pressure. *Journal of Psychosomatic Research, 51*(4), 597–605.

Baron Short, E., Kose, S., Mu, Q., Borckardt, J., Newberg, A., George, M. S., et al. (2010). Regional brain activation during meditation shows time and practice effects: An exploratory fMRI study. *Evidence-Based Complementary and Alternative Medicine, 7*(1), 121–127.

Baxter, L. R., Jr., Schwartz, J. M., Phelps, M. E., Mazziotta, J. C., Guze, B. H., Selin, C. E., et al. (1989). Reduction of prefrontal cortex glucose metabolism common to three types of depression. *Archives of General Psychiatry, 46*(3), 243–250.

Beauchemin, J., Hutchins, T., & Patterson, F. (2008). Mindfulness meditation may lessen anxiety, promote social skills, and improve academic performance among adolescents with learning disabilities. *Complementary Health Practice Review, 13*(1), 34–45.

Bedard, M., Felteau, M., Mazmanian, D., Fedyk, K., Klein, R., Richardson, J., et al. (2003). Pilot evaluation of a mindfulness-based intervention to improve quality of life among individuals who sustained traumatic brain injuries. *Disability and Rehabilitation, 25*(13), 722–731.

Bench, C. J., Friston, K. J., Brown, R. G., Frackowiak, R. S., & Dolan, R. J. (1993). Regional cerebral blood flow in depression measured by positron emission tomography: The relationship with clinical dimensions. *Psychological Medicine, 23*(3), 579–590.

Berkovich-Ohana, A., Glicksohn, J., & Goldstein, A. (2011). Mindfulness-induced changes in gamma band activity: Implications for the default mode network, self-reference and attention. *Clinical Neurophysiology, 123*(4), 700–710.

Biegel, G., Brown, K., & Shapiro, S. (2009). Mindfulness-based stress reduction for the treatment of adolescent psychiatric outpatients: A randomized clinical trial. *Journal of Consulting and Clinical Psychology, 77*(5), 855–866.

Blair, C., & Diamond, A. (2008). Biological processes in prevention and intervention: The promotion of self-regulation as a means of preventing school failure. *Developmental Psychopathology, 20*(3), 899–911.

Blair, C., & Peters, R. (2003). Physiological and neurocognitive correlates of adaptive behavior in preschool among children in Head Start. *Developmental Neuropsychology, 24*(1), 479–497.

Blair, C., & Razza, R. P. (2007). Relating effortful control, executive function, and false belief understanding to emerging math and literacy ability in kindergarten. *Child Development, 78*(2), 647–663.

Blumberg, H. P., Kaufman, J., Martin, A., Charney, D. S., Krystal, J. H., & Peterson, B. S. (2004). Significance of adolescent neurodevelopment for the neural circuitry of bipolar disorder. *Annals of the New York Academy of Sciences, 1021,* 376–383.

Bondolfi, G., Jermann, F., der Linden, M. V., Gex-Fabry, M., Bizzini, L., Rouget, B. W., et al. (2010). Depression relapse prophylaxis with mindfulness-based cognitive therapy: Replication and extension in the Swiss health care system. *Journal of Affective Disorders, 122*(3), 224–231.

Brefczynski-Lewis, J. A., Lutz, A., Schaefer, H. S., Levinson, D. B., & Davidson, R. J. (2007). Neural correlates of attentional expertise in long-term meditation practitioners. *Proceedings of the National Academy of Sciences of the USA, 104*(27), 11483–11488.

Brewer, J. A., Sinha, R., Chen, J. A., Michalsen, R. N., Babuscio, T. A., Nich, C., et al. (2009). Mindfulness training and stress reactivity in substance abuse: Results from a randomized, controlled stage I pilot study. *Substance Abuse, 30*(4), 306–317.

Brewer, J. A., Worhunsky, P. D., Gray, J. R., Tang, Y. Y., Weber, J., & Kober, H. (2011). Meditation experience is associated with differences in default mode network activity and connectivity. *Proceedings of the National Academy of Sciences of the USA, 108*(50), 20254–20259.

Britton, W. B., Haynes, P. L., Fridel, K. W., & Bootzin, R. R. (2010). Polysomnographic and subjective profiles of sleep continuity before and after mindfulness-based cognitive therapy in partially remitted depression. *Psychosomatic Medicine, 72*(6), 539–548.

Britton, W. B., Lindahl, J., Cahn, B., Davis, J., & Goldman, R. (2013). Awakening is not a metaphor: The effects of Buddhist meditation practices on basic wakefulness *Annals of the New York Academy of Sciences, 1307*, 64–81.

Britton, W. B., Shahar, B., Szepsenwol, O., & Jacobs, W. J. (2012). Mindfulness-based cognitive therapy improves emotional reactivity to social stress: Results from a randomized controlled trial. *Behavior Therapy, 43*(2), 365–380.

Broderick, P. (2005). Mindfulness and coping with dysphoric mood: Contrasts with rumination and distraction. *Cognitive Therapy and Research, 29*, 501–510.

Buckner, R. L., & Vincent, J. L. (2007). Unrest at rest: Default activity and spontaneous network correlations. *NeuroImage, 37*(4), 1091–1099.

Burke, C. A. (2009). Mindfulness-based approaches with children and adolescents: A preliminary review of current research in an emergent field. *Journal of Child and Family Studies, 19*, 133–144.

Bushell, W. C. (2009). New beginnings: Evidence that the meditational regimen can lead to optimization of perception, attention, cognition, and other functions. *Annals of the New York Academy of Sciences, 1172*, 348–361.

Campbell-Sills, L., Barlow, D., Brown, T., & Hofmann, S. (2006). Effects of suppression and acceptance on emotional responses of individuals with anxiety and mood disorders. *Behaviour Research and Therapy, 44*, 1251–1263.

Carlson, L. E., Speca, M., Faris, P., & Patel, K. D. (2007). One year pre–post intervention follow-up of psychological, immune, endocrine and blood pressure outcomes of mindfulness-based stress reduction (MBSR) in breast and prostate cancer outpatients. *Brain, Behavior, and Immunity, 21*(8), 1038–1049.

Carlson, S. M., Mandell, D. J., & Williams, L. (2004). Executive function and theory of mind: Stability and prediction from ages 2 to 3. *Developmental Psychology, 40*(6), 1105–1122.

Carlson, S. M., & Moses, L. J. (2001). Individual differences in inhibitory control and children's theory of mind. *Child Development, 72*(4), 1032–1053.

Carter, C. S., Perlstein, W., Ganguli, R., Brar, J., Mintun, M., & Cohen, J. D. (1998). Functional hypofrontality and working memory dysfunction in schizophrenia. *American Journal of Psychiatry, 155*(9), 1285–1287.

Castillo, R. (1990). Depersonalization and meditation. *Psychiatry Research: Neuroimaging Section, 53*, 158–168.

Chadwick, P., Hughes, S., Russell, D., Russell, I., & Dagnan, D. (2009). Mindfulness groups for distressing voices and paranoia: A replication and randomized feasibility trial. *Behavioural and Cognitive Psychotherapy, 37*(4), 403–412.

Chambers, R., Lo, B. C. Y., & Allen, N. B. (2008). The impact of intensive mindfulness training on attentional control, cognitive style, and affect. *Cognitive Therapy and Research, 32*(3), 303–322.

Chan, D., & Woollacott, M. (2007). Effects of level of meditation experience on attentional focus: Is the efficiency of executive or orientation networks improved? *Journal of Alternative and Complementary Medicine, 13*(6), 651–657.

Chan-Ob, T., & Boonyanaruthee, V. (1999). Meditation in association with psychosis. *Journal of the Medical Association of Thailand, 82*(9), 925–930.

Clark, L., Chamberlain, S. R., & Sahakian, B. J. (2009). Neurocognitive mechanisms in depression: Implications for treatment. *Annual Review of Neuroscience, 32,* 57–74.

Clark, L., Iversen, S. D., & Goodwin, G. M. (2002). Sustained attention deficit in bipolar disorder. *British Journal of Psychiatry, 180,* 313–319.

Cordon, S., Brown, K., & Gibson, P. (2009). The role of mindfulness-based stress reduction on perceived stress: Preliminary evidence for the moderating role of attachment style. *Journal of Cognitive Psychotherapy, 23*(3), 258–269.

Couyoumdjian, A., Sdoia, S., Tempesta, D., Curcio, G., Rastellini, E., de Gennaro, L., et al. (2009). The effects of sleep and sleep deprivation on task-switching performance. *Journal of Sleep Research, 19,* 64–70.

Creswell, J., Way, B., Eisenberger, N., & Lieberman, M. (2007). Neural correlates of dispositional mindfulness during affect labeling. *Psychosomatic Medicine, 69,* 560–565.

Dahlin, E., Nyberg, L., Backman, L., & Neely, A. S. (2008). Plasticity of executive functioning in young and older adults: Immediate training gains, transfer, and long-term maintenance. *Psychology and Aging, 23*(4), 720–730.

Davidson, R. J. (2000). Affective style, psychopathology, and resilience: Brain mechanisms and plasticity. *American Psychologist, 55*(11), 1196–1214.

Davidson, R. J., Goleman, D. J., & Schwartz, G. E. (1976). Attentional and affective concomitants of meditation: A cross-sectional study. *Journal of Abnormal Psychology, 85*(2), 235–238.

Davidson, R. J., Jackson, D. C., & Kalin, N. H. (2000). Emotion, plasticity, context, and regulation: Perspectives from affective neuroscience. *Psychological Bulletin, 126,* 890–909.

Desbordes, G., Negi, L. T., Pace, T. W., Wallace, B. A., Raison, C. L., & Schwartz, E. L. (2012). Effects of mindful-attention and compassion meditation training on amygdala response to emotional stimuli in an ordinary, non-meditative state. *Frontiers in Human Neuroscience, 6,* 292.

Diamond, A. (2013). Executive functions. *Annual Review of Psychology, 64,* 135–168.

Diamond, A., & Lee, K. (2011). Interventions shown to aid executive function development in children 4 to 12 years old. *Science, 333*(6045), 959–964.

Draganski, B., Gaser, C., Busch, V., Schuierer, G., Bogdahn, U., & May, A. (2004). Neuroplasticity: Changes in grey matter induced by training. *Nature, 427*(6972), 311–312.

Dreyfus, G. (2003). *The sound of two hands clapping: The education of a Tibetan Buddhist monk.* Berkeley: University of California Press.

Eigsti, I. M., Zayas, V., Mischel, W., Shoda, Y., Ayduk, O., Dadlani, M. B., et al. (2006). Predicting cognitive control from preschool to late adolescence and young adulthood. *Psychological Science, 17*(6), 478–484.

Engler, J. (1984). Therapetic aims in psychotherapy and meditation: Developmental stages in the representation of self. *Journal of Transpersonal Psychology, 16,* 25–61.

Epstein, M., & Lieff, J. (1981). Psychiatric complications of meditation practice. *Journal of Transpersonal Psychology, 13*(2), 137–147.

Erisman, S. M., & Roemer, L. (2010). A preliminary investigation of the effects of experimentally induced mindfulness on emotional responding to film clips. *Emotion, 10*(1), 72–82.

Evans, S., Ferrando, S., Findler, M., Stowell, C., Smart, C., & Haglin, D. (2008). Mindfulness-based cognitive therapy for generalized anxiety disorder. *Journal of Anxiety Disorders, 22*(4), 716–721.

Farb, N. A., Anderson, A. K., Mayberg, H., Bean, J., McKeon, D., & Segal, Z. V. (2010). Minding one's emotions: Mindfulness training alters the neural expression of sadness. *Emotion, 10*(1), 25–33.

Farb, N. A., Segal, Z. V., Mayberg, H., Bean, J., McKeon, D., Fatima, Z., et al. (2007). Attending to the present: Mindfulness meditation reveals distinct neural modes of self-reference. *Social Cognitive and Affective Neuroscience, 2*(4), 313–322.

Flook, L., Smalley, S. L., Kitil, M. J., Galla, B. M., Kaiser-Greenland, S., Locke, J., et al. (2010). Effects of mindful awareness practices on executive functions in elementary school children. *Journal of Applied School Psychology, 26*(1), 70–95.

Fox, M. D., Snyder, A. Z., Vincent, J. L., Corbetta, M., Van Essen, D. C., & Raichle, M. E. (2005). The human brain is intrinsically organized into dynamic, anticorrelated functional networks. *Proceedings of the National Academy of Sciences of the USA, 102*(27), 9673–9678.

Gallagher, S. (2000). Philosophical conceptions of the self: Implications for cognitive science. *Trends in Cognitive Science, 4*, 14–21.

Gentili, C., Ricciardi, E., Gobbini, M. I., Santarelli, M. F., Haxby, J. V., Pietrini, P., et al. (2009). Beyond amygdala: Default mode network activity differs between patients with social phobia and healthy controls. *Brain Research Bulletin, 79*(6), 409–413.

Goldin, P. R., & Gross, J. J. (2010). Effects of mindfulness-based stress reduction (MBSR) on emotion regulation in social anxiety disorder. *Emotion, 10*(1), 83–91.

Goldin, P. R., Ramel, W., & Gross, J. (2009). Mindfulness meditation training and self-referential processing in social anxiety disorder: Behavioral and neural effects. *Journal of Cognitive Psychotherapy, 23*(3), 242–257.

Goldin, P. R., Ziv, M., Jazaieri, H., & Gross, J. J. (2012). Randomized controlled trial of mindfulness-based stress reduction versus aerobic exercise: Effects on the self-referential brain network in social anxiety disorder. *Frontiers in Human Neuroscience, 6*, 295.

Goldstein, R. Z., Craig, A. D., Bechara, A., Garavan, H., Childress, A. R., Paulus, M. P., et al. (2009). The neurocircuitry of impaired insight in drug addiction. *Trends in Cognitive Science, 13*(9), 372–380.

Greenberg, M., & Harris, A. (2012). Nurturing mindfulness in children and youth: Current state of research. *Child Development Perspectives, 6*(2), 161–166.

Gregoski, M. J., Barnes, V. A., Tingen, M. S., Dong, Y., Zhu, H., & Treiber, F. A. (2012). Differential impact of stress reduction programs upon ambulatory blood pressure among African American adolescents: Influences of endothelin-1 gene and chronic stress exposure. *International Journal of Hypertension, 2012*(510291), 1–12.

Hamilton, J. P., Furman, D. J., Chang, C., Thomason, M. E., Dennis, E., & Gotlib, I. H. (2011). Default-mode and task-positive network activity in major depressive disorder: Implications for adaptive and maladaptive rumination. *Biological Psychiatry, 70*(4), 327–333.

Harter, S. (2006). The self. In N. Eisenberg (Ed.), *Handbook of child psychology: Vol. 3. Social, emotional, and personality development* (pp. 505–570). New York: Wiley.

Hasenkamp, W., & Barsalou, L. W. (2012). Effects of meditation experience on functional connectivity of distributed brain networks. *Frontiers in Human Neuroscience, 6*, 38.

Hasenkamp, W., Wilson-Mendenhall, C. D., Duncan, E., & Barsalou, L. W. (2012). Mind wandering and attention during focused meditation: A fine-grained temporal analysis of fluctuating cognitive states. *NeuroImage, 59*(1), 750–760.

Heeren, A., Van Broeck, N., & Philippot, P. (2009). The effects of mindfulness on executive processes and autobiographical memory specificity. *Behaviour Research and Therapy, 47*(5), 403–409.

Hester, R., & Garavan, H. (2004). Executive dysfunction in cocaine addiction: Evidence for discordant frontal, cingulate, and cerebellar activity. *Journal of Neuroscience, 24*(49), 11017–11022.

Holmes, D. S. (1984). Meditation and somatic arousal reduction. *American Psychologist, 39*(1), 1–10.

Hölzel, B. K., Carmody, J., Vangel, M., Congleton, C., Yerramsetti, S. M., Gard, T., et al. (2011). Mindfulness practice leads to increases in regional brain gray matter density. *Psychiatry Research: Neuroimaging, 191*(1), 36–43.

Hölzel, B. K., Ott, U., Gard, T., Hempel, H., Weygandt, M., Morgen, K., et al. (2008). Investigation of mindfulness meditation practitioners with voxel-based morphometry. *Social Cognitive and Affective Neuroscience, 3*(1), 55–61.

Hsu, S. H., Grow, J., & Marlatt, G. A. (2008). Mindfulness and addiction. *Recent Developments in Alcoholism, 18*, 229–250.

Huttenlocher, P., & Dabholkar, A. (1997). Regional differences in synaptogenesis in human cerebral cortex. *Journal of Comparative Neurology, 387*, 167–178.

Ivanov, I., Schulz, K. P., London, E. D., & Newcorn, J. H. (2008). Inhibitory control deficits in childhood and risk for substance use disorders: A review. *American Journal of Drug and Alcohol Abuse, 34*(3), 239–258.

Jazaieri, H., Goldin, P. R., Werner, K., Ziv, M., & Gross, J. J. (2012). A randomized trial of MBSR versus aerobic exercise for social anxiety disorder. *Journal of Clinical Psychology, 68*(7), 715–731.

Jha, A. P., Krompinger, J., & Baime, M. J. (2007). Mindfulness training modifies subsystems of attention. *Cognitive, Affective, and Behavioral Neuroscience, 7*(2), 109–119.

Johnson, D. P., Penn, D. L., Fredrickson, B. L., Kring, A. M., Meyer, P. S., Catalino, L. I., et al. (2011). A pilot study of loving-kindness meditation for the negative symptoms of schizophrenia. *Schizophrenia Research, 129*(2–3), 137–140.

Josipovic, Z., Dinstein, I., Weber, J., & Heeger, D. (2012). Influence of meditation on anti-correlated networks in the brain. *Frontiers in Human Neuroscience, 5*, 183.

Kabat-Zinn, J. (1990). *Full catastrophe living: Using the wisdom of your body and mind to face stress, pain, and illness.* New York: Delacorte Press.

Kabat-Zinn, J. (2011). Some reflections on the origins of MBSR, skillful means, and the trouble with maps. *Contemporary Buddhism, 12*, 281–306.

Kabat-Zinn, J., Lipworth, L., & Burney, R. (1985). The clinical use of mindfulness meditation for the self-regulation of chronic pain. *Journal of Behavioral Medicine, 8*(2), 163–190.

Kaiser-Greenland, S. (2010). *The mindful child.* New York: Free Press.

Kaul, P., Passafiume, J., Sargent, C., & O'Hara, B. (2010). Meditation acutely improves psychomotor vigilance, and may decrease sleep need. *Behavioral and Brain Functions, 6,* 47–56.

Kennedy, R. (1976). Self-induced depersonalization syndrome. *American Journal of Psychiatry, 133*(11), 1326–1328.

Kim, Y. W., Lee, S. H., Choi, T. K., Suh, S. Y., Kim, B., Kim, C. M., et al. (2009). Effectiveness of mindfulness-based cognitive therapy as an adjuvant to pharmacotherapy in patients with panic disorder or generalized anxiety disorder. *Depression and Anxiety, 26*(7), 601–606.

Kuehner, C., Huffziger, S., & Liebsch, K. (2009). Rumination, distraction, and mindful self-focus: Effects on mood, dysfunctional attitudes, and cortisol stress response. *Psychological Medicine, 39*(2), 219–228.

Kuijpers, H., van der Heijden, F., Tuinier, S., & Verhoeven, W. (2007). Meditation-induced psychosis. *Psychopathology, 40,* 461–464.

Kuyken, W., Byford, S., Taylor, R. S., Watkins, E., Holden, E., White, K., et al. (2008). Mindfulness-based cognitive therapy to prevent relapse in recurrent depression. *Journal of Consulting and Clinical Psychology, 76*(6), 966–978.

Lansky, E. (2006). Transcendental meditation: A double-edged sword in epilepsy? *Epilepsy and Behavior, 9,* 394–400.

Lazar, S. W., Bush, G., Gollub, R. L., Fricchione, G. L., Khalsa, G., & Benson, H. (2000). Functional brain mapping of the relaxation response and meditation. *NeuroReport, 11*(7), 1581–1585.

Lazar, S. W., Kerr, C. E., Wasserman, R. H., Gray, J. R., Greve, D. N., Treadway, M. T., et al. (2005). Meditation experience is associated with increased cortical thickness. *NeuroReport, 16*(17), 1893–1897.

Lazarus, A. (1976). Psychiatric problems precipitated by transcendental meditation. *Psychological Reports, 39,* 601–602.

Lefevre, J. A., Berrigan, L., Vendetti, C., Kamawar, D., Bisanz, J., Skwarchuk, S. L., et al. (2013). The role of executive attention in the acquisition of mathematical skills for children in grades 2 through 4. *Journal of Experimental and Child Psychology, 114*(2), 243–261.

Lemogne, C., Delaveau, P., Freton, M., Guionnet, S., & Fossati, P. (2010). Medial prefrontal cortex and the self in major depression. *Journal of Affective Disorders, 136*(1–2), e1–e11.

Lewis, M., & Carmody, D. P. (2008). Self-representation and brain development. *Developmental Psychology, 44,* 1329–1334.

Lopez, D. S., Jr. (2009). *Buddhism and science: A guide for the perplexed.* Chicago: University of Chicago Press.

Luders, E., Toga, A., Lepore, N., & Gaser, C. (2009). The underlying anatomical correlates of long-term meditation: Larger frontal and hippocampal volumes of gray matter. *NeuroImage, 45,* 672–678.

Lustyk, M., Chawla, N., Nolan, R., & Marlatt, G. (2009). Mindfulness meditation research: Issues of participant screening, safety procedures, and researcher training. *Advances in Mind–Body Medicine, 24*(1), 20–30.

Lutz, A., Slagter, H. A., Dunne, J. D., & Davidson, R. J. (2008). Attention regulation and monitoring in meditation. *Trends in Cognitive Science, 12*(4), 163–169.

Lutz, A., Slagter, H. A., Rawlings, N. B., Francis, A. D., Greischar, L. L., & Davidson, R. J. (2009). Mental training enhances attentional stability: Neural and behavioral evidence. *Journal of Neuroscience, 29*(42), 13418–13427.

Ma, S. H., & Teasdale, J. D. (2004). Mindfulness-based cognitive therapy for depression: Replication and exploration of differential relapse prevention effects. *Journal of Consulting and Clinical Psychology, 72*(1), 31–40.

MacDonald, A. W., 3rd, & Carter, C. S. (2003). Event-related fMRI study of context processing in dorsolateral prefrontal cortex of patients with schizophrenia. *Journal of Abnormal Psychology, 112*(4), 689–697.

MacDonald, A. W., 3rd, Carter, C. S., Kerns, J. G., Ursu, S., Barch, D. M., Holmes, A. J., et al. (2005). Specificity of prefrontal dysfunction and context processing deficits to schizophrenia in never-medicated patients with first-episode psychosis. *American Journal of Psychiatry, 162*(3), 475–484.

Maclean, C., Walton, K., Wenneberg, S., Levitsky, D., Mandarino, J., Waziri, R., et al. (1994). Altered responses of cortisol, GH, TSH, and testosterone in acute stress after four months' practice of transcendental meditation (TM). *Annals of the New York Academy of Sciences, 746*, 381–384.

MacLean, K. A., Ferrer, E., Aichele, S. R., Bridwell, D. A., Zanesco, A. P., Jacobs, T. L., et al. (2010). Intensive meditation training improves perceptual discrimination and sustained attention. *Psychological Science, 21*(6), 829–839.

Maguire, E. A., Woollett, K., & Spiers, H. J. (2006). London taxi drivers and bus drivers: A structural MRI and neuropsychological analysis. *Hippocampus, 16*(12), 1091–1101.

Mahone, E. M., & Hoffman, J. (2007). Behavior ratings of executive function among preschoolers with ADHD. *Clinical Neuropsychology, 21*(4), 569–586.

Masuda, A., Feinstein, A. B., Wendell, J. W., & Sheehan, S. T. (2010). Cognitive defusion versus thought distraction: A clinical rationale, training, and experiential exercise in altering psychological impacts of negative self-referential thoughts. *Behavior Modification, 34*(6), 520–538.

Mayberg, H. S., Liotti, M., Brannan, S. K., McGinnis, S., Mahurin, R. K., Jerabek, P. A., et al. (1999). Reciprocal limbic–cortical function and negative mood: Converging PET findings in depression and normal sadness. *American Journal of Psychiatry, 156*(5), 675–682.

McKee, L., Zvolensky, M. J., Solomon, S., Bernstein, A., & Leen-Feldner, E. (2007). Emotional-vulnerability and mindfulness: A preliminary test of associations among negative affectivity, anxiety sensitivity, and mindfulness skills. *Cognitive Behaviour Therapy, 36*(2), 91–101.

Meiklejohn, J., Phillips, C., Freedman, M., Griffin, M., Biegel, G., Roach, A., et al. (2012). Integrating mindfulness training into K–12 education: Fostering the resilience of teachers and students. *Mindfulness, 3*(4), 1–17, 291–307.

Meyer, S. E., Carlson, G. A., Wiggs, E. A., Martinez, P. E., Ronsaville, D. S., Klimes-Dougan, B., et al. (2004). A prospective study of the association among impaired executive functioning, childhood attentional problems, and the development of bipolar disorder. *Developmental Psychopathology, 16*(2), 461–476.

Miller, E. K., & Cohen, J. D. (2001). An integrative theory of prefrontal cortex function. *Annual Review of Neuroscience, 24*, 167–202.

Mind and Life Education Research Network (MLERN), Davidson, R., Dunne, J., Eccles, J., Engle, A., Greenberg, M., et al. (2012). Contemplative practices and mental training: Prospects for American education. *Child Development Perspectives, 6*(2), 146–153.

Moffitt, T. E., Arseneault, L., Belsky, D., Dickson, N., Hancox, R. J., Harrington, H., et al. (2011). A gradient of childhood self-control predicts health, wealth, and public safety. *Proceedings of the National Academy of Sciences of the USA, 108*(7), 2693–2698.

Morgane, P. J., Galler, J. R., & Mokler, D. J. (2005). A review of systems and networks of the limbic forebrain/limbic midbrain. *Progress in Neurobiology, 75*(2), 143–160.

Mularski, R. A., Munjas, B. A., Lorenz, K. A., Sun, S., Robertson, S. J., Schmelzer, W., et al. (2009). Randomized controlled trial of mindfulness-based therapy for dyspnea in chronic obstructive lung disease. *Journal of Alternative and Complementary Medicine, 15*(10), 1083–1090.

Napoli, M., Krech, P., & Holley, L. (2005). Mindfulness training for elementary school students: The attention academy. *Journal of Applied School Psychology, 21*(1), 99–123.

Ochsner, K. N., Bunge, S. A., Gross, J. J., & Gabrieli, J. D. (2002). Rethinking feelings: An fMRI study of the cognitive regulation of emotion. *Journal of Cognitive Neuroscience, 14*(8), 1215–1229.

Ochsner, K. N., & Gross, J. J. (2005). The cognitive control of emotion. *Trends in Cognitive Science, 9*(5), 242–249.

Ochsner, K. N., Ray, R. D., Cooper, J. C., Robertson, E. R., Chopra, S., Gabrieli, J. D., et al. (2004). For better or for worse: Neural systems supporting the cognitive down- and up-regulation of negative emotion. *NeuroImage, 23*(2), 483–499.

Ortner, C. M. N., Kilner, S., & Zelazo, P. D. (2007). Mindfulness meditation and emotional interference in a simple cognitive task. *Motivation and Emotion, 31*, 271–283.

Ospina, M. B., Bond, K., Karkhaneh, M., Tjosvold, L., Vandermeer, B., Liang, Y., et al. (2007). *Meditation practices for health: State of the research.* Evidence Report/Technology Assessment No. 155 (Prepared by the University of Alberta Evidence-Based Practice Center under Contract No. 290-02-0023). AHQR Publication No. 07-E010. Rockville, MD: U.S. Department of Health and Human Services.

Pace, T. W., Negi, L. T., Adame, D. D., Cole, S. P., Sivilli, T. I., Brown, T. D., et al. (2009). Effect of compassion meditation on neuroendocrine, innate immune, and behavioral responses to psychosocial stress. *Psychoneuroendocrinology, 34*(1), 87–98.

Pagnoni, G., & Cekic, M. (2007). Age effects on gray matter volume and attentional performance in Zen meditation. *Neurobiology of Aging, 28*(10), 1623–1627.

Papageorgiou, C., & Wells, A. (2000). Treatment of recurrent major depression with attention training. *Cognitive and Behavioral Practice, 7*, 407–413.

Penades, R., Catalan, R., Salamero, M., Boget, T., Puig, O., Guarch, J., et al. (2006). Cognitive remediation therapy for outpatients with chronic schizophrenia: A controlled and randomized study. *Schizophrenia Research, 87*, 323–331.

Perner, J., Kain, W., & Barchfeld, P. (2002). Executive control and higher-order theory of mind in children at risk of ADHD. *Infant and Child Development, 11,* 141–158.

Proulx, K. (2008). Experiences of women with bulimia nervosa in a mindfulness-based eating disorder treatment group. *Eating Disorders, 16,* 52–72.

Qin, P., & Northoff, G. (2011). How is our self related to midline regions and the default-mode network? *NeuroImage, 57*(3), 1221–1233.

Raes, F., Dewulf, D., Van Heeringen, C., & Williams, J. M. (2009). Mindfulness and reduced cognitive reactivity to sad mood: Evidence from a correlational study and a non-randomized waiting list controlled study. *Behaviour Research and Therapy, 47*(7), 623–627.

Rapgay, L., & Bystrisky, A. (2009). Classical mindfulness: An introduction to its theory and practice for clinical application. *Annals of the New York Academy of Sciences, 1172,* 148–162.

Riggs, N. R., Blair, C. B., & Greenberg, M. T. (2003). Concurrent and 2-year longitudinal relations between executive function and the behavior of 1st and 2nd grade children. *Child Neuropsychology, 9*(4), 267–276.

Ritskes, R., Ritskes-Hoitinga, M., Stodkilde-Jorgensen, H., Baerntsen, K., & Hartman, T. (2003). MRI scanning during Zen meditation: The picture of enlightenment? *Constructivism in Human Sciences, 8,* 85–90.

Rodrigues, A., Loureiro, M., & Paulo Caramelli, P. (2010). Musical training, neuroplasticity and cognition. *Dementia and Neuropsychology, 4*(4), 277–286.

Roth, R. M., Koven, N. S., Randolph, J. J., Flashman, L. A., Pixley, H. S., Ricketts, S. M., et al. (2006). Functional magnetic resonance imaging of executive control in bipolar disorder. *NeuroReport, 17*(11), 1085–1089.

Santorelli, S. F., & Kabat-Zinn, J. (Eds.). (2003). *MBSR curriculum guide and supporting materials: Mindfulness-based stress reduction professional training.* Worcester, MA: Center for Mindfulness.

Sasson, V. (Ed.). (2013). *Little Buddhas: Children and childhoods in Buddhist texts and traditions.* Oxford, UK: Oxford University Press.

Schoeberlein, D., Koeffler, T., & Jha, A. (2005). *Contemplation and education: The current status of programs using contemplative techniques in K–12 educational settings: A mapping report.* Garrison, NY: Garrison Institute.

Schonert-Reichl, K., & Lawlor, M. S. (2010). The effects of a mindfulness-based education program on pre- and early adolescents' well-being and social and emotional competence. *Mindfulness, 1,* 137–151.

Segal, Z. V. (1988). Appraisal of the self-schema construct in cognitive models of depression. *Psychological Bulletin, 103*(2), 147–162.

Segal, Z. V., Williams, J. M., & Teasdale, J. D. (2002). *Mindfulness-based cognitive therapy for depression: A new approach to preventing relapse.* New York: Guilford Press.

Semple, R., Lee, J., Rosa, D., & Miller, L. (2010). A randomized trial of mindfulness-based cognitive therapy for children: Promoting mindful attention to enhance social–emotional resiliency in children. *Journal of Child and Family Studies, 19*(2), 218–229.

Sethi, S. (2003). Relationship of meditation and psychosis: Case studies. *Australian and New Zealand Journal of Psychiatry, 37*(3), 382.

Shapiro, D. H., Jr. (1992). Adverse effects of meditation: A preliminary investigation of long-term meditators. *International Journal of Psychosomatics, 39*(1–4), 62–67.

Shapiro, S. L., Brown, K., & Astin, J. (2011). Toward the integration of meditation into higher education: A review of research evidence. *Teachers College Record, 113*(3), 493–528.

Shapiro, S. L., Carlson, L. E., Astin, J. A., & Freedman, B. (2006). Mechanisms of mindfulness. *Journal of Clinical Psychology, 62*(3), 373–386.

Sharf, R. (1995). Buddhist modernism and the rhetoric of meditative experience. *Numen, 42*(3), 228–283.

Sheline, Y. I., Barch, D. M., Price, J. L., Rundle, M. M., Vaishnavi, S. N., Snyder, A. Z., et al. (2009). The default mode network and self-referential processes in depression. *Proceedings of the National Academy of Sciences of the United States of America, 106*(6), 1942–1947.

Siegle, G. J., Ghinassi, F., & Thase, M. E. (2007). Neurobehavioral therapies in the 21st century: Summary of an emerging field and an extended example of cognitive control training for depression. *Cognitive Therapy and Research, 31*, 235–262.

Siegle, G. J., & Hasselmo, M. E. (2002). Using connectionist models to guide assessment of psychological disorder. *Psychological Assessment, 14*(3), 263–278.

Siegle, G. J., Steinhauer, S. R., Thase, M. E., Stenger, V. A., & Carter, C. S. (2002). Can't shake that feeling: Event-related fMRI assessment of sustained amygdala activity in response to emotional information in depressed individuals. *Biological Psychiatry, 51*(9), 693–707.

Siegle, G. J., Thompson, W., Carter, C. S., Steinhauer, S. R., & Thase, M. E. (2007). Increased amygdala and decreased dorsolateral prefrontal BOLD responses in unipolar depression: Related and independent features. *Biological Psychiatry, 61*(2), 198–209.

Slagter, H. A., Lutz, A., Greischar, L. L., Francis, A. D., Nieuwenhuis, S., Davis, J. M., et al. (2007). Mental training affects distribution of limited brain resources. *PLoS Biology, 5*(6), e138.

Soler, J., Valdeperez, A., Feliu-Soler, A., Pascual, J. C., Portella, M. J., Martin-Blanco, A., et al. (2012). Effects of the dialectical behavioral therapy–mindfulness module on attention in patients with borderline personality disorder. *Behaviour Research and Therapy, 50*(2), 150–157.

Spek, A. A., van Ham, N. C., & Nyklicek, I. (2013). Mindfulness-based therapy in adults with an autism spectrum disorder: A randomized controlled trial. *Research in Developmental Disabilities, 34*(1), 246–253.

Srinivasan, N., & Baijal, S. (2007). Concentrative meditation enhances preattentive processing: A mismatch negativity study. *NeuroReport, 18*(16), 1709–1712.

Sudsuang, R., Chentanez, V., & Veluvan, K. (1991). The effect of Buddhist meditation on serum cortisol and total protein levels, blood pressure, pulse rate, lung volume, and reaction time. *Physiology and Behavior, 50*, 543–548.

Tang, Y. Y., Ma, Y., Wang, J., Fan, Y., Feng, S., Lu, Q., et al. (2007). Short-term meditation training improves attention and self-regulation. *Proceedings of the National Academy of Science of the USA, 104*(43), 17152–17156.

Tang, Y. Y., Yang, L., Leve, L., & Harold, G. T. (2012). Improving executive function and its neurobiological mechanisms through a mindfulness-based intervention: Advances within the field of developmental neuroscience. *Child Development Perspectives, 6*(4), 361–366.

Taylor, V. A., Grant, J., Daneault, V., Scavone, G., Breton, E., Roffe-Vidal, S., et al.

(2011). Impact of mindfulness on the neural responses to emotional pictures in experienced and beginner meditators. *NeuroImage, 57*(4), 1524–1533.

Teasdale, J. D., Moore, R. G., Hayhurst, H., Pope, M., Williams, S., & Segal, Z. V. (2002). Metacognitive awareness and prevention of relapse in depression: Empirical evidence. *Journal of Consulting and Clinical Psychology, 70*(2), 275–287.

Teasdale, J. D., Segal, Z. V., Williams, J. M., Ridgeway, V., Soulsby, J., & Lau, M. (2000). Prevention of relapse/recurrence in major depression by mindfulness-based cognitive therapy. *Journal of Consulting and Clinical Psychology, 68*, 615–623.

Travis, F., Haaga, D. A., Hagelin, J., Tanner, M., Arenander, A., Nidich, S., et al. (2010). A self-referential default brain state: Patterns of coherence, power, and eLORETA sources during eyes-closed rest and transcendental meditation practice. *Cognitive Processes, 11*(1), 21–30.

Urry, H. L., van Reekum, C. M., Johnstone, T., Kalin, N. H., Thurow, M. E., Schaefer, H. S., et al. (2006). Amygdala and ventromedial prefrontal cortex are inversely coupled during regulation of negative affect and predict the diurnal pattern of cortisol secretion among older adults. *Journal of Neuroscience, 26*(16), 4415–4425.

Valentine, E., & Sweet, P. (1999). Meditation and attention: A comparison of the effects of concentrative and mindfulness meditation on sustained attention. *Mental Health, Religion, and Culture, 2*(1), 59–70.

van den Heuvel, O. A., Veltman, D. J., Groenewegen, H. J., Cath, D. C., van Balkom, A. J., van Hartskamp, J., et al. (2005). Frontal–striatal dysfunction during planning in obsessive–compulsive disorder. *Archives of General Psychiatry, 62*(3), 301–309.

Wanden-Berghe, R. G., Sanz-Valero, J., & Wanden-Berghe, C. (2011). The application of mindfulness to eating disorders treatment: A systematic review. *Eating Disorders, 19*(1), 34–48.

Watkins, E., Teasdale, J. D., & Williams, R. M. (2000). Decentring and distraction reduce overgeneral autobiographical memory in depression. *Psychological Medicine, 30*(4), 911–920.

Way, B., Creswell, J., Eisenberger, N., & Lieberman, M. (2010). Dispositional mindfulness and depressive symptomatology: Correlations with limbic and self-referential neural activity at rest. *Emotion, 10*, 12–24.

Weinstein, N., Brown, K., & Ryan, R. M. (2009). A multi-method examination of the effects of mindfulness on stress attribution, coping, and emotional well-being. *Journal of Research in Personality, 43*, 374–385.

Wenk-Sormaz, H. (2005). Meditation can reduce habitual responding. *Advances in Mind–Body Medicine, 21*(3–4), 33–49.

White, L. (2012). Reducing stress in school-age girls through mindful yoga. *Journal of Pediatric Health Care, 26*(1), 45–56.

Whitfield-Gabrieli, S., Thermenos, H. W., Milanovic, S., Tsuang, M. T., Faraone, S. V., McCarley, R. W., et al. (2009). Hyperactivity and hyperconnectivity of the default network in schizophrenia and in first-degree relatives of persons with schizophrenia. *Proceedings of the National Academy of Sciences of the USA, 106*(4), 1279–1284.

Williams, J. M., Alatiq, Y., Crane, C., Barnhofer, T., Fennell, M. J., Duggan, D. S., et al. (2008). Mindfulness-based cognitive therapy (MBCT) in bipolar disorder:

Preliminary evaluation of immediate effects on between-episode functioning. *Journal of Affective Disorders, 107*(1–3), 275–279.

Williams, J. M., Duggan, D. S., Crane, C., & Fennell, M. J. (2006). Mindfulness-based cognitive therapy for prevention of recurrence of suicidal behavior. *Journal of Clinical Psychology, 62*(2), 201–210.

Wood, A. G., & Smith, E. (2008). Pediatric neuroimaging studies: A window to neurocognitive development of the frontal lobes. In V. Anderson, R. Jacobs, & P. J. Anderson (Eds.), *Executive functions and the frontal lobes: A lifespan perspective* (pp. 203–216). Philadelphia: Taylor & Francis.

Yorston, G. (2001). Mania precipitated by meditation: A case report and literature review. *Mental Health, Religion, and Culture, 4*, 209–214.

Zeidan, F., Johnson, S. K., Diamond, B. J., David, Z., & Goolkasian, P. (2010). Mindfulness meditation improves cognition: Evidence of brief mental training. *Consciousness and Cognition, 19*(2), 597–605.

Zhao, X. H., Wang, P. J., Li, C. B., Hu, Z. H., Xi, Q., Wu, W. Y., et al. (2007). Altered default mode network activity in patient with anxiety disorders: An fMRI study. *European Journal of Radiology, 63*(3), 373–378.

Zylowska, L., Ackerman, D., Yang, M., Futrell, J., Horton, N., Hale, T., et al. (2008). Mindfulness meditation training in adults and adolescents with ADHD: A feasibility study. *Journal of Attention Disorders, 11*(6), 737–746.

Index

Page numbers followed by an *f*, *t*, or, *n* indicate figures, tables, or footnotes.